VLSI-SoC: ADVANCED TOPICS ON SYSTEMS ON A CHIP

IFIP – The International Federation for Information Processing

IFIP was founded in 1960 under the auspices of UNESCO, following the First World Computer Congress held in Paris the previous year. An umbrella organization for societies working in information processing, IFIP's aim is two-fold: to support information processing within its member countries and to encourage technology transfer to developing nations. As its mission statement clearly states,

> *IFIP's mission is to be the leading, truly international, apolitical organization which encourages and assists in the development, exploitation and application of information technology for the benefit of all people.*

IFIP is a non-profitmaking organization, run almost solely by 2500 volunteers. It operates through a number of technical committees, which organize events and publications. IFIP's events range from an international congress to local seminars, but the most important are:

• The IFIP World Computer Congress, held every second year;
• Open conferences;
• Working conferences.

The flagship event is the IFIP World Computer Congress, at which both invited and contributed papers are presented. Contributed papers are rigorously refereed and the rejection rate is high.

As with the Congress, participation in the open conferences is open to all and papers may be invited or submitted. Again, submitted papers are stringently refereed.

The working conferences are structured differently. They are usually run by a working group and attendance is small and by invitation only. Their purpose is to create an atmosphere conducive to innovation and development. Refereeing is less rigorous and papers are subjected to extensive group discussion.

Publications arising from IFIP events vary. The papers presented at the IFIP World Computer Congress and at open conferences are published as conference proceedings, while the results of the working conferences are often published as collections of selected and edited papers.

Any national society whose primary activity is in information may apply to become a full member of IFIP, although full membership is restricted to one society per country. Full members are entitled to vote at the annual General Assembly. National societies preferring a less committed involvement may apply for associate or corresponding membership. Associate members enjoy the same benefits as full members, but without voting rights. Corresponding members are not represented in IFIP bodies. Affiliated membership is open to non-national societies, and individual and honorary membership schemes are also offered.

VLSI-SoC: ADVANCED TOPICS ON SYSTEMS ON A CHIP

IFIP TC 10/WG 10.5 and IEEE/CEDA
A Selection of Extended Versions of the Best Papers
of the Fourteenth International Conference on
Very Large Scale Integration of Systems on Chip
(VLSI-SoC2007), October 15-17, 2007,
Atlanta, USA

Edited by

Ricardo Reis
Universidade Federal do Rio Grande do Sul
Brazil

Vincent Mooney
Georgia Institute of Technology
USA

Paul Hasler
Georgia Institute of Technology
USA

 Springer

VLSI-SoC: Advanced Topics on Systems on a Chip

Edited by Ricardo Reis, Vincent Mooney and Paul Hasler

p. cm. (IFIP International Federation for Information Processing, a Springer Series in Computer Science)

ISSN: 1571-5736 / 1861-2288 (Internet)
ISBN: 978-0-387-89557-4
eISBN: 978-0-387-89558-1

Printed on acid-free paper

9 8 7 6 5 4 3 2 1

springer.com

CONTENTS

Contents

PREFACE

This book contains extended and revised versions of the best papers that were presented during the fifteenth edition of the IFIP/IEEE WG10.5 International Conference on Very Large Scale Integration, a global System-on-a-Chip Design & CAD conference. The 15th conference was held at the Georgia Institute of Technology, Atlanta, USA (October 15-17, 2007). Previous conferences have taken place in Edinburgh, Trondheim, Vancouver, Munich, Grenoble, Tokyo, Gramado, Lisbon, Montpellier, Darmstadt, Perth and Nice.

The purpose of this conference, sponsored by IFIP TC 10 Working Group 10.5 and by the IEEE Council on Electronic Design Automation (CEDA), is to provide a forum to exchange ideas and show industrial and academic research results in the field of microelectronics design. The current trend toward increasing chip integration and technology process advancements brings about stimulating new challenges both at the physical and system-design levels, as well in the test of these systems. VLSI-SoC conferences aim to address these exciting new issues.

The 2007 edition of VLSI-SoC maintained the traditional structure, which has been successful at the previous VLSI-SoC conferences. The quality of submissions (109 papers) made the selection process difficult, but finally 46 papers and 13 posters were accepted for presentation in VLSI-SoC 2007. Out of the 46 full papers presented at the conference, 16 regular papers were chosen by a selection committee to have an extended and revised version included in this book. These selected papers have authors from Brazil, France, Germany, Italy, Israel, The Netherlands, Portugal, Serbia, Spain, Switzerland and the United States of America.

VLSI-SoC 2007 was the culmination of many dedicated volunteers: paper authors, reviewers, session chairs, invited speakers and various committee chairs, especially the local arrangements organizers. We thank them all for their contribution.

This book is intended for the VLSI community mainly to whom that did not have the chance to take part in the VLSI-SOC 2007 Conference. The papers were selected to cover a wide variety of excellence in VLSI technology and the advanced research they describe. We hope you will enjoy reading this book and find it useful in your professional life and to the development of the VLSI community as a whole.

The Editors

June 2008

Statistical Analysis of Normality of Systematic and Random Variability of Flip-Flop Race Immunity in 130nm and 90nm CMOS Technologies

Gustavo Neuberger, Gilson Wirth, Fernanda Kastensmidt, Ricardo Reis

Universidade Federal do Rio Grande do Sul (UFRGS)
Instituto de Informática
Av. Bento Gonçalves, 8500
Porto Alegre, RS, Brazil
{neuberg, wirth, fglima, reis}@inf.ufrgs.br

Abstract. Statistical process variations are a critical issue for circuit design strategies to ensure high yield in sub-100nm technologies. In this work we investigate the variability of flip-flop race immunity in 130nm and 90nm low power CMOS technologies. An on-chip measurement technique with resolution of ~1ps is used to characterize hold time violations of flip-flops in short logic paths, which are generated by clock-edge uncertainties in synchronous designs. Statistical die-to-die variations of hold time violations are measured in various register-to-register configurations and show overall 3σ die-to-die standard deviations of 12-16%. Mathematical methods to separate the measured variability between systematic and random variability are discussed, and the results presented. They show that while systematic variability is the major issue in 130nm, it is significantly decreased in 90nm technology due to better process control. Another important point is that the race immunity decreases about 30% in 90nm, showing that smaller clock skews can lead to violations in 90nm. Normality tests to check if the variability follows a normal Gaussian distribution are also presented.

Introduction

Modern synchronous digital designs necessarily include a large amount of flip-flops (FF) in pipeline stages to improve data throughput. FF timing is determined by the CLK-Q propagation time, setup time and hold time. Complying with the specified setup and hold times is a pre-requisite for a stable sampling of the data signal around the clock edge. Due to the increasing relevance of process, voltage and temperature variations for robust circuit operation in modern CMOS technologies on the one hand and the frequent use of FFs in microprocessor, DSP cores and dedicated hardware on the other hand, a precise statistical characterization of FF is mandatory. This has motivated investigations of variability of the FF propagation time using Monte Carlo simulation [1]. Statistical variations of setup and FF propagation times in critical paths are essential for maximum chip performance. In contrast to this, a violation of the hold time in short FF-logic-FF paths lead to complete chip failure. In this case

Please use the following format when citing this chapter:

Neuberger, G., Wirth, G., Kastensmidt, F. and Reis, R., 2009, in IFIP International Federation for Information Processing, Volume 291; *VLSI-SoC: Advanced Topics on Systems on a Chip*; eds. R. Reis, V. Mooney, P. Hasler; (Boston: Springer), pp. 1–16.

races in short pipeline stages are generated by a combination of clock skew and jitter between sending and receiving FFs, and process variations within the circuits. The internal race immunity is a figure of merit to characterize the robustness of a FF against race conditions and is defined as the difference between clock-to-Q delay and hold time. Hence, the race immunity strongly depends on the specific FF type [2].

Especially scan chains for DFT schemes [3] are sensitive circuit structures since no logic is placed between the FFs. Several techniques for diagnosis of hold time failures in scan chains [3-6] as well as in generic short logic paths [7] are proposed. These techniques are applied for buffer insertion, i.e. hold time fixing, to increase the delay of these paths during chip design [8]. However, depending on the design and FF properties, without detailed analysis of the critical clock skew and process variability, the extra delay introduced during hold-time fixing can be over or under estimated. In this work, we therefore present a statistical analysis of the race immunity in several test paths, due to process variability in 130nm and 90nm CMOS technologies. The experimental data is obtained using a precise on-wafer measurement technique with ~1ps resolution. This measurement technique has been presented in [9] for a 130nm CMOS technology and is here transferred to 90nm CMOS to facilitate a comparison between both technologies.

Test Circuit and Timing Issues

To evaluate the impact of statistical variations on hold time violations four different logic paths are considered. The two basic configurations are two simple pipeline stages with two master-slave edge-triggered FFs without logic between them, similar to one stage of a scan chain. Further pipelines including six small inverters between the FFs, represent short logic paths. The FFs used in this work are conventional rising edge-triggered master-slave FFs composed of CMOS transmission gates in the forward propagation path and C^2MOS latches in the feedback loops [10] with typical library extensions such as input and output node isolations and local clock buffers.

For each configuration a version with the weakest FF of the standard cell library, i.e. smallest transistor sizes and hence largest sensitivity to process variations, and a version with 8x increased driving strength is used. Comparing the results of both it is possible to analyze the impact of different transistor dimensions on the variability. The inverters used in both versions are of the minimum size, since these configurations represent typical non-critical paths where large driving capability is not required.

To emulate clock uncertainties, the sending and receiving FFs are controlled by different clock signals. The clock signal CLK2 of the receiving FFs is generated from the launching clock CLK1 of the sending FF by a programmable delay line as shown in fig. 1. If this artificial clock skew is large enough, i.e. CLK2 arrives after CLK1 and exceeds the internal race immunity tCLK-Q-tHOLD of the FF, a race is produced and detected if the output of both FFs are of same value at same time (Q1(t)=Q2(t)). The violation can be detected by initializing the FFs with opposite values, and applying a pulse in the data input, as shown in fig. 2. As long as Q1(t)≠Q2(t) pipeline operation is correct. Equation (1) describes the timing conditions in the case of a violation:

$$t_{CLK-Q} - t_{hold} - t_{CLKskew} - \Delta t_{var} < 0 \tag{1}$$

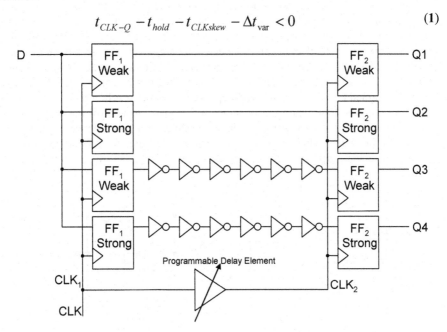

Fig. 1. Different test circuits with sensitivity to race conditions

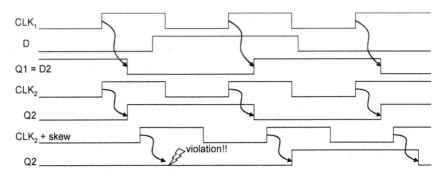

Fig. 2. Timing diagram showing hold time violation

Δt_{var} includes variations from different sources.

It is possible to see that the probability of a hold time violation receives contribution of the FF race immunity (that is inherent to the FF type and size used in the design), the maximum clock skew found in the circuit, and process variations. If the clock uncertainty is very well controlled and race immunity is large enough, process variability plays a minor role, but this is not the case of the majority of semi-custom designs that have to meet a short time-to-market. Usually, the clock uncertainty and race immunity are of about the same order of magnitude.

Measurement Scheme

To specify the critical clock skew producing a hold time violation, the artificial skew is programmable over a wide range of 80 steps corresponding to a resolution of ~1ps. The programmable delay line is composed of two inverters, and 80 NMOS/PMOS gate capacitances as load elements connected to the inverters via pass transistors. Using capacitances as programmable electrical fan out elements is advantageous since a sub-gate delay resolution is achieved. The capacitances and transistors have been carefully designed to be able to achieve steps of the desired resolution.

Programming is done using an 80-stage shift register to control the inputs of the pass transistors. For coarse-grain clock skew shifting a multiplexer to enable or disable a further buffer chain is added. It is needed because the versions with 0 or 6 inverters have very different critical clock skews. Fig. 3 shows the implemented circuit.

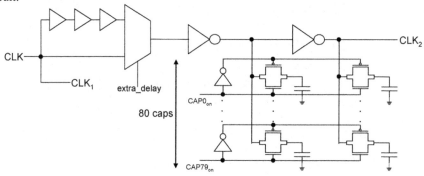

Fig. 3. Schematics of the programmable delay line for the clock skew emulation

To measure the absolute time produced by a specific setting of the programmable delay line, it is additionally placed in the middle of a ring oscillator. The ring oscillator is connected to an 11-stage frequency divider to monitor the output frequency. Thus, it is possible to determine the programmed delay based on measuring and comparing the frequencies achieved with different numbers of capacitances. Fig. 4 shows the final layout of the different circuits in the 130nm CMOS technology.

For the measurement, first the settings for all combinations of the 80 capacitances are written into the shift register. Then the frequencies of the ring oscillator on each die are measured for all configurations to calibrate the programmable skews and to eliminate impact of systematic variations from the measurement accuracy. For measurement of the delay variations of the logic path, the delay line is initialized with minimum delay, and the delay is stepwise increased until a violation in the pipeline is detected. The corresponding delay estimated from the ring oscillator measurements is the critical clock skew for the given die and operating conditions. The procedure is repeated for each of the 4 test circuits considering the rising and falling input transitions. Fig. 5 shows the measurement flow. The flow was repeated at different voltages: 1.5 V (nominal voltage), 1.2 V and 0.9 V.

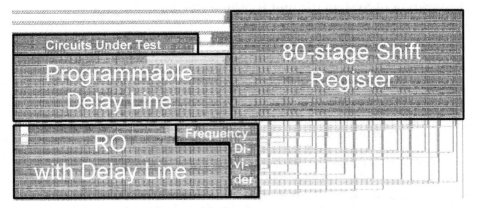

Fig. 4. Final Layout

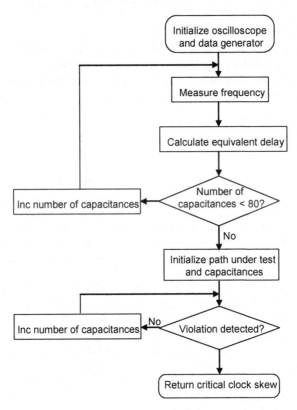

Fig. 5. Measurement flow

Separation of Systematic and Random Residual Variations

With the discussed measurement technique, it is possible to measure the overall variability on the wafer. However, for a deeper analysis, it is necessary to make mathematical transformations in the obtained data. Several methods to make the separation between the different components of the variability are present in the literature [11, 12]. In this work, we will focus in how to separate the data between systematic (over the wafer) variability and residual (within-die, local, or residuals due to imperfection in the measurement) variability.

A simple but widely used method is the moving average. In this method, the measured value in each die is substituted by the average of the value in the die itself with the values of the neighbor dies. If the number of dies is large, the average window can be expanded. We will analyze the results using a 3x3 window (the die with its direct adjacent neighbors) and a 5x5 window (with neighbors up to 2 dies of distance). The drawback of this method is some deterioration in the borders, since we do not have all neighbors available for the average.

Another common method is curve fitting. In this method, we take the measured data and apply a linear regression to find the curve that it approximates better. The curve can be a paraboloid, a plane, a Gaussian, and many others, depending on specific issues of the fabrication process. This is a more complex method, and requires a mathematic intensive computation.

Normality Tests

To evaluate the randomness and check if the measured variability data is a normal Gaussian, mathematical normality tests were performed in the results. There are several tests that are designed to check this normality [13]. Although it is possible to see that our data have strong systematic component and is clearly not normal Gaussian, after the separation between systematic and random residual variability in the previous section, the random residual component can possibly be normal Gaussian.

The first test used in the data was the Wilks-Shapiro (W-S) test. It returns a number called p-value, which may lay between 0 and 1. The larger this number, more likely is the distribution to be normal. A p-value larger than 0.05 is said to be a normal Gaussian curve at the 95% confidence level.

Another common test is the Anderson-Darling (A-D) normality test. The result of this test is a number larger than 0. But now, the smaller this number, more likely is the distribution to be normal. It is considered that a value smaller than 0.787 gives a normal Gaussian distribution with 95% confidence. The A-D normality test is a modification of the Kolmogorov-Smirnov (K-S) test and gives more weight to the tails than the K-S test.

An alternative way to check the normality is to calculate the kurtosis and the skewness of the data. Kurtosis is based on the size of a distribution's tails. A kurtosis of about 3 means a distribution very close to a normal distribution. Skewness is the measure of the asymmetry of the distribution. A normal distribution should be symmetrical and present a skewness value equal to 0.

For the measured data, these tests were made for all test circuits, using the total data, but also both systematic and random parts separated. The software used to make the tests was DataPlot from NIST/Sematech [14].

Experimental Results

The circuits are fabricated in 130nm and 90nm low power CMOS technologies using regular-VT core devices. For the 130nm CMOS technology, 182 chips are measured on one wafer, while only 36 dies are available in 90nm CMOS due to a larger reticle size. Nominal supply voltages are Vdd = 1.5V for 130nm CMOS, and Vdd = 1.32V for in 90nm CMOS, respectively. The temperature was 25°C in both cases.

First, the variability of the ring oscillator frequency over the wafers is analyzed, with different results (fig. 6). The 130nm wafer shows a typical global wafer variation with slower dies in the center of the wafer, while in 90nm the distribution seems to be more random, with smaller systematic variability, probably due to the larger reticle size and better controlled manufacturing process. The frequencies are normalized to omit confidential technology data. The faster circuits achieve resolutions less than 1ps, while none of the chips had a resolution of more than 1.2ps. It is important to note that the 90nm wafer was a test and not a production wafer, and the systematic variability was further reduced before the technology entered in production, even though the test wafer presented an improvement in systematic variability, if compared to 130nm.

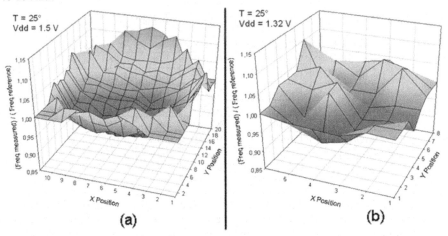

Fig. 6. Normalized frequency variability of the RO (a) over the 130nm wafer, (b) over the 90nm wafer

Fig. 7 shows the die-to-die distribution of the critical clock skew for 0-1 transitions in all 4 test circuits in 130nm wafers. The expected Gaussian curve for normal distributions is observed. The 90nm wafer shows similar Gaussian curve. Based on this data and repeating the measurement procedure for 1-0 transitions, the mean critical clock skew and the standard deviation are extracted. Table 1 summarizes the results for 130nm. The results are normalized again.

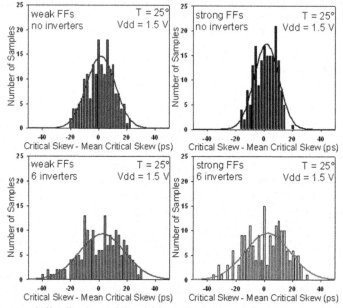

Fig. 7. Measured distribution of the critical clock skews for rising transitions in 130 wafer. The mean critical skew is set to 0 ps

Table 1. Normalized hold time violations in 130nm wafer at V_{DD}=1.5V and T=25°

Circuit	Transition	μ	σ	σ / μ (%)
weak FFs,	Rising	100.00	4.96	4.96
no inverters	Falling	109.95	4.87	4.43
strong FFs,	Rising	88.87	4.02	4.52
no inverters	Falling	95.00	4.09	4.31
weak FFs,	Rising	181.70	7.92	4.36
6 inverters	Falling	192.71	7.73	4.01
strong FFs,	Rising	170.54	7.48	4.39
6 inverters	Falling	177.52	7.41	4.17

The σ deviation of the delay can be up to 5% of the nominal value. The critical skews are in the range of the clock skew that can be expected in circuits using the same technology, showing that these statistical effects have to be considered during hold-time fixing at the end of the layout generation. It is important to note that using larger FFs, the absolute variation of the critical skew decreases, but the relative value remains similar, since these circuits are faster. This indicates that larger FFs have an increased probability of violation, since the clock skew needed to provoke the failure is smaller.

The test circuits with extra inverters have an expected larger absolute variability, but relatively it is smaller, showing that the FFs are more sensitive to process variations than the inverters, or a large number of inverters average the variability.

Another important point is that the master-slave FFs used in the experiment typically have a small or even negative hold time, and consequently larger race immunity. Repeating the experiments for faster FFs that are used in high-speed designs and have larger hold times, the results would be even more critical.

The impact of the supply voltage in the race immunity variability was also analyzed. Figure 8 shows the results for both race immunity average and standard deviation for all 8 test path combinations at 130nm technology. In the average, it can be observed that the race immunity average more than doubles when the supply voltage changes from 1.5V to 0.9V, which is a typical operating range for SoCs with dynamic voltage scaling. If the clock skew more than doubles also for the same voltage drop, the probability of hold time violation increases. However, if the change of clock skew is less than double, the probability will decrease. On the other hand, analyzing the standard deviation, it is possible to see that it increases from almost 5% to almost 7%. Considering that it is relative to the average, the increase in the variability is relatively larger than the increase in the average.

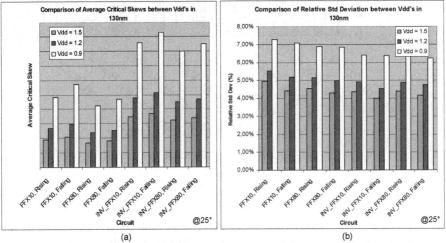

Fig. 8. Dependence of race immunity on different voltages: (a) average race immunity, (b) relative standard deviation of race immunity

Figure 9 shows a graphical comparison of the results of race immunity found for both technologies. It is possible to see that the race immunity decreases about 30% from 130nm to 90nm. This is an expected value, since it is the speed-up from one technology to another. However, it is much more difficult to scale the clock skew in the same percentage in the scaling. It shows that the problem of hold time violations becomes more critical, and the clock skew and variability must be better controlled in newer technologies.

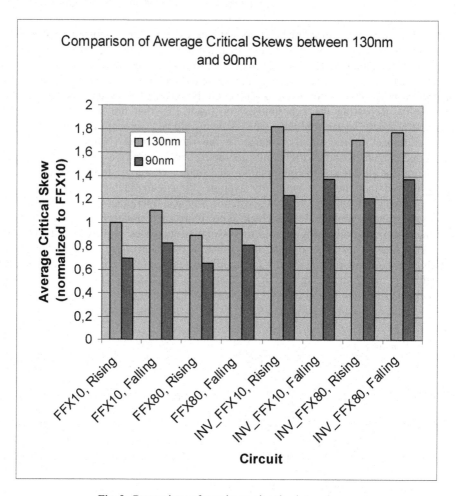

Fig. 9. Comparison of race immunity absolute value

The next step in the analysis was to apply the separation methods described in the previous section in the RO frequency variability. The three methods were compared: moving average with a 3x3 window, moving average with a 5x5 window, and curve fitting. Figure 10 shows the curves obtained for the 130nm wafer. In 130nm, the curve obtained was a paraboloid, what could be observed already in the original data. However, in the 90nm wafer, the original data was very random and difficult to see any systematic dependence, but the mathematical methods showed a slightly inclined plane, with ring oscillator frequency increasing slightly from one side of the wafer to the other.

Regarding the numerical results, the standard deviation calculated with the 3x3 moving average method was very close to the one found with the curve fitting method. However, the 5x5 moving average method presented results more than 20% different from the other, always decreasing systematic variability while increasing the random residuals, showing that a 5x5 window may be too large for the available data, masking part of the systematic variability, and especially leading to a deformation at the corners.

Based on these results, we decided to continue the analysis using only the 3x3 moving average method, due to its simplicity and very close results compared to curve fitting. The final step was to apply the method in the data obtained for the critical clock skew distribution in all circuit configurations. Table 2 shows the results of the total measured variability, and the systematic and residual variability calculated with the method.

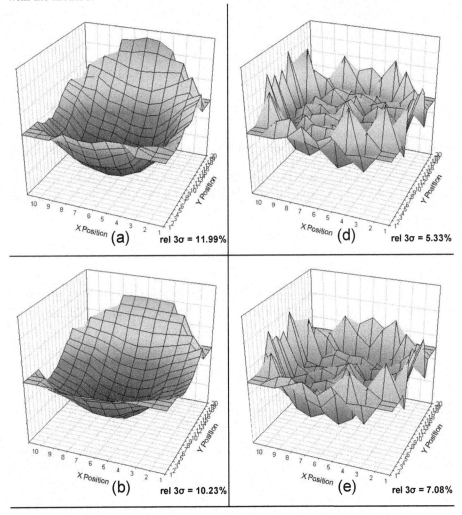

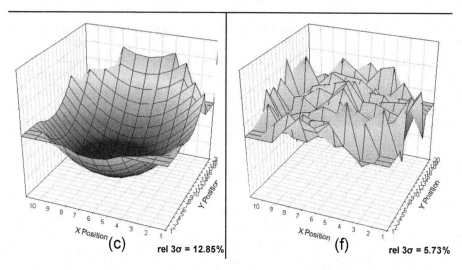

(c)   rel 3σ = 12.85%   (f)   rel 3σ = 5.73%

Fig. 10. Frequency variability curves in 130nm wafer: (a) systematic variability using the method Moving Average with 3x3 window, (b) systematic variability using the method Moving Average with 5x5 window, (c) systematic variability using the method Curve Fitting, (d) residual variability using the method Moving Average with 3x3 window, (e) residual variability using the method Moving Average with 5x5 window, (f) residual variability using the method Curve Fitting.

Table 2. Total, systematic and residual variability in the critical clock skew using the 3x3 moving average method in 130nm wafer

Circuit	Transition	σ Total (%)	σ Systematic (%)	σ Residual (%)
weak FFs,	Rising	4.96	4.04	2.50
no inverters	Falling	4.43	3.64	2.23
strong FFs,	Rising	4.52	3.47	2.53
no inverters	Falling	4.31	3.35	2.37
weak FFs,	Rising	4.36	3.56	2.15
6 inverters	Falling	4.01	3.33	1.89
strong FFs,	Rising	4.38	3.65	1.94
6 inverters	Falling	4.17	3.45	1.86

The results show that the systematic variability is dominant in 130nm technology, but the residual, probably influenced by the local and within-die variability, is expected to become much more important in 90nm and 65nm CMOS technologies, while the systematic variability probably will decrease due to a better process control. From table 2 it can be seen that using larger transistors (stronger FFs) and inverters between the flip-flops decreases the residual variability. This may result from a decrease in the local and within-die variability in larger transistors, and the averaging effect found if a larger number of gates (inverters) is used.

The next step was to apply the normality test to the set of data. All 8 test paths and also the ring oscillator frequency were tested, using the methods described previously.

Dies that were clear outliers were removed. Table 3 shows the results of these tests applied to the ring oscillator frequency data from the 130nm wafer, while tables 4, 5, 6 and 7 show the results for the different test paths.

Table 3. Wilks-Shapiro and Anderson-Darling normality tests, kurtosis and skewness for total, systematic and random residual variability for frequency data in 130nm wafer 2 at $V_{DD}=1.5V$ and $T=25°$

	Frequency		
	Total	Syst	Residual
W-S p-value	0.0001	0.0004	0.000056
Conclusion	Reject	Reject	Reject
A-D value	1.806	1.084	2.376
Conclusion	Reject	Reject	Reject
Kurtosis	2.393	2.565	3.105
Skewness	0.456	0.417	0.685

Table 4. Wilks-Shapiro and Anderson-Darling normality tests, kurtosis and skewness for total, systematic and random residual variability for test path of weak FFs, no inverters, in 130nm wafer at $V_{DD}=1.5V$ and $T=25°$

	Weak FFs, No Inv's, Rising			Weak FFs, No Inv's, Falling		
	Total	Syst	Residual	Total	Syst	Residual
W-S p-value	0.1907	0.0011	0.447	0.114	0.001	0.269
Conclusion	Accept	Reject	Accept	Accept	Reject	Accept
A-D value	0.464	0.987	0.25	0.673	1.128	0.672
Conclusion	Accept	Reject	Accept	Accept	Reject	Accept
Kurtosis	2.396	2.317	2.89	2.434	2.313	3.062
Skewness	-0.134	-0.25	0.00372	-0.188	-0.356	0.167

Table 5. Wilks-Shapiro and Anderson-Darling normality tests, kurtosis and skewness for total, systematic and random residual variability for test path of strong FFs, no inverters, in 130nm wafer at $V_{DD}=1.5V$ and $T=25°$

	Strong FFs, No Inv's, Rising			Strong FFs, No Inv's, Falling		
	Total	Syst	Residual	Total	Syst	Residual
W-S p-value	0.0259	0.0023	0.0783	0.0012	0.0003	0.957
Conclusion	Reject	Reject	Accept	Reject	Reject	Accept
A-D value	0.941	0.919	0.682	1.284	1.299	0.208
Conclusion	Reject	Reject	Accept	Reject	Reject	Accept
Kurtosis	2.224	2.526	2.197	2.111	2.346	2.786
Skewness	-0.149	-0.359	-0.00355	-0.227	-0.344	-0.0489

Table 6. Wilks-Shapiro and Anderson-Darling normality tests, kurtosis and skewness for total, systematic and random residual variability for test path of weak FFs, 6 inverters, in 130nm wafer at V_{DD}=1.5V and T=25°

| | Weak FFs, 6 Inv's, Rising | | | Weak FFs, 6 Inv's, Falling | | |
	Total	Total	Total	Total	Syst	Residual
W-S p-value	0.0247	0.00201	0.00201	0.00201	0.0003	0.957
Conclusion	Reject	Reject	Reject	Reject	Reject	Accept
A-D value	0.674	1.015	1.015	1.015	1.299	0.208
Conclusion	Accept	Reject	Reject	Reject	Reject	Accept
Kurtosis	2.595	2.419	2.419	2.419	2.346	2.786
Skewness	-0.335	-0.358	-0.358	-0.358	-0.344	-0.0489

Table 7. Wilks-Shapiro and Anderson-Darling normality tests, kurtosis and skewness for total, systematic and random residual variability for test path of strong FFs, 6 inverters, in 130nm wafer at V_{DD}=1.5V and T=25°

| | Strong FFs, 6 Inv's, Rising | | | Strong FFs, 6 Inv's, Falling | | |
	Total	Syst	Residual	Total	Syst	Residual
W-S p-value	0.0169	0.0027	0.0681	0.0007	0.0003	0.111
Conclusion	Reject	Reject	Accept	Reject	Reject	Accept
A-D value	1.009	0.873	0.759	1.451	1.344	0.718
Conclusion	Reject	Reject	Accept	Reject	Reject	Accept
Kurtosis	2.351	2.392	2.533	2.245	2.281	2.877
Skewness	-0.259	-0.306	-0.27	-0.329	-0.336	-0.329

Analysing the results, it is possible to see some similarities between the results of different test circuits. First, Wilks-Shapiro and Anderson-Darling tests produced consistent conclusions in all cases. In all cases, random variability is more normal than the equivalent systematic variability, while the total data is located somewhere between them. The only exception is the ring oscillator composed of 17 stages, where the random variability is strongly reduced due to the use of large transistor widths. Moreover, since the relative random variation of the total propagation delay of a delay chain or ring oscillator decreases according to $1/\sqrt{n}$, where n is the logic depth of the circuit, for the ring oscillator used in the test circuit the logic depth between two rising edges, which are used for frequency measurement at the input of the frequency divider, is n=34 and therefore random variations are suppressed due to averaging.

In all cases except for the ring oscillator frequency, the random variability is considered normal in the conclusion of the tests, while systematic variability is not normal (as expected, since it has a strong spatial dependence from the middle to the corners of the wafer). The total data is considered normal in the cases with weak FFs and no inverters, since these are the cases where random variability prevails, while it is not normal in other cases. In the case where we have large FFs and inverters, the role of random (local) variability is diminished and the role of systematic variability increases.

Analysing the kurtosis and skewness results, it is possible to see that in all cases, they are close to the values of 3 and 0, respectively, as expected for normal Gaussian curves.

Conclusions

This work presents an experimental analysis of the variability of hold time violations of edge-triggered master-slave FFs due to process variations in 130nm and 90nm low power CMOS technology. For accurate on-wafer characterization, a test circuit and a measurement technique with ~1ps resolution are presented. The proposed methodology provides detailed information about the circuit robustness of FFs under realistic operating conditions. This precise FF characterization then enables designers to perform hold-time fixing for short paths considering statistical variations of FFs as well as delay increasing inverters during buffer insertion. Moreover, during standard cell library development, the methodology is beneficial to optimize the FF portfolio, i.e. to balance race immunity and clock-to-Q propagation delay for various cell driving strengths and different FF topologies.

The proposed technique can be extended to characterize other timing constraints. Finally, statistical timing violations in edge-triggered master-slave flip flops are investigated experimentally, at different supply voltages. Mathematical methods to isolate systematic and random residual variations from the experimental data are discussed and compared. Results show that the absolute race immunity reduces by about 30% from 130nm to 90nm CMOS technology due to speed improvement, leading to a faster CLK-Q delay. This indicates that hold time violations are a harder problem in newer technologies if the clock skew is not expected to scale in the same way.

The results also show that the systematic variability is larger than random variability in a 130nm CMOS technology, but this trend is expected to not continue in newer technologies. However, there are design techniques available to reduce the impact of systematic variations, and the trend may be different between logic circuits and SRAMs. The normality tests performed in the results showed that, in general, random variability is a normal Gaussian distribution, while systematic variability is not, except in the cases with weak FFs and no inverters.

Future work includes the investigation of the impact of different temperature and supply voltage on variability.

References

[1] H. Q. Dao, K. Nowka, and V. G. Oklobdzija, "Analysis of clocked timing elements for dynamic voltage scaling effects over process parameter variation", Proc. Intl. Symposium on Low Power Electronics and Design (ISLPED), 2001, pp. 56-59.

[2] D. Marković, B. Nikolić, and R. W. Brodersen, "Analysis and design of low-energy flip-flops", Proc. Intl. Symposium on Low Power Electronics and Design (ISLPED), 2001, pp. 52-55.

[3] Y. Huang, W. T. Cheng, S. M. Reddy, C. J. Hsieh, and Y. T. Hung, "Statistical diagnosis for intermittent scan chain hold-time fault", Proc. Intl. Test Conf, 2003, pp. 319-328.

[4] S. Edirisooriya, and G. Edirisooriya, "Diagnosis of scan failures", Proc. VLSI. Test Symposium, 1995, pp. 250-255.

[5] R. Guo, and S. Venkataraman, "A technique for fault diagnosis of defects in scan chains", Proc. Intl. Test Conf, 2001, pp. 268-277.

[6] J. C.-M. Li, "Diagnosis of multiple hold-time and setup-time faults in scan chains", IEEE Transactions on Computers, Nov. 2005, Vol 54 Issue 11, pp. 1467-1472.

[7] Z. Wang, M. Marek-Sadowska, K.-H. Tsai, and J. Rajski, "Diagnosis of hold time defects", Proc. IEEE Intl. Conf. on Computer Design (ICCD), 2004, pp. 192-199.

[8] N. V. Shenoy, R. K. Brayton, and A. L. Sangiovanni-Vincentelli, "Minimum padding to satisfy short path constraints", Proc. IEEE/ACM Intl. Conf. on Computer Aided Design (ICCAD), 1993, pp. 156-161.

[9] G. Neuberger, F. Kastensmidt, R.Reis, G. Wirth, R. Brederlow, C. Pacha, "Statistical characterization of hold time violations in 130nm CMOS technology", IEEE European Solid-State Circuits Conference (ESSCIRC), 2006.

[10] G. Gerosa et al., "A 2.2W, 80 MHz superscalar RISC Microprocessor", IEEE J. Solid-State Circuits, 1994, pp. 1440-1454.

[11] B. E. Stine, D. S. Boning, and J. E. Chung, "Analysis and decomposition of spatial variation in integrated circuit processes and devices", IEEE Transactions on Semiconductor Manufacturing, Feb. 1997, Vol 10 Issue 1, pp. 24-41.

[12] D. S. Boning, and J. E. Chung, "Statistical metrology: understanding spatial variation in semiconductor manufacturing", Proc. Microelectronic Manufacturing Yield, Reliability and Failure Analysis II: SPIE 1996 Symposium on Microelectronic Manufacturing, 1996, pp. 16-26.

[13] P. Mach, and H. Hochlova, "Testing of normality of data files for application of SPC tools", 27th International Spring Seminar on Electronics Technology: Meeting the Challenges of Electronics Technology Progress, 2004, pp. 318-321.

[14] http://www.itl.nist.gov/div898/software/dataplot/homepage.htm.

Use of Gray Decoding for Implementation of Symmetric Functions

Osnat Keren[1] Ilya Levin[2] and Radomir S. Stankovic[3]

[1] Bar-Ilan University, Israel, kereno@eng.biu.ac.il
[2] Tel-Aviv University, Israel, ilia1@post.tau.ac.il
[3] Nis University, Serbia, radomir.stankovic@gmail.com

Abstract. We study a problem of reduction of the number of product terms in representation of totally symmetric Boolean functions by Sum of Products (SOP) and Fixed Polarity Reed-Muller (FPRM) expansions. We propose a method, based on the Gray decoding, for reduction of the number of product terms, and, consequently, the implementation cost of the symmetric functions. The method is founded on the principles of linear transformations of the input variables of an initial function. It provides significant simplification both of the SOPs and the FPRMs representations of the functions. Mathematical analysis as well as experimental results demonstrate the efficiency of the proposed method.

1 Introduction

Linearization of switching functions based on linear transformation of variables is a classical method of optimization in circuit synthesis originating already in 1958 [22]. It has been recently efficiently exploited by several authors and discussed for different aspects due to its:

1. *Effectiveness.* The method provides considerable simplification of the representation of functions with respect to different optimization criteria.
2. *Simplicity of the implementation.* The overhead comprises EXOR circuits required to perform the selected linear combination of variables. The overhead is usually quite negligible compared to the overall complexity of the implementation [12].

The linearization can be performed over different data structures used to represent functions. For example, it has been performed over Sum-of-Product (SOP) expressions [10, 13, 15, 29], AND-EXOR expressions [5], word-level expressions [28] as well as decision diagrams [7, 14, 18].

In spectral techniques, the linearization is studied as a mean to reduce the number of non-zero coefficients in spectral expressions for discrete functions [8], [12]. In [12, 20], and [21] the extensions to multiple-valued logic functions are discussed. The complexity of determining an optimal non-singular binary matrix that defines the optimal linear transformation of variables is NP-complete. For this reason a number of alternative strategies have been suggested in exploiting this method.

Please use the following format when citing this chapter:

Keren, O., Levin, I. and Stankovic, R.S., 2009, in IFIP International Federation for Information Processing, Volume 291; *VLSI-SoC: Advanced Topics on Systems on a Chip*; eds. R. Reis, V. Mooney, P. Hasler; (Boston: Springer), pp. 17–32.

For achieving the exact optimum, some restrictions should to be made on the number of variables in functions processed. For example, it has been reported in [7] that the complete search over all possible linear transformations is feasible for functions up to seven variables within reasonable space and time resources. Another strategy in using the linearization is to apply the method for particular classes of functions. For instance, in [10, 28] a method has been used for specific circuits, such as n-bit adders. The optimal linear transform has been found for this adder.

Sometimes, nearly optimal solutions can be provided by deterministic algorithms if analysis of additional information about the functions is available ([8, 12] and [14] and references therein).

In this paper, we develop a compromising approach. We deal with symmetric Boolean functions and demonstrate that for such functions an efficient linear transformation of variables can be determined analytically without intense computations. In particular, we show that a Gray decoding of the input variables provides a significant reduction in the number of product terms.

Symmetric Boolean functions represent an important fraction of Boolean functions. They are characterized by the fact that their outputs only depend on the Hamming weights of their inputs. These functions can be represented in a compact way both for their algebraic normal forms and for their value vectors. As symmetric functions are the only functions having a known implementation with a number of gates which is linear in the number of input variables [1], they might be good candidates in term of implementation complexity. There are efficient circuit-based methods and complete BDD-based methods for identifying symmetries of completely and incompletely specified functions [11, 17, 19, 23, 30, 33].

In last several years, symmetric functions have been studied from different aspects. Optimal Fixed Polarity Reed-Muller (FPRM) expansions for totally symmetric functions are discussed in [4, 32] and references therein. A lower bound on the number of gates in conjunctive (disjunctive) normal form representation of symmetric Boolean functions is given in [31] and a method for generating a minimal SOP cover is presented in [3]. A multilevel synthesis of symmetric functions which exploits the disjoint decomposability and weight dependency of the functions is presented in [16] and a mapping of symmetric and partially symmetric functions to the CA-type FGPAs was suggested in [2]. A new expansion of symmetric functions and their application to non-disjoint functional decompositions for LUT-type FPGAs is presented in [26].

In this paper we study a specific case of symmetric functions, and show that for these functions, a linear transformation based on Gray decoding of the input variables is very effective. We show that the Gray decoding almost always reduces the complexity in terms of the following three criteria: the number of gates in two-level realization, the number of FPRM terms and the number of FPGA LUTs. Additionally we show that not only symmetric functions but also partially symmetric functions may be efficiently implemented by using the proposed technique. This technique can be considered as a combination of a well-known classical decomposition technique of the partially symmetric functions ([24]) with the proposed linear transformation.

The paper is organized as follows. Section 2 gives basic definitions of symmetric Boolean functions and Gray codes. Section 3 presents the implementation of a symmetric function as a superposition of a Gray decoder and a non-linear function. Section 4 presents an illustrative example discussing in detail application of the proposed method. In Section 5 we discuss features of the proposed method and prove that the solutions produced can never increase complexity of representation of SOPs compared to the given initial representations. In Section 6 we discuss the use of the Gray decoding for partially symmetric functions. Section 7 contains experimental results and Section 8 concludes the paper.

2   Preliminaries

2.1   Totally symmetric functions

Let $f(x) = f(x_{n-1}, \ldots x_0)$ a Boolean function of $n \geq 2$ inputs and a single output. The function f is *symmetric* in x_i and x_j iff

$$f(x_{n-1} \ldots x_i \ldots x_j \ldots x_0) = f(x_{n-1} \ldots x_j \ldots x_i \ldots x_0). \tag{1}$$

The function f is *totally* symmetric iff it is symmetric in all pairs of its variables.

A function $f(x) = S_i(x)$ is called an *elementary* symmetric function with working parameter i iff

$$S_i(x) = \begin{cases} 1 & ||x|| = i \\ 0 & otherwise \end{cases}$$

where $||x||$ is the Hamming weight of x. There are $n + 1$ elementary symmetric functions satisfying

$$\sum_x S_i(x)S_j(x) = \begin{cases} \binom{n}{i} & i = j \\ 0 & otherwise \end{cases}.$$

Any symmetric function can be represented as a linear combination of elementary symmetric functions, i.e. $f(x) = \oplus_{i=0}^n a_i S_i(x)$ where $a_i \in \{0, 1\}$. Hence, there are 2^{n+1} symmetric functions out of 2^{2^n} functions.

Example 1. Consider an elementary 5-inputs symmetric function $f(x) = S_3(x)$. The K-map of the function is given in Table 3. The minimal SOP representation of the function consists of 10 minterms of 5 literals.

A Fixed Polarity Reed-Muller (FPRM) expansion is an EXOR of product terms, where no two products consists of the same variables and each variable appears in complemented or un-complemented form, but not in both [25]. In matrix notation [1], the FPRM expansion of a function $f(x_{n-1}, \ldots x_0)$ with a given polarity vector $h = (h_{n-1}, \ldots h_1, h_0)$, is defined as

$$f(x_{n-1}, \ldots x_0) = \left(\otimes_{i=0}^{n-1} [1, x_{n-1-i}^{h_{n-1-i}}] \right) \left(\otimes_{i=0}^{n-1} R^{h_{n-1-i}}(1) \right) F$$

where $\otimes$ is a Kronecker product,

$$x_i^{h_i} = \begin{cases} x_i & if\ h_i = 0 \\ x_i' & otherwise \end{cases}$$

and

$$R^{h_i}(1) = \begin{cases} \begin{pmatrix} 1 & 0 \\ 1 & 1 \end{pmatrix} & if\ h_i = 0 \\[2ex] \begin{pmatrix} 0 & 1 \\ 1 & 1 \end{pmatrix} & otherwise \end{cases}$$

and F is the truth vector. The number of product terms in the FPRM depends on the polarity vector.

Example 2. The FPRM expansion of the *3-out-of-5* function in Example 1 with a positive polarity $(h = 0)$ comprises 10 terms,

$$f = x_4x_3x_2 \oplus x_4x_3x_1 \oplus x_4x_2x_1 \oplus x_3x_2x_1 \oplus x_4x_3x_0$$
$$\oplus\ x_4x_2x_0 \oplus x_3x_2x_0 \oplus x_4x_1x_0 \oplus x_3x_1x_0 \oplus x_2x_1x_0.$$

The positive polarity produces the minimal number of terms, all the other 31 polarity vectors produces FPRM expansions of at least 16 product terms.

2.2   Gray code

The reflected binary code, also known as Gray code after Frank Gray [6], is used for listing n-bit binary numbers so that successive numbers differ in exactly one bit position. The definition of the Gray encoding and decoding is the following: Elements of a binary vector of length n, $z = (z_{n-1}, \ldots z_0)$ and the vector $x = (x_{n-1}, \ldots x_0)$ derived by Gray encoding are related as

$$x_i = \begin{cases} z_i & i = n - 1 \\ z_i \oplus z_{i+1} & otherwise \end{cases}$$

and

$$z_i = \begin{cases} x_i & i = n - 1 \\ x_i \oplus z_{i+1} & otherwise \end{cases}.$$

This relation can be written using matrix notation as $x = G_E\ z$ and $z = G_D\ x$ where $G_E = (\tau_{n-1}, \ldots, \tau_1, \tau_0)$ is a non-singular matrix of the form

$$G_E = \begin{pmatrix} 1 & 0 \ldots 0\ 0 \\ 1 & 1\ 0 \ldots 0\ 0 \\ 0 & 1\ 1 \ldots 0\ 0 \\ \vdots & \vdots\ \vdots \ldots \vdots\ \vdots \\ 0 & 0\ 0 \ldots 1\ 0 \\ 0 & 0\ 0 \ldots 1\ 1 \end{pmatrix}. \tag{2}$$

and $G_D = G_E^{-1}$. The matrices G_E and G_D are called the Gray encoding and the Gray decoding matrices, respectively. The implementation of the Gray encoder (decoder) requires $n - 1$ two-input EXOR gates.

Example 3. Let $n = 4$ and $z = (1, 1, 0, 1)$ then

$$x_3 = z_3 = 1$$
$$x_2 = z_3 \oplus z_2 = 0$$
$$x_1 = z_2 \oplus z_1 = 1$$
$$x_0 = z_1 \oplus z_0 = 1$$

or

$$x = (\tau_3, \tau_2, \tau_1, \tau_0)z = \begin{pmatrix} 1\ 0\ 0\ 0 \\ 1\ 1\ 0\ 0 \\ 0\ 1\ 1\ 0 \\ 0\ 0\ 1\ 1 \end{pmatrix} \begin{pmatrix} 1 \\ 1 \\ 0 \\ 1 \end{pmatrix} = \begin{pmatrix} 1 \\ 0 \\ 1 \\ 1 \end{pmatrix}.$$

3   Implementation of totally symmetric functions by Gray decoded inputs

In this paper we introduce an implementation of a symmetric function as a superposition of two functions: a Gray decoder defined by the matrix G_D, and the corresponding function f_{G_D} whereas $f(x) = f_{G_D}(G_D x)$ (see Figure 3).

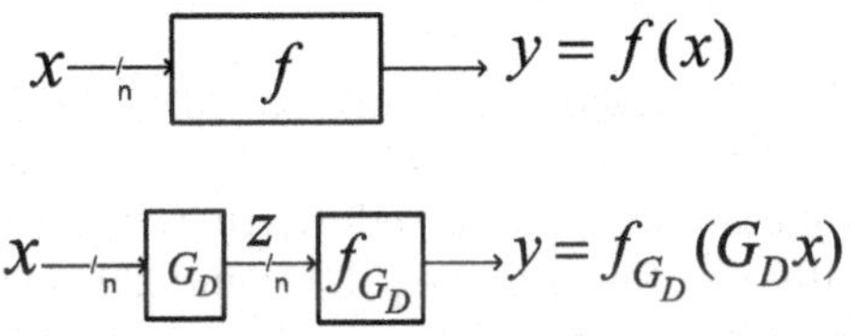

Fig. 1. Implementation of a Boolean function with a Gray decoding of the input variables

The main idea behind this approach is the following: A Boolean function maps elements of the vector space $\{0, 1\}^n$ to $\{0, 1\}$. The vector space $\{0, 1\}^n$ is spanned by n base vectors, usually the binary vectors $\{\delta_i\}_{i=0}^{n-1}$ corresponding to the integer value 2^i are used. The set of δ_i's is called the initial basis. This basis is used in definition of SOP expressions.

Any set of n linearly independent vectors forms a basis, and in particular, the columns $\{\tau_i\}_{i=0}^{n-1}$ of the matrix G_E.

Since $Ix = G_E z$, the vector x can be interpreted as the coefficient vector that defines an element of $\{0, 1\}^n$ using the initial basis, and z can be interpreted as the coefficient vector representing an element with the set of τ's. Thus, the matrices G_E and G_D define a linear transformation between the coefficient vectors.

Example 4. In Example 3, the element $(1, 0, 1, 1) \in \{0, 1\}^4$ can be represented as a linear combination of the initial base vectors $\delta_3 = (1, 0, 0, 0), \delta_2 = (0, 1, 0, 0), \delta_1 = (0, 0, 1, 0)$ and $\delta_0 = (0, 0, 0, 1)$, or as a linear combination of the columns of G_E. Namely,

$$(1, 0, 1, 1) = 1 \cdot \delta_3 + 0 \cdot \delta_2 + 1 \cdot \delta_1 + 1 \cdot \delta_0 = 1 \cdot \tau_3 + 1 \cdot \tau_2 + 0 \cdot \tau_1 + 1 \cdot \tau_0,$$

thus, $x = (1011)$ and $z = (1101)$.

In theoretical considerations, complexity of circuit realization of a Boolean function is usually estimated without referring to a specific implementation technology. It is, therefore, often expressed in the number of two-input gates (AND/OR) that are required for the realization of the function considered. Formally, this criterion can be written in terms of a cost function [12, 27]

$$\mu(f) = |\{x | x, \tau \in \{0, 1\}^n, f(x) = f(x + \tau), ||\tau|| = 1\}|$$

where $+$ stands for a bitwise EXOR of two binary vectors and $||\tau||$ is the Hamming weight of a binary vector τ. The autocorrelation function of f, is defined as $R(\tau) = \sum_{x \in \{0,1\}^n} f(x) f(x \oplus \tau)$. For a given function f, the value of μ can be related to the values of the autocorrelation function of f, at points corresponding to the base vectors,

$$\mu(f) = \sum_{i=0}^{n-1} R(\delta_i).$$

In the case of initial basis, these are points 2^i, and linear transformation of variables performs the shift of these values.

There is a variety of minimization procedures that construct a linear transformation deterministically, see, for instance [14, 15] and [29] and references therein. It should be noticed that implementation of such procedures may be a space and time demanding task, and therefore, it is useful to take into considerations specific features of functions to be realized. In particular, we point out that for totally symmetric Boolean functions the linear transformation of variables derived from the Gray code almost always reduce the implementation cost. The same transformation often reduces the number of terms in Fixed polarity Reed-Muller expressions.

4   Motivation example

Consider the *3-out-of-5* function in Example 1. Let G_E and the G_D be the 5×5 Gray encoding and decoding matrices. The columns of G_E are binary vectors of length 5 corresponding to the integer values $1, 3, 6, 12$ and 24. Let $z = G_D x$ be the Gray decoded inputs. Table 4 shows the K-map of f_{G_D}. The minimal SOP representation of f_{G_D} consists of 5 products,

$$f_{G_D}(z_4, z_3, z_2, z_1, z_0) =$$
$$z_3 z_2' z_0 + z_3 z_1' z_0 + z_4 z_2' z_0 + z_4' z_2 z_1' z_0 + z_4 z_3' z_1 z_0.$$

The FPRM expansion of f_{G_D} with a polarity vector $h = (11000)$ is

$$f_{G_D}(z_4, z_3, z_2, z_1, z_0) = z_0 \oplus z_2 z_1 z_0 \oplus z_3' z_2 z_0 \oplus z_4' z_3' z_0.$$

Table 1. K-map of a *3-out-of-5* function

$x_4 x_3 x_2$ / $x_1 x_0$	000	001	011	010	110	111	101	100
00						1		
01			1		1		1	
11		1		1				1
10			1		1		1	

Table 2. K-map of Gray coded *3-out-of-5* function

$z_4 z_3 z_2$ / $z_1 z_0$	000	001	011	010	110	111	101	100
00								
01		1	1	1	1	1		1
11				1	1		1	1
10								

The values of the autocorrelation function of the original *3-out-of-5* function are shown in Figure 2 (top figure). The values of $R(\tau)$ at positions $\tau = 1, 2, 4, 8$ and 16 corresponding to the initial base vectors are all zero , thus, the minimal SOP comprises 10 minterms. The autocorrelation values at positions $\tau = 1, 3, 6, 12$ corresponding to the new base vectors (τ_0, τ_1, τ_2 and τ_3) are equal to 6.

Applying the Gray decoding on the inputs is equivalent to permuting the autocorrelation values so that high autocorrelation values are now placed at positions 2^i. The autocorrelation function of f_{G_D} is shown at the bottom of Figure 2. The sum of the autocorrelation values of f_{G_D} at positions 2^i ,$i = 0, \dots, 4$ is $4 \cdot 6 + 0$, therefore, the number of pairs in the first merging step of the Quine-McClusky minimization algorithm is now 12 which leads to a minimal SOP representation.

5   Analysis

Let $f(x) = f(x_{n-1}, \dots x_0) \sum_{i=0}^{n} a_i S_i(x)$, $a_i \in \{0, 1\}$, a totally symmetric Boolean function of n variables and a single output. The autocorrelation function of $S_i(x)$

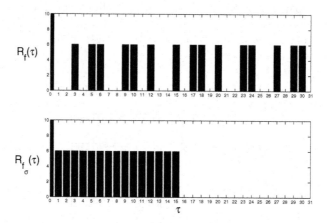

Fig. 2. Autocorrelation function values of the original *3-out-of-5* symmetric function f (top) and the values of the autocorrelation function corresponding to f_{G_D} with the Gray decoded inputs (bottom).

is [12]

$$R_{S_i}(\tau) = \sum_{x \in \{0,1\}^n} S_i(x) S_i(x \oplus \tau)$$

$$= \begin{cases} \binom{n-||\tau||}{i-||\tau||/2} \binom{||\tau||}{||\tau||/2} & ||\tau|| \text{ is even} \\ 0 & otherwise \end{cases}$$

where $\binom{a}{b} = 0$ for $b < 0$.

The cross correlation between $S_i(x)$ and $S_j(x)$ is

$$R_{S_i, S_j}(\tau) = \sum_{x \in \{0,1\}^n} S_i(x) S_j(x \oplus \tau)$$

$$= \begin{cases} \binom{n-||\tau||}{i-w} \binom{||\tau||}{w} & i - j + ||\tau|| \text{ is even} \\ 0 & otherwise \end{cases}$$

where $w = (i - j + ||\tau||)/2$.

The autocorrelation function of f is

$$R_f(\tau) = \sum_{x \in \{0,1\}^n} f(x) f(x \oplus \tau)$$

$$= \sum_{i=0}^{n} a_i R_{S_i}(\tau) + \sum_{\substack{i,j=0 \\ i \neq j}}^{n} a_i a_j R_{S_i, S_j}(\tau). \qquad (3)$$

Therefore, the autocorrelation values in positions corresponding the the initial set of base vectors $\{\delta_i\}_{i=0}^{n-1}$ is

$$R_f(\delta_i) = 2\sum_{k=1}^{n-1} a_k a_{k+1} R_{S_k, S_{k+1}}(\tau)$$

$$= 2\sum_{k=1}^{n-1} a_k a_{k+1}\binom{n-1}{k}. \tag{4}$$

On the other hand, the autocorrelation values at positions corresponding to the base vectors $\tau_i = \delta_i + \delta_{i+1}$, $i = 0,\ldots n-2$, defined by the columns of the Gray encoding matrix G_E, are

$$R_f(\tau_i) = 2\sum_{k=0}^{n} a_k \binom{n-2}{k-1} + 2\sum_{k=1}^{n-2} a_k a_{k+2}\binom{n-2}{k} \tag{5}$$

The following Theorem states that the realization cost of f_{G_D} with the Gray decoded inputs is less or equal to the realization cost of f for any totally symmetric function.

Theorem 1. *Let $f(x) = \sum_{i=1}^{n} a_i S_i(x)$, $a_i \in \{0,1\}$ a totally symmetric function, and let f_{G_D} the corresponding function with the Gray decoded inputs, i.e. $f(x) = f_{G_D}(G_D x)$. Then,*

$$\mu_f \le \mu_{f_{G_D}}.$$

Proof. The proof is based the fact that $R_{f_{G_D}}(\delta_i) = R_f(G_D^{-1}\delta_i) = R_f(\tau_i)$. Let $\Delta_i = R_f(\tau_i) - R_f(\delta_i)$, clearly, $\Delta_{n-1} = 0$ and for $0 \le i < n-1$, $\Delta_i = 2\sum_{k=0}^{n} d_k$ where

$$d_k = a_k\left(\binom{n-2}{k-1} - a_{k+1}\binom{n-1}{k} + a_{k+2}\binom{n-2}{k}\right). \tag{6}$$

We now show that $\Delta_i \ge 0$ for all i. From 6, if $a_k = 0$ than $d_k = 0$, otherwise, there are four possible cases:

1. If $a_{k+1} = a_{k+2} = 0$ than $d_k > 0$.
2. If $a_{k+1} = a_{k+2} = 1$ than $d_k = 0$ since

$$\binom{a}{b} = \binom{a-1}{b} + \binom{a-1}{b-1}.$$

3. If $a_{k+1} = 0$ and $a_{k+2} = 1$ than $d_k > 0$.
4. If $a_{k+1} = 1$ and $a_{k+2} = 0$ than we may consider the sum $d_k + d_{k+1}$ and get

$$\binom{n-2}{k-1} - \binom{n-1}{k} + \binom{n-2}{k} + a_{k+2}\binom{n-2}{k} \ge 0 \tag{7}$$

Therefore, $R_{f_{G_D}}(\delta_i) = R_f(\tau_i) \ge R_f(\delta_i)$. From [12], the cost function μ_f of a function $f : \{0,1\}^n \rightarrow \{0,1\}$ equals to $\mu_f = 2^n - 2R_f(0) + 2\sum_{i=0}^{n-1} R_f(\delta_i)$, and thus $\mu_{f_{G_D}} \ge \mu_f$. □

6 Implementation of partially symmetric functions by Gray decoded inputs

In this section we extend the use of the Gray decoder to the case of partially symmetric functions. We start with the definition of partially symmetric functions, and then we present a three-level implementation of partially symmetric functions which is based on a set of Gray decoders.

A function is said to be symmetric with respect to a set λ, $\lambda \subseteq \{x_{n-1} \ldots x_0\}$, if it is invariant under all the permutations of the variables in λ. The variables of the function can be partitioned into disjoint symmetry sets $\lambda_1, \ldots, \lambda_k$. A function is called *partially symmetric* if it has at least one symmetry set λ_i of size $|\lambda_i| > 1$. Without loss of generality, we assume that the input variables are ordered, i.e. the first $|\lambda_1|$ variables are elements of the first symmetry set λ_1, the next $|\lambda_2|$ variables are elements of the second symmetry set λ_2 etc.

A partially symmetric function f may be represented as a superposition of two functions: a linear function defined by a matrix σ, and a function f_σ whereas $f(x) = f_\sigma(z)$ and $z = \sigma x$. The linear transformation matrix σ represents k Gray decoders that work on each symmetric set separately (see Figure 3). The matrix σ is defined through its inverse matrix T as follows,

$$
T = \begin{pmatrix} G_{D,k} & \cdots & 0 & 0 \\ \vdots & & \vdots & \vdots \\ 0 & \cdots & G_{D,2} & 0 \\ 0 & \cdots & 0 & G_{D,1} \end{pmatrix} \tag{8}
$$

where $G_{D,i}$ is a Gray decoding matrix corresponding to $|\lambda_i|$ variables. The overall implementation cost of the Gray decoders is $(n - k)$ XOR gates.

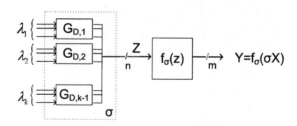

Fig. 3. The original function (top) and its linear decomposition with a set of Gray decoders (bottom)

Recall that we are not interested in the optimal solution to the general minimization problem of partially symmetric functions. Rather, we suggest a specific linear transformation matrix based on the Gray decoder which is suitable for partially symmetric functions. The following example clarifies this point.

Example 5. Consider a single-output partially symmetric function $f(x_4, x_3, x_2, x_1, x_0)$ that has two symmetry sets $\lambda_1 = \{x_4, x_3, x_2\}$ and $\lambda_2 = \{x_1, x_0\}$. The K-map of the function is given in Table 3. The SOP representation of the function consists of 13 product terms and 62 literals.

Let T be the Gray encoding matrix as defined in Eq. 8 and $\sigma = T^{-1}$ the Gray decoding matrix. The columns of T are binary vectors of length 5 corresponding to the integer values $1, 3, 4, 12$ and 24, that is,

$$T = \begin{pmatrix} 1 & 0 & 0 & 0 & 0 \\ 1 & 1 & 0 & 0 & 0 \\ 0 & 1 & 1 & 0 & 0 \\ 0 & 0 & 0 & 1 & 0 \\ 0 & 0 & 0 & 1 & 1 \end{pmatrix}.$$

Let $z = \sigma x$ be the Gray decoded inputs. The K-map of $f_\sigma(z)$ is given in Table 4. The minimal SOP representation of f_σ consists of 5 products and only 16 literals.

Note that the values of $R(\tau)$ at positions $\tau = 1, 2, 4, 8$ and 16 corresponding to the initial base vectors, are $0, 0, 2, 2$ and 2 respectively. However, the auto-correlation values at positions $\tau = 1, 3, 4, 12$ and 24 corresponding to the new base vectors are equal to $0, 12, 2, 10$ and 10. Therefore, the cost function of the original function is $\mu(f) = 6$ and it is smaller than $\mu(f_\sigma) = 34$. Nevertheless, the linear transformation corresponding to the Gray decoder is not optimal. It is possible to choose a different set of base vectors, for example, $3, 30, 5, 4$ and 8, that is,

$$\hat{T} = \begin{pmatrix} 0 & 0 & 0 & 1 & 0 \\ 1 & 0 & 0 & 1 & 0 \\ 0 & 1 & 1 & 1 & 0 \\ 0 & 0 & 0 & 1 & 1 \\ 0 & 0 & 1 & 0 & 1 \end{pmatrix},$$

for which the autocorrelation values are $12, 12, 10, 2$ and 2, respectively. Thus, the matrix $\hat{\sigma} = \hat{T}^{-1}$ defines a function $f_{\hat{\sigma}}$ having $\mu(f_{\hat{\sigma}}) = 36$. Consequently, the minimal SOP representation of $f_{\hat{\sigma}}$ comprises 4 product terms and 13 literals. Clearly, this additional reduction in the number of literals (from 16 to 13) is negligible.

Table 3. K-map of the original function in Example 5

$x_4x_3x_2$ x_1x_0	000	001	011	010	110	111	101	100
00	1		1		1		1	
01		1		1				1
11			1		1	1	1	
10		1		1				1

The following lemma states that the Gray decoding of the inputs of a partially symmetric function cannot increase the implementation cost.

Table 4. K-map of Gray coded function in Example 5

$z_4 z_3 z_2$ $z_1 z_0$	000	001	011	010	110	111	101	100
00	1			1	1			1
01		1	1			1		
11		1	1			1		
10				1	1		1	1

Lemma 1. *Let f be a partially symmetric function that has $k \geq 1$ symmetric sets $\lambda_1, \ldots, \lambda_k$. Let σ be the linear transformation matrix as defined in Eq. 8, and f_σ be the corresponding linearized function, $f(x) = f_\sigma(\sigma x)$. Then $\mu(f_\sigma) \geq \mu(f)$.*

The proof of the lemma is similar to the proof of Theorem 1.

7 Experimental results

In this section, we compare the implementation cost of the original and Gray-coded functions in terms of:

a) The number of Look-Up-Tables ($LUTs$) required to implement the function by *SPARTAN3 xcs200ft256* as computed by LeonardoSpectrum.

b) The number of literals (L) in its minimal SOP representation as produced by ESPRESSO.

c) The number of nonzero terms in the optimal Fixed-Polarity Reed-Muller ($FPRM$) expansion.

Tables 5 and 6 show the number LUTs for several totally symmetric functions of 8 and 12 input variables, the number of literals in the minimal SOP expression and the number of non-zero FPRM terms as computed with and without the Gray decoding. The improvement in those parameters is given in percentage. The symmetric functions $f = \sum_i a_i S_i(x)$ are specified by a set I, $I = \{i | a_i \neq 0\}$, of working parameters, I is written in the left column of Tables 5 and 6. The simulation results show an average reduction of 70% in the number of LUTs, an average reduction of 88% in the munber of literals, and 68% in the number of non-zero FPRM coefficients.

Table 7 shows how the Gray decoding reduces the implementation cost of several totally symmetric LGSynth93 benchmark functions. Given a polarity vector, the number of non-zero FPRM terms of a k-output function is defined as the size of the union of the non-zero terms in the FPRM expansion of each one of the k single-output functions. For example, the original benchmark function *rd84* has four outputs, the number of non-zero FPRM terms of each is $28, 8, 1$ and 70 and the size of the union of these terms is 107. The number of non-zero terms of the corresponding Gray coded single-output functions is $14, 4, 1$ and 38 and the size of their union is 39.

Simulation results that demonstrate the efficiency of Gray decoding on a number of partially symmetric functions are shown in Table 8. The simulation results show an average reduction of 86% in the number of literals and an average reduction of 60% in the number of non-zero FPRM coefficients. The first column in the table is the benchmark name, the second column shows the number of inputs, the third column specifies which single-output function is simulated, and the forth column shows the number of symmetry sets in that function.

Table 5. Totally symmetric functions of 8 inputs

I	LUT orig	LUT Gray	% improv.	L orig	L Gray	% improv.	$FPRM$ orig	$FPRM$ Gray	% improv.
3	12	7	41.7	448	92	79.5	64	24	62.5
4	13	9	30.8	560	106	81.1	107	15	86.0
3, 4	18	13	27.8	490	185	62.2	96	31	67.7
3, 5	15	8	46.7	896	45	95.0	104	17	83.6
3, 4, 5	18	15	16.7	336	123	63.4	162	49	69.7
2, 3, 5, 7	19	10	47.4	904	74	91.8	36	40	-11.1
0, 2, 3, 5, 8	18	11	38.9	856	109	87.3	107	25	76.6

Table 6. Totally symmetric functions of 12 inputs

I	LUT orig	LUT Gray	% improv.	L orig	L Gray	% improv.	$FPRM$ orig	$FPRM$ Gray	% improv.
3	65	26	60.0	2640	470	82.2	232	200	13.8
4	32	41	-28.1	5940	800	86.5	794	166	79.1
3, 4	143	71	50.3	5445	1225	77.5	562	306	45.6
3, 5	37	57	-54.1	12144	584	95.2	1024	136	86.7
3, 4, 5	204	118	40.2	7920	1170	85.2	1354	356	73.7
0, 2, 3, 5, 8	217	101	53.5	17876	1582	91.1	738	328	55.6

Table 7. Totally symmetric benchmark functions

	in	out	LUT orig	LUT Gray	L orig	L Gray	$FPRM$ orig	$FPRM$ Gray
rd53	5	3	6	4	140	35	20	12
rd73	7	3	24	8	756	141	63	24
rd84	8	4	51	13	1774	329	107	39
9sym	9	1	36	36	504	135	173	33
total			117	61	3174	640	363	108

Table 8. Partially symmetric benchmark functions

	in	out func.	sets	L orig	L Gray	$FPRM$ orig	$FPRM$ Gray
z4	7	1	2	12	1	3	1
z4	7	2	3	48	12	5	4
z4	7	3	3	136	22	9	6
radd	8	1	4	64	14	15	7
radd	8	2	4	184	27	9	6
radd	8	3	4	68	13	5	4
adr4	8	2	3	20	7	3	2
adr4	8	3	4	68	13	5	4
add6	12	1	6	63	6	63	11
add6	12	3	6	456	40	17	8
total				1119	155	134	53

8   Conclusions

The problem of linearization of logic functions may be considered as a determining a linear transform for variables in a given function, which produces a
representation of the function appropriate for particular applications. However,
it is not always necessary to determine the best possible linear transformation
for a class of functions. For many practical applications it is sufficient to find a
suitable transform producing acceptable solutions.

In this paper we consider the class of symmetric functions and point out
a suitable linear transformation of variables resulting in considerably reduced
number of product terms in AND-OR and Reed-Muller expressions.

We propose a method to represent a symmetric logic function as a superposition of a linear portion that realize the Gray decoding of input vectors and
a non-linear portion. Being a particular case of the linear transformation, the
described Gray decoding transform enables to achieve very compact implementations of the initial symmetric function.

We have shown that the use of the Gray transform improves the complexity
of the initial function implementation in terms of a specific cost function. Experimental results show that for majority of benchmarks the proposed method
improves also a LUT based implementation of the function. The suggested approach can be extended to partially symmetric functions. In addition, we have
shown that it provides an average reduction of about 86% in the number of literals and an average reduction of about 60% in the number of non-zero FPRM
coefficients.

References

1. J.T. Astola and R.S. Stankovic, *Fundamentals of Switching Theory and Logic Design: A Hands on Approach,* Springer-Verlag New York, 2006.

2. M. Chrzanowska-Jeske and Z. Wang, " Mapping of symmetric and partially-symmetric functions to theCA-type FPGAs" *proc. of the 38th Midwest Symposium on Circuits and Systems*, vol. 1, pp. 290-293, Aug 1995.

3. D. L. Dietmeyer, "Generating minimal covers of symmetric functions," *IEEE Transactions on Computer-Aided Design of Integrated Circuits and Systems*, Vol. 12, No. 5, pp. 710-713, May 1993.

4. R. Drechsler, B. Becker, "Sympathy: fast exact minimization of fixed polarity Reed-Muller expressions for symmetric functions," *Proc. of the European Design and Test Conference*, pp. 91 - 97, March 1995.

5. R. Drechsler and B. Becker, "EXOR transforms of inputs to design efficient two-level AND-EXOR adders," *IEE Electronic Letters*, vol. 36, no. 3, pp. 201-202, Feb. 2000.

6. F. Gray, " Pulse code communication," March 17, 1953 (filed Nov. 1947). U.S. Patent 2,632,058.

7. W. Günther, R. Drechsler, "BDD minimization by linear transforms", *Advanced Computer Systems*, pp. 525-532, 1998.

8. S.L. Hurst,D.M. Miller, J.C. Muzio, *Spectral Techniques in Digital Logic*, Academic Press, Bristol, 1985.

9. J. Jain, D. Moundanos, J. Bitner, J.A. Abraham, D.S. Fussell and D.E. Ross, "Efficient variable ordering and partial representation algorithm," *Proc. of the 8th International Conference on VLSI Design*, pp. 81-86, Jan. 1995.

10. J. Jakob, P.S. Sivakumar, V.D. Agarwal, "Adder and comparator synthesis with exclusive-OR transform of inputs", *Proc. 1st Int. Conf. VLSI Design*, pp. 514-515, 1997.

11. S. Kannurao and B. J. Falkowski, "Identification of complement single variable symmetry in Boolean functions through Walsh transform," *Proceedings of the International Symposium on Circuits and Systems* (ISCAS), 2002.

12. M.G. Karpovsky, *Finite Orthogonal Series in the Design of Digital Devices*, John Wiley, 1976.

13. M.G. Karpovsky, E.S. Moskalev, "Utilization of autocorrelation characteristics for the realization of systems of logical functions," *Avtomatika i Telemekhanika*, No. 2, 1970, 83-90, English translation *Automatic and Remote Control*, Vol. 31, pp. 342-350, 1970.

14. M.G. Karpovsky, R.S. Stankovic and J.T. Astola, "Reduction of sizes of decision diagrams by autocorrelation functions," *IEEE Trans. on Computers*, vol. 52, no. 5, pp. 592-606, May 2003.

15. O. Keren, I. Levin and R.S. Stankovic, "Linearization of Functions Represented as a Set of Disjoint Cubes at the Autocorrelation Domain," *Proc. of the 7th International Workshop on Boolean Problems*, pp. 137-144, Sept. 2006.

16. B. G. Kim, D.L. Dietmeyer, "Multilevel logic synthesis of symmetric switching functions," *IEEE Trans. on Computer-Aided Design of Integrated Circuits and Systems*, Vol.10, No. 4O, pp. 436-446, Apr. 1991.

17. E.J., Jr. McCluskey, "Detection of group invariance or total symmetry of a Boolean function," *Bell Systems Tech. Journal*, vol. 35, no. 6, pp. 1445-1453, 1956.

18. Ch. Meinel, F. Somenzi, T. Tehobald, "Linear sifting of decision diagrams and its application in synthesis," *IEEE Trans. CAD*, Vol. 19, No. 5, 2000, 521-533.

19. D. Moller, J. Mohnke, and M. Weber, "Detection of symmetry of Boolean functions represented by ROBDDs," *Proc. of the International Conference on Computer-Aided Design (ICCAD)*, 1993, pp. 680684.

20. C. Moraga, "Introducing disjoint spectral translation in spectral multiple-valued logic design", *IEE Electronics Letters*, 1978, Vol. 14, No. 8, pp. 248-243, 1978.

21. C. Moraga, "On some applications of the Chrestenson functions in logic design and data processing", *Mathematic and Computers in Simulation*, Vol. 27, pp. 431-439, 1985.

22. E.I. Nechiporuk, "On the synthesis of networks using linear transformations of variables", *Dokl. AN SSSR*. Vol. 123, No. 4, pp. 610-612, Dec. 1958.

23. S. Panda, F. Somenzi, and B. Plessier, "Symmetry detection and dynamic variable ordering of decision diagrams," *Proc. of the International Conference on Computer-Aided Design (ICCAD)*, 1994.

24. T. Sasao, *Logic Synthesis and Optimization*, Springer, 1993.

25. T. Sasao, *Switching Theory for Logic Synthesis*, Kluwer Academic Publishers, Feb. 1999

26. T. Sasao, "A new expansion of symmetric functions and their application to non-disjoint functional decompositions for LUT type FPGAs", *IEEE Int. Workshop on Logic Synthesis, IWLS-2000*, May 2000.

27. C. E. Shannon, "The Synthesis of Two-Terminal Switching Circuits," *Bell System Technical Journal*, Vol. 28, pp. 59-98, Jan. 1949.

28. R.S. Stankovic,J.T. Astola, "Some remarks on linear transform of variables in adders," *Proc. 5th Int. Workshop on Applications of Reed-Muller Expression in Circuit design*, Starkville, Mississippi, USA, Aug. 10-11, pp. 294-302, 2001.

29. D. Varma and E.A. Trachtenberg, "Design automation tools for efficient implementation of logic functions by decomposition," *IEEE Transactions on Computer-Aided Design of Integrated Circuits and Systems*, vol. 8, no. 8, pp. 901-916, Aug. 1989.

30. K.H. Wang and J.H. Chen, "Symmetry Detection for Incompletely Specified Functions," *Proc. of the 41st Conference on Design Automation Conference, (DAC'04)*, pp. 434-437, 2004.

31. G. Wolfovitz "The complexity of depth-3 circuits computing symmetric Boolean functions," *Information Processing Letters*, vol. 100, No. 2, pp. 41 - 46, Oct. 2006.

32. S.N. Yanushkevich, J.T. Butler, G.W. Dueck, V.P. Shmerko, "Experiments on FPRM expressions for partially symmetric logic functions", *Proc.30th Int. Symp. on Multiple-Valued Logic*, Portland, Oregon USA, 141-146, May 2000.

33. J. S. Zhang, A. Mishchenko, R. Brayton, M. Chrzanowska-Jeske, "Symmetry detection for large Boolean functions using circuit representation, simulation, and satisfiability", *Proceedings of the 43rd annual conference on Design automation*, pp. 510 - 515, 2006.

A Programmable Multi-Dimensional Analog Radial-Basis-Function-Based Classifier

Sheng-Yu Peng, Paul E. Hasler, and David V. Anderson

School of Electrical and Computer Engineering
Georgia Institute of Technology
Atlanta, Georgia 30332–0250

Abstract. A compact analog programmable multidimensional radial-basis-function (RBF)-based classifier is demonstrated in this chapter. The probability distribution of each feature in the templates is modeled by a Gaussian function that is approximately realized by the bell-shaped transfer characteristics of a proposed floating-gate bump circuit. The maximum likelihood, the mean, and the variance of the distribution are stored in floating-gate transistors and are independently programmable. By cascading these floating-gate bump circuits, the overall transfer characteristics approximate a multivariate Gaussian function with a diagonal covariance matrix. An array of these circuits constitute a compact multidimensional RBF-based classifier that can easily implement a Gaussian mixture model. When followed by a winner-take-all circuit, the RBF-based classifier forms an analog vector quantizer. Receiver operating characteristic curves and equal error rate are used to evaluate the performance of the RBF-based classifier as well as a resultant analog vector quantizer. It is shown that the classifier performance is comparable to that of digital counterparts. The proposed approach can be at least two orders of magnitude more power efficient than the digital microprocessors at the same task.

1 Motivations for Analog RBF Classifier

The aggressive scaling of silicon technologies has led to transistors and many sensors becoming faster and smaller. The trend toward integrating sensors, interface circuits, and microprocessors into a single package or into a single chip is more and more prevalent. Fig. 1**A** illustrates the block diagram of a typical microsystem, which receives analog inputs via sensors and performs classification, decision-making, or, in a more general term, information-refinement tasks in the digital domain. Although fabrication and packaging technologies enable an unprecedented number of components to be packed into a small volume, the accompanying power density can be higher than ever, which has become one of the bottle-neck factors in the microsystem development. If the information-refinement tasks can be performed in the analog domain with less power consumption, the specifications for the analog-to-digital-converters, which are usually power-hungry, can be relaxed. In some cases, analog-to-digital conversion can

Please use the following format when citing this chapter:

Peng, S.-Y., Hasler, P.E. and Anderson, D.V., 2009, in IFIP International Federation for Information Processing, Volume 291;
VLSI-SoC: Advanced Topics on Systems on a Chip; eds. R. Reis, V. Mooney, P. Hasler; (Boston: Springer), pp. 33–52.

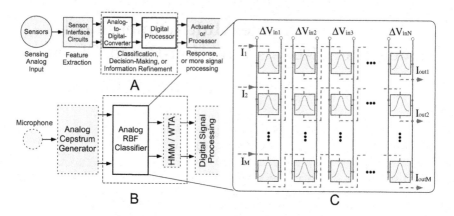

Fig. 1. A: The block diagram of a typical microsystem. **B:** An analog RBF-based classifier in an analog front-end for speech recognition includes a band-pass-filter bank based analog Cepstrum generator, an analog RBF-based classifier, and a continuous-time hidden Markov model. **C:** The block diagram of an analog RBF-based classifier which is composed of an array of the proposed floating-gate bump cells. Followed by a winner-take-all circuit, it results in a highly compact and power-efficient analog vector quantizer.

be avoided altogether. In such systems, multivariate Gaussian response functions are critical building blocks for a variety of applications, such as radial-basis-function(RBF)-based classifiers, Gaussian mixture modeling of data, and vector quantizers. This chapter discusses the development of an analog Gaussian response function having a diagonal covariance matrix and demonstrates its application to vector quantization.

Fig. 1**B** illustrates one possible application of this work as part of an analog speech recognizer [1] that includes a band-pass-filter bank based analog Cepstrum generator, an analog RBF-based classifier, and a winner-take-all (WTA) stage, or a continuous-time hidden Markov model (HMM) block built from programmable analog waveguide stages. The input to the HMM stage could represent the RBF response directly or it could pass through a logarithmic element first. By performing analog signal processing in the front end, not only the computational load of the subsequent digital processor can be reduced, but also the required specifications for the analog-to-digital converters can be relaxed in terms of speed, accuracy, or both. As a result, the entire system can be more power efficient.

In this chapter, a highly compact and power-efficient, programmable analog RBF-based classifier is demonstrated. It is at least two orders of magnitude more power efficient than the digital counterparts. As illustrated in Fig. 1**C**, the analog RBF-based classifier is composed of an array of proposed floating-gate bump cells having bell-shaped transfer characteristics that can realize the Gaussian functions. The height, the width, and the center of a bump circuit transfer curve, which represent the maximum likelihood, the variance, and the

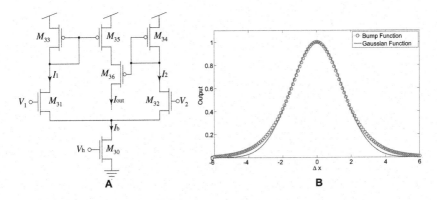

Fig. 2. A: Schematic of a conventional bump circuit introduced in [7]. **B:** Comparison between the normalized Gaussian function and the normalized Bump function.

mean of a template distribution respectively, can be independently programmed. The ability to program these three parameters empowers the classifiers to fit into different scenarios with the full use of statistical information up to the second moment. When followed by a winner-take-all stage, an RBF-based classifier forms a multi-dimensional analog vector quantizer.

A vector quantizer compares distances or similarities between an input vector and the stored templates. It classifies the input data to the most representative template. Vector quantization is a typical technique used in pattern recognition and data compression. Crucial issues of the vector quantizer implementation concern the storage efficiency and the computational cost for searching the best-matching template. In the past decade, efficient digital [2, 3] and analog [4–6] hardware vector quantizers have been developed. In general, the analog vector quantizers have been shown to be more power efficient than their digital counterparts. However, in a previous design [4], the computational efficiency is partially due to the fact that only the mean absolute distances between the input vector and the templates are compared instead of considering the possible feature distributions. To have better approximation to the Gaussian distribution, many variations of analog RBF circuits are designed [6–11]. Among these previous works, the simple "bump" and "anti-bump" circuits in [7] are the most classic because of their simplicity.

2   Bump circuits

The schematic of a conventional bump circuit in [7] is shown in Fig. 2**A**. If all transistors operate in the subthreshold region, the branch currents in the differential pair can be expressed as

$$I_1 = \frac{I_b}{1 + e^{-\kappa \Delta V_{in}/U_T}}, \quad I_2 = \frac{I_b}{1 + e^{\kappa \Delta V_{in}/U_T}}, \tag{1}$$

where κ is the subthreshold slope factor, U_T is the thermal voltage, and $\Delta V_{in} = V_{in1} - V_{in2}$. The output current is the harmonic mean of I_1 and I_2 and can be described as

$$I_{out} = \frac{I_1 I_2}{I_1 + I_2} = \frac{I_b}{2 + e^{\kappa \Delta V_{in}/U_T} + e^{-\kappa \Delta V_{in}/U_T}} = \frac{I_b}{2} \text{sech}^2 \left(\frac{\kappa \Delta V_{in}}{2U_T} \right). \quad (2)$$

The normalized bump function is compared with the normalized Gaussian function as shown in Fig. 2**B**. This simple circuit can implement the exponential decay behavior of a Gaussian function. It is noticeable that, from (2), the width of the transfer characteristic is fixed by the ratio of κ/U_T.

The analog RBF or vector quantization circuits reported in [6–11] require extra circuits to store or to periodically refresh template data. In [5, 12, 13], floating-gate transistors are used to implement the bump and anti-bump circuits. Because the template data are stored in the form of charges on floating gates, the circuits are very compact. Particularly in [12, 13], two adaptive versions of the floating-gate bump and anti-bump circuits are introduced to implement competitive learning. Although the bump centers in these circuits are adaptive to the mean values, the bump widths are still constant. As will be shown later, the floating-gate bump circuit introduced in this chapter has the potential to adapt to both the mean and the variance of the distribution.

3   Programmable Floating-gate Bump circuit

In the proposed analog classifier, the Gaussian response function is approximated by the bell-shaped transfer characteristics of a floating-gate bump circuit. The height, the width, and the center of the transfer curve represent the maximum likelihood, the variance, and the mean of a distribution respectively. Adjusting these parameters is equal to pre-scaling input signals in the analog fashion so that the circuit outputs can fall into the effective input range of the following stage. For example, in the analog vector quantizer implementation, despite the different distributions in different applications, the required precision of the following WTA circuit can remain relaxed if the input signals can be scaled properly.

The schematics of the proposed floating-gate bump circuit and its bias generation block are shown in Fig. 3. All floating-gate transistors have two input capacitances and all input capacitances are of the same size. The proposed floating-gate bump circuit is composed of three parts: an inverse generation block, a conventional bump circuit, and in between a fully differential variable gain amplifier (VGA).

The inverse generation block, made up of two floating-gate summing amplifiers, provides the complementary input voltages to the VGA so that the floating-gate common-mode voltage of M_{21} and M_{22} as well as the outputs of the VGA are independent of the input signal common-mode level. If the charges on M_{13} and M_{14} are matched and the transistors are in the saturation region,

$$V_{in1} + V_{1c} = V_{in2} + V_{2c} = V_{const}, \quad (3)$$

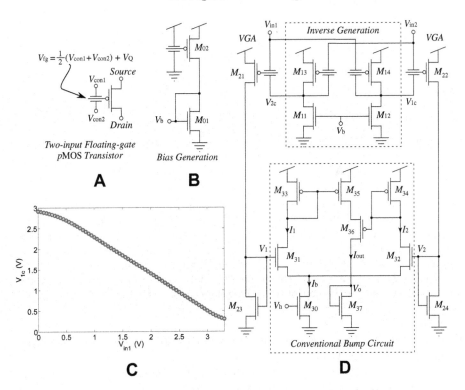

Fig. 3. A: The symbol of a two-input floating-gate pMOS transistor. **B:** The schematic of the bias generation circuit for the proposed floating-gate bump circuit. **C:** The transfer characteristic of the inverse generation block. **D:** The schematic of the proposed bump circuit that is composed of an inverse generation block, a fully differential variable gain amplifier (VGA), and a conventional bump circuit.

where V_{const} only depends on the bias voltage, V_b, and the charges on M_{13} and M_{14}. If the charge on M_{02} in the bias generation circuit also matches that on M_{13} and M_{14}, the generated voltage, V_b, provides the summing amplifiers an operating range that is one V_{DSsat} away from the supply rails, as shown in Fig. 3C.

The floating-gate voltages on M_{21} and M_{22} can be expressed as

$$V_{fg,21} = \frac{1}{2}(V_{in1} + V_{const} - V_{in2}) + \frac{Q_{21}}{C_T} = \frac{1}{2}\Delta V_{in} + V_{Q,cm} + \frac{1}{2}V_{Q,dm} \qquad (4)$$

$$V_{fg,22} = \frac{1}{2}(V_{in2} + V_{const} - V_{in1}) + \frac{Q_{22}}{C_T} = -\frac{1}{2}\Delta V_{in} + V_{Q,cm} - \frac{1}{2}V_{Q,dm}, \qquad (5)$$

where $\Delta V_{in} = V_{in1} - V_{in2}$, Q_{21} and Q_{22} are the amounts of charge on M_{21} and M_{22} respectively, C_T is the total capacitance seen from a floating gate, and

$$V_{Q,cm} = \frac{1}{2}\left(\frac{Q_{21} + Q_{22}}{C_T} + V_{const}\right), V_{Q,dm} = \frac{Q_{21} - Q_{22}}{C_T}. \qquad (6)$$

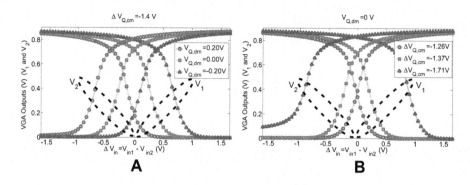

Fig. 4. Measured variable gain amplifier transfer characteristics. V_{in2} is fixed at $V_{DD}/2$ and V_{in1} is swept from 0V to V_{DD}, where V_{DD} is 3.3V. In the programming mode, the control gate voltages are set to be $-\Delta V_{Q,cm} \mp V_{Q,dm}/2$ and the floating-gate transistors are programmed to have $1\,\mu A$ of current. **A:** The differential charge on M_{21} and M_{22} are programmed to several different levels and the amount of the common-mode charge is fixed. **B:** The common-mode charge on M_{21} and M_{22} are programmed to several different levels and the amount of the differential charge is fixed.

From (4) and (5), these two floating-gate voltages do not depend on the input signal common-mode level.

The variable gain of the VGA stems from the nonlinearity of the transfer function from the floating-gate voltage, $V_{fg,21}$ (or $V_{fg,22}$), to the diode-connected transistor drain voltage, V_1 (or V_2). Several pairs of the transfer curves corresponding to different amounts of the charge on the floating gates are measured and are shown in Fig. 4. The value of ΔV_{in} at the intersection indicates the center of the bell-shaped transfer curve. As shown in Fig. 4A, the value of ΔV_{in} at the intersection shifts as the differential charge changes, but the slopes at the intersection are invariant. Thus, by programming the differential charge, the center of the transfer function can be tuned without altering the width. On the other hand, as shown in Fig. 4B, the slopes at the intersection point varies with the common-mode charge while the value of ΔV_{in} at the intersection does not. Therefore, we can program the common-mode charge to tune the width of the bell-shaped transfer characteristics without affecting the center. Because the template information are stored in a pair of floating-gate transistors as in [12,13], this circuit has the potential to implement adaptive learning algorithms with not only an adaptive mean but also an adaptive variance.

The detailed derivations of the relation between the VGA gain and the common-mode charge are given in the appendix. The final equation is

$$\frac{\Delta V_{out}}{\Delta V_{in}} \approx -\gamma \left(1 + e^{-\frac{\gamma \kappa_p}{2U_T}(V_{DD} - V_{Q,cm} - V_{T0,p})}\right) = \eta, \qquad (7)$$

where $\gamma = \frac{\kappa_p}{\kappa_n}\sqrt{\frac{I_{0,p}W_pL_n}{I_{0,n}L_pW_n}}$, the subscripts "p" and "n" refer to the pMOS and nMOS transistors respectively, I_0 is the subthreshold pre-exponential current

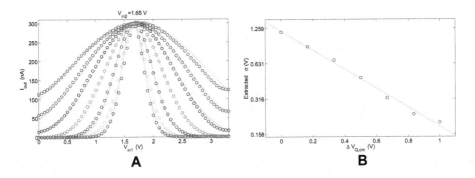

Fig. 5. Gaussian fits of the transfer curves and the width dependance. **A:** Comparison of the measured 1D bumps (circles) and the corresponding Gaussian fits (dashed lines). One of the bump input voltages is fixed at $V_{DD}/2$, where V_{DD} is 3.3V through the measurement. The extracted standard deviation varies 5.87 times and the mean only shifts 4.23%. The minimum achievable extracted standard deviation is 0.199V. **B:** The width and common-mode charge relation in the semi-logarithmic scale. The width is characterized by the extracted standard deviation, σ. The shift of the programmed common-mode floating gate voltage, $\Delta V_{Q,cm}$, represents the common-mode charge level. The dashed line is the exponential curve fit.

factor, W and L are the dimensions of a transistor, κ is the subthreshold slope factor, V_{T0} is the threshold voltage, and U_T is the thermal voltage. From (2), the transfer function of the complete bump circuit can be expressed as

$$I_{out} = \frac{2I_b}{2 + e^{\kappa\eta\Delta V_{in}/U_T} + e^{-\kappa\eta\Delta V_{in}/U_T}}, \tag{8}$$

which is used to approximate a Gaussian function. By adjusting $V_{Q,cm}$, the magnitude of the VGA gain increases exponentially and the extracted standard deviation decreases exponentially.

In Fig. 5**A**, the common-mode charge is programmed to several different levels and the transfer curves with different widths are measured. The bell-shaped curves are compared with their correspondent Gaussian fits. In Fig. 5, the extracted standard deviation varies 5.87 times and the mean only shifts 4.23%. In the semi-logarithmic plot of Fig. 5**B**, the extracted standard deviation, σ, exponentially depends on the common-mode charge as predicted by (7). The minimum achievable extracted standard deviation from the measurements is 0.199V, which is set by the maximum gain of the VGA. If two diode-connected nMOS transistors are used as the load, the maximum VGA gain will be doubled and the minimum achievable standard deviation can be reduced by half.

A diode-connected transistor, M_{37}, in the bump circuit converts the output current into a voltage. By feeding this voltage to the tail transistor, M_{30}, in the next stage bump circuit as shown in Fig. 6, the final output current approximates a multivariate Gaussian function with a diagonal covariance matrix. Although

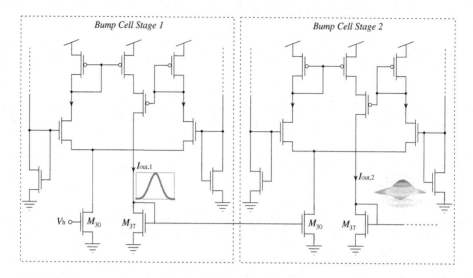

Fig. 6. By connecting the diode-connected output transistor to the tail transistor of the next stage bump cell, the resulting output current can approximate a multivariate Gaussian function with a diagonal covariance matrix.

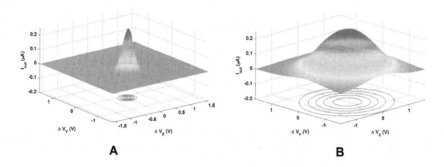

Fig. 7. Measurement results from two cascading floating-gate bump circuits. ΔV_X is the input voltage difference $\Delta V_{in} = V_{in1} - V_{in2}$ of the first stage floating-gate bump circuit and ΔV_Y is the input voltage difference of the second stage. In both stages, $V_{in2} = V_{DD}/2$. The common-mode charges are programmed to different levels to approximate bivariate Gaussian functions with different variance.

the feature dimension can be increased by cascading more floating-gate bump cells, the bandwidth of the classifier decreases. The mismatches between the floating-gate bump circuits can be trimmed out by using floating-gate programming techniques. In Fig. 7, two 2-D "bumps" with different widths approximating bivariate Gaussian functions with different standard deviations are shown. The output currents of an array of these floating-gate bump circuits can easily be summed up to implement GMMs.

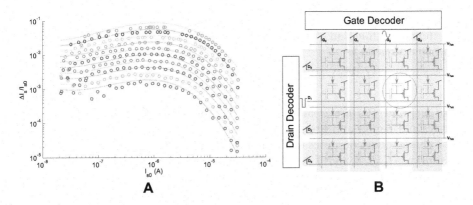

Fig. 8. A: Measured injection characterization points (circles) and the corresponding curve fits (dashed lines). The pulse width is fixed at 200μsec. 10 different values of V_{ds} ranging from 5.6V to 6.5V and 30 channel current levels ranging from 20nA to 20μA are used to obtain the curve fits for each curve. Cubic functions are used to regress the nonlinear functions $g(\cdot)$ and $f(\cdot)$ in (10). **B:** The block diagram of programming an array of floating-gate transistors. Drain-lines and gate-lines are shared in rows and in columns respectively. By applying V_{DD} to unselected drain-lines and gate-lines, floating-gate transistors can be programmed individually.

4   Programming Floating-gate Transistor Array

How to accurately programming an array of floating-gate transistors is a critical technique in the development of the proposed analog classifier. Fowler-Nordheim tunneling and channel hot electron injection mechanisms are used to program charge on floating gates. The techniques of programming an array of floating-gate transistors have been detailed in many previous works [14, 15]. The floating-gate programming method and the way to program an array of floating-gate transistors will be briefly reviewed in this section.

Fowler-Nordheim tunneling removes electrons from the floating gates through tunneling junctions, which are schematically represented by arrowheaded capacitors shown in Fig. 8**B**. Because of the poor selectivity, tunneling currents are used as the global erase. To accurately program charges on floating gates, channel hot electron injection are employed. As detailed in [16], the injection current can be modeled as

$$I_{inj} = I_{inj0} \left(\frac{I_s}{I_{s0}} \right)^{\alpha} e^{-\Delta V_{ds}/V_{inj}}, \qquad (9)$$

where I_s is the channel current, V_{inj} is a device and bias dependent parameter, and α is very close to 1. Instead of using this computationally complex physical model as in [14], an empirical model proposed in [15] is used to perform floating-gate transistor characterization and algorithmic programming.

Given a short pulse of V_{ds} across a floating-gate device, the injection current is proportional to $\Delta I_s/I_{s0}$, where $\Delta I_s = I_s - I_{s0}$ is the increment of the channel current. From (9), logarithmic of this ratio should be a linear function of V_{ds} and a nonlinear function of $\log(I_{s0}/I_u)$, where I_u is an arbitrary unity current. It can be expressed as

$$\log\left(\frac{\Delta I_s}{I_{s0}}\right) = g\left(\log\left(\frac{I_{s0}}{I_u}\right)\right) V_{ds} + f\left(\log\left(\frac{I_{s0}}{I_u}\right)\right), \tag{10}$$

where $g(\cdot)$ and $f(\cdot)$ are weakly linear functions when the transistor is in the subthreshold region and are nonlinear when the transistor is above threshold. In the characterization process, V_{ds} and I_{s0} are given and ΔI_s can be measured. Thus, $g(\log(I_{s0}/I_u))$ and $f(\log(I_{s0}/I_u))$ can be regressed by high order polynomial functions. After the characterization process, we obtain the resulting polynomial regressive functions, $\hat{f}(\log(I_{s0}/I_u))$ and $\hat{g}(\log(I_{s0}/I_u))$. In the programming process, with the regressive functions, the appropriate V_{ds} value for injection can be predicted by

$$V_{ds} = \frac{\log\left(\frac{\Delta I s}{I_{s0}}\right) - \hat{f}\left(\log\left(\frac{I_{s0}}{I_u}\right)\right)}{\hat{g}\left(\log\left(\frac{I_{s0}}{I_u}\right)\right)}, \tag{11}$$

where I_{s0} is the given starting point and I_s is the target value.

The measured and the regressive results for the injection characterization are compared in Fig. 8A. Only one floating-gate transistor in the floating-gate array is used in the characterization, and the regressive functions are cubic. The measured regressive coefficient mismatches in the array are less than 10%. To avoid overshooting the target value, we always apply slightly shorter and smaller pulses of V_{ds} than the predicted values. Therefore, despite the mismatches and the discrepancy between the curve fits and the measured data, the current level of the floating-gate transistor approaches the target value asymptotically. The precision of the programmed current level can be as accurate as 99.5%, which is consistent with other approaches [14, 15]. As presented in [17], the retention time for the charges on floating gates can last over 10 years at room temperature. Because the bump circuit is a differential structure, the center of the transfer curve would not vary with the temperature. However, its width depends on the temperature because of the U_T term in (7).

To program an array of the floating-gate bump circuits, floating-gate transistors are arranged as in Fig. 8B in the programming mode. There are two conditions required for injection: a channel current and a high channel-to-drain field. We can deactivate the unselected columns (or rows) by applying V_{DD} to the corresponding gate-lines (or drain-lines) so that there are no currents through (or no fields across) the devices for injection. In this manner, each floating-gate transistor can be isolated from others and can be programmed individually.

5   A Programmable Analog Vector Quantizer

A "FG-pFET & Mirror" block shown in Fig. 9A is added in front of the first bump cell to program its tail current, which sets the height of the "bump."

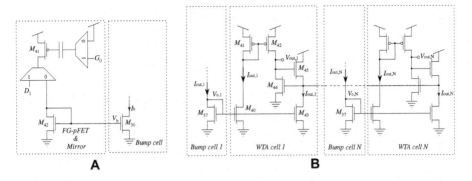

Fig. 9. A: The schematic of the *"FG-pFET & Mirror"* block. The charge on the *p*MOS transistor can be programmed to set the height of the bell-shaped transfer curve. **B:** The schematic of a current mode winner-take-all circuit. Only the output voltage of the winning cell will be high to indicate the best-matching template.

For the analog vector quantizer implementation, the final output currents of the RBF-based classifier are duplicated and are fed into a simple current mode winner-take-all circuit, the schematic of which is shown in Fig. 9**B**. Only the output voltage of the winning cell will be high to indicate the best-matching template.

To have the access to all drain and gate terminals of floating-gate transistors in the programming mode, multiplexers are inserted into the circuits as shown in Fig. 10. Most of the multiplexers are in the inverse generation and bias generation blocks. Since only one bias generation block is needed for the whole system, when the system is scaled up, the bias generation block does not cost extra complexity. In the analog RBF-based classifier and the vector quantizer, the same input voltage vector is compared with all stored templates. Therefore, the inverse generation can be shared by the same column of bump cells, each of which only includes a VGA and a conventional bump circuit. The number of inverse generation blocks is equal to the dimension of the feature space. Together with the gate-line and drain-line decoders, most of the programming overhead circuitries are at the peripheries of the floating-gate bump cell array; therefore the system can be easily scaled up and maintain high compactness. The compactness and the ease of scaling up are important issues in the implementation of an analog speech recognizer that requires more than a thousand of bump cells. The final architecture of our analog vector quantizer is shown in Fig. 11.

Two examples are used to demonstrate the reconfigurability of the classifiers as shown in Fig. 12. Four templates are used and their outputs are superposed in a 3-D plot. The floating-gate transistors of other unused templates are tunneled off. Four bell-shaped output currents emulate the bivariate Gaussian likelihood functions of four templates. The thick solid lines at the bottom, indicate the boundaries determined by the WTA outputs.

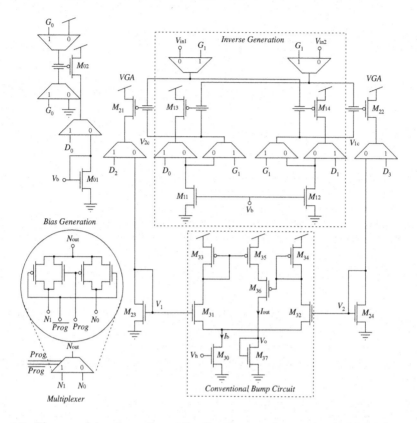

Fig. 10. The complete schematics of the floating-gate bump circuit. Multiplexers for floating-gate programming are inserted into the original circuits. The "1" on the multiplexer indicates the connection in the programming mode and the "0" indicates the connection in the operating mode. The tunneling junction capacitors are not shown for simplicity. Most of the multiplexers are in the bias generation and inverse generation blocks. Only two multiplexers are added in the bump cell that includes the VGA and the conventional bump circuit.

6   Performance of The Analog Vector Quantizer

We have fabricated a prototyped analog vector quantizer in a $0.5\,\mu$m CMOS process. We also fabricated a 16×16 highly compact low-power version of an analog vector quantizer in the $0.5\,\mu$m CMOS process occupying less than $1.5 \times 1.5mm^2$. Some important parameters and measured results are listed in the TABLE 1.

To measure the power consumption, several "bumps" are programmed with identical width while other "bumps" are deactivated by tunneling their floating-gate transistors off. The power consumption is averaged over the entire 2-D input space. The slope of the curve in Fig. 13**A** indicates the average power consump-

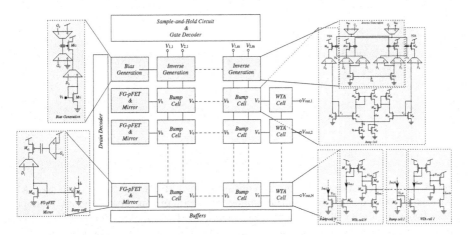

Fig. 11. Architecture of an analog vector quantizer. The core is the bump cell array followed by a WTA circuit. The main complexity from programming are at the peripheries and the system can be scaled up easily.

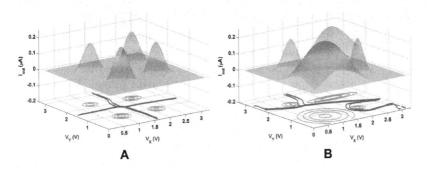

Fig. 12. Configurable classification results. The measured bump output currents (circle contours) and the WTA voltages (thick solid lines at the bottom) of four templates are superposed in a single plot. V_X and V_Y are the V_{in1} in the first stage and the second stage floating-gate bump circuits respectively. Both of their V_{in2} terminals are fixed at $V_{DD}/2$. **A:** Four templates are programmed to have the same variance and evenly spaced means. **B:** Four templates are programmed to have different variances with evenly spaced means.

tion per bump cell with a specific value of width. The relation between the power consumption and the extracted standard deviation is shown in Fig. 13B.

The VGA is the main source of the power consumption. The gain is tunable when the nMOS transistors in the VGA operate in the transition between above threshold and subthreshold regions. The width tunability can also result from the nonlinearity of the pMOS transistors when they are in transition between saturation and ohmic region. From simulation, to save the power consumed in

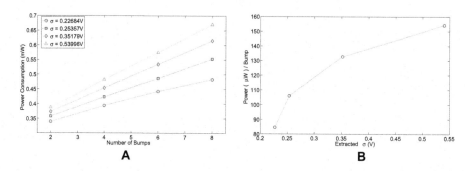

Fig. 13. Relation between the power consumption and the extracted variance. **A:** Measured power consumption of the analog vector quantizer with different number of floating-gate bump cells being activated with a fixed width. The slope of the curves indicate the average power consumption per bump cell. **B:** The relation between the power consumption per bump and the extracted variance of the bell-shaped transfer curve. The larger the variance is, the more the power consumption.

the VGA, we can make nMOS transistors longer to reduce the above-threshold currents and raise the source voltages of M_{23} and M_{24} to reduce the headroom.

Because the RBF output current is in the nano-amp range and the bandwidth of our current preamplifier for measurement is approximately 1KHz at that current level, we can not measure the speed of our floating-gate bump circuit directly, which is expected to be around mega-Hz range. We can only measure the response time from the input to the WTA outputs. The measured transient response of the analog vector quantizer is shown in Fig. 14**A**. One of the speed bottlenecks of the system is the inverse generation block. For a given width, the speed and the power depend on the amount of charge on M_{13} and M_{14}. With more electrons on the floating gates, the circuit can achieve higher speed but with the cost of more power consumption as shown in Fig. 14**B**. The

Table 1. Analog Vector Quantizer Parameters

Size of VQ	7(templates)×2(components)
Area/Bump Cell	$42 \times 82 \, \mu\text{m}^2$
Area/WTA Cell	$20 \times 35 \, \mu\text{m}^2$
Power Supply Rail	$V_{\text{DD}} = 3.3V$
Power Consumption/Bump Cell	$90\mu W \sim 160\mu W$
Response Time	$20\mu \sim 40\mu\text{sec}$
Floating-gate Programming Accuracy	99.5%
Retention Time	10 years @ $25°$C

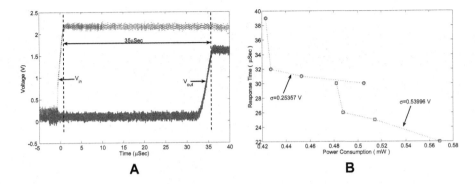

Fig. 14. Response time and speed-power trade-off of an analog vector quantizer. **A:** The response time between the input voltage and the WTA output. **B:** The relation between the response time and the power consumption for a given bump width. The inverse generation block dominates the response time in the steep region. The VGA dominates in the flat region. Charge on M_{13} and M_{14} can be programmed to optimize the speed-power trade-off.

steep portion of the curve implies that the inverse generation block dominates. In this region, we can increase the speed by consuming more power in the inverse generation block. The flat region in Fig. 14**B** indicates the VGA dominant region. In this region, burning more power in the inverse generation block does not improve the speed of the system. Thus, given a variance, we can program the charges on M_{13} and M_{14} so that the system operates at the knee of the curve to optimize the trade-off between the speed and the power consumption in the inverse generation block.

Finally, we evaluate the computational accuracy of the analog RBF. Since the computation method and errors are different from those of traditional digital approaches, generic comparisons of effective bit-accuracy do not make sense. Rather, we choose to evaluate the impact of using the analog RBFs on system performance. To this end receiver operating characteristic (ROC) curves and equal error rate (EER) are adopted. Two separate 2D bumps are programmed to have the same variance with a fixed separation as shown in Fig. 15. The corresponding Gaussian fits are used as the actual probability density functions (pdf) of two classes. Comparing these two pdf's using different thresholds renders a ROC curve of these two Gaussian distributed classes that is used as the evaluation reference. With the knowledge of the class distributions, comparing the output currents using different thresholds generates a ROC curve for the 2D bumps. Comparing each of the two WTA output voltages with different thresholds generates two ROC curves that characterize the classification results of the vector quantizer. The EER, which is the intersection of the ROC curve and the $-45°$ line as shown in Fig. 16**A**, is the usual operating point of classifiers. In

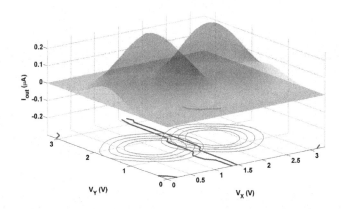

Fig. 15. Distributions of two "bumps" used to evaluate the classifier performance. In the measurements for performance evaluation, the separation of the center is kept constant but the widths of these two "bumps" varies. The measured bump output currents (circle contours) and the WTA voltages (thick solid lines at the bottom) of two templates are superposed in a single plot. V_X and V_Y are the values at the V_{in1} input terminals of the first and the second floating-gate bump circuits respectively. The V_{in2} terminals in both stages are fixed at $V_{DD}/2$.

Fig. 16**B**, both the ROC areas and the EER are plotted to investigate the effect of the bump width on the performance. At the EER point, the performance of the analog RBF classifier, which uses floating-gate bump circuits to approximate Gaussian likelihood functions, is undistinguishable from that of an ideal RBF-based classifier. Despite the finite gain of the WTA circuit, the performance of the analog vector quantizer is still comparable to an ideal maximum likelihood (ML) classifier. By optimizing the precision and speed of the WTA circuit, the performance can be improved but it is beyond the scope of this chapter.

7   Power Efficiency Comparison

To compare the efficiency of our analog system with the DSP hardware, we estimate the metric of millions of multiply accumulates per second per milli-watt (MMAC/s/mW) of our classifiers. When the system is scaled up, the efficiency of the bump cells dominates the performance. Therefore, we consider the performance of a single bump cell only.

Each Gaussian function is estimated as 10 MACs and can be evaluated by a bump cell in less than 10μ sec (which is still an overestimate) with the power consumption of $120\mu W$ or so. This is equivalent to 8.3 MMAC/s/mW. The performance of commercial low-power DSP microprocessors ranges from 1 MMAC/s/mW to 10 MMAC/s/mW and a special designed high performance DSP microprocessor in [18] is better than 50 MMAC/s/mW. If this comparison

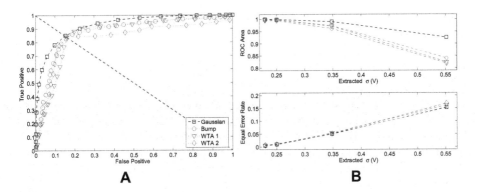

Fig. 16. ROC and EER performance of the classifiers. **A:** The ROC curves of the Gaussian fits (squares), output currents of the 2D bumps (circles) and WTA output voltages (triangles and diamonds) with the extracted $\sigma = 0.55$V. The Gaussian fits are used as the actual pdf's of the two classes and the corresponding ROC curve is used as a reference. The intersection of the ROC curve and the $-45°$ line is the EER point, which is the usual operating point. **B:** The effects of different bump widths on the receiver operating characteristic (ROC) area and the equal error rate (EER) performance. The separation of the means of two classes is 1.2V. The results show that the analog VQ is comparable to an ideal maximum-likelihood (ML) classifier.

is expanded to include the WTA function, the efficiency of the proposed analog system will improve even more relative to the digital system.

Although our power efficiency is comparable to the digital system, our classifier consumes much more power compared to other analog vector-matrix-multiplication systems [19,20], the efficiency of which ranges from 37 to 175 MMAC/s/μW. The reason is that the transistors M_{23} and M_{24} are operating far above threshold. By making M_{21} and M_{22} long and raising the source voltages of M_{23} and M_{24} (which is not available in the current chip), from simulation, the power consumption can be easily reduce by at least two orders of magnitude. If the WTA circuit is also optimized, it is anticipated that future ICs will be at least two to three orders of magnitude more efficient than DSP microprocessors at the same task.

8   Conclusion

In this chapter, a new programmable floating-gate bump circuit is demonstrated. The height, the center and the width of its bell-shaped transfer characteristics can be programmed individually. A multivariate radial basis function with a diagonal matrix can be realized by cascading these bump cells. Based on the new bump circuit, a novel compact RBF-based soft classifier is built. By adding a simple current mode winner-take-all circuit, we implement an analog vector quantizer. The performance and the efficiency of the classifiers are comparable to the digital system. With slight modifications, the overall efficiency is anticipated to be improved by at least two to three orders of magnitude better than DSP microprocessors.

Appendix

The nMOS transistors in the VGA are assumed in the transition between the above-threshold and the subthreshold regions. The pMOS transistors are assumed in the above-threshold region. Because the transfer characteristics of the two branches are symmetric, we can use the half circuit technique to analyze the VGA gain. By equating the currents flowing through the pMOS and nMOS transistors, we can have

$$
I_{0,p} \left(\frac{W_p}{L_p} \right) \frac{1}{4U_T^2} \left[\kappa_p (V_{DD} - V_{fg,21} - V_{T0,p}) \right]^2
$$
$$
= I_{0,n} \left(\frac{W_n}{L_n} \right) \ln^2 \left(1 + e^{\frac{\kappa_n}{2U_T}(V_1 - V_{T0,n})} \right) \tag{12}
$$

where the subscripts of "p" and "n" refer to pMOS and nMOS transistors respectively, I_0 is the subthreshold pre-exponential current factor, κ is the subthreshold slope factor, V_{T0} is the threshold voltage, and U_T is the thermal voltage. At the peak of the bell-shaped transfer curve, $V_{Q,dm} = 0$ and

$$
V_{fg,21} = \frac{1}{2} \Delta V_{in} + V_{Q,cm}
$$
$$
V_1 = V_{out,cm} + \frac{1}{2} \Delta V_{out},
$$

where $V_{out,cm} = (V_1 + V_2)/2$, $\Delta V_{out} = V_1 - V_2$. We can obtain the gain of the VGA by differentiating (12) with respect to $V_{fg,21}$ and have

$$
\frac{\Delta V_{out}}{\Delta V_{in}} = \frac{dV_1}{dV_{fg,21}} = -\gamma \left(1 + e^{-\frac{\kappa_n}{2U_T}(V_1 - V_{T0,n})} \right)
$$
$$
= \frac{-\gamma}{1 - e^{-\frac{\gamma \kappa_p}{2U_T}(V_{DD} - V_{fg,21} - V_{T0,p})}}
$$
$$
\approx -\gamma \left(1 + e^{-\frac{\gamma \kappa_p}{2U_T}(V_{DD} - V_{Q,cm} - V_{T0,p})} \right), \tag{13}
$$

where $\gamma = \frac{\kappa_p}{\kappa_n} \sqrt{\frac{I_{0,p} W_p L_n}{I_{0,n} L_p W_n}}$. Therefore, the gain increases approximately exponentially with the common-mode charge and, accordingly, we can expect the exponential relation between the extracted standard deviation of the transfer curve and the common-mode charge.

References

1. P. Hasler, P. D. Smith, D. Graham, R. Ellis, and D. V. Anderson, "Analog Floating-Gate, On-Chip Auditory Sensing System Interfaces," in *IEEE J. Sensors*, vol. 5, no. 5, pp.1027-1034, Oct. 2005.

2. M.Ogawa, K. Ito, and T. Shibata, "A general-purpose vector-quantization processor employing two-dimensional bit-propagating winner-take-all," in *Symposium on VLSI Circuits*, pp.244-247, 13-15 June 2002.
3. M. Bracco, S. Ridella, and R. Zunino, "Digital Implementation of Hierarchical Vector Quantization," in *IEEE Trans. Neural Networks*, vol. 14, no. 5, pp.1072-1084, Sep. 2003.
4. G. Cauwenberghs and V. Pedron, "A low-power CMOS analog vector quantizer," in *IEEE J. Solid-State Circuits*, vol. 32, no. 8, pp.1278-1283, Aug. 1997.
5. P. Hasler, P. Smith, C. Duffy, C. Gordon, J. Dugger, D. Anderson, "A floating-gate vector-quantizer," in *Midwest Symposium on Circuits and Systems*, Vol.1,4-7, Aug. 2002, pp. I-196-9.
6. T. Yamasaki and T. Shibata, "Analog soft-pattern-matching classifier using floating-gate MOS technology," in *IEEE Trans. Neural Networks*, vol. 14, no. 5, pp.1257-1265, Sep. 2003.
7. T. Delbruck, "Bump circuits for computing similarity and dissimilarity of analog voltage," in *Proc. Int. Neural Network Society*, Seattle, WA, 1991.
8. S. S. Watkins and P. M. Chau, "A radial basis function neurocomputer implemented with analog VLSI circuits," in *Int. Joint Conf. Neural Networks*, 1992, vol. 2, pp. 607V612.
9. J. Choi, B. J. Sheu, and J. C.-F. Chang, "A Gaussian synapse circuit for analog neural networks," in *IEEE Trans. VLSI Syst.*, vol. 2, pp. 129V133, Mar. 1994.
10. S.-Y. Lin, R.-J. Huang, and T.-D. Chiueh, "A Tunable Gaussian/Square Function Computation Circuit for Analog Neural Networks" in *IEEE Transactions on Circuits and System II*, vol. 45, no. 3, 1998, pp. 441-446.
11. D. S. Masmoudi, A. T. Dieng, and M. Masmoudi, "A subthreshold mode programmable implementation of the Gaussian function for RBF neural networks applications", in *Intelligent Control, 2002. Proceedings of the 2002 IEEE International Symposium on*, Vancouver, Cananda, Oct. 2002, pp. 454-459.
12. D. Hsu, M. Figueroa, and C. Diorio, "A silicon primitive for competitive learning," in *Conference on Neural Information Processing Systems*, Dec. 2000.
13. P. Hasler, "Continuous-Time Feedback in Floating-Gate MOS Circuits," in *IEEE Trans. Circuit and system II*, Vol. 48, No. 1, pp. 56-64, Jan. 2001.
14. M. Kucic, A. Low, P. Hasler, and J. Neff, "A programmable continuous-time floating-gate Fourier processor," in *IEEE Trans. Circuit and system II*, pp. 90-99, Jan. 2001.
15. A. Bandyopadhyay, G.J. Serrano, and P. Hasler, "Adaptive Algorithm Using Hot-Electron Injection for Programming Analog Computational Memory Elements Within 0.2% of Accuracy Over 3.5 Decades," in *IEEE J. Solid-State Circuits*, vol. 41, no. 9, pp.2107-2114, Sept. 2006.
16. P. Hasler and J. Dugger, "Correlation Learning Rule in Floating-Gate pFET Synapses," in *IEEE Trans. Circuit and system II*, vol. 48, no. 1, pp.65-73, Jan. 2001.
17. V. Srinivasan, G. J. Serrano, J. Gray, and P. Hasler, "A precision cmos amplifier using floating-gates for offset cancellation," in Proc. CICC05, Sept. 2005, pp. 734737.
18. J. Glossner, K. Chirca, M. Schulte, H. Wang, N. Nasimzada, D. Har, S. Wang; A. J. Hoane, G. Nacer, M. Moudgill, M., S. Vassiliadis, "Sandblaster low power DSP," in *IEEE Prec. Custom Integrated Circuits Conference*, pp.575-581, oct. 2004.
19. R. Chawla, A. Bandyopadhyay, V. Srinivasan, and P. Hasler, "A 531nW/MHz, 128x32 current-mode programmable analog vector-matrix multiplier with over two decades of linearity," in *IEEE Prec. Custom Integrated Circuits Conference*, pp.651-654, oct. 2004.

20. R. Karakiewicz, R. Genov, A. Abbas, and G. Cauwenberghs, "175 GMACS/mW Charge-Mode Adiabatic Mixed-Signal Array Processor," in *Symposium on VLSI Circuits*, June, 2006.

Compression-based SoC Test Infrastructures

Julien DALMASSO, Marie-Lise FLOTTES, Bruno ROUZEYRE

LIRMM, Univ. Montpellier II/CNRS, 161 rue Ada, 34932 Montpellier cedex 5, France
{dalmasso, flottes, rouzeyre}@lirmm.fr

Abstract.

Test Data Compression techniques have been developed for reducing requirements in terms of Automatic Test Equipments. In this paper, we explore the benefits of using these techniques in the context of core-based SoCs. Test Data Compression is used to reduce the system test time by increasing the test parallelism of several cores without the expense of additional tester channels. In this paper, we first discuss the constraints on test architectures and on the design flow inferred by the use of compressed test data. We propose a method for seeking an optimal architecture in terms of total test application time. The method is independent of the compression scheme used for reduction of core test data. The gain in terms of test application time for the SoC is over 50% compared to a test scheme without compression.

1. Introduction

Testing a SoC mainly consists in testing each core in the system. In order to provide accessibility to these cores, the SoC architecture is completed by a Test Access Mechanism (TAM) and wrappers interfacing cores with the TAM (IEEE 1500 standard [1]). The TAM is generally a bus whose bandwidth fits the number of SoC test IOs. TAM and wrappers are preferably co-designed in order to reduce the global Test Application Time (TAT): several methods formulated as optimization problems have been proposed for establishing the best trade-off between the number of test buses, the bus bandwidth, the wrapper size and the test parallelism (e.g. [2], [3], [4], [5], [6]). However, as the complexity of SoC design keeps on growing, testing becomes more and more expensive with regard to test time and test pin requirements. While increasing the number of scan chains in a core helps to reduce its test time, it also increases the bandwidth of the core interface with the TAM. The consequence of this local test time improvement is to either reduce the test parallelism possibilities at system level, or increase test resources requirements: larger TAM, larger numbers of test inputs and higher requirements in terms of tester channels.

Several Test Data Compression (TDC) techniques aiming at reducing the number of visible scan chains have been developed. Concerning test pattern compression, also called horizontal compression, those techniques consist in compressing test patterns off line (i.e. reducing their bit width), storing the compressed test data in the ATE,

Please use the following format when citing this chapter:

Dalmasso, J., Flottes, M.-L. and Rouzeyre, B., 2009, in IFIP International Federation for Information Processing, Volume 291; *VLSI-SoC: Advanced Topics on Systems on a Chip*; eds. R. Reis, V. Mooney, P. Hasler; (Boston: Springer), pp. 53–67.

and decompressing test data on-chip for restoring initial test patterns (see Figure 1). Input-data compression schemes rely on the fact that test patterns originally contain don't-care bits. These don't care bits do not have to be stored into ATE but can be supplied on-chip in some other ways. LFSRs [7][8], Xor networks [9] [10], ring generator [11], RAM [12] [13], arithmetic units [14] and test pattern broadcasting among multiple scan chains [15] [16] [19] constitute a range of solutions for minimizing the number of data to be stored into ATE. All these methods reduce therefore the number of necessary ATE channels (W_{ATE}) required to test a standalone core including N scan chains ($N > W_{ATE}$).

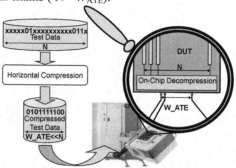

Fig. 1. Compression/Decompression scheme

Note that as mentioned earlier, increasing the number of internal scan chains in a core, and therefore its interface with the TAM, allows reducing its test time since the resulting test scheme requires fewer scan-in clock cycles. However, if a compression technique is used for keeping the number of visible scan chains W_{ATE} as low as possible ($W_{ATE} < N$), the core test time may be affected compared to a solution where the number of visible scan chain is equal to the number of real scan chains ($W_{ATE} = N$). Because no matter the TDC technique is used, compressing an N-bits vector on a W_{ATE}-bits word to be stored in the ATE is not always possible. Consequently, it is necessary to serialize the non-compressible vectors with the help of a decompressor-bypass mechanism, or to look for additional compressible test patterns for keeping the fault coverage obtained with the original non-compressed test sequence. In any case, a side-effect is an increase in TAT of the core under test.

Concerning test responses, several methods have been proposed (e.g. [17], [18]). Conversely to TDC, those test responses compaction techniques do not impact TAT and are independent of the core netlist and of the test responses sequence. Thus, they can be directly employed in the framework of SoCs design. In the remainder of this paper, we focus on test pattern compression only.

Several TDC approaches can be considered at system level. In a bottom-up approach, TDC is applied at core level by the core designer, and then wrapped cores (including decompressors) are embedded in the SoC by the system integrator. In this case, the test infrastructure design resumes to the classical TAM optimization problem since individual test times and number of visible scan chains on the core interfaces are known, and fixed, before system integration. The second approach consists in questioning test time optimization and compression schemes at system level. In this case, the cores come with their uncompressed test sequences and the system integrator must determine the compression ratio on every core, define the test infrastructure and resulting test time. This approach should allow optimizing the test of the system with regard to the test resources constraints and not only with regards to the pre-fixed test times of the individual cores as in the bottom-up approach.

Concerning TDC at system level, several approaches focus on memory depth requirements using different forms of stream compression (e.g. [19], [20]), or on test pattern broadcasting among multiple cores (test time savings up to 23% are reported in [21]). TAM architectures using horizontal compression have been presented in [23], [24], [25] but the proposed methods rely on specific TDC techniques. Moreover, all architectural solutions are not considered since these techniques essentially target TAM architectures with a single decompressor for all cores, or architectures with a dedicated decompressor per core (or connected to duplicated versions of the same core).

In this paper, we propose a method for exploring all TAM/TDC architectures including solutions with a dedicated decompressor per core and architectural solutions with shared decompressors. The final goal is to generate test architectures and test schedules that minimize the system TAT. The proposed technique is independent of the adopted compression scheme.

Section 2 discusses the implication of TDC insertion at SoC level. The problem formulation as well as notations are given is Section 3. The algorithm is detailed is Section 4 whereas experimental results are reported in Section 5. Finally, Section 6 draws some conclusions.

2.   SoC test architecture and compression

2.1   Test infrastructure design

A SoC test architecture is proposed by the IEEE 1500 Standard. It mainly consists of a TAM bus and wrappers around cores. The TAM links the SoC's test IOs to the cores. Each core wrapper interfaces the core and the TAM bus. As in [2] and [3], we assume a TAM architecture organized around a partitioned test bus, each core being connected to one sub-bus, as depicted in Figure 2 in which the TAM is split into two sub-buses TAM1 and TAM2. Cores connected to the same sub-bus are tested serially (e.g. C1, C2, C3), cores assigned to different TAMs can be tested in parallel (e.g. C1 and C4 or C1 and C5). We do not make any assumption about the wrappers of the cores : they can be designed when building the test infrastructure at system level or pre-defined by the 1500-ready cores. In the rest of this paper, W_{TAM} denotes the TAM bandwidth, and W_{TAMi} the bandwidth of sub-bus i.

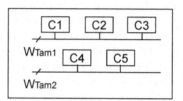

$$W_{ATE} = W_{Tam} = \sum W_{Tami}$$

Fig. 2. TAM architecture

Let's recall that, under the chosen TAM model, building the test infrastructure mainly consists in: 1) finding a partition of the bus into p sub-buses and determining their bandwidth, 2) assigning the cores to the p sub-buses, and designing their wrappers 3) deriving a test schedule so that the total test time is minimized. An underlying data of these tasks is the test times of cores.

The test time of a core depends, among other things, on the size of its wrapper in terms I/Os interfaces with the TAM. The test time of the core and its wrapper size are linked by the following relation:

$$T_{core} = V \times [1+\max\{si,so\}] + \min\{si,so\}$$

where V is the number of test patterns, and si (so) the number of scan cycles required to load (unload) a test vector (test response). In Figure 3 for instance, two wrappers configurations of the same core are depicted. On the left hand side, the core is connected to the TAM through 2 visible scan chains and the test time is 13p+12 cycles. On the right hand side, the wrapper interface is enlarged to 3 scan chains at the benefit of the test time, which is reduced to 10p+6 cycles.

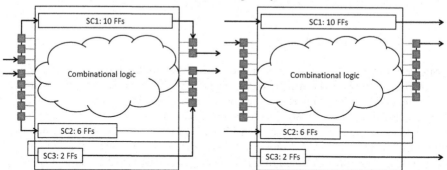

Fig. 3. Wrapper designs

2.2   Compression and test infrastructure

The TAM bandwidth can be increased thanks to TDC techniques without changing the requirements in terms of ATE channels (W_{ATE}). The tests parallelism can therefore be increased without additional cost and should result in a shorter test time. However, as explained in the introduction, TDC may also increase the test times of individual cores. More precisely, for a fixed number N of scan chains (or equivalently for a fixed wrapper size), the test time of a core increases when the number of bits at the input of the decompressor gets smaller. For instance, using the TDC technique presented in [14], the test of the S38417 benchmarks circuit with N=16 scan chains needs 21451 clock cycles when $W_{ATE} = 10$ and increase to 38867 clocks cycles when $W_{ATE} = 3$ (see for instance, results given in Figure 9).

The use of TDC impacts the building of the test infrastructure in two aspects:

- 1) Since TDC modifies the test times of individual cores, the decompression ratios must be established *during* the design of the test infrastructure and not after.
- 2) Since decompressors can be shared between several cores, test sequences to compress must be defined before decompressor assignation.

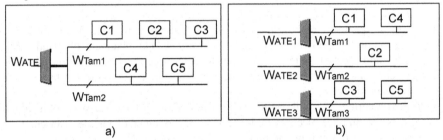

a)   b)

Fig. 4. TAM/decompressors architectures

Let's discuss this last point on the Figure 4 example: either a decompressor feeds several sub-buses (Figure 4.a) or one decompressor feeds a single sub-bus (in Figure 4.b). The evaluation in terms of test time of a solution requires defining the bus partitioning, the core assignment, the test parallelism, the test sequence, and finally the compression of this sequence. Figure 4.a for instance depicts only one bus partitioning and core assignment possibility. It includes several test parallelism solutions (e.g. either C1 and C4 tested in parallel or C1 and C5). In turn, each one necessitates building the actual test sequence by concatenating the test sequences of the cores tested in parallel, C1 and C4 for instance. Finally the resulting test sequence has to be compressed in order to obtain the actual test time. Another way of dealing with this model is 1) to build the optimal test infrastructure and related test schedule without looking at compression 2) derive the whole SoC test sequence and compress it. Doing so, there is no chance to obtain an optimal solution since the test infrastructure (without decompressor) is built given the original test times of cores which are latter modified by the compression. We did such an experiment with the example given in section 5. Doing so, the obtained test time is 65699 cycles while a solution with 57941 cycles has been obtained using the method we propose here.

Conversely, the cores connected downstream a decompressor in the second architecture style (Figure 4.b) are tested one after the other. The test sequences to compress are simply those of the cores and not issued from the concatenation of several ones. The compression of the test sequences can therefore be done independently of the test infrastructure building process. This alleviates the problems raised by the first model.

So in the remaining, we consider the second architecture style and we propose a method for *conjunctly* building up the TAM, the wrappers (if needed) and the decompressors.

Each path for the ATE channels, through a decompressor, up to sub-bus is called a *line*. The architecture depicted in Figure 4.b) is composed of three lines for instance. It must be noted that within this architectural model and in the absence of additional constraints such as power limit for instance, the test scheduling is trivial (as without compression). The test time on a line is simply the sum of the individual test times of the cores since there is no test parallelism on the line. The total TAT at system level is the maximal test times over the lines.

3.   Problem statement and notations

We state the problem of building the test infrastructure with decompressors as an optimization problem. Given the number of available ATE channels, the bandwidth of the TAM, and the test patterns, we want to determine the best partition of the test infrastructure into p lines and the interconnection of the cores to the sub-buses so that the TAT is minimized.

In the remaining, we will use the following notations. the ratio W_{ATE}/N is denoted by ρ. n is the number of cores under test, w_c the number of visible scan chains for every core c=1…n. Let p be the number of lines, and let W_{ATE_i} and W_{TAM_i}, i=1,…,p be respectively the number of ATE channels and the bandwidth of the sub-bus on line i. Let $\rho_i = W_{ATE\_i}/W_{TAM\_i}$ be the decompression ratio of line i. $t^c_{w_c,\rho}$ denotes the test time of core c with a w_c bits wrapper for a ratio ρ.

The problem is to determine:
- the line number p;
- the bitwidths W_{ATE_i} and W_{TAM_i} for i=1,…,p;
- an assignment of the cores to the lines;
- optionally, the wrapper size w_c of each core,
- and a test schedule so that TAT is minimal.

The following constraints must be obeyed:

$$W_{ATE} = \sum_{i=1,..,p} W_{ATE\_i} \qquad\qquad \text{cons.1}$$

$$W_{TAM} \geq \sum_{i=1,..,p} W_{TAM\_i} \qquad\qquad \text{cons.2}$$

$$W_{TAM\_i} \geq W_{ATE\_i}, \ i=1,..,p \qquad\qquad \text{cons.3}$$

$$w_c \leq W_{TAM\_i} \ \text{if c is connected to line i.} \qquad \text{cons.4}$$

Variables to be determined are given in italic in Figure 5 (.W_{ATE} and W_{TAM} being given)

Concerning core wrappers, there are two cases: either the cores are wrapper-ready or their wrappers have to be designed. In the later case, it must be noted first that $1 \leq w_c \leq \max(\#PIs,\#POs) + \#scan$ chains. Secondly, once w_c is determined, designing the wrapper so that the test time of the core is minimized resumes simply to balance the lengths of the visible scan chains. This won't be detailed in the remaining.

In the scenario where the wrappers are already fixed, if a core is assigned to a line i for which W_{TAM_i} is strictly greater than the wrapper size w_c, only w_c bits of TAM_i are connected to the wrapper, the test time of the core is considered to be the same as if TAM_i was w_c bits wide. For instance, and for a core c with $w_c =4$, its test time $t^c_{w_c,\rho}$ is the same whether it is assigned to a line with $W_{ATE} = 2$ and $W_{TAM} =6$, or to a line with $W_{ATE} = 2$ and $W_{TAM} =4$, i.e. $\rho = 2/4$.

The test time $t^c_{w_c,\rho}$ of a core c must be pre-computed for all possible values of ρ (from 1 to $1/w_c$). (cf. section 4 to see how this process can be speeded up). For examining the benefit of using TDC when designing the test infrastructure of a SoC, we developed the heuristic presented hereafter.

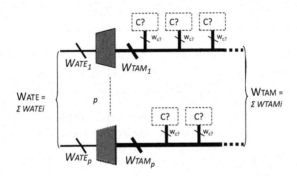

Fig. 5. Problem statement

4.   Algorithm

The general flow chart of the method is depicted in Figure 6. First, all the possible combinations of lines are explored (line 1 and 2). The ATE channels partition can be easily determined knowing the total W_{ATE} width and the number of lines p by applying the formula of the partition of integer numbers. Namely, the number $X(n,p)$ of partitions of a set of n elements into p subsets can be computed as:

$$X(n, p) = \sum_{k=1}^{p} X(n-p,k) \text{ with } X(n,n) = X(n,1) = 1 \tag{1}$$

and $X(n,p) = 0$ if $p > n$

For instance, 10 ATE channels can be partitioned into p=3 subsets in X(10,3)=8 different ways (1+1+8, 1+2+7, 1+3+6, etc...).

Then for each ATE channels partition, all the compatible partitions of the TAM are calculated. A partition of the TAM is said to be compatible with a partition of the ATE channels if cons.3 is verified for all p lines. Furthermore, if cores are wrapper-ready i.e. w_c are fixed, the number of TAM partitions to be explored can be further reduced by considering cons.4. In other words, the narrowest TAM must be large enough to support the narrowest wrapper. It must be noticed that if $W_{TAM\_i} = W_{ATE\_i}$, no decompressor is present on this line. For a pair of partition, (ATE channels partition and TAM partition), cores must be assigned and the scheduling performed to obtain the TAT of this architecture (line 3 in Figure 6).

---

1. For all ATE channels partitions into p parts
2.   For each compatible TAM partition into p parts
3.   Find the best assignment of the cores to the p lines (that minimize TAT) ->cf Fig 5.
If this assignment reduces the global TAT, memorize this assignment and ATE/TAM architecture

Fig. 6. Partition algorithm

Seeking for the assignment of cores to lines that minimizes TAT is an NP-complete problem. So we developed the heuristic given in Figure 7.

// Initial Solution
–   Sort cores by decreasing test data volume
–   Assign each core to the largest bus so that TAT increases as few as possible.
// Improvement of the solution
• While TAT is reduced
–   Find the line i with the highest TAT_i
–   For each core c assigned to i,
     •   For all other lines k ($k \neq i$)
          –   Move core c from i to k
          –   Compute newTAT and memorize i, k, c and newTAT
          –   Move back core c from k to i
–   Move core c from i to k such that:
          1) the smallest TAT has been obtained
          2) the number of useless bits on k is minimized
          3) the standard deviation between TAT_i of all lines is maximized

Fig. 7. Assignment algorithm

The first step determines an initial solution of the architecture, i.e an initial assignment of cores to the TAMs. Each core is positioned on the largest possible TAM i.e. and its wrapper size is set according to (cons.4). If the core is wrapper-ready, it is assigned to the smallest bus i.e. respecting cons.4. For instance, in case of 3 TAMs having resp. 5, 7 and 10 bits, a core with a 6-bits wrapper will be assigned to the 7 bits TAM. The first bus is not large enough to be connected to the core's wrapper (cons.4). The second bus is preferred to the third one since, a priori, it is beneficial to reserve the larger one for cores with larger wrappers.

The second step consists in improving this initial solution. For this, the cores are moved to other lines to reduce the global TAT.

The principle is to move a core from the line with the highest TAT to another line so that the global TAT gets reduced as much as possible. For that, all cores of the line are virtually shifted to other lines and TATs are computed accordingly. The move that gives the highest benefit is chosen. In case of equality, the algorithm chooses (Core c, Line i) such that the number of useless bits on the line is minimized i.e. $W_{TAM\_i} - w_c$ is minimal. This is done for getting more room to move cores with larger wrappers to large buses, in next steps. Similarly, a third order criterion is used to unbalance test times over lines.

Let's recall that the computation of TAT is straightforward (TAT_i denotes the test application time on line i):

$$TAT = \max(TAT_i, i = 1,...,p) \text{ and } TAT_i = \sum_{\text{cores assigned to i}} t^c_{w_c,\rho_i} \qquad (2)$$

Note that the test times $t^c_{w_c,\rho}$ for all cores and for all compression ratios (W_{ATE_i}/w_c) are inputs of the proposed algorithm. These data are necessary to compute the system TAT (i.e. schedule the tests). Thus, as a pre-process, the compression algorithm must be performed for all compression ratios, for all cores and all wrapper sizes. This can be very CPU expensive depending on the compression technique used. We propose here an alternative to the exhaustive computation

First, when the wrapper size is questioned, let's recall that as reported by many authors, the test time of a core, in the absence of compression i.e. $\rho=1$, is a stepwise decreasing function of the wrapper size. Furthermore it depends on the number of test vectors and not on the vectors themselves. Figure 8 reports the test time versus w_c for the 10th core of the D695 ITC'02 benchmark. In general the number of steps is small. Only 15 optimal values of w_c have to be considered for this core.

Fig. 8. ITC'02 d695 benchmark (core 10) Test time vs wrapper size

Secondly, whatever the TDC technique is used, the same behavior of the test time of cores versus decompression ratio can be observed (for a given wrapper size w_c). It can be identified to the function:

$$t^c_{w_c,\rho} = \frac{\alpha}{\rho} + \beta \qquad (3)$$

Only two values of t for one core are sufficient to identify α and β. The estimated values of $t^c_{w_c,\rho}$ for several decompression ratios are thus obtained from only two measured values instead of w_c computations. In order to improve the precision of the estimation, the compression algorithm is performed with the first and last decompression ratio values.

This property has been validated with the TDC method [14]. This compression scheme is applicable with intellectual property cores and it is Test Suite independent, i.e. it does not required specific test generation or fault simulation.

The measured and estimated $t_{c,\rho}$ values are reported on Figure 9 for the ISCAS'89 s38417 benchmark (16-bits wrapper). The maximum error between measured and estimated values is smaller than 1%. Similar results have been obtained for all ISCAS'89 benchmarks and several configurations of wrappers.

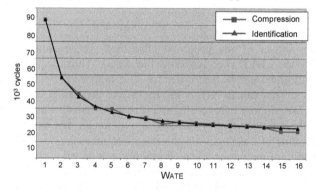

Fig. 9. S38417 (w_c = 16) computed/estimated test times

As a final remark let's note that the proposed heuristic can be adapted to additional constraints such as power limit, precedence constraints, etc.... Concerning the power consumption constraint for instance, two levels of optimization can be envisaged. At core level, the don't care values not assigned by the compression scenari can be assigned in such a way that power consumption is limited during scan shifting. At system level, core test parallelism is not totally fixed by our architectural solution since cores assigned to the same line must be serially tested but there is no constraint on the test order. In Figure 2 for instance, cores on the first line can be tested in the following order C1, C2 and C3 or C1,C3 and C2 for instance. The best solution in terms of power consumption depends of the test order on the second line C4, C5 or C5, C4.

5.   Results

The first SoC used for experiments is the one described in [9][23] and depicted in Figure 10. It is composed of 16 ISCAS'89 benchmark circuits used as cores (i.e. with wrappers).

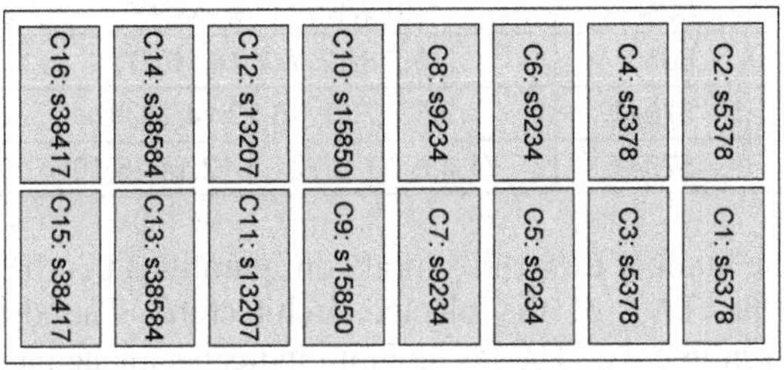

Fig. 9. SoC example from [23]

The test sequences of the circuits have been obtained with the Synopsis ATPG tool TETRAMAX [26] and compressed with our TDC technique described in [14]. The characteristics of the cores are given in table 1.

Table 1. Characteristics of the cores

Core number	#scan chains (wc)	test cycles
1 to 4	5	9331
5 to 8	6	9030
9, 10	10	8804
11,12	12	16048
13,14	14	19845
15,16	16	45760

As explained before, the proposed method able to deal with either wrapper ready cores or with cores for which the 1500 wrapper has to be designed. The 2 following sub-sections present experimental results in both cases.

5.1 Fixed wrapper

In a first series of experiments, we assume that the wrappers are already designed. Wrappers sizes are equal to the number of scan chains. We have set the number of ATE channels to 32 and the maximal total TAM bitwidth to 64. The algorithm has been applied with a number of lines ranging from 2 to 6. Results are reported in Table 2.

Table 2. Architectures exploration results

#lines	# conf.	TAT	Lines' parameters (W_{ATE_i} / W_{TAM_i})	#bits used on TAM
2	522	127413	(16,16) / (16, 48)	30
3	44639	90457	(8,9,15) / (14,16,34)	42
4	1345142	68361	(5,7,8,12) / (7,14,16,27)	53
5	18605924	57941	(5,5,7,7,8) / (6,12,14,16,16)	64
6	142238520	57941	(1,4,5,7,7,8) / (1,5,12,14,16,16)	63

Col.2 indicates the number of architectural configurations that have been explored while col.3 gives the TAT of the elected architecture. The details of the test infrastructure are given in col.4. The last column indicates the actual number of TAM bits.

For instance, for architecture with 3 lines, 44639 configurations have been explored. The optimal one leads to a TAT equal to 90457 test cycles. The architecture is composed of 3 lines with 3 decompressors such that (W_{ATE_1}, W_{TAM_1}) = (8,14), (W_{ATE_2}, W_{TAM_2}) = (9,16), and (W_{ATE_3}, W_{TAM_3}) = (15,34).

From this table, some observations can be done:

- All potential test infrastructures are explored including those that do not contain decompressors. For instance, for the 2 lines configuration, the optimal architecture does not include a decompressor on the first bus $W_{ATE\_1} = W_{TAM\_1} = 16$.

- While a budget of a 64 bits TAM has been given, all those bits are not necessarily connected to cores (and thus are useless). This is the case for p=2, 3, 4, 6. This is mainly due to the wrapper sizes chosen for the cores. This means that the actual bitwidth of the TAM is smaller than 64 bits.

Among all compressor/TAM architectures, the best TAT is obtained with p=5 lines. The corresponding test schedule and architecture are given in Figure 11 and Figure 12. Test parallelism cannot be fully exploited with smaller values of p since at most p cores can be tested in parallel. For larger values of p (6, 7, …), further experiments have shown that TAT increases.

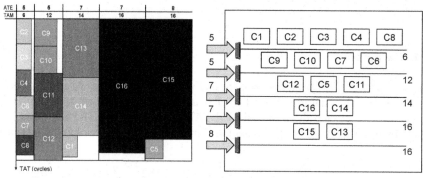

Fig 11 Test schedule for a 32 → 64 bits decompression with 5 lines TAT = 57941 cycles

Fig. 12 Final architecture

The reason is that the sizes of the wrappers relatively to the possible TAM_i widths act as a brake on parallelisation.

We measured the benefit of using compressors in SoCs test architectures by comparing them to standard architectures i.e. without using compression, while setting the same environmental constraints. In the first case, we assumed the same limit on the numbers of available ATE channels (32 bits and thus a TAM of 32 bits), in a second case, the same area budget for building the TAM (64 bits wide and thus 64 ATE channels).

For the first case, the TAT is 127413 cycles for a standard TAM architecture when a number of sub-buses p ranges from 2 to 4 and 131210 cycles when p equals 5 or 6. These results have to be compared with the 57941 cycles when compression is used. Thus, the use of TDC technique in the context of SoC infrastructure design leads to a gain of 54.5% in terms of TAT for this example (at the expense of area overhead: larger TAM, decompressors).

In the second case, i.e. a TAM of 64 bits (which means 64 ATE channels for a standard architecture vs 32 ATE channels with compression), comparative results are reported in Table 3. At the evidence, TDC has allowed to divide by two the number of ATE channels at the expense of only a 4% increase on TAT.

Table 3. Architectures Comparison (fixed wrappers)

	Proposed architecture: $W_{ATE} = 32$, $W_{TAM} = 64$		Standard architecture: $W_{ATE} = 64$, $W_{TAM} = 64$	
# lines	TAT	actual TAM bitwidth	# lines	TAT
2	127413	30	2	127413
3	90457	42	3	90457
4	68361	53	4	68361
5	57941	64	5	57941
6	57941	63	6	55738

5.2 Unfixed wrapper

We did the same experiments, but without assuming fixed wrappers size i.e. letting the method determines the most adequate wrappers structures. TAT are reported in Table 4. It can be fist noted that since wrappers structures are questioned, bus width can be better utilized leading to shorter TAT. Secondly, as in the previous case, the use of TDC leads to a large TAT improvement.

The same kind of experiments has been performed on the g1023 ITC'02 benchmark. Unfortunately, in the ITC'02 suite, neither cores netlists nor test patterns are provided, all information necessary to perform compression. Only the number of test vectors is specified. We have randomly chosen test sequences including the given number of vectors. To be conservative, the patterns are such that they include 80% of don't care bits (many authors report a don't care bits percentage ranging from 95% to 99% on industrial circuits). Comparative results are given in table 5.

Table 4. Architectures Comparison

p	32→64 Decomp. Architecture	Standard 64 bits Architecture	Standard 32 bits Architecture
2	66596	52953	97216
3	61277	49814	96624
4	57337	49129	96736
5	55101	48592	96624
6	54140	48517	96563

Table 5. g1023 Comparison results

p	Decomp. Architecture		Standard Architecture		
	32→64	16→32	64 bits	32 bits	16 bits
2	17492	26256	15153	19633	33952
3	14185	23084	11274	17892	33718
4	12996	21409	11274	17235	33824
5	12399	20719	11274	17215	33824
6	12138	20667	11274	17235	33824

6.   Conclusion

In this paper, we explored the benefits of horizontal test data compression techniques in the context of the design of SoC test infrastructures. The increase in parallelism allowed by compression is fully exploited to reduce the test application time of the SoC. We propose a method that explores all architectural solutions from one single decompressor for all cores to architectures with a dedicated decompressor per core. Results obtained on a SoC based on ISCAS'89 benchmarks circuits have confirmed this TAT reduction with a ratio of more than 50%. While the experiments have been performed using a particular TDC technique, the method is independent of the used TDC.

Presently, this method is geared to minimize the test time. Area overhead induced by decompressors and TAM is not taken into account. Seeking the best trade-off is a direction for future research.

References

[1]   IEEE standard for embedded core test – IEEE Std. 1500-2004.
[2]   V. Iyengar et al.. "Test wrapper and test access mechanism co-optimization for

system-on-a-chip". J. Electronic Testing, vol. 18, no. 2, pp. 213-230, April 2002

[3]   V. Iyengar et al., "Efficient Wrapper/TAM Co-Optimization for Large SOCs", DATE'02, pp: 491-497.

[4]   V. Iyengar et al. "Wrapper/TAM co-optimization, constraint-driven test scheduling, and tester data volume reduction for SOCs", DAC '02. pp: 685-690.

[5]   S.K. Goel, E.J. Marinissen, "Effective and Efficient Test Architecture Design for SOCs", ITC'02, p: 529- 535.

[6]   G. Zeng, H. Ito, "Concurrent core test for SOC using shared test set and scan chain disable", DATE'06, pp: 1045-1050.

[7]   A. Jas, B. Pouya, N.A. Touba, "Virtual Scan Chains: a means for reducing scan length in cores", VTS'00, pp: 73-78.

[8]   L-T Wang et al., "VirtualScan: a new compressed scan technology for test cost reduction", ITC'04, pp: 916-924.

[9]   I. Bayraktaroglu, A. Orailoglu, "Test volume application time reduction through scan chain concealment", DAC'01, pp: 151-155.

[10]   K.J. Balakrishman, N.A. Touba, "Reconfigurable linear decompressor using symbolic Gaussian elimination", DATE'05, pp: 1130-1135.

[11]   J. Rajski et al., "Embedded deterministic test for low cost manufacturing Test", ITC'02, pp: 916-922.

[12]   L. Li, K. Chakrabarty, N. A. Touba "Test data compression using dictionaries with selective entries and fixed-length indices", ACM TODAES, Vol. 8, No. 4, October 2003, pp: 470-490.

[13]   A. Würtenberger, C.S.Tautermann, S.Hellebrand, "Data compression for multiple scan chains using dictionaries with corrections", ITC'04, pp: 926-935.

[14]   J. Dalmasso, M.L. Flottes, B. Rouzeyre, "Fitting ATE Channels with Scan Chains: a Comparison between a Test Data Compression Technique and Serial Loading of Scan Chains", DELTA'06, pp: 295-300.

[15]   N. Sitchinava et al., "Changing the scan enable during shift", Proc. VTS'04, pp: 73-78.

[16]   H. Tang, S.M. Reddy, I. Pomeranz, "On reducing test data volume and test application time for multiple scan chain designs", Proc. ITC'03, pp: 1079-1088.

[17]   S. Mitra, K.S. Kim, "X-compact, an efficient response compaction technique for test cost reduction", ITC 02, pp: 311-320

[18]   J. Rajski,et al., "Finite memory test response compactors for embedded test applications", IEEE Trans. on CAD, April 2005, Vol. 24-4, pp: 622- 634.

[19]   A. Chandra and K. Chakrabarty, "Test Data Compression and Test Resource Partitioning for System-on-a-Chip Using Frequency-Directed Run-Length (FDR) Codes," IEEE Trans. Computers, vol. 52, no. 8, Aug. 2003, pp. 1076-1088.

[20]   P.T. Gonciari, B.M. Al-Hashimi, and N. Nicolici, "Variable-Length Input Huffman Coding for System-on-a-Chip Test," IEEE Trans. Computer-Aided Design, vol.22, no. 6, June 2003, pp. 783-796.

[21]   A. Larsson, E. Larsson, P. Eles, Z. Peng, "SOC Test Scheduling with Test Set Sharing and Broadcasting", Proc. ATS'05, Session A4: SoC Testing

[22]   B. Arslan, A. Orailoglu, "CircularScan: a scan architecture for test cost reduction", DATE'04, pp: 1290-1295.

[23]   V. Iyengar, A. Chandra, "A Unified SOC Test Approach Based on Test Data Compression and TAM Design", Proc. IEEE DFT'03, pp: 511-518

[24]   P.T. Gonciari, B.M. Al-Hashimi, "A Compression-Driven Test Access Mechanism Design Approach", ETS'04, pp: 100-105.

[25]   P.T. Gonciari, B.M. Al-Hashimi, N. Nicolici, "Integrated Test Data Decompression and Core Wrapper Design for Low-Cost System-on-a-Chip Testing", ITC'02, p: 64-70.

[26]   www.synopsys.com/products/test/tetramax_ds.html

Parametric Structure-Preserving
Model Order Reduction [*]

Jorge Fernández Villena[**,1], Wil H.A. Schilders[2,3], and L. Miguel Silveira[1,4]

[1] INESC ID / IST - Tech. University of Lisbon, Rua Alves Redol 9 1000-029 Lisbon, Portugal
[2] NXP Semiconductors Research, High Tech Campus 37, 56656 AE Eindhoven
[3] Dept. of Mathematics and Computer Science, Tech. University of Eindhoven, 5600 MB, Eindhoven, The Netherlands
[4] Cadence Research Labs, Rua Alves Redol 9 1000-029 Lisbon, Portugal
{jorge.fernandez,lms}@inesc-id.pt   wil.schilders@nxp.com

Abstract. Analysis and verification environments for next-generation nano-scale RFIC designs must be able to cope with increasing design complexity and to account for new effects, such as process variations and Electromagnetic (EM) couplings. Designed-in passives, substrate, interconnect and devices can no longer be treated in isolation as the interactions between them are becoming more relevant to the behavior of the complete system. At the same time variations in process parameters lead to small changes in the device characteristics that may directly affect system performance. These two effects, however, cannot be treated separately as the process variations that modify the physical parameters of the devices also affect those same EM couplings. Accurately capturing the effects of process variations as well as the relevant EM coupling effects requires detailed models that become very expensive to simulate. Reduction techniques able to handle parametric descriptions of linear systems are necessary in order to obtain better simulation performance. In this work we discuss parametric Model Order Reduction techniques based on Structure-Preserving formulations that are able to exploit the hierarchical system representation of designed-in blocks, substrate and interconnect, in order to obtain more efficient simulation models.

1 Introduction

New coupling and loss mechanisms, including EM field coupling and substrate noise as well as process-induced variability, are becoming too strong and too relevant to be neglected, whereas more traditional coupling and loss mechanisms are more difficult to describe given the wide frequency range involved and the greater variety of structures to be modeled. The performance of each device in the circuit is strongly affected by the environment surrounding it. In other words, the response of each circuit part depends not only on its own physical and electrical characteristics, but to a great extent also on its positioning in the IC, i.e. on the devices to which it is directly connected to or coupled with. The high level of integration available in current RFIC designs leads to proximity effects between the devices, which induce EM interactions, that can

---

[*] Work partially supported by the EU/IST/FP6/027378 STREP CHAMELEON RF project.
[**] Also supported by EC/IST/FP6/019417 COMSON Network under a Marie Curie Fellowship.

Please use the following format when citing this chapter:

Villena, J.F., Schilders, W.H.A. and Silveira, L.M., 2009, in IFIP International Federation for Information Processing, Volume 291; *VLSI-SoC: Advanced Topics on Systems on a Chip*, eds. R. Reis, V. Mooney, P. Hasler; (Boston: Springer), pp. 69–88.

lead to different behaviors of the affected parts. In any manufacturing process there is always a certain degree of uncertainty involved given our limited control over the environment. For the most part this uncertainty was previously ignored when analyzing or simulating complete systems, or assumed to be accounted for in the individual device models. However, as we step towards the nano-scale and higher frequency eras, such environmental, geometrical and electromagnetic fluctuations become more significant. Nowadays, parameter variability can no longer be disregarded, and its effect must be accounted for in early design stages so that unwanted consequences can be minimized. This leads to parametric descriptions of systems, including the effects of manufacturing variability, which further increases the complexity of such models. Reducing this complexity is paramount for efficient simulation and verification. However, the resulting reduced models must retain the ability to capture the effects of small fluctuations, in order to accurately predict behavior and optimize designs. This is the realm of *Parametric Model Order Reduction* (pMOR). Furthermore, these parametric fluctuations of the physical characteristics of the devices can affect not only the performance of such devices, but also the coupling between devices. For this reason the parametric models of the individual blocks of a system can no longer be simulated in isolation but must be treated as one entity and verified together. Such reduction must take advantage of the hierarchical description of those systems, namely to account for designed-in elements as well as interconnect effects. To this end, structure-preserving techniques must be used which not only retain structural properties of the individual systems but also its connections and couplings.

The goal of this paper is therefore to present and discuss techniques for model order reduction of interconnect, substrate or designed-in passives, taking into account their dependence on relevant process or fabrication parameters and their coupling and connections. The paper is structured as follows: Section 2 gives an introduction to Model Order Reduction. In Section 3 an overview of several existing pMOR techniques will be presented. In Section 4 an introduction to two-level hierarchical MOR will be done, and an extension to improve the reduction will be presented. In Section 5 the proposed methodology for combining the parametric techniques with the hierarchical reduction will be proposed. To illustrate the procedure, its pros and cons, in Section 6 some reduction results will be presented for several real-life structures. Finally conclusions will be drawn in Section 7.

2   Model Order Reduction

Model Order Reduction (MOR) is a framework whose aim is to efficiently find a behavioral equivalent yet reduced representation of a system. The system is usually represented in its state-space representation, which in descriptor form can be written as

$$Cẋ(t) + Gx(t) = Bu(t)$$
$$y(t) = Lx(t) \tag{1}$$

where $C, G \in \mathbb{R}^{n \times n}$ are respectively the dynamic and static matrices describing circuit behavior, $B \in \mathbb{R}^{n \times m}$ is the matrix that relates the input vector $u \in \mathbb{R}^m$ to the inner states

$x \in \mathbb{R}^n$ and $L \in \mathbb{R}^{n \times p}$ is the matrix that links those inner states to the outputs $y \in \mathbb{R}^p$. This time-domain descriptor yields a frequency response modeled via the transfer function

$$H(s) = L(sC + G)^{-1}B \tag{2}$$

for which we seek to generate a reduced order approximation, able to accurately capture the input-output behavior of the system,

$$\hat{H}(s) = \hat{L}(s\hat{C} + \hat{G})^{-1}\hat{B}. \tag{3}$$

Existing methods for linear model reduction can be broadly characterized into two types: those based on balancing techniques (sometimes also referred to as SVD[5]-based [1]), and those that are based on projection methods.

The first set of techniques, those in the truncated balanced realization (TBR) family [2], perform reduction based on the concept of controllability and observability of the system states. They rely on balancing the system and then truncating the states with small controllability and observability, information given by the Hankel Singular Values of the product of the system Gramians, which are obtained by solving a pair of Lyapunov equations. These methods are purported to produce nearly optimal models and have easy to compute *a-posteriori* error bounds. There are also known techniques [3] that extent this framework in order to guarantee the passivity of the *Reduced Order Model* (ROM), independently of the structure of its representation. However, the TBR procedures are awkward to implement and expensive to apply, which limits their applicability to small and medium sized problems. Hybrid techniques that combine some of the features of each type of methods have also been presented [4–6].

Among the second set of techniques, Krylov subspace projection methods such as PVL [7] and PRIMA [8] have been the most widely studied over the past decade. They are very appealing because of their simplicity and performance in terms of efficiency and accuracy. They rely on the computation of a basis for the Krylov subspace, $colspan\{V\} = Kr\{A, R, q \times m\}$, which encloses information about the transfer function, with $A = G^{-1}C$, $R = G^{-1}B$, and q the number of block moments matched (each block with m columns). The projection of the high-dimensional original system in the lower-dimensional generated subspace guarantees such implicit moment matching and avoids numerical errors in the reduction process.

$$\hat{G} = V^T GV \qquad \hat{C} = V^T CV \qquad \hat{B} = V^T B \qquad \hat{L} = LV \tag{4}$$

Furthermore, this orthogonal projection (and congruence transformation), performed in PRIMA, guarantees the preservation of the passivity in the reduction process if C, G are positive definite and $B = L^T$ (see [8] for details). However the procedures in this framework exhibit several known shortcomings. The lack of a general strategy for error control and order selection, as well as a dependence on the original model's structure if passivity is to be guaranteed after the reduction are among the more obvious ones.

A different technique that attempts to establish a bridge between the two families of methods was also proposed. The Poor Man's TBR [9] is based on a projection scheme

---

[5] SVD – Singular value decomposition.

where the projection matrix approximately spans the dominant eigenspaces of the controllability and observability matrices and provides an interesting platform for bridging between the two types of techniques. The controllability Gramian is estimated via a frequency-based quadrature rule of its integral form

$$X = \int_{-\infty}^{\infty} (j\omega C + G)^{-1} BB^T (j\omega C + G)^{-H} d\omega \tag{5}$$

where X is the controllability Gramian, and ω is the frequency. The Gramian can be estimated by

$$\bar{X} = \sum_k z_k z_k^H = ZZ^H \tag{6}$$

where $Z = [z_1\ z_2\ \dots]$ and $z_k = \left(j\omega^{(k)} C + G \right)^{-1} B$, with $\omega^{(k)}$ the kth frequency sample. In [9] it was shown that if the quadrature scheme is accurate enough, then the estimated Gramian $\bar{X}$ in (6) converges to the original one X, which implies that the dominant eigenspace of $\bar{X}$ converges to the dominant eigenspace of X (and in fact it converges faster than the Gramian).

Still the technique is not without drawbacks, as it relies on proper choice of sampling points, a non-trivial task in general.

3   Parametric Model Order Reduction

Actual fabrication of physical devices is susceptible to the variation of technological and geometrical parameters due to deliberate adjustment of the process or from random deviations inherent to the manufacturing procedures. This variability leads to a dependence of the extracted circuit elements on several parameters, of electrical or geometrical origin. This dependence results in a parametric state-space system representation, which in descriptor form can be written as

$$\begin{aligned} C(\lambda)\dot{x}(t,\lambda)(\lambda) + G(\lambda)x(t,\lambda) &= Bu(t) \\ y(t,\lambda) &= Lx(t,\lambda) \end{aligned} \tag{7}$$

where the various elements have the meaning described for (1). The elements of the matrices C and G, as well as the states of the system x, depend on a set of Q parameters $\lambda = [\lambda_1, \lambda_2, \dots, \lambda_Q]$ which model the effects of the mentioned uncertainty. Usually the system is formulated so that the matrices related to the inputs and outputs (B and L) do not depend on the parameters. This time-domain descriptor yields a parametric dependent frequency response modeled via the transfer function

$$H(s,\lambda) = L(sC(\lambda) + G(\lambda))^{-1} B \tag{8}$$

for which we again seek to generate a reduced order approximation, able to accurately capture the input-output behavior of the system for any point in the multidimensional frequency-parameter space.

$$\hat{H}(s,\lambda) = \hat{L}(s\hat{C}(\lambda) + \hat{G}(\lambda))^{-1} \hat{B} \tag{9}$$

In general, one attempts to generate a ROM whose structure is as much similar to the original as possible, i.e. exhibiting a similar parametric dependence and retaining as much of the original structure as possible. In this situation, the generated models can be efficiently combined and used inside simulation environments.

3.1   Representation of the Parametric System

The treatment of the system matrices as appear in (7) is quite inappropriate, as the parameter dependence can vary from element to element inside the matrices, and the reduction methodology will likely not maintain this dependence. For this reason, an approximate representation is generally used as the original system. An affine model based on a Taylor Series expansion can be used for accurately approximating the behavior of the static and dynamic matrices, $G(\lambda)$ and $C(\lambda)$, expressed as a function of the parameters.

$$
\begin{aligned}
G(\lambda_1,\ldots,\lambda_Q) &= \sum_{k_1=0}^{\infty} \cdots \sum_{k_Q=0}^{\infty} G_{k_1,\ldots,k_Q} \lambda_1^{k_1} \cdots \lambda_Q^{k_Q} \\
C(\lambda_1,\ldots,\lambda_Q) &= \sum_{k_1=0}^{\infty} \cdots \sum_{k_Q=0}^{\infty} C_{k_1,\ldots,k_Q} \lambda_1^{k_1} \cdots \lambda_Q^{k_Q}
\end{aligned}
\tag{10}
$$

where $G_{k_1,\ldots,k_Q}$ and $C_{k_1,\ldots,k_Q}$ are, respectively, the sensitivities of the static and dynamic system matrices. The Taylor series can be extended up to the desired (or required) order, including cross derivatives, for the sake of accuracy.

The techniques here presented can be combined with any order of the Taylor Series in (10). However, for simplicity, in the following a first order approximation, with first order sensitivities and no cross terms, will be used to illustrate the procedure.

$$
\begin{aligned}
G(\lambda_1,\ldots,\lambda_Q) &= G_0 + G_{\lambda_1}\lambda_1 + G_{\lambda_2}\lambda_2 + \ldots + G_{\lambda_Q}\lambda_Q \\
C(\lambda_1,\ldots,\lambda_Q) &= C_0 + C_{\lambda_1}\lambda_1 + C_{\lambda_2}\lambda_2 + \ldots + C_{\lambda_Q}\lambda_Q
\end{aligned}
\tag{11}
$$

where G_0 and C_0 are the nominal matrices, whereas G_{λ_i} and C_{λ_i} represent the 1st order derivatives of the original matrices with respect to the ith parameter. Under this representation of the parametric system, the structure for parameter dependence may be maintained under a projection scheme, as long as the projection is not only applied to the nominal matrices, but to the sensitivities as well.

$$
\begin{aligned}
\hat{G}(\lambda_1,\ldots,\lambda_Q) &= \hat{G}_0 + \hat{G}_{\lambda_1}\lambda_1 + \hat{G}_{\lambda_2}\lambda_2 + \ldots + \hat{G}_{\lambda_Q}\lambda_Q \\
\hat{C}(\lambda_1,\ldots,\lambda_Q) &= \hat{C}_0 + \hat{C}_{\lambda_1}\lambda_1 + \hat{C}_{\lambda_2}\lambda_2 + \ldots + \hat{C}_{\lambda_Q}\lambda_Q
\end{aligned}
\tag{12}
$$

where $\hat{C}_0 = V^T C_0 V$, $\hat{G}_0 = V^T G_0 V$, $\hat{C}_{\lambda_i} = V^T C_{\lambda_i} V$, and $\hat{G}_{\lambda_i} = V^T G_{\lambda_i} V$, with V the projector whose columns span the desired subspace basis. This is one of the main features that make the projection-based reduction the procedure followed by most of the parametric model order reduction techniques.

Another important issue is the passivity of the system. Taylor Series is not globally accurate, and, under large parameter variations, can lead to loss of accuracy, and more important, passivity. To avoid such pitfalls, the building of the Taylor Series formulation must be done such that under any expected parameter setting, the system matrices retain

their positive definiteness. A simple scheme for ensuring this is to compute the derivatives element-wise, i.e. for each resistor, capacitor, etc..., consistently with the nominal,
and thus under any possible parameter setting the stamping of this value still yields a
positive definite matrix. Projection techniques are able to guarantee the passivity of the
reduced models under certain circumstances (as pointed in Section 2), usually fulfilled
in the case of electric models (for details see [8]).

3.2   Reduction via Multi-Dimensional Moment Matching

Some of the most appealing techniques for the reduction of the parametric systems
are multi-dimensional moment matching algorithms. These techniques appear as extensions to nominal moment-matching ones [8, 7, 10]. Moment matching algorithms have
gained a well deserved reputation in nominal MOR due to their simplicity and efficiency. The extensions of these techniques to the parametric case feature a similar simplicity. They are usually based in the implicit or explicit matching of the moments of the
parametric transfer function (8). These moments depend not only on the frequency, but
on the set of parameters affecting the system, and thus are denoted as multi-dimensional
moments.

Some schemes, denoted as Multi-Parameter Moment Matching [11], rely on matching, via different approaches, the multi-parameter moments of (8).

$$x(s,\lambda_1,\ldots,\lambda_Q) = \sum_{k=0}^{\infty} \sum_{k_s=0}^{k} \sum_{k_1=0}^{k-k_s} \cdots \sum_{k_Q=0}^{k-k_s-k_1\ldots-k_{Q-1}} M_{k,k_s,k_1,\ldots,k_Q} s^{k_s} \lambda_1^{k_1} \ldots \lambda_Q^{k_Q} \qquad (13)$$

where $M_{k,k_s,k_1,\ldots,k_Q}$ is a k-th ($k = k_s + k_1 + \ldots + k_Q$) order multi-parameter moment corresponding to the coefficient term $s^{k_s} \lambda_1^{k_1} \ldots \lambda_Q^{k_Q}$. Following the same idea used in the
nominal moment matching techniques, a basis for the subspace formed from these mo-
ments can be built

$$colspan[V] = colspan\{M_{0,0,0,\ldots,0}, M_{1,1,0,\ldots,0}, \ldots, M_{k,k_s,k_1,\ldots,k_Q}\} \qquad (14)$$

and the resulting matrix V can be used as a projection matrix for reducing the original system. The generated parameterized ROM matches up to the k-th order multi-
parameter moment of the original system. The main inefficiencies of these techniques
arise from the fact that the same number of moments is matched for all the parameters
(including the frequency), and the expansion is performed around a single point. However, it should be noticed that the parameters usually fluctuate in small ranges around
their nominal values, whereas the frequency has a much wider range of variation. To
match the number of moments required to maintain the accuracy for large frequency
ranges may lead to large basis, and thus oversized reduced models. Some schemes have
been proposed to cope with this issue [12], but still suffer from some drawbacks.

A slightly different approach, that provides more compact ROMs, is presented in
[13], which relies on the computation of several subspaces, built separately for each
dimension, i.e. the frequency s and the parameter set λ. Given a parametric system
(7), the first step of the algorithm is to obtain the k_s block moments of the transfer
function with respect to the frequency when the parameters take their nominal value (for

example, via [8]). These block moments will be denoted as V_s. The next step is to obtain the subspace which matches the k_{λ_i} block moments of x with respect to each of the parameters λ_i (with the values for the rest of the parameters $j \neq i$ fixed to their nominal values), and will be denoted by V_{λ_i}. Once all the subspaces have been computed, an orthonormal basis can be obtained so that its columns span the union of all previously computed subspaces.

$$colspan[V] = colspan\{V_s, V_{\lambda_1}, \ldots, V_{\lambda_Q}\} \qquad (15)$$

Applying the resulting matrix in a projection scheme ensures that the parametric ROM matches k_s moments of the original system with respect to the frequency, and k_{λ_i} moments with respect to each parameter λ_i. If the cross-term moments are needed for accuracy reasons, the subspace that spans these moments can be also included by following the same procedure.

Still a different alternative was proposed in [14], where the number of multi-parameter moments matched is increased by applying a two step moment matching scheme. The first step matches the parameter moments explicitly, and a second projection step is applied to capture the frequency moments (for details see [14]). Unfortunately, the parameter dependence is lost and the passivity is not preserved.

Recent approaches [15, 16] were presented to overcome these shortcomings. They rely on a recursive procedure to compute the same moments spanned by the approach in [14]. Basically, the frequency moments of the nominal transfer function are generated, and from these moments, in a recursive fashion, the frequency moments for each parameter moment are also generated. As an example, for first order moment with respect to the parameters

$$colspan[V_0] = colspan\{V_0^0, V_0^1, \ldots, V_0^{\alpha_0-1}\}$$
$$colspan[V_{\lambda_i}] = colspan\{V_{\lambda_i}^0, V_{\lambda_i}^1, \ldots, V_{\lambda_i}^{\alpha_i-1}\} \qquad (16)$$
$$V_{\lambda_i}^j = -(G_0 + s_e C_0)^{-1}(G_{\lambda_i} V_0^j + s_e C_{\lambda_i} V_0^{j-1} + s_e C_0 V_{\lambda_i}^{j-1})$$

where V_0 is the basis that allows matching α_0 frequency moments for the nominal system (V_0^j is related to the jth moment of the nominal system with respect to frequency), and V_{λ_i} is the basis that allows matching α_i frequency moments for the first moment of the ith parameter, that is $M_{1,0,\ldots,1,\ldots}$ up to $M_{\alpha_i,\alpha_i-1,\ldots,1,\ldots}$ in Eqn.(13 ($V_{\lambda_i}^j$ is related to the jth frequency moment for the first moment of the ith parameter; see [15, 16] for further details). This adds flexibility as the number of moments to match with respect to each parameter and the frequency can be different. Furthermore, the number of frequency moments generated for each parameter moment can be also different. Both techniques differ in the methodology for selecting the most relevant moments, either by applying sampling on a tree scheme [15], or by generating the moments exhaustively until no rank is added [16]. The moments generated are orthonormalized and applied as an overall basis, V, in a projection scheme on the Taylor Series matrices.

$$colspan[V] = colspan\{V_0, V_{\lambda_1}, \ldots, V_{\lambda_Q}\} \qquad (17)$$

These schemes avoid or minimize the growth of the ROM with the number of parameters and moments to match.

3.3   Reduction via Variational PMTBR

A different approach was also proposed that extends the PMTBR [9] algorithm to include variability [17]. This approach is based on the statistical interpretation of the algorithm (see [9] for details) and enhances its applicability. In this interpretation, the approximated Gramian is seen as a covariance matrix for a Gaussian variable, $x(0)$, obtained by exciting the underlying system description with white noise. Rewriting the Gramian from (5) as

$$X_\lambda = \int_{S_\lambda} \int_{-\infty}^{\infty} (j\omega C(\lambda) + G(\lambda))^{-1} BB^T (j\omega C(\lambda) + G(\lambda))^{-H} p(\lambda) d\omega d\lambda \qquad (18)$$

where $p(\lambda)$ is the joint *Probability Density Function* (PDF) of λ in the parameter space, S_λ. Just as in the original PMTBR algorithm, a quadrature rule can be applied in the parameter plus frequency space to approximate the Gramian via numerical computation

$$z_k = z(s = s^{(k)}, \lambda = \lambda^{(k)}) = (s^{(k)} C(\lambda^{(k)}) + G(\lambda^{(k)}))^{-1} B \qquad (19)$$

where z_k is the kth sample, obtained for a frequency value of $s^{(k)}$ and a parameter set $\lambda^{(k)}$ (i.e. $\lambda^{(k)} = [\lambda_1^{(k)} \ldots \lambda_Q^{(k)}]$). The sampling scheme can be combined with any representation, i.e. does not require the computation of the sensitivities of the Taylor Series representation as in the case of multi-dimensional moment matching techniques. On the other hand, the Taylor Series representation exhibits further advantages in terms of maintenance of the parametric dependence and reuse, which are useful for efficient use of the reduced models in simulation environments. Note that the accuracy of the resulting ROM does not depend on the accuracy of the approximation of the integral, but on the projection subspace. After the quadrature is performed in the overall variational subspace, the deterministic procedure is followed and the most relevant vectors are selected via *Singular Value Decomposition* (SVD) in order to build a projection matrix

$$Z = [z_1, \ldots, z_k, \ldots] \longrightarrow VSU = SVD(Z) \qquad (20)$$

where S is the diagonal matrix with the singular values σ_i in its entries, and V and U are the unitary matrices that span the vectors associated with such singular values. The vectors of V whose associated singular values do not fall below a desired tolerance, are used in a congruence transformation on the parametric system matrices (7) (and thus retain the projection-based reduction advantages when applied to a Taylor Series representation). As in the deterministic case, an error analysis and control can be included, via the singular values, but in this variational case, only a bound on the expected error can be given (as we are working with statistical analysis)

$$E\{\|\hat{x}_0 - x_0\|_2^2\} \le \sum_{i=r+1}^{n} \sigma_i^2 \qquad (21)$$

where r is the reduced order, n the original number of states, and σ_i are the singular values obtained from (20). The complexity and computational cost is generally the same as that of the deterministic PMTBR plus the previous quadrature operations, and, it has been shown that the size of the reduced model is less sensitive to the number of

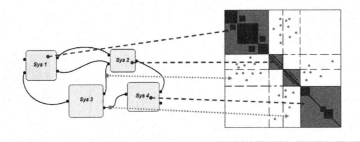

Fig. 1. Illustration of two-level block hierarchy in the system matrix.

parameters in the description, and to how this parameter dependence is modeled. On the other hand, the issue of sample selection, already an important one in the non-parametric context, becomes even more relevant, since the sampling must now be done in a potentially much higher-dimensional space.

4   Block Hierarchical Model Order Reduction

4.1   Structure Preservation

As pointed out, individual blocks inside an RFIC can no longer be treated in isolation, and for this reason the complete system must be treated as an entity. Considering the linear system composed of all these interconnected component blocks including designed-in passives, interconnect, etc, the joint description has an interesting structure, where the diagonal blocks correspond to the individual block matrices, whereas the off-diagonal blocks correspond to the static interconnections (in the G matrix) and dynamic couplings (C matrix), as shown in Figure 1. Standard model order reductions techniques can be applied to this joint, global system and while the resulting reduced model will usually be able to accurately capture the input-output behavior of the complete set of blocks, this approach leads to full reduced matrices. Furthermore, the original two-level hierarchy with interconnections and couplings, in where the individual sub-systems can be recognized, can no longer be recovered (as seen in top of Figure 2).

An alternative approach is to perform the reduction of the individual models in a hierarchical fashion, i.e to reduce each model independently without taking into account the rest of the models or the environment (as seen in bottom of Figure 2). Hence every model is reduced separately and thus the hierarchy and structure of the global system is maintained. However, to apply MOR to each model implies capturing its individual behavior, not the global one. This can be inefficient as too much effort may be spent capturing some local behavior that is not relevant for the global response (maybe filtered by another model). Furthermore certain aspects of the global response might be missed as it is not clear at the component level how relevant they are.

To avoid these problems, one can reduce each component block separately but oriented to capture the global input-output response. This approach will provide us with more control in the reduction stage while also preserving the structure of the interconnections. The transfer function to match is the global one, so the most relevant behavior

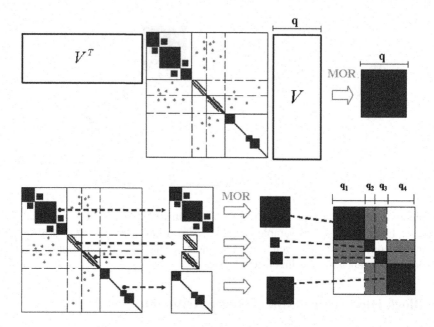

Fig. 2. Illustration of flat reduction in a Block Structured System (Up), and illustration of independent reduction of each system (Down).

for the complete RF system is captured. Hence the global matrices are used in the process of generating the basis for the projector, and thus only the global inputs and outputs of the complete interconnected system are relevant. Therefore, the inefficiencies caused by the large number of ports of the individual component blocks can be avoided. The basis is later used for the reduction of the individual blocks, so the hierarchy can be maintained.

Some recent methods have advocated this approach. In [18] a control theoretic viewpoint of reduction of interconnected systems was presented, but it has the disadvantage that it is unable to treat capacitive couplings, and it is cumbersome to define the interconnections in complex settings. A generalization that overcomes such problems is the *Block Structure Preserving* (BSP) framework, first presented in [19], in which it was applied to separate variables of different nature, and later generalized in [20, 21].

Considering a system composed of N_b sub-systems, the resulting description matrices can be written as

$$G = \begin{bmatrix} G_{11} & \cdots & G_{1N_b} \\ \vdots & \ddots & \vdots \\ G_{N_b1} & \cdots & G_{N_bN_b} \end{bmatrix} \quad C = \begin{bmatrix} C_{11} & \cdots & C_{1N_b} \\ \vdots & \ddots & \vdots \\ C_{N_b1} & \cdots & C_{N_bN_b} \end{bmatrix}$$

$$B = \begin{bmatrix} B_1^T & \cdots & B_{N_b}^T \end{bmatrix}^T \quad L = \begin{bmatrix} L_1 & \cdots & L_{N_b} \end{bmatrix}. \tag{22}$$

The main idea is to retain the system block structure, i.e. the two-level hierarchy and thus some degree of sparsity, after reduction via projection, allowing for a more efficient

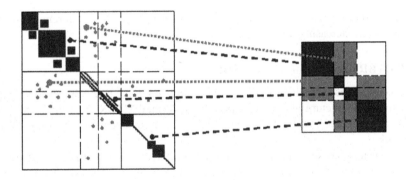

Fig. 3. Illustration of the effect of the Block Structure Preserving reduction.

reduction and use of the reduced model. The procedure relies on expanding the projector of the global system (obtained via any classical MOR projection technique) into a block diagonal matrix, with block sizes equal to the sizes of its N_b individual component blocks (22). A basis that spans a suitable subspace for reduction via projection is then computed (for example a Krylov subspace). The projector built from that basis can be split and restructured into a block diagonal one so that the 2-level structure is preserved under congruence transformation.

$$V = \begin{bmatrix} V_1 \\ \vdots \\ V_{N_b} \end{bmatrix} \qquad \check{V} = \begin{bmatrix} V_1 & & \\ & \ddots & \\ & & V_{N_b} \end{bmatrix} \qquad (23)$$
$$V = colsp\left[Kr\{A,R,q\}\right] \rightarrow colspan\left[V\right] \subset colspan\left[\check{V}\right]$$

where $Kr\{A,R,q\}$ is the q column Krylov subspace of the complete system ($A = G^{-1}C$ and $R = G^{-1}B$). The block-wise congruence transformation is (see Figure 3)

$$\hat{G}_{ij} = V_i^T G_{ij} V_j \qquad \hat{C}_{ij} = V_i^T C_{ij} V_j \qquad \hat{B}_i = V_i^T B_i \qquad \hat{L}_j = L_j V_j \qquad (24)$$

It should be noticed that the above projection matrix $\check{V}$ has N_b (number of blocks) times more columns than the original projector. This leads to an N_b times larger reduced system. On the other hand, this technique maintains the block structure of the original system and gives us some flexibility when choosing the size of the reduced model depending on the block layout and relevance. The reduced system will be able to match up to N_b times q block moments of the original complete transfer function (see [20] for details) under the best conditions (i.e. with very weak entries in the off-diagonal blocks). Under the worst conditions, only q block moments are matched, i.e. the same number than in the *flat* reduction.

This technique is applicable to the global system, composed of the individual blocks and their connections (including both resistive as well as capacitive or inductive couplings between the blocks). The BSP technique therefore preserves the block structure of the system. However, the inner structure of the blocks themselves is lost since the procedure turns any non-empty block in the original system into a full block, but it is still possible to identify the blocks and relate them to the original device or interaction block. Nevertheless, if any block is empty in the global system matrix, it remains empty after reduction, increasing the sparsity.

4.2   PMTBR in Block Structure MOR

Any projection-based MOR procedure can be extended in the BSP manner to maintain the hierarchical structure of a system. In the case of the PMTBR algorithm, additional characteristics of the procedure can be further taken advantageous of in the current framework.

If the system has some internal structure, then the matrix Z that is computed from the vector samples of the global system can be split into blocks. The estimated Gramian can be written block-wise as

$$\begin{bmatrix} Z_1 \\ \vdots \\ Z_{N_b} \end{bmatrix} \rightarrow ZZ^H = \begin{bmatrix} Z_1 Z_1^H & \cdots & Z_1 Z_{N_b}^H \\ \vdots & \ddots & \vdots \\ Z_{N_b} Z_1^H & \cdots & Z_{N_b} Z_{N_b}^H \end{bmatrix} = \bar{X} \tag{25}$$

But if we expand the matrix Z into diagonal blocks

$$\check{Z} = \begin{bmatrix} Z_1 & & \\ & \ddots & \\ & & Z_{N_b} \end{bmatrix} \rightarrow \check{Z}\check{Z}^H = \begin{bmatrix} Z_1 Z_1^H & & \\ & \ddots & \\ & & Z_{N_b} Z_{N_b}^H \end{bmatrix} = \check{X}. \tag{26}$$

From (25) it can be seen that $Z_i Z_i^H = \bar{X}_{ii}$, i.e. the matrix $\check{X} = \check{Z}\check{Z}^H$ is a block diagonal matrix whose entries are the block diagonal entries of the matrix $\bar{X}$. Under a good quadrature scheme, the matrix $\bar{X}$ converges to the original X, and therefore $\check{X}$ will converge to the block diagonals of X. This means that the dominant eigenspace of $\check{X}$ converges to the dominant eigenspace of the block diagonals of X. We can then apply an SVD to each block of the Z matrix

$$Z_i = V_i S_i U_i \rightarrow \check{X}_{ii} = \bar{X}_{ii} = V_i S_i^2 V_i^T \tag{27}$$

where S_i is real diagonal, and V_i and U_i are unitary matrices. The dominant eigenvectors of V_i in 27 corresponding to the dominant eigenvalues of S_i, can be used as a projection matrix in a congruence transformation over the system matrices for model order reduction. The elements of S_i can also be used for *a priori* error estimation in a way similar to how *Hankel Singular Values* are used in TBR procedures. Of course, the convergence of these singular values, and therefore the error bounds, depends on the *strength* of the coupling and the interconnections, but it is supposed that the impact of the systems (placed in the block diagonals) in the global behavior *dominates* the impact the couplings and interconnections may have in such global behavior. Using these block projectors V_i, a structure preserving projector for the global system can be built (23) which will capture the most relevant behavior of each block (revealed by the SVD) with respect to the global response (recall that Z is composed of sample vectors of the complete system). This approach provides us with more flexibility when reducing a complete system composed of several blocks and the interactions between them, as it allows to control the reduced size of each device via an error estimation on the global response.

5   Parametric Block Structure MOR

From the two-level hierarchical description of a system it is possible to have some extra block information that allows us to perform a more efficient MOR. But the behavior of the individual blocks that compose the system is subject to the effect of process variations, both geometrical and electrical. Such variations, as previously pointed out, also affect the interactions and couplings between these blocks. Any system-wide EM simulations must address these effects. Therefore, the variability study must be done over the complete system, and after model generation, a two-level parametric system will be obtained, with the block matrices in the block diagonals and the interactions between them in the off-diagonals. All these blocks will be functions of the relevant process and geometrical parameter.

$$G = \begin{bmatrix} G_{11}(\lambda_{\{11\}}) & \cdots & G_{1N_b}(\lambda_{\{1N_b\}}) \\ \vdots & \ddots & \vdots \\ G_{N_b1}(\lambda_{\{N_b1\}}) & \cdots & G_{N_bN_b}(\lambda_{\{N_bN_b\}}) \end{bmatrix} \quad C = \begin{bmatrix} C_{11}(\lambda_{\{11\}}) & \cdots & C_{1N_b}(\lambda_{\{1N_b\}}) \\ \vdots & \ddots & \vdots \\ C_{N_b1}(\lambda_{\{N_b1\}}) & \cdots & C_{N_bN_b}(\lambda_{\{N_bN_b\}}) \end{bmatrix}$$

$$B = \begin{bmatrix} B_1^T & \cdots & B_{N_b}^T \end{bmatrix}^T \qquad\qquad L = \begin{bmatrix} L_1 & \cdots & L_{N_b} \end{bmatrix}$$

$$(28)$$

where $\lambda_{\{ij\}}$ represents the subset of parameters affecting block G_{ij} in (28) (it is supposed that some parameters are local, and thus only affect some localized blocks). From (28) is clear that we have a parametric system depending on $\lambda = \bigcup_{i=1,j=1}^{N_b} \lambda_{\{i,j\}}$. Therefore we can apply parametric MOR reduction. Note that any parameter affecting several blocks (diagonal blocks and their interactions) is treated as a single parameter (this avoids the treatment of the same parameter affecting different systems as several different ones).

In this circumstances, BSP techniques can be applied in order to maintain the system structure. This is possible as long as the selected pMOR technique is based on a projection scheme, which is the case for most of the existing procedures (as already presented in Section 3). The extension is very simple: obtain a suitable basis for projection from the *complete system*, and then split and expand it into a block structure preserving projector. If the basis spans the most relevant behavior of the parametric system, then the expanded BSP projector will capture those as well.

All the advantages and disadvantages mentioned in Section 4 hold here. But there is an extra and important advantage in the parametric case: **the BSP technique maintains the block parametric dependence**, i.e. if a block C_{ij} depends on a subset of parameters $\lambda_{\{ij\}}$, then the reduced block $\hat{C}_{ij} = V_i^T C_{ij} V_j$ will depend on the same parameter subset and no other. This fact has inherent advantages in terms of storage and use of the sensitivities, as the reduced sensitivities are even sparser than the nominal matrices. On the other hand, as previously discussed, some pMOR algorithms yield very large ROMs, and therefore their combination with BSP techniques will lead to an extremely large ROM.

However, it was shown in Section 3.3 that the ROM sizes obtained with the Variational PMTBR method are usually less sensitivity to the number of parameters, and such method is an extension of the PMTBR framework to handle parametric systems;

Algorithm I: Block Structure Preserving VPMTBR

Starting from a Block Structured System C, G, B, L with N_b blocks:

1: Select a quadrature rule of K points in the space $[s,\ \lambda]$

2: For each point compute: $z_k = \left(s^{(k)} C(\lambda^{(k)}) + G(\lambda^{(k)}) \right)^{-1} B$

3: Form the matrix columns $Z = [z_1 \dots z_K]$

4: Split it into N_b blocks, according to the system structure

$$Z = \begin{bmatrix} Z_1 \\ \vdots \\ Z_{N_b} \end{bmatrix}$$

5: For each block Z_j obtain the SVD: $Z_j = V_j S_j U_j$

6: For each matrix V_j drop the columns whose singular values falls bellow the desired global tolerance

7: Build a Block Structure Preserving Projector from the remaining columns

$$\check{V} = \begin{bmatrix} V_1 & & \\ & \ddots & \\ & & V_{N_b} \end{bmatrix}$$

8: Apply $\check{V}$ in a congruence transformation on the Block Structured System C, G, B, L

---

the main difference is that the sampling scheme for obtaining the matrix whose columns span the desired subspace is extended to the multidimensional space of the parameters and the frequency, the rest of the procedure being exactly the same.

For this reason, the Variational PMTBR framework can be easily extended and combined with the BSP methodology, by direct use of the technique presented in Section 4.2 in the variational case. The advantages of the block size control and error estimation provided in such case are still valid, although in this case, as in [17], only a bound on the expected error can be given. This block-wise control is very useful when the various component models of a complete system have very different relevant rank: if the same ROM size is applied to every block, the reduction may grow unnecessarily large. In contrast, the complexity of the proposed methodology is exactly the same as that for the non-structure-preserving techniques. The only difference is that the SVD (or orthonormalization in the moment matching approaches) must be done block-wise in order to avoid numerical errors (e.g. the expansion of a orthogonal matrix to a block diagonal does not guarantee the orthogonality of this new basis). This can become an advantage, because for some blocks the number of vectors needed is lower, so less computational effort is required in orthonormalization steps.

6   Results

To illustrate the proposed procedure we present results from two examples to which several pMOR techniques were applied. These include [17] denoted as VPMTBR, [13]

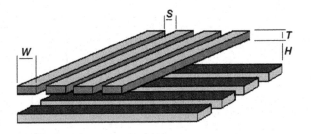

Fig. 4. Bus topology for Example 1.

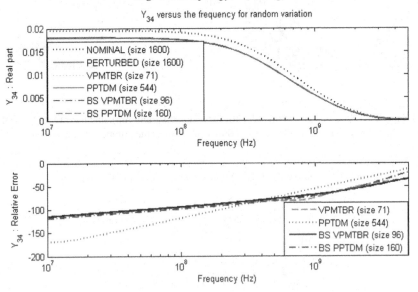

Fig. 5. (Up) Y_{34} versus the frequency for Example 2 for the nominal, pertubed and parametric ROMs with random parameter variation set. (Down) Relative Error of the ROMs w.r.t. the perturbed response.

denoted as PPTDM, and two Block Structure preserving methods: *Algorithm I*, denoted as BS VPMTBR, and block structure based on [13], denoted as BS PPTDM. The non-reduced model response will be denoted as Original or Perturbed, depending on whether a parameter variation has been applied.

6.1 Example 1 - Coupled Buses

This example, depicted in Figure 4, is composed of 16 blocks: 2 buses of 8 parallel lines each (each line modeled as an RC ladder of 100 segments) are on different metal layers, and cross at a square angle. The inputs and outputs are taken at the edges of each line of the first bus, so the system will have 16 ports. In this case there is no interconnection, just coupling effects. Each line is assumed coupled to the previous and the next line of their bus, and to every line of the other bus in the crossing area. Each

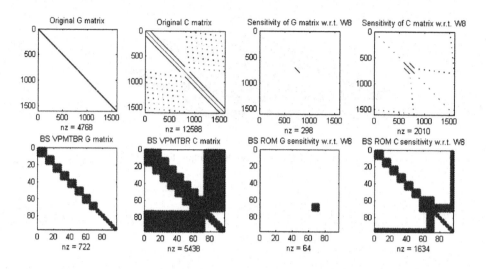

Fig. 6. Example 1 - Structure of the matrices for the original system (up), and the ROM obtained with BS VPMTBR (down). Note the different dimensions (nz is the number of nonzero elements in matrix).

Table 1. Characteristics of the pMOR methods applied in Example 1

MOR Method	Size	NNZ (G C)	Sparsity Ratio
NONE	1600	4768 12588	0.0018 0.0049
VPMTBR	71	5041 5041	1.000 1.000
PPTDM	544	295936 295936	1.000 1.000
BS VPMTBR	96	722 5438	0.078 0.590
BS PPTDM	160	1600 17200	0.062 0.672

line has its width (W) as a parameter, which implies 16 independent parameters. The width variation affects the line model, as well as the in-bus coupling (width variation also affects the interline spacing), and the inter-bus coupling (the crossing area varies).

Figure 5 shows the frequency response of the nominal system, the pertubed response of the non-reduced system, and the responses of ROMs for VPMTBR, PPTDM, BS VPMTBR and BS PPTDM. Again, the main characteristics of the resulting ROMs are shown in Table 1. The PPTDM based algorithms result in very large ROMs even for small number of moments to match (2 w.r.t. the frequency and 2 w.r.t. each parameter). For these reasons each block moment from PPTDM was truncated to 10 vectors to keep the size manageable (otherwise no reduction would be possible). While this seems to produce acceptable results, there is little control over the result. On the other hand, the PMTBR based techniques leads to more compressed ROMs, as the SVD reveals the most relevant vectors. In the case of the BS VPMTBR, the control of each block allows different reduction sizes for each bus: since the ports of the 2nd bus are not taken into account, less effort is needed to capture its behavior. In fact, the models for the 1st bus

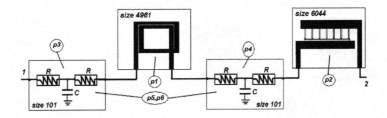

Fig. 7. Interconnection scheme for Example 2, with original sizes and parameter indication.

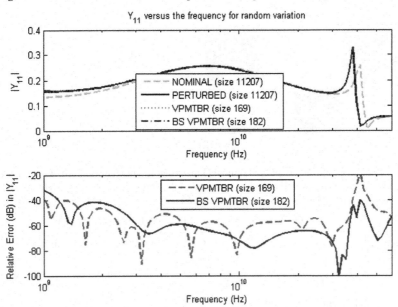

Fig. 8. Example 2 - (Up) Magnitude in dB of Y_{11} versus the frequency of Example 1 for the nominal, the pertubed and the parametric ROMs for a random parameter variation. (Down) Relative Error (in dB) of Y_{11} for the ROMs w.r.t. the perturbed response.

are of sizes 8 to 10, while models for the 2nd bus are all size 3. The ability to control reduction locally is clearly an advantage of the method. The effect of this control can be seen in Figure 6, which shows the structure for the original (nominal and one sensitivity) matrices (up), and the structure obtained with BS VPMTBR reduction.

6.2   Example 2 - EM based models

The second example system is composed of four blocks: a *Multiple Input Multiple Output* (MIMO) RC ladder of size 101, with 2 ports, a MIMO EM based model of a planar Spiral Inductor of size 4961, with 2 ports, another RC ladder of size 101 and 2 ports, and an MIMO EM-based model for a metal-insulator-metal (MIM) capacitor. The four systems are connected in series as shown in Figure 7, so the global inputs and outputs are taken in the first port of the first RC and the second port of the CMIM model.

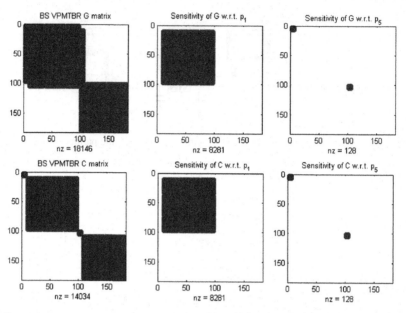

Fig. 9. Example 2 -(Up) Structure of the nominal G matrix (left), and the structure of the sensitivities of G w.r.t. p_1 (centre, affecting the block related to the spiral), and w.r.t. p_5 (right, affecting the RC ladders) for the BSP-based reduction. (Down) Same matrices, but for the dynamic part.

Table 2. Example 2 - Characteristics of the pMOR methods applied

MOR Method	Size	NNZ (G C)	Max. RE	Generation Cost
	(Blocks)	(Sparsity Ratio)		
NONE	11207	49305 13708	0	*none*
	$(101,4961,101,6044)$	$(0.00039 \ 0.00011)$		
VPMTBR	169	28561 28561	$-18.7dB$	$90Samples(s+\lambda)$
	(169)	(1.00 1.00)		$SVD(n \times 169)$
BS VPMTBR	182	18146 14034	$-31.9dB$	$90Samples(s+\lambda)$
	$(8,91,8,75)$	(0.55 0.42)		$SVD(n \times \{8,91,8,75\})$

The system depends on six parameters, affecting different blocks. Figure 8 shows the frequency response of the self-admittance Y_{11} of the nominal system, the pertubed response of the non-reduced system, and the responses of the PMTBR-based models (the PPTDM and BS PPTDM models do not produce competitive results sizewise, and therefore were omitted). Table 2 shows the main characteristics of the obtained ROMs. The BS VPMTBR yields a slightly bigger ROM, but it maintains the block structure, both of the nominal matrices and the sensitivities (see Figure 9), of the original system, and is able to control the size of each reduced block depending on its relevance on the global response. Furthermore, the block parameter dependence is clearly maintained. Figure 9 shows the structure of the matrices obtained with BS VPMTBR, for the nominal matrices (left, G up and C down), where the effect of the block order control can be seen, and for two sensitivities, one affecting only the block related to the Spiral (centre), and other affecting the RC ladders (right), which are extremely sparse. On the other hand, the *flat* reduction via VPMTBR yields full matrices, both for the nominal and the sensitivities. The accuracy is also better for the BSP based approach, and the procedure requires similar computational effort.

7 Conclusion

In this paper we have presented a block structure-preserving parametric model order reduction technique, as an extension of existing parametric MOR techniques, in order to improve the reduction when a two-level hierarchical structure is available in the system description. This type of structure is common in coupled or interconnected systems, and can lead to simulation advantages. The methodology presented here is general in the sense that it can be used with any projection parametric MOR technique to maintain the two-level hierarchy and the block-parameter dependence. The presented extension of the PMTBR-based procedures into the Block Structure Preserving framework, allows more control on the reduction, provided by the inclusion of estimated error bounds on the single blocks oriented to the global response.

Acknowledgment

The authors gratefully acknowledge the support from the EU, and would like to thank the CHAMELEON RF consortium, and in particular Wim Schoenmaker (MAGWEL), Nick van der Meijs and Kees-Jan van der Kolk (TU Delft), and Daniel Ioan and Gabriela Ciuprina (PU Bucharest) for many helpful discussions, and for providing some of the simulation examples.

References

1. Antoulas, A.C.: Approximation of Large-Scale Dynamical Systems. Society for Industrial and Applied Mathematics, Philadelphia, PA, USA (2005)
2. Moore, B.: Principal Component Analysis in Linear Systems: Controllability, Observability, and Model Reduction. IEEE Transactions on Automatic Control **AC-26** (1981) 17–32
3. Phillips, J., Daniel, L., Silveira, L.M.: Guaranteed passive balancing transformations for model order reduction. In: 39th ACM/IEEE Design Automation Conference, New Orleans, Louisiana (2002) 52–57
4. Li, J.R., Wang, F., White, J.: Efficient model reduction of interconnect via approximate system grammians. In: International Conference on Computer Aided-Design, San Jose, CA (1999) 380–383
5. Jaimoukha, I.M., Kasenally, E.M.: Krylov subspace methods for solving large Lyapunov equations. SIAM Journal on Numerical Analysis **31** (1994) 227–251
6. Kamon, M., Wang, F., White, J.: Generating nearly optimally compact models from Krylov-subspace based reduced-order models. IEEE Transactions on Circuits and Systems II: Analog and Digital Signal Processing **47** (2000) 239–248

7. Feldmann, P., Freund, R.W.: Efficient linear circuit analysis by Padé approximation via the Lanczos process. IEEE Transactions on Computer-Aided Design of Integrated Circuits and Systems **14** (1995) 639–649

8. Odabasioglu, A., Celik, M., Pileggi, L.T.: PRIMA: passive reduced-order interconnect macromodeling algorithm. IEEE Trans. Computer-Aided Design **17** (1998) 645–654

9. Phillips, J.R., Silveira, L.M.: Poor Man's TBR: A simple model reduction scheme. IEEE Trans. Computer-Aided Design **24** (2005) 43–55

10. Elfadel, I.M., Ling, D.L.: A block rational arnoldi algorithm for multipoint passive model-order reduction of multiport rlc networks. In: International Conference on Computer Aided-Design, San Jose, California (1997) 66–71

11. Daniel, L., Siong, O.C., Low, S.C., Lee, K.H., White, J.K.: A multiparameter moment-matching model-reduction approach for generating geometrically parametrized interconnect performance models. IEEE Trans. Computer-Aided Design **23** (2004) 678–693

12. Li, P., Liu, F., Li, X., Pileggi, L., Nassif, S.: Modeling interconnect variability using efficient parametric model order reduction. In: Proc. Design, Automation and Test in Europe Conference and Exhibition. (2005)

13. Gunupudi, P., Khazaka, R., Nakhla, M., Smy, T., Celo, D.: Passive parameterized time-domain macromodels for high-speed transmission-line networks. IEEE Trans. On Microwave Theory and Techniques **51** (2003) 2347–2354

14. Li, X., Li, P., Pileggi, L.: Parameterized interconnect order reduction with Explicit-and-Implicit multi-Parameter moment matching for Inter/Intra-Die variations. In: International Conference on Computer Aided-Design, San Jose, CA (2005) 806–812

15. Zhu, Z., Phillips, J.: Random sampling of moment graph: a stochastic krylov-reduction algorithm. In: Proc. Design, Automation and Test in Europe Conference and Exhibition, Nice, France (2007) 1502–1507

16. Li, Y.T., Bai, Z., Su, Y., Zeng, X.: Parameterized model order reduction via a two-directional arnoldi process. In: International Conference on Computer Aided-Design, San Jose, CA, USA (2007) 868–873

17. Phillips, J.: Variational interconnect analysis via PMTBR. In: International Conference on Computer Aided-Design, San Jose, CA, USA (2004) 872–879

18. Vandendorpe, A., Dooren, P.V.: Model reduction of interconnected systems. In: Proc. of 16th International Symposium on Mathematical Theory of Networks and Systems (MTNS 2004), Leuven, Belgium (2004) THP3–4

19. Freund, R.W.: Sprim: Structure-preserving reduced-order interconnect macro-modeling. In: International Conference on Computer Aided-Design, San Jose, CA. U.S.A (2004) 80–87

20. Yu, H., He, L., Tan, S.X.D.: Block structure preserving model order reduction. In: BMAS - IEEE Behavioral Modeling and Simulation Wokshop. (2005) 1–6

21. Li, R.C., Bai, Z.: Structure-preserving model reduction using a krylov subspace projection fomulation. Comm. Math. Sci. **3** (2005) 179–199

ReCPU: a Parallel and Pipelined Architecture for Regular Expression Matching

Marco Paolieri[1], Ivano Bonesana[1], and Marco Domenico Santambrogio[2]

[1] ALaRI, Faculty of Informatics
University of Lugano, Lugano, Switzerland
{paolierm, bonesani}@alari.ch

[2] Dipartimento di Elettronica e Informazione
Politecnico di Milano, Milano, Italy
marco.santambrogio@polimi.it

Abstract. Text pattern matching is one of the main and most computation intensive tasks of applications such as Network Intrusion Detection Systems and DNA Sequencing Matching. Even though software solutions are available, they do not often satisfy the performance requirements, therefore specialized hardware designs can represent the right choice. This paper presents a novel hardware architecture for efficient regular expression matching: *ReCPU*.

This special-purpose processor is able to deal with the common regular expression semantics by treating the regular expressions as a programming language. With the parallelism exploited by the proposed solution a throughput of more than one character comparison per clock cycle (maximum performance of current state of the art solutions) is achieved and just $O(n)$ memory locations (where n is the length of the regular expression) are required.

In this paper we are going to expose our complete framework for efficient regular expression matching, both in its architecture and compiler. We present an evaluation of area, time and performance by synthesizing and simulating the configurable VHDL description of the proposed solution. Furthermore, we performed a design space exploration to find the optimal architecture configuration given some initial constraints. We present these results by explaining the idea behind the adopted cost-function.

1 Introduction

1.1 State of the Art

Searching for a set of strings that match a given pattern in a large input text - i.e. pattern matching - is a well known computation intensive task present in several application fields. Nowadays, there is an increasing demand for high performance pattern matching. In network security and QoS applications [1][2][3][4][5] it is required to detect multiple packets which payload matches a predefined set of patterns. In Network Intrusion Detection Systems (NIDS) regular expressions are

Please use the following format when citing this chapter:

Paolieri, M., Bonesana, I. and Santambrogio, M.D., 2009, in IFIP International Federation for Information Processing, Volume 291;
VLSI-SoC: Advanced Topics on Systems on a Chip; eds. R. Reis, V. Mooney, P. Hasler; (Boston: Springer), pp. 89–108.

used to identify network attacks by predefined patterns. Software solutions are not feasible to perform this task without a sensible reduction of the throughput, therefore dedicated hardware architecture can overcome this (e.g. as described in [1]). Bioinformatics - as in case of the Human Genome project - requires DNA sequence matching [6][7]: searching DNA patterns among millions of sequences is a very computationally expensive task. Different alternative solutions to speedup software approaches have been proposed (e.g. like in [7] where the DNA sequences are compressed and a new research-algorithm is described).

For these application domains it is reasonable to move towards a full hardware implementation, overcoming the performance achievable with any software solution. Several research groups have been studying hardware architectures for regular expression matching. They are mostly based on Non-deterministic Finite Automaton (NFA) as described in [8] and [9]. In [5] a software that translates a RE into a circuit description has been developed. A Non-deterministic Finite Automaton is used to dynamically create efficient circuits for the pattern matching task.

FPGAs solutions have been presented: in the parallel implementation described in [4] multiple comparators are used to increase the throughput for parallel matching of multiple patterns. In [8] another FPGA implementation is proposed, it requires $O(n^2)$ memory space and processes one text character in $O(1)$ time (one clock cycle), it is based on an hardware implementation of Non-deterministic Finite Automaton (NFA). Additional time and space are necessary to build the NFA structure starting from the given regular expression, therefore the overall execution time is not constant: it can be linear in best cases and exponential in worst ones. That is not the case for the solution proposed in this paper: regular expressions are stored using $O(n)$ memory locations. Furthermore, it does not require any additional time to start the regular expressions matching. In [9] an architecture that allows extracting and sharing common sub-regular expressions, with the goal of reducing the area of the circuit, is presented. In [6] a DNA sequence matching processor using FPGA and Java interface is addressed. Parallel comparators are used for the pattern matching. They do not implement the regular expression semantics (i.e. complex operators), but just simple text search based on exact string matching. The work proposed in [3] focuses on pattern matching engines implemented with reconfigurable hardware. The implementation is based on Non-deterministic Finite Automaton and it includes a tool for automatic generation of the VHDL description.

These approaches require the re-generation of the HDL description, whenever a new regular expression needs to be executed. Each description is strictly dependent on the given pattern. The time needed for the re-generation increases the overall execution time and reduces the performance.

1.2 An Overview of ReCPU

This paper presents, to the best of our knowledge, a novel approach to solve the pattern matching problem. Regular expressions are considered the programming language of a dedicated CPU. We do not build either Deterministic nor Non-deterministic Finite Automaton of the given regular expression: so we have the advantage that any modification on the regular expression does not require any change on the HDL description. This way any additional setup time is avoided and a considerable overall speed-up is achieved.

ReCPU - the proposed architecture - is a dedicated processor able to fetch a regular expression from the instruction memory and to perform the pattern matching with the text stored in the data memory. The architecture is optimized to execute comparisons in parallel by means of several parallel units and a two-stage pipeline. This architecture has several advantages: on average it compares more than one character per clock cycle and it requires linear memory occupation (i.e. for a given regular expression of size n, the memory required is just $O(n)$). In our solution it is easily possible to change the pattern at run-time just updating the content of the instruction memory, without any modification of the underlying hardware. Since it is based on a CPU-like approach a *compiler* is necessary to obtain the machine executable code from a given regular expression (i.e. a low-level operational description starting from a high-level representation). This guarantees much more flexibility than the other solutions described in Sect. 1.1.

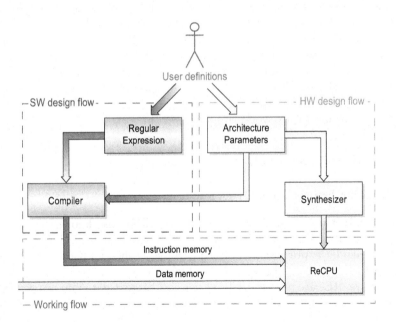

Fig. 1. ReCPU framework flows.

The ReCPU framework (i.e. CPU and compiler) has been inspired from the VLIW design style [10]. This has several advantages: it is easily possible to configure the design to achieve a particular trade-off between performance, area, power, etc. Moreover since some architectural parameters are exposed to the compiler, it can automatically compile the portable high-level regular expression description to a set of instructions targeted for a custom design.

In Fig. 1 the complete working flow of the proposed framework is shown: the user defines the regular expression and the architectural parameters specifying the number of parallel units. These information are used to synthesize ReCPU on the hardware design flow and to compile the regular expression following the software design flow. ReCPU works on the content of instructions and data memory as it is visible in the bottom part of Fig. 1: the former is automatically generated by the compiler, while the latter is specified by the user.

1.3 Organization of the Paper

This paper is organized as follows: in Sect. 1.2 the general concepts of ReCPU design are described. A brief overview of regular expressions focusing first on a formal definition and then on the semantics that has been implemented in hardware, is addressed in Sect. 2.1. The idea behind considering regular expressions as a programming language is fully covered in Sect. 2.2, by means of some examples.

Section 3 provides a top-down detailed description of the hardware architecture: the *Data Path* in Sect. 3.1 and the *Control Unit* in 3.2.

Results of synthesis on ASIC technology are discussed in terms of critical path, maximum working frequency and area in Sect. 4.1, a comparison of the performance with other solutions is also proposed. In Sect. 4.2 a *Design Space Exploration* (DSE) for FPGA synthesis is provided. A possible cost function is defined and applied to the DSE.

Conclusions and future works are addressed in Sect. 5.

2 Proposed Approach

2.1 Regular Expressions Overview

Formal Definition. A *regular expression* [11] (RE), also known as *pattern*, is an expression that describes the elements of a set of strings. The theoretical concept of regular expression was introduced by Stephen C. Kleene in the 1950s as a model to describe and classify formal languages.

Nowadays, REs are used to perform searches on text data and are commonly present in programming languages, text-editors and word processors for text editing. In this section we propose a brief review of the basic concepts of formal languages to be able to expose formally the concept of regular expression. This helps to understand the different features of ReCPU that we are going to describe in the next sections.

Given a finite alphabet Σ of elementary symbols, we define a *string* as an ordered combination of some elements of Σ. A particular string, belonging to any Σ, is the *empty string*, containing no elements and indicated with ϵ.

Let us define Σ^* as the set of all possible strings generated with the elements of Σ. A language L over Σ is a set of strings generated by the alphabet, thus it is a subset of Σ^*. In other words

$$L(\Sigma) \subset \Sigma^*$$

The simplest language L contains only strings composed by a single element of the alphabet and the empty string. It can be used to generate other languages, called *regular languages*, by applying three basic operators

- concatenation, denoting the set $\{\{a,b\} \,|\, a \in L_1 \wedge b \in L_2\}$;
- union (or alternation), denoting the set $\{L_1 \cup L_2\}$;
- star (or closure), denoting the set that can be made by concatenating zero or more strings of L.

Using the strings of the language and the operators, it is possible to write formulas representing regular languages (i.e. a new set of strings derived from the regular language). This formula is known as *regular expression*. A language can be titled as *regular* only if it exists a regular expression able to describe the whole set of strings composing it.

We can define formally regular expressions as follows [12]:

Definition 1. *A regular expression over the alphabet Σ is defined as:*

1. *$\emptyset$ is a regular expression corresponding to the empty language $\emptyset$.*
2. *ϵ is a regular expression corresponding to the language ϵ.*
3. *For each symbol $a \in \Sigma$, a is a regular expression corresponding to language a.*
4. *For any regular expression R and S over Σ, corresponding to the languages L_R and L_S respectively, each of the following is a regular expression corresponding to the indicated language:*
   (a) concatenation: $(RS) \Leftrightarrow L_R L_S$;
   (b) union: $(R|S) \Leftrightarrow L_R \cup L_S$;
   (c) star: $R^* \Leftrightarrow L_R^*$.
5. *Only the formulas produced applying rules 1-4 are regular expressions over Σ.*

Given an arbitrary set of strings T and a regular expression R, the pattern matching problem can be defined as follows:

Definition 2. *To find the elements of T, if there are any, which are also elements of the regular language described by R.*

The Syntax. In the IEEE POSIX 1003.2 document, a standard syntax for REs has been proposed. Even though it is a bit different from the formal definition, it recalls the same concepts. In an RE single characters are considered regular expressions that match themselves and additional operators are defined. Let us consider two REs: a and b, the operators that have been implemented in our architecture are:

- $a \cdot b$: it matches all the strings that match a and b;
- $a|b$: matches all strings that match either a or b ;
- $a*$: matches all strings composed by zero or more occurrences of a[3];
- $a+$: matches all strings composed by one or more occurrences of a;
- (a): parenthesis are used to define the scope and precedence of the operators (e.g. to match zero or more occurrences of a and b, it is necessary to define the following RE: $(ab)*$).

2.2 Regular Expressions as a Programming Language

The novel idea we propose is to translate a given RE into a set of low-level instructions (i.e. *machine code*) part of a program stored in the instruction memory and executed by ReCPU. This approach is the same used in general purpose processors: a program is coded using a high-level language - that is more readable by programmers - and then compiled, optimized and linked to produce an efficient low-level set of instructions executed by the microprocessor. An example of this, is to code a program using C, then build it using *gcc* to obtain the compiled binary program that is executed by the CPU.

In our case the high-level representation is the RE defined according to the standard syntax described in [11] or in [13]. The compilation flow is inspired by the VLIW style [10], because some architectural parameters are exposed to the compiler, that is able to exploit an high level of parallelism issuing the instructions to different parallel units (i.e. the *clusters*). Similarly, the *Regular Expression compiler* (REc) is aware of the number and the structure of configurable units in the ReCPU architecture and based on this it splits the RE into different low-level instructions, issuing as many character comparisons as the number of parallel comparators available in the architecture.

Given a regular expression, REc[4] generates the sequence of instructions that are executed by the core of the architecture on the text stored in the data memory. REc provides in output two binary images: one for the instruction memory and the other one for the data memory, with the input text adapted to the configuration of the architecture. The compiler does not need to perform many optimizations due to the simplicity of the *RE programming language*. However, some controls are performed to detect syntactical mistakes and possible problems of stack-overflow. Given the stack-size (see Sect. 3 for more details) REc computes the maximum level of nested parenthesis allowed and determines whether the architecture can execute the specified RE or not. A RE is completely matched whenever a NOP instruction is fetched from the instruction memory. If any instruction fails during the execution, the RE is considered completely failed and it is restarted. The binary code of a low-level instruction produced by the compiler is composed by an *opcode* and a *reference text* as shown in Fig. 2. The *opcode* is divided in three different parts:

---

[3] Please notice that this operator is different from the formal *star* operator previously defined.

[4] REc is the Regular Expression compiler written in Python

– the most significant bit (MSB) used to indicate an open parenthesis;
– the next 2-bits for the internal operand used within the reference;
– the last bits for the external operand for describing loops and close parenthesis.

The complete list of the opcodes is shown[5] in Table 1.

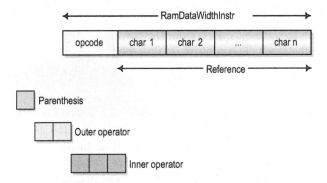

Fig. 2. Instruction Structure.

Table 1. Bitwise representation of the opcodes.

Opcode	Associated Operator
0 00 000	nop
1 -- ---	(
0 01 ---	and
0 10 ---	or
0 -- 001	)*
0 -- 010	)+
0 -- 011	)|
0 -- 1--	)

The novel idea of considering REs as a programming language is clarified by
the following examples: operators like * and + correspond to *loop* instructions.
Such operators find more occurrences of the same pattern (i.e. a loop on the same
RE instruction). This technique guarantees the possibility to handle complex
REs looping on more than one instruction. The loop terminates whenever the
pattern matching fails. In case of + at least one valid iteration of the loop is
required to validate the RE, while for * there is no limitation to the minimum
number of iterations.

---

[5] Please notice that *don't care* values are expressed as '-'.

Another characteristic of complex REs that can be perfectly managed considering REs as a programming language is the use of nested parenthesis (e.g. $(((ab) * (c|d))|(abc)))$. This can be handled with the *function call paradigm* of common programming languages, so that we can deal with it as in the majority of processors. We consider an open parenthesis as a *call* instruction and a closed one as a *return*. Whenever an open parenthesis is encountered, the current context is pushed into an entry of a stack data structure and the execution continues normally. Whenever a close parenthesis is found, a pop operation is performed on the stack and the overall validity of the RE is checked by combining the outer operator of the the current instruction, the current context and the previous one popped from the stack. The context is composed by the internal registers of the *Control Unit* that contain the memory location and the partial matching result (see Sect. 3.2 for further details). This way, our architecture can tackle very complex nested REs using a well and widely known approach.

A simple example of translating a RE into a sequence of instructions is listed in Table 2 (where it has been hypothesized to have a ReCPU that compares 4 characters per comparison unit - see Sect. 3 for further details). The given RE is *(ABCD)|(aacde)*, the open parenthesis are translated into *call*s, while the closed parenthesis are translated into *return*s. The original RE is split into several sub-expressions. This mechanism allows us to exploit the maximum possible capacity of the internal parallel comparators. The overall RE result is computed by combining the partial results of each sub-expression. If during the execution the RE does not match, the program is restarted from the first instruction with a different starting address in the data memory. Otherwise, the execution continues until the NOP instruction is fetched. At this point the RE is considered completed.

Table 2. Translation of the RE=(ABCD)|(aacde), into ReCPU instructions using 4 cluster units.

SubRE	Translated Instructions
(	call
ABCD	compare text with "ABCD"
)|	return: process OR
(	call
aacd	compare text with "aacd"
e)	compare text with "e" and return, overall evaluation
NOP	end of RE

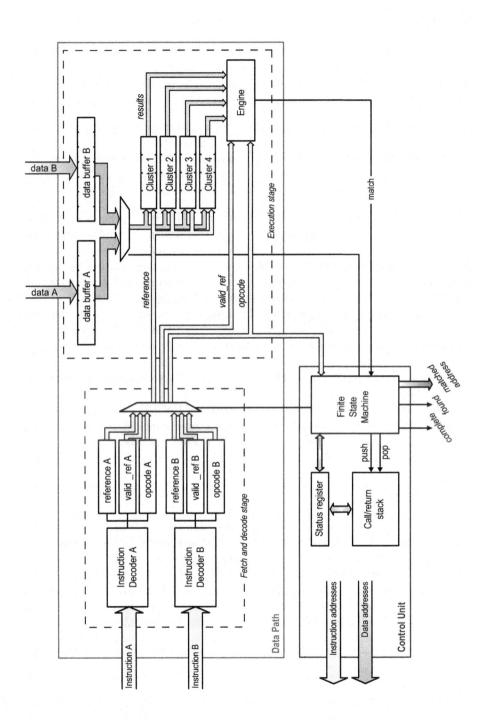

Fig. 3. Block diagram of ReCPU with 4 Clusters, each of those has a ClusterWidth of 4. The main blocks are: Control Path and Data Path (composed by a Pipeline with Fetch/Decode and Execution stages).

3 Architecture Description

ReCPU has a Harvard based architecture that uses two separate memory banks: one storing the text and the other one the instructions (i.e. the RE). Both RAMs are dual port to allow parallel accesses to the parallel buffers described in Sect. 3.1. As shown in Fig. 3, the structure of ReCPU is divided into two parts:

- The *Data Path* is in charge of decoding the instructions, executing the comparisons and producing the partial matching result.
- The *Control Unit* selects the next instruction to be executed, collects the partial matching results to check the correctness of the RE and is in charge of executing complex instructions such as loops and parenthesis.

One of the main features of ReCPU is the capability to process more than one character comparison per clock cycle. In this design we applied some well known computer architecture techniques - such as pipelining and prefetching - to provide a higher throughput. We achieved this goal by incrementing the level of data and instruction parallelism and by limiting the number of stall conditions, which are the largest waste of computation time during the execution.

The architecture is adaptable by the designer who can specify the number of parallel units, their internal structure as well as the width of the buffers and the memory ports. To adapt the architecture to the requirements is necessary to trade-off performance, area, power, etc. To find the optimal architecture a *cost-function* has been defined and a *Design Space Exploration* has been carried out (see Sect. 4).

This section overviews the internal structure of ReCPU - shown in the block diagram of Fig. 3 - focusing on the microarchitectural implementation. A detailed description of the two main blocks: the *Data Path* and the *Control Unit*, is provided in the sections 3.1 and 3.2.

3.1 Data Path

We applied some techniques from processor architecture field to increase the parallelism of ReCPU: *pipelining*, data and instructions *prefetching*, and use of multiple memory ports. The pipeline is composed by two stages: *Fetch/Decode* and *Execute*. The *Control Unit*, as explained in Sect. 3.2, takes one cycle to fill the pipeline and then it starts taking advantage of the prefetch mechanism without any further loss of cycles. Moreover we introduced duplicated buffers in each stage to avoid stalls. This solution is advantageous because the replicated blocks and the corresponding control logic are not so complex: the increase in terms of area is acceptable, and no overhead in terms of critical path. This way, we have a reduction of the execution latency with a consequent performance improvement.

Due to the regular flow of the instructions a good prediction technique with duplicated instruction fetching structures is able to avoid stalls. In the *Fetch/Decode* stage, two instruction buffers load two sequential instructions: when an RE starts matching, one buffer is used to prefetch the next instruction and the other is used as *backup* of the first one. In case the matching process fails (i.e. prefetching is useless) the content of the second buffer - the backup of the first one - can be used without the need of stalling the pipeline. Similarly, the parallel data buffers reduce the latency of the access to the data memory.

According to this design methodology in the *Fetch/Decode* stage, the decoder and the pipeline registers are duplicated. By means of a multiplexer, just one set of pipeline register values are forwarded to the *Execution* stage. As shown in Fig. 3, the multiplexer is controlled by the *Control Unit*. The decoder logic extracts from the instruction the reference string (i.e. the characters of the pattern that must be compared with the text), its length - indicated as valid_ref and necessary because the number of characters composing the sub-RE can be lower than the width of the cluster - and the operators used.

The second stage (see Fig. 3) of the pipeline is the *Execute*: it is a fully combinatorial circuit. The reference coming from the previous stage is compared with the data read from the RAM and previously stored in one of the two parallel buffers. Like in *Fetch/Decode* stage this technique reduces the latency of the access to the memory avoiding the need of a stall if a jump in the data memory is required. A jump in the data memory is required whenever one or more instructions are matching the text and then the matching fails (because the current instruction is not satisfied). In this case a jump in the data memory restarts the search from the address where the first match occurred.

The core of ReCPU is based on sets of parallel bitwise comparators grouped in units called *Clusters*, which are shown in Fig. 4. Each comparator compares an input text character with a different one coming from the reference of the instruction (see Fig. 2). The number of elements of a *Cluster* is indicated as *ClusterWidth* and represents the number of characters that can be compared every clock cycle whenever a sub-RE is matching. This figure influences the throughput whenever a part of the pattern starts matching the input text. The *Execute* stage is composed by several *Clusters* - the total number is indicated as *NCluster* - used to compare a sub-RE. Each *Cluster* is shifted one character from the previous cluster in order to cover a wider set of data in a single clock cycle. This influences the throughput whenever the pattern is not matching. The results of each comparator *Cluster* are collected and evaluated by the block called *Engine*. It produces a match/not-match signal to the *Control Unit*.

Our approach is based on a fully-configurable VHDL implementation. It is possible to modify some architectural parameters such as: number and dimensions of the parallel comparator units (*ClusterWidth* and *NCluster*), width of buffer registers and memory addresses. This way it is possible to define the best architecture according to the user requirements, finding a good trade-off between timing, area constraints and desired performance. Each parameter is propagated through the modules using the VHDL *generics* technique. Moreover, we defined some packages to define some constants, types and other values used in entities and architectures.

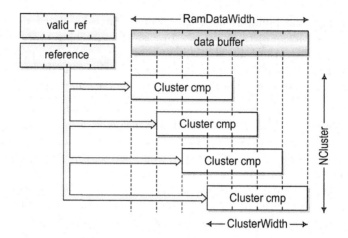

Fig. 4. Detail of comparator clusters.

3.2 Control Unit

In Sect. 2, we defined an RE as a sequence of instructions that represent a set of conditions to be satisfied. If all the instructions of an RE are matched, then the RE itself is matched. Essentially, the ReCPU *Data Path* fetches an instruction, decodes it and verifies whether it matches the current part of the text or not. But it cannot identify the result of the whole RE. Moreover the *Data Path* does not have the possibility to request data or instructions from the external memories, because it does not know the next address to be loaded.

To manage the execution of the RE we designed a *Control Unit* block based on some specific hardware components. The core of the *Control Unit* is the *Finite State Machine* (FSM) shown in Fig. 5. The execution of an RE requires two input addresses: the RE and the text start addresses. The FSM is designed in such a way that after the preload of the pipeline (FD state), two different cases can occur. When the first instruction of an RE does not match the text, the FSM loops in the EX_NM state, as soon as a match is detected the FSM goes into the EX_M state.

While the text is not matching, the same instruction address is fetched and the data address advances exploiting the comparisons with the clusters of the *Data Path*. If no match is detected the data memory address is incremented by the number of clusters. This way, multiple characters are compared every single clock cycle leading to a throughput clearly greater than one character per clock cycle. Further details are presented in Sect. 4.

When an RE starts matching, the FSM goes into *EX_M* state and the ReCPU switches to the matching mode by using a single cluster to perform the pattern matching task on the data memory. As for the previous case more than one character per clock cycle is checked by the different comparators of a cluster. When the FSM is in this state and one of the instructions of the RE fails the whole process has to be restarted from the point where the RE started to match.

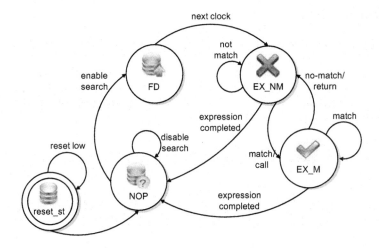

Fig. 5. Finite state machine of the *Control Path.*

In both cases (matching or not matching), whenever a NOP instruction is detected the RE is considered complete, so the FSM goes into the NOP state and the overall result is given as output. The ReCPU returns a signal indicating the matching of the RE and the memory location of the first character matching the string. We conceived an operation mode able to find more than one pattern in a text: each time a RE is matched, ReCPU stops until an input signal requests another RE matching. In such case the RE is reloaded and the sequence of operations is restarted.

A particular case is represented by loops (i.e. + or * operators). We exploit these operators with a call and return paradigm. When an open parenthesis is detected a call is performed: the *Control Unit* saves the content of the status register (i.e. the actual matching value, the current program counter and the current internal operator) in the stack module drawn in Fig. 3. The RE is then executed normally until a return instruction is detected. A return is basically a closed parenthesis followed by +, * or |. It restores the old context and updates the value of the global matching. If a not matching condition is verified while the FSM is processing a call, the stack is erased and the whole RE is considered not matching. The process is restarted as in the simple not matching case.

Problems of overflow in the number of elements stored in the stack are avoided by the compiler. It knows the size of the stack and computing the maximum level of nested parenthesis it is able to determine whether the architecture can execute the RE or not.

4 Experimental Results

4.1 Analysis of Synthesis and Simulation Results

ReCPU has been synthesized using Synopsys Design Compiler[6] on the STMicro-electronics HCMOS8 ASIC technology library featuring 0.18μm silicon process. The proposed architecture has been synthesized setting *NCluster* and *Cluster-Width* equal to 4. The synthesis results are presented in Table 3:

Table 3. Synthesis results for ReCPU architecture with NCluster and ClusterWidth set to 4.

Critical Path	Area	Max Clock Frequency
3.14 ns	51082 μm^2	318.47 MHz

The papers describing the hardware solutions covered in Sect. 1 show a maximum clock frequency between 100MHz and 300MHz. The results show how our solution is competitive with the others having the advantage of processing in average more than one character per clock cycle (i.e. the case for all the other solutions like [8] and [9]).

Let us analyze different scenarios to figure out the performance of our implementation: whenever the input text is not matching the current instruction and the opcode represents a · operator the maximum level of parallelism is exploited and the performance in terms of time required to process a character are up to

$$T_{cnm} = \frac{T_{cp}}{NCluster + ClusterWidth - 1} \qquad (1)$$

where the T_{cnm}, expressed in $ns/char$, depends on the number of clusters, the width of the cluster and the critical path delay T_{cp}. If the input text is not matching the current instruction and the opcode is a | then the performance are given by the following formula:

$$T_{onm} = \frac{T_{cp}}{NCluster} \cdot \qquad (2)$$

If the input text is matching the current instruction then the performance depends on the width of one cluster (all the other clusters are not used)

$$T_m = \frac{T_{cp}}{ClusterWidth} \cdot \qquad (3)$$

For each different scenarios, using the time per character computed with the formulas (1), (2) and (3) it possible to compute the corresponding bit-rate to evaluate the maximum performance. The bit-rate B_x represents the number of bits[7] processed in one second and can be computed as follows:

---

[6] www.synopsys.com
[7] It is computed considering that 1 character = 8 bits.

$$B_x = \frac{1}{T_x} \cdot 8 \cdot 10^9 \qquad (4)$$

where T_x is any of the quantities (1), (2) and (3).

The numerical results for the implementation we have synthesized are shown in Table 4.

Table 4. Time requested to process one character and corresponding bit-rate for the synthesized architecture.

T_{cnm}	T_{onm}	T_m	B_{cnm}	B_{onm}	B_m
ns/char	ns/char	ns/char	Gbit/s	Gbit/s	Gbit/s
0.44	0.78	0.78	18.18	10.19	10.19

The results summarized in Table 4 represent the maximum achievable throughput with different scenarios. Whenever there is a function call (i.e. nested parenthesis) one additional clock cycle of latency is required. The throughput of the proposed architecture depends on the RE as well as on the input text so it is not possible to compute a fixed throughput but just to provide the maximum performance achievable in different cases.

In our experiments we compared ReCPU with the popular software *grep*[8] using three different text files of 65K characters each. For those files we chose a different content trying to stress the behavior of ReCPU. We ran *grep* on a Linux Fedora Core 4.0 PC with Intel Pentium 4 at 2.80GHz, 512MB RAM measuring the execution time with Linux *time* command and taking as result the *real* value. The results are presented in Table 5.

Table 5. Performance comparison between grep and ReCPU on a text file of 65K characters.

Pattern	*grep*	ReCPU	Speedup
$E|F|G|HAA$	19.1 *ms*	32.7 μs	584.8
$ABCD$	14.01 *ms*	32.8 μs	426.65
$(ABCD)+$	26.2 *ms*	393.1 μs	66.74

We noticed that if loop operators are not present our solution performs equal either with more than one instruction and OR operators or with a single AND instruction (see the first two entries of the table). In these cases the *speedup* is more than 400 times, achieving extremely good results with respect to software solutions. In case of loop operators it is possible to notice a slow-down in the performance but still achieving a *speedup* of more than 60 times.

---

[8] www.gnu.org/software/grep

To prove the performance improvements of our approach respect to the other published solutions, we compare the bit-rates described in the Table 6. It was not possible to compare the bit-rate for [6], [9] because this quantity was not published in the papers.

In Table 6 and in Fig. 6, the bit-rate range for different solutions is shown. We compared it with the one of ReCPU computing a speedup factor that underlines the goodness of our approach. It is shown that the performance achievable with our solution is n times faster than the other published research works. Our solution guarantees several advantages apart from the bit-rate improvement: $O(n)$ memory locations are necessary to store the RE and it is possible to modify the pattern at run-time just updating the program memory. It is interesting to notice - analyzing the results in the table - that in the worst case we are performing pattern matching almost two times faster.

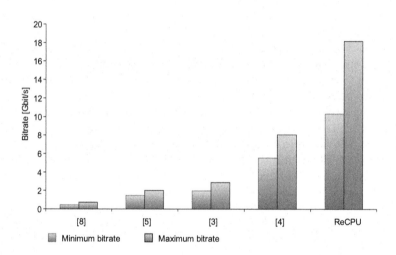

Fig. 6. Comparison of the bitrates of ReCPU and the state of the art solutions.

Table 6. Bit-Rate comparison between literature solutions and ReCPU.

Solution published in	bit-rate Gbit/s	ReCPU Gbit/s	Speedup factor (x)
[3]	$(2.0, 2.9)$	$(10.19, 18.18)$	$(5.09, 6.26)$
[5]	$(1.53, 2.0)$	$(10.19, 18.18)$	$(6.66, 9.09)$
[4]	$(5.47, 8.06)$	$(10.19, 18.18)$	$(1.82, 2.25)$
[8]	$(0.45, 0.71)$	$(10.19, 18.18)$	$(22, 25)$

4.2   Design Space Exploration

In this section we present a Design Space Exploration used to find the optimal ReCPU architecture configuration synthesized on a Xilinx Virtex-II FPGA[9]. Taking advantage of the fully configurable VHDL description, we modified the structure altering the number of parallel comparator clusters - i.e. NCluster (NC) - and the number of bitwise comparator units - i.e. ClusterWidth (CW). We analyzed how area and performance scale.

We performed the Design Space Exploration with NCluster in the range $\{2, 4, 8, 16, 32, 64\}$ and ClusterWidth in $\{4, 8\}$. Also the width of the memory ports (i.e. RWD: RamWidthData, RWI: RamWidthInstruction) must be adapted according to the following rules:

$$RWI = CW$$

$$RWD = CW + NC$$

Increasing the number of NCluster, more characters are compared simultaneously, and so ReCPU results to be faster whenever the pattern is not matching the input text. Nevertheless, due to the higher hardware complexity, the *Critical Path* raises up and thereby the maximum possible clock frequency decreases. On the other side, a larger ClusterWidth corresponds to much better performance whenever the input string starts matching, since a wider sub-RE is processed in a single clock cycle. The results of the synthesis are shown in Table 7.

Table 7. Results of the synthesis of ReCPU with different parameters on Xilinx Virtex-II FPGA.

NC	CW	RWD	RWI	Critical Path ns	Max Freq. MHz	Norm. Area	T_{cnm} ns	T_{onm} ns	T_m ns	Cost	Norm. Cost
2	4	6	4	8.938	111.88	0.1334	1.8	4.4	2.2	2.68	1.00
4	4	8	4	9.722	102.86	0.1619	1.4	2.4	2.4	2.17	0.97
8	4	12	4	10.078	99.23	0.2086	0.9	1.3	2.5	1.8	0.81
16	4	20	4	11.157	89.63	0.3128	0.6	0.7	2.8	1.72	0.77
32	4	36	4	11.583	86.33	0.4944	0.3	0.4	2.9	1.62	0.73
64	4	68	4	12.974	77.08	1	0.2	0.2	3.2	1.72	0.77
2	8	10	8	8.938	111.88	0.1334	1.0	4.5	1.1	1.92	0.86
4	8	12	8	9.722	102.87	0.1619	0.9	2.4	1.2	1.44	0.65
8	8	16	8	10.078	99.23	0.2086	0.7	1.3	1.3	1.11	0.50
16	8	24	8	11.157	89.63	0.3128	0.5	0.7	1.4	0.99	0.45
32	8	40	8	11.583	86.33	0.4944	0.3	0.4	1.4	0.89	0.40
64	8	72	8	12.974	77.08	1	0.2	0.2	1.6	0.91	0.41

In the Design Space Exploration to evaluate the different configurations that have been synthesized and listed in Table 7, we defined a *cost function* that

---

[9] A Virtex-II pro, technology xc2vp30-fg676-7.

takes into account the previously described scenarios considering the area and the performance. It is defined as follows:

$$costf = p_1 \cdot T_{cnm} + p_2 \cdot T_{onm} + p_3 \cdot T_m \ . \tag{5}$$

The function $costf(\cdot)$ evaluates the different performance indexes (see Sect. 4.1) with a corresponding probability. To better analyze the overall implementation it is necessary to distinguish among different cases. We have not performed a statistical analysis on the utilization of the operators as well as on the probabilities of having or not a matching. This would be necessary to compute an average performance index, but it is strictly dependent on the input search text.

Let us consider an input text and an RE such that the probability of having an *and* operator in the current instruction and the probability of having an *or* operator in the current instruction are the same (i.e. $p_{and} = p_{or} = 0.5$). Among these cases there is respectively the probability $p_m = 0.25$ of matching the pattern and 0.25 of not matching. We actually consider all the cases equiprobable. The $costf(\cdot)$ is the resulting average time per character based on the previous probabilities. Let us define

- p_1 as the probability of having an *and* operator with a not matching pattern ($p_1 = 0.25$);
- p_2 as the probability of having an *or* operator with a not matching pattern ($p_2 = 0.25$);
- p_3 as the probability of having a matching with any operator (0.5).

The Design Space Exploration optimizes the $costf(\cdot)$ given these probabilities for the inputs (i.e. search text and RE). We choose to optimize the cost function with respect to the area of the design. The normalized values computed in Table 7 are plotted in Fig. 7, where the *Pareto* optimal points have been highlighted. Each point in the graph is a synthesis of ReCPU with a different set of values for the generics VHDL parameters. It is easily possible to identify which points belong to the *Pareto* front, and which others are the dominated ones. The best configuration out-coming from this analysis is listed in Table 8.

Table 8. The best configuration out-coming from the analysis of the *Pareto* points generated by the Design Space Exploration.

NC	CW	RWD	RWI	Critical Path ns	Max Freq. MHz	Norm. Area	T_{cnm} ns	T_{onm} ns	T_m ns	Cost	Norm. Cost
8	8	16	8	10.078	99.23	0.2086	0.7	1.3	1.3	1.11	0.50

5 Conclusions and Future Works

Nowadays the need of high performance computing is growing up. An example of this is represented by biological sciences (e.g. Humane Genome Project) where

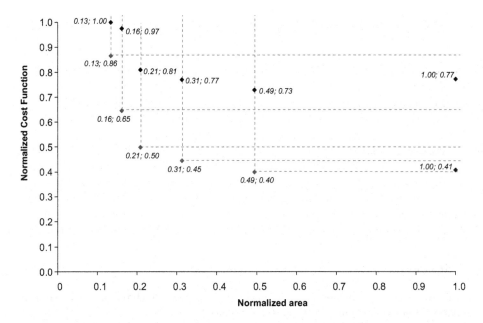

Fig. 7. This plot shows the normalized values of area and cost function of Table 7. The optimal points belonging to the *Pareto front* are colored in red while the non-optimal are in blue.

DNA sequence matching is one of the main applications. To achieve higher performance it is necessary to use hardware solutions for pattern matching tasks. In this paper we presented a novel architecture for hardware regular expression matching.

Our contribution involves a completely different approach of dealing with the regular expressions. REs are considered the programming language of a parallel and pipelined architecture. This guarantees the possibility of changing the RE at run-time just modifying the content of the instruction memory and it involves a high improvement in terms of performance.

Some features, like the multiple characters checking, instructions prefetching and parallelism exposure to the compiler level are inspired from the VLIW design style.

The current state of the art solutions guarantee a fixed performance of one character per clock cycle. Our goal was to figure out a way of extract additional parallelism to achieve in average much better performance. We proposed a solution that has a bit-rate of at least 10.19 Gbit/s with a peak of 18.18 Gbit/s.

We presented the results of the synthesis on ASIC technology to compare the performance with the other state of the art solutions. Moreover, we exploited the configurable VHDL design of ReCPU to perform a Design Space Exploration, proposing a possible cost function based on the probabilities of matching or not a pattern with different RE operators. We provided the results of the exploration by optimizing the cost function respect to the area requested to synthesize our design on an FPGA.

Future works are focused on the definition of a reconfigurable version of the proposed architecture based on FPGA-devices. This way, we could exploit the possibility to dynamically reconfigure the architecture at run-time. The study of possible optimizations of the *Data Path* to reduce the critical path and increase the maximum possible clock frequency is an alternative. We would also like to explore the possibility of adding some optimizations in the compiler.

Another possible development is to use ReCPU in a parallel multi-core environment. This way it could be possible to create a cluster of pattern matching processors working together and increasing the throughput. The advantages include the possibility of having a ReCPU cluster in a single System-On-Chip, achieving considerable high performance at a contained cost due to the density of the actual silicon technology that offer large areas with contained costs.

References

1. Yadav, M., Venkatachaliah, A., Franzon, P.: Hardware architecture of a parallel pattern matching engine. In: Proc. ISCAS. (2007)
2. Liu, R.T., Huang, N.F., Kao, C.N., Chen, C.H., Chou, C.C.: A fast pattern-match engine for network processor-based network intrusion detection system. In: Proc. ITCC. (2004)
3. Bispo, J., Sourdis, I., Cardoso, J., Vassiliadis, S.: Regular expression matching for reconfigurable packet inspection. In: IEEE International Conference on Field Programmable Technology (FPT). (2006) 119–126
4. Sourdis, I., Pnevmatikatos, D.: Fast, large-scale string match for a 10Gbps FPGA-based network intrusion. In: International Conference on Field Programmable Logic and Applications, Lisbon, Portugal (2003)
5. Cho, Y., Mangione-Smith, W.: A pattern matching coprocessor for network security. In: DAC 05: Proceedings of the 42nd annual conference on Design automation, New York, NY, USA, ACM Press (2005) 234–239
6. Brown, B.O., Yin, M.L., Cheng, Y.: DNA sequence matching processor using FPGA and JAVA interface. In: Annual International Conference of the IEEE EMBS. (2004)
7. Chen, L., Lu, S., Ram, J.: Compressed pattern matching in DNA sequences. In: Proc. CSB. (2004)
8. Sidhu, R., Prasanna, V.: Fast regular expression matching using FPGAs. In: IEEE Symposium on Field-Programmable Custom Computing Machines (FCCM01). (2001)
9. Lin, C.H., Huang, C.T., Jiang, C.P., Chang, S.C.: Optimization of regular expression pattern matching circuits on FPGA. In: DATE 06: Proceedings of the conference on Design, automation and test in Europe, 3001 Leuven, Belgium, Belgium, European Design and Automation Association (2006) 12–17
10. Fisher, J.A., Faraboschi, P., Young, C.: Embedded Computing: A VLIW Approach to Architecture, Compilers and Tools. Morgan Kaufmann (2004)
11. Friedl, J.: Mastering Regular Expressions. 3 edn. OReilly Media (2006)
12. Hopcroft, J., Motwani, R., Ullman, J.: Introduction to Automata Theory, Languages and Computation. 2 edn. Pearson Education (2001)
13. GNU USA: Grep Manual. (2002)

QoS in Networks-on-Chip - Beyond Priority and Circuit Switching Techniques

Aline Mello, Ney Calazans, Fernando Moraes

Pontifícia Universidade Católica do Rio Grande do Sul (FACIN-PUCRS)
Av. Ipiranga, 6681 - Prédio 30 / BLOCO 4 - 90619-900 - Porto Alegre – RS – BRASIL
{alinev, calazans, moraes}@inf.pucrs.br

Abstract. The idea behind the proposition of Networks-on-Chip (NoCs) for modern and future systems on chip capitalizes on the fact that busses do not scale well when shared by a large number of cores. Even if NoC research is a relatively young field, the literature abounds with propositions of NoC architectures. Several of these propositions claim providing quality of service (QoS) guarantees, which is essential for real time and multimedia applications. The most widespread approach to attain some degree of QoS guarantee relies on a two-step process. The first step is to characterize application performance through traffic modeling and simulation. The second step consists in tuning a given network template to achieve some degree of QoS guarantee. These QoS targeted NoC templates usually provide specialized structures to allow either the creation of connections (circuit switching) or the assignment of priorities to connectionless flows. It is possible to identify three drawbacks in this two-step process approach. First, it is not possible to guarantee QoS for new applications expected to run on the system, if those are defined after the network design phase. Second, even with end-to-end delay guarantees, connectionless approaches may introduce jitter. Third, to model traffic precisely for a complex application is a very hard task. If this problem is tackled by oversimplifying the modeling phase, errors may arise, leading to NoC parameterization that is poorly adapted to achieve the required QoS. This Chapter has two main objectives. The first one is to evaluate the area-performance trade-off and the limitations of circuit switching and priority scheduling to meet QoS. This evaluation will show where such implementations are really suited for QoS, and when more elaborate mechanisms to meet QoS are needed. The second objective comprises proposing a method, called *rate-based scheduling*, to approach QoS requirements considering the execution time state of the NoC. The evaluation of circuit switching and priority scheduling show that: (*i*) circuit switching can guarantee QoS only to a small number of flows; the technique do not scale well, and can potentially waste significant bandwidth; (*ii*) priority-based approaches may display best-effort behavior and, in worst-case situations, may lead to unacceptable latency for low priority flows, besides being subject to jitter. In face of these limitations, rate-based scheduling arises as an option to improve the performance of QoS flows when varying traffic scenarios are used.

Key words: quality of service, QoS, network-on-chip, NoC, circuit switching, priority scheduling, rate-based scheduling.

Please use the following format when citing this chapter:

Mello, A., Calazans, N. and Moraes, F., 2009, in IFIP International Federation for Information Processing, Volume 291;
VLSI-SoC: Advanced Topics on Systems on a Chip; eds. R. Reis, V. Mooney, P. Hasler; (Boston: Springer), pp. 109–130.

1   Introduction

As described in [1], networks on-chip (NoCs) are a promising way to implement future interconnection architectures, due to their: (*i*) energy efficiency and reliability [2]; (*ii*) scalability of bandwidth when compared to bus architectures; (*iii*) reusability; (iv) distributed routing decisions [2]. Network interfaces, routers and point-to-point links define a NoC infrastructure. A network interface connects IPs to the NoC, and is responsible to prepare and deliver packets or entire messages to other IPs through the NoC and to receive packets/messages from the network to the IP [2].

Currently, most NoC implementations only provide support to best effort (BE) services [1], even those proposed by NoC companies like Arteris [3]. BE services guarantee delivery of all packets from a source to a target, but provide no bounds for throughput, jitter or latency. This kind of service usually assigns the same priority to all packets, leading to unpredictable transmission delays. The term Quality of Service (QoS) refers to the capacity of a network to control traffic constraints to meet design requirements of an application or of some of its specific modules. Thus, BE services are inadequate to satisfy QoS requirements for applications/modules with tight performance requirements, as in the case of multimedia streams. To meet performance requirements and thus guarantee QoS, the network needs to include specific characteristics at some level in its protocol stack. Accessing the relative priority and requirements of each flow enables an efficient assignment of resources to flows [4].

Present NoC implementations providing support to QoS try to achieve performance requirements at *design time*. The network is designed according to the application, requiring accurate traffic modeling and simulation to obtain the desired bandwidth and latency figures for the target application. The simulation results allow dimensioning the network to support application requirements. Network synthesis occurs after simulation. However, it is still possible that QoS guarantee is not met for new applications. Modern SoCs, such as 3G phones, support different application profiles. Designing the network to support all possible traffic scenarios is unfeasible in terms of power and area. Thus, some mechanism has to be used at *execution time* to enable meeting QoS requirements for a wide range of applications. Some examples of mechanisms are those long used in IP and ATM networks, including admission control and traffic shaping. The main advantage of using such mechanisms is to support new applications after network design, at the cost of extra area and power.

NoCs proposed to meet QoS (e. g. [5] [6] [7] [8] [9] [10] [11] [12]) employ circuit switching and/or priority scheduling in their router architectures to attain performance requirements. Nonetheless, these techniques are implemented at *design time* for some devised traffic scenarios. For real applications, there can be a significant uncertainty during execution time: some flows may disappear and re-appear randomly or periodically, and they may also be interdependent [13]. To the knowledge of the Authors, there is no NoC implementation with built-in mechanisms to meet QoS taking into account the state of the network at *execution time*.

This Chapter has two objectives. The first is to evaluate area-performance trade-off and limitations of circuit switching and priority scheduling to meet QoS. This shows where such implementations are really suited for achieving QoS, and where more elaborate mechanisms are needed. The second is to propose a method, *rate-based scheduling*, to approach QoS requirements considering the NoC *execution time* state.

The rest of this Chapter is organized as follows. Section 2 is an overview of NoCs that offer guarantees of QoS. Section 3 details four NoC designs: (*i*) a best effort NoC; (*ii*) a static priority scheduling NoC; (*iii*) a NoC employing dynamic priority scheduling to meet QoS; and (*iv*) a NoC employing circuit and packet switching. Section 4 proposes the rate-based scheduling policy. Section 5 analyzes latency, jitter and throughput for all NoCs. Section 6 gives conclusions and suggests future works.

2   Related Work

Current NoC designs employ at least one of three methods to provide QoS: (*i*) dimensioning the network to provide enough bandwidth to satisfy all IP requirements; (*ii*) providing support to circuit switching for all or selected IPs; (*iii*) making available priority scheduling for packet transmission.

Harmanci et al. [14] present a quantitative comparison between circuit switching and priority scheduling, showing that the prioritization of flows on top of a connectionless communication network is able to guarantee end-to-end delays in a more stable form than circuit switching. However, the reference does not quantify results. A possible explanation for this is the use of a TLM SystemC modeling, instead of clock cycle accurate models. Also, structural limitations of circuit switching and priority scheduling are not depicted.

The first method to provide QoS mentioned above is advocated e. g. by the Xpipes NoC [6]. The designer sizes Xpipes according to application requirements, adjusting each channel bandwidth to fulfill the requirements. However, applying this method alone does not guarantee avoidance of local congestions (hot spots), even if bandwidth is largely increased. This fact, coupled to ever-increasing performance requirements [15], makes the method improper to satisfy a wide range of applications.

The second method, support to circuit switching[1], provides a connection-oriented distinction between flows. This method is used in Æthereal [7], aSOC [8], Octagon [9], Nostrum [10] and SoCBUS [11] NoCs. For example, the Nostrum NoC [10] employs virtual circuits (VC), with the routing of QoS flows decided at design time. The communications on the physical channels are globally scheduled in time slots using TDM. The VCs guarantee throughput and constant latency at execution time, even with variable traffic rates. Circuit switching NoCs create connections for all or to selected flows. The establishment of connections requires allocation of resources such as buffers and/or channel bandwidth. This scheme has the advantage of guaranteeing tight temporal bounds for individual flows. However, the method has two main disadvantages: (*i*) poor scalability [14]; (*ii*) inefficient bandwidth usage. The router area is proportional to the number of supported connections, penalizing

---

[1] Here, the term *circuit switching* is used to refer to both, networks providing physical level structures to establish connection between source and destination, as well as to packet switched networks employing higher level services (such as virtual circuits) to create connections.

scalability. Resource allocation for a given flow is based on worst case scenarios. Consequently, network resources may be wasted, particularly for bursty flows.

QNoC [5], DiffServ-NoC [14] and RSoC [12] are examples of NoCs adopting the third method, packet switching with priorities. This connectionless technique groups traffic flows into different classes, with different service levels for each class. It requires separate buffering to manipulate packets according to the services levels. To each service level corresponds a priority class. The network serves non-empty higher priority buffers first. Packets stored in lower priority buffers are transmitted only when no higher priority packets is waiting to be served. This scheme offers better adaptation to varying network traffic and a potentially better utilization of network resources. However, end-to-end latency and throughput cannot be guaranteed, except to higher priority flows. Also, it is necessary to devise some form of starvation prevention for lower priority flows. When flows share resources, even higher priority flows can have an unpredictable behavior. Thus, this method often provides a poorer QoS support than circuit switching.

Neither circuit switching nor priority methods guarantee QoS for *multiple concurrent flows*. When using circuit switching, the network may reject flows, due to a limited amount of simultaneously supported connections, even if bandwidth is available. When multiple flows with the same priority compete for resources, priority-based networks have behavior similar to BE networks (see Section 5). As mentioned before, networks using any of the three methods above employ techniques at design time to guarantee QoS through traffic modeling, simulation-based network sizing and network synthesis. The drawbacks of sizing the network at design time are: (*i*) the complexity of traffic modeling and system simulation is very high, being thus error-prone; and (*ii*) the network designed in this way may not guarantee QoS for new applications. The first drawback may force the use of simplified application/environment models, which can in turn lead to incorrect dimensioning of the NoC parameters for synthesis. The second drawback may arise if new applications must execute after product delivery, as occurs in reconfigurable or systems.

The main performance figures used in the above reviewed NoCs are end-the-end latency and throughput. But when QoS is considered, another concept can be of relevance, *jitter*, the variation in latency, caused by network congestion, or route variations [16]. In connectionless networks, buffers introduce jitter. When packets are blocked, latency increases. Once the network can release packets from blocking, latency reduces, due to burst packet diffusion. Thus, networks using only priorities cannot guarantee jitter control. Some works advocate different methods to enhance QoS. For example, Andreasson and Kumar proposed a *slack-time aware* routing [13] [17], a source routing technique to improve overall network utilization by dynamically controlling the injection of BE packets in the network at specific paths, while guaranteed throughput (GT) packets are not employing these. However, this work does not aim at QoS achievement.

The NoCs to be described in the next two Sections share a basic set of common features: 2D mesh topology, wormhole packet switching, deterministic distributed routing, and physical channels multiplexed in at least two virtual channels (VC). This certainly does not cover all possible features found in NoC architectures proposed in the literature. But many of these features are found in several NoCs [18] [19].

3   Reference NoC Designs

This Section presents four NoC designs. The first is a NoC supporting BE services only (BE-NoC). The second and third add priority schemes to the BE-NoC, to enable differentiating flows. The fourth design adds circuit-switching to the BE-NoC.

3.1   Best Effort NoC - *BE-NoC*

The BE-NoC is based on Hermes [19], a parameterizable infrastructure used to implement low area overhead packet switching NoCs with 2D mesh or torus topology, which allows to select the routing algorithm, the flit size and the buffer depth. This work employs Hermes with a parameterizable number of virtual channels (VCs) [20]. The first and the second flits of a packet are header information, respectively containing the target address, and the payload size (up to $2^{(\text{flit size, in bits})}$) in flits. The remainder flits are payload.

Credit based is the flow control algorithm assumed here. **Fig. 1** shows the credit-based interface between routers. The output port signals are: (*1*) clock_tx: synchronizes data transmission; (*2*) tx: indicates data availability; (*3*) lane_tx: indicates the VC or lane transmitting data; (*4*) data_out: data to be sent; (*5*) credit_in: indicates available buffer space, for each lane.

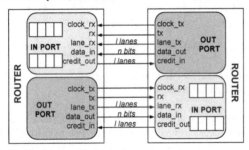

Fig. 1. Physical router interface for the BE-NoC.

The router has centralized switching control logic and five bi-directional ports: East, West, North, South, and Local. The Local port establishes a communication between the router and its local core. The other ports connect to neighbor routers. Any physical channel may support multiplexed VCs. **Fig. 2** presents the internal router structure, with two lanes per physical channel. Although physical channel multiplexing may increase switching performance [1], it is important to keep a compromise among performance, complexity and router area.

Each input port has a depth *d* buffer for temporary flit storage. When *n* lanes are used, a buffer with *d/n* depth is associated to each lane. The input port receives flits, storing them in the buffer indicated by signal *lane_rx* (**Fig. 1**). Next, it decrements the amount of lane credits. When an output port transmits a flit, this flit is removed from the buffer and the credit counter is incremented. Credit availability reaches a neighbor router through signal credit_out (**Fig. 1**).

The XY routing algorithm sends packets in the X direction up to the target X coordinate, and then proceeds in the Y direction until reaching the target router. The behavior of this algorithm allows the use of the partial crossbar of **Fig. 2**. Packets coming from the Local, East or West ports may go to any output port. Packets coming from the North port can only be transmitted to the South and Local ports, and packets coming from the South port can only be follow to the North and Local ports. A partial crossbar reduces router area by up to 3%, compared to a full crossbar.

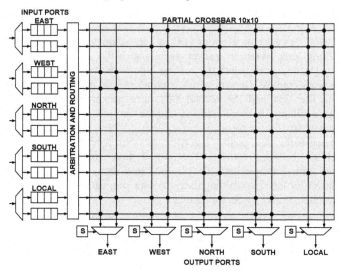

Fig. 2. Router internal structure, for two virtual channels Hermes NoC. "Solder points" indicate existing connections in the partial crossbar.

Multiple packets may arrive simultaneously in a given router. A centralized round-robin arbitration grants access to incoming packets. The priority of a lane is a function of the last lane having a routing request granted. If the incoming packet request is granted by the arbiter, the XY routing algorithm is executed to connect the input port to the correct output port. When the algorithm returns a busy output port, the header flit and all subsequent flits of this packet are blocked.

After routing execution, the output port allocates the bandwidth among the n lanes. Each lane with flits to transmit occupies at least $1/n$ of the physical channel bandwidth. If only one lane satisfies this condition, it occupies the whole physical channel bandwidth. After all flits in a packet are transmitted, the port is released.

3.2   Static Priority NoC – *SP-NoC*

The objective of this design is to add the ability to provide differentiated services to the flows, using a resource allocation mechanism based on static priorities (similar to QNoC [5]). This design modifies the arbitration and scheduling router policies without modifying the BE-NoC router interface.

In the *SP-NoC*, each lane is associated to a priority and is served according to it. The priority of each lane is given by its index, as defined by Equation 1. In this way, this NoC allows the network to differentiate *n* flows, where *n* is the number of lanes per physical channel.

$$priority\ of\ L_i = i - 1,\ \text{for all i} \geq 1 \tag{1}$$

To differentiate flows, the packet header is extended by a new field, named *priority*. This field determines which lane is used for packet transmission. For example, lane L2 transmits packets with priority 1. The user may assign to the priority field a value between *0* (lowest priority) and *n-1* (highest priority) . Only the source router verifies the priority field. The remaining routers transmit packets using the same lane allocated by the source router.

The assignment of priorities to virtual channels requires modification of router arbitration and scheduling algorithms. In priority-based arbitration, when multiple packets arrive simultaneously at the router input ports, the packet with higher priority is served first, even if other packets are waiting to be served. In priority-based scheduling[2], packets with higher priority are also served first. Then, data transmission in lower priority lanes depends on the load of the higher priority lanes, which can vary dynamically. For this reason, end-to-end latency bounds cannot be determined for all lanes, only for the highest priority lane. Consequently, it is hard to support multiple services with guaranteed QoS using priorities [21].

Priority-based arbitration and scheduling are effective for a small number of virtual channels [21]. For example, it is possible to reserve a virtual channel for real-time flows, a second one for non-real-time flows with controlled losses, and a third one for best-effort traffic. The drawback of the approach is the fact that the router area increases approximately with the square of the number of virtual channels [20].

3.3   Dynamic Priority NoC – *DP-NoC*

In a *DP-NoC*, priority is assigned to *flows* as opposed to the *SP-NoC*, where priority is assigned to *lanes*. Thus, *SP-NoCs* statically reserve NoC resources at design time to certain types of flows (e. g., the lane L2 is reserved for the flow with priority 1). In *DP-NoCs* such reservation does not exist.

In *DP-NoCs*, lane priority varies according to the packet priority. This allows: (*i*) transmitting packets through any lane; (*ii*) transmitting packets through different lanes along the packet path; (*iii*) transmitting packets with the same priority through different lanes in the same physical link using time division multiplexing (TDM). In *DP-NoCs*, the priority field is also included in the packet header, being possible to assign to this field any value between zero and (2^t-1), where *t* is the flit width.

DP-NoCs keep the same external router interface of previous designs, requiring modifications in arbitration, routing table and scheduling. The arbitration method serves the packets with higher priority first, as in *SP-NoCs*. However, as the priority is

---

[2] Scheduling defines which flow can use a given output port.

defined in the packet, it is necessary to compare the priority field of all incoming packets, increasing the time to perform arbitration by two clock cycles. The routing table is extended with a new field, named *priority*. This field determines the priority of the output port lanes. The scheduling policy verifies the packets waiting to be transmitted to the free lanes in decreasing priority order. A round-robin algorithm is used to solve conflicts when packets with the same priority dispute the same lane. In *SP-NoCs*, this kind of conflict never arises.

3.4   Circuit Switching NoC – *CS-NoC*

The *Circuit switching* NoC adds differentiated services by enabling connection establishment. The network offers a guaranteed throughput (GT) service to flows with QoS requirements. To flows without QoS requirements, the network offers a best effort (BE) service. This approach, GT plus BE, is similar to the one implemented in the Æthereal NoC.

This design employs two lanes, L1 and L2. Lane L1 carries circuit switching data, while lane L2 is used to transmit packet switching data. GT flows have priority higher than BE flows, with end-to-end latency guarantee. When a given GT flow leaves the physical channel idle, BE flows may use this channel, without incurring in any significant penalty to GT data arriving while a BE flow is using the channel.

The physical interface between routers in CS-NoC has all signals of the previous NoC, plus an additional signal, *ack_in* (and *ack_out* respectively), to signal connection establishment (*ack_in* asserted) and connection release (*ack_in* unasserted).

A GT flow requires connection establishment before starting data transmission. A connection between a source and a target node require the reservation of lane L1 along the path between their respective routers. The path reservation avoids the establishment of other connections in the same path.

The hardware to implement circuit switching is simpler than in packet switching, since a register can be used instead of a buffer, and the control flow is simplified, requiring neither handshake nor credit control. Some NoCs, such as Æthereal, store in a table data such as the required bandwidth of the GT flows, but this table increases router area significantly. Multiple flows may use the physical channel, multiplexing the bandwidth (TDM). In the CS-NoC only one connection can be established per physical channel, not requiring this additional area. A specific protocol is used to establish and release connections. In summary, connections are established or released using BE control packets. These packets are differentiated from BE data packets by the most significant bit of the first header flit. When this bit is asserted, the BE packet has control function, and the second flit indicates the command to be executed (connection establishment or release). BE control packets do not contain payload.

4   A NoC Supporting Rate-Based Scheduling – *RB-NoC*

This Section proposes the design of a router with a built-in mechanism which overcomes circuit switching and priority scheduling limitations stated in Section 3. BE flows are transmitted using a single specific VC per channel, while QoS flows may use any VC. This resource reservation for QoS flows is needed to avoid that multiple BE flows momentarily block some channel for a QoS flow.

Telecom networks have employed rate-based scheduling policies to control congestion. Examples of such policies are virtual clock (VC) [21], weighted fair queuing (WFQ) and the method proposed in [22]. The rate-based scheduling policy proposed here comprises two steps: admission control followed by dynamic scheduling.

The admission step determines if the network may accept a new QoS flow without penalizing performance guarantees already assigned to other QoS flows. It starts by sending a control packet from the source router to the target router, containing the rate required by the IP. The QoS flow is admitted into the network if and only if all routers in the path to the target can transmit at the required rate. When the control packet arrives at the target, an acknowledgment signal is back propagated to the source router. This process is similar to the connection establishment in circuit switching but, differently from circuit switching, there is no static resource reservation.

When the QoS flow is admitted, a *virtual connection* is established between the source and target router, as in ATM networks. This virtual connection corresponds to a line in the *flow* table (see **Fig. 3**) of each router in the connection path. Each line of the flow table identifies the QoS flow using the following fields: source router, target router, required rate, and used rate.

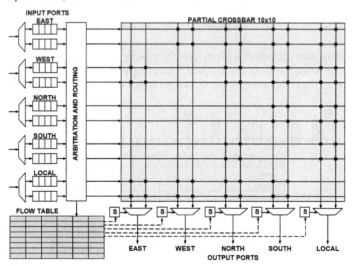

Fig. 3. Router architecture with support for rate-based scheduling.

The *flow table* depth determines how many simultaneous QoS flows can be admitted by each router. The virtual connection is released by the source router with another control packet. Once the virtual path is established, the source router may start sending QoS flow packets. When packets arrive at a router input port they are stored in input buffers, arbitrated and routed to an output port (**Fig. 3**). Packets assigned to the same output port are served according to the proposed scheduling policy.

In the implemented scheduling policy, BE flows are transmitted only when no QoS flow requires the physical channel. The RB-NoC employs a notion of priority to differentiate QoS flows among them, but priority is defined in a different way from SP-NoC and DP-NoC definitions. In an RB-NoC, a QoS flow *priority* is the difference between the required rate and the rate currently used by it. When two or more QoS flows compete, the higher priority flow is scheduled first.

As illustrated in **Fig. 3**, the flow table is read by the scheduler (blocks named S in **Fig. 3**) to find the priority of each QoS flow assigned to a same output port. The flow priority is periodically updated according to Equation 2. A positive priority means that the flow used less than its required rate in the considered sampling period. A negative priority means that the flow violates its rate in the sampling period.

$$priority_i = required\ rate - used\ rate_i, \quad \text{where } i \text{ designates a given flow} \qquad (2)$$

The required rate is fixed during the admission control step. The used rate (UR) is *periodically* computed according to Equation 3, where CR is the *current rate* used during the current period, and UR is the average of the previous used rate and the current used rate.

$$UR_i = \begin{cases} CR_i, & if\ UR_{i-1} = 0 \\ \dfrac{UR_{i-1} + CR_i}{2}, & if\ UR_{i-1} \neq 0 \end{cases} \qquad (3)$$

Fig. 4 illustrates packets of a given QoS flow being transmitted. Timestamps T0 to T4 designate when the rates are sampled, assuming in this example 10 time units in each interval. The table in the Figure shows the behavior of one flow, from T0 to T4.

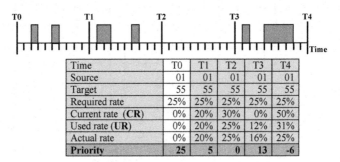

Time	T0	T1	T2	T3	T4
Source	01	01	01	01	01
Target	55	55	55	55	55
Required rate	25%	25%	25%	25%	25%
Current rate (CR)	0%	20%	30%	0%	50%
Used rate (UR)	0%	20%	25%	12%	31%
Actual rate	0%	20%	25%	16%	25%
Priority	25	5	0	13	-6

Fig. 4. Transmission of packets for a given QoS flow.

In this example, the 4th line of the table contains the required rate (25%) for this flow. At timestamp T1 the current rate (5th line) is 20%, corresponding to the channel bandwidth used by the flow in the previous interval (T0-T1). According to the Equation 3, it is possible to obtain the used rate (6th line of the table). The 8th line of the table contains the flow priority, which is updated according to Equation 2.

The interval between timestamps is an important parameter of the proposed method. The 7th line contains the actual flow rate (shown here for comparison purposes, not physically present in the flow table). If the chosen interval is too short, the computed used rate may not correspond to the actual rate, compromising the scheduling method. If the interval is too long, the computed used rate will be accurate, but the flow priority will remain fixed for a long period, also compromising the method.

To minimize the error induced by the sampling period, the method in fact employs two sample intervals. In the previously presented example, consider a second current rate ($CR2$) and a sample interval 4 times larger than the original one. In this example, $CR2$ will be equal to 100% (summation of CR from T0 to T4) in T4. Dividing $CR2$ by 4, the corrected used rate is obtained (CUR, Equation 4). It can be observed that applying CUR to UR each n intervals (4 in this example), the error is minimized.

$$CUR = \frac{CR2}{n} = \frac{\sum_{i=0}^{n-1} CR_i}{n} \tag{4}$$

Consequently, in Equation 3, UR_i receives CUR when $i \bmod n$ is zero, where n corresponds to the result of dividing the longer sample interval value by the shorter. If the used rate is considered alone in the priority computation ($priority_i = 100 - UR_i$), the scheduling policy tends to balance physical channel use, which implies disregarding that distinct QoS flows may require distinct rates, and should thus be avoided.

5   Experimental Results

The behavior of a network depends on its architecture as well as on the running application. For example, in some applications (e.g. streaming) long messages may dominate, while in others (e.g. controllers) short messages dominate traffic characteristics. According to [4], the influence of traffic in system performance is greater than that of network structural parameters. Thus, it is important to dispose of traffic generators to model the behavior of real traffic. This Section shows experiments comparing the performance of the described NoCs through functional VHDL simulation. The parameters for all NoCs are: 8x8 mesh topology; XY routing; 16-bit flits; 2 virtual channels; 8-flit buffers associated to each input lane. An 8x8, 64-router NoC is big enough to provide significant results on which to draw conclusions about future SoC interconnects, while allowing reasonable RTL simulation time. The flit with has no influence here on the QoS behavior. Thus, a close to minimum value was chosen. Buffer sizing is a complex subject, but previous experiments [19] have showed that 8 is a minimum size that does not impair NoC performance.

5.1   Experimental setup

Table 1 presents the flows used in the experiments. Flow *A* is characterized as a CBR (constant bit rate) service, i. e. a flow transmitting at a fixed rate [23]. Flow *B* is a variable bit rate (VBR) service [23]. This flow is modeled using a Pareto distribution [24]. According to [24], Pareto distributions are observable in bursty traffic between on-chip modules in typical MPEG-2 video and networking applications. Flows *A* and *B* have QoS requirements of latency and jitter. Nodes generating flows *A* and *B* transmit 2000 packets. The results do not take consider the first 100 packets, which correspond to the warm-up period. Also, the last 100 packets are discarded from results, since the traffic by end of simulation does not correspond to regular load operation. Flow *C* is a BE flow, also modeled using a Pareto distribution. This flow disturbs flows with QoS requirements (*A* and *B*), being considered as *noise* traffic. For this reason, results for the *C* flow are not discussed.

Table 1. Characterization of the flows used in the experiments.

Type	Service	QoS	Distribution	Number of Packets	Packet Size	Target
A	CBR	Yes	Uniform (20%)	2000	50	Fixed
B	VBR	Yes	Pareto (40% in the ON period)	2000	50	Fixed
C	BE	No	Pareto (20% in the ON period)	Random	20	Random

All simulations scenarios were repeated for different amounts of packets per flow (100, 200, 1000 and 2000) and different packet sizes (50 and 500 flits). The same results were observed for latency, throughput and jitter for every experiment counting 200 flits per flow or more. This means that the network reaches a steady state in this situation. Results for long packets (500 flits) are proportional to the results for short packets (50 flits). From the results included below it is easy to infer other behaviors.

Two evaluation scenarios are defined. In the first, two QoS flows (F1 and F2) originated at different nodes share part of the path to targets. In the second, three QoS flows (F1, F2 and F3) generate traffic, all sharing part of the path. All remaining network nodes transmit disturbing C flows. **Fig. 5** presents the spatial distribution of source and target nodes. The placement of source and target nodes aims to evaluate situations where the flows with QoS requirements compete for network resources.

Spatial traffic distributions and the experimental scenarios were chosen to highlight the limitations of priority scheduling and circuit switching when resources are shared among flows. Models CBR (e.g. non-compacted video) and VBR (MPEG) are artificial but relevant workload models [10]. Equation 5 gives the minimal latency to transfer a packet from a source to a target, in clock cycles.

$$minimal \ \ latency \ = (R \times N) + P \qquad\qquad (5)$$

In this Equation: (*i*) R is the router minimal latency (arbitration and routing), equal to 5 for the BE, SP, DP and CS NoCs; for the RB-NoC this value is 13; (*ii*) N is the number of routers in the path; (*iii*) P is the packet size. **Table 2** summarizes the conducted experiments. Column Priority (P) has no meaning for BE-NoC and RB-NoC. In the CS-NoC, flows with P=1 are GT flows and flows with priority 0 are BE flows.

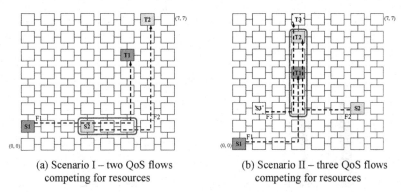

(a) Scenario I – two QoS flows
competing for resources

(b) Scenario II – three QoS flows
competing for resources

Fig. 5. Spatial traffic distribution of source and target nodes for flows with QoS requirements. Dotted lines indicate the path of each flow. Rounded rectangles highlight the area where flows compete for network resources. All other nodes transmit C flows, disturbing the QoS flows.

Table 2. Experimental scenarios. NA stands for Not Applicable.

Experiment	Traffic Distribution	Flow F1 (QoS)		Flow F2 (QoS)		Flow F3 (QoS)		Noise flows (BE)	
		Type	P	Type	P	Type	P	Type	P
I	I	A (CBR)	1	A (CBR)	0	NA	NA	C	0
II	I	A (CBR)	1	A (CBR)	1	NA	NA	C	0
III	I	B (VBR)	1	B (VBR)	1	NA	NA	C	0
IV	II	A (CBR)	1	A (CBR)	1	A (CBR)	0	C	0
V	II	B (VBR)	1	B (VBR)	1	B (VBR)	0	C	0

P = Priority   NA = Not Applicable

The number of virtual channels (VCs) defines how many flows compete for resources in the same channel. As all NoC designs have two VCs, there are three options when more than one QoS flow coexist: all flows with low priority (using BE-NoC), some flows with high priority (I, IV and V for SP-NoC, DP-NoC, CS-NoC), or all flows with high priority (II and III for SP-NoC, DP-NoC, CS-NoC).

5.2   SP-NoC priority mechanism analysis

This Section compares SP-NoC to BE-NoC with regard to latency, jitter, latency spreading and throughput. **Fig. 6** gives the average latency and jitter for Experiment I. BE-NoC does not differentiate flows; i. e. average latency and jitter of packets depend on the transmission traffic conditions. Thus, BE-NoC gives no guarantees to any flow.

In SP-NoC, the highest priority flow F1 has average latency near the optimum minimum latency (5(10)+50) and jitter is close to zero. This occurs because F1 has higher priority and exclusive usage of the virtual channel L2. Therefore, whenever F1 has data to send, it has access to the physical channel. However, F2 is always blocked while F1 is delivering flits. F2 shows an average latency of about 50 clock cycles greater that the minimum latency and its jitter is about 40 clock cycles, representing 80% of the packet size. This experiment shows that a priority mechanism helps guaranteeing QoS, if flows with a same priority do not compete.

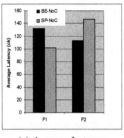
(a) Average Latency

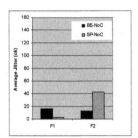
(b) Average Jitter

Fig. 6. Results for flows F1 and F2, Experiment I.

Fig. 7 shows average latency, jitter and latency spreading for Experiment II. Flows F1 and F2 have the same priority, competing for lane L2. It is noticeable that F2 has average latency near to minimum and F1 latency is around 50% larger than the minimum. This occurs because F1 and F2 are CBR flows, i. e. they insert packets in the network at fixed intervals. As F2 source node is closer to the disputed region, it is served first. For the same reason, F1 and F2 have jitter near zero and small spreading.

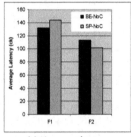
(a) Average latency

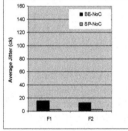
(b) Average Jitter

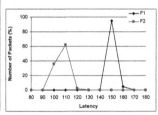
(c) Latency spreading of SP-NoC flows

Fig. 7. Results for flows F1 and F2, Experiment II, CBR traffic.

However, when F1 and F2 are VBR flows (Experiment III) results are quite different (see **Fig. 8**). Here, packets enter the network at variable intervals, using a 40% load for the ON period, representing a 20% effective load. The ON-OFF traffic model randomizes the packet injection instants. Thus, there is no flow always served first. This has two consequences: (*i*) the jitter of both flows increases, and (*ii*) due to the duration of the OFF periods, both latencies approach the minimum value.

Fig. 7 and **Fig. 8** show the priority mechanism behavior when flows with a same priority compete for network resources. In the case of CBR flows (Experiment II), one of the flows has unpredictable behavior, similar to a BE flow. In the case of VBR flows (Experiment III), the priority mechanism guarantees latencies close to minimum for the flows with higher priority. However, these present high values of jitter. Depending on the parameters that specify QoS for the flows, the usage of priority mechanism should be limited to specific situations, where competition among equal priority flows is avoidable or kept to a minimum.

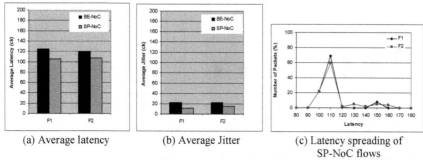

(a) Average latency   (b) Average Jitter   (c) Latency spreading of
SP-NoC flows

Fig. 8. Results for flows F1 and F2, Experiment III, VBR traffic.

Fig. 9 illustrates the average latency, the jitter and the throughput for Experiment IV. Here, two high priority flows compete for resources with a third low priority flow. It is possible to observe that average latency and jitter of priority flows (F1 and F2) have the same behavior of **Fig. 7**. These flows have 99% of packets with throughput between 15% and 20%, in accordance with the insertion rates. However, the low priority flow (F3) has higher average latency (about 2.5 times the minimum latency (5(8)+50) and highest jitter.

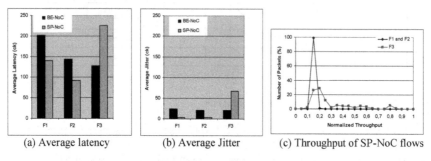

(a) Average latency   (b) Average Jitter   (c) Throughput of SP-NoC flows

Fig. 9. Results for flows F1, F2 and F3, Experiment IV, CBR traffic.

The F3 packets throughput presents large variation, having packets with rate superior to the injection rate. This is due to the fact that packets are sent in burst after the release of the blocking condition. If F3 had some attached throughput QoS requirement, using a priority mechanism would not be adequate.

Fig. 10 shows results of Experiment V, where 3 VBR flows compete for resources. Priority flows are transmitted with near to minimum latency (90 clock cycles) and jitter close to 0. These flows have 90% of the packets with throughput between 35% and 45%, and 10% of the packets with throughput between 0% and 5%. This occurs because a VBR flow uses an ON-OFF Pareto distribution. Here, the flow with low priority (F3) is penalized, showing high latency and jitter, and erratic throughput (excessive throughput spreading).

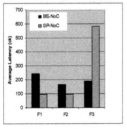 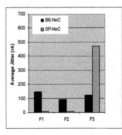 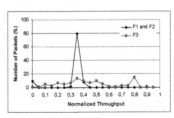

   (a) Average latency   (b) Average Jitter   (c) Throughput of SP-NoC flows

Fig. 10. Results for flows F1, F2 and F3, Experiment V, VBR traffic.

Table 3 summarizes the evaluation of the static priority mechanism.

Table 3. SP-NoC evaluation summary (all flows compete with BE packets).

Experiment	Description	QoS guarantee			
		Latency	Jitter	Throughput	Reason
I	One priority CBR flow, *without* competition with priority flows	Yes	Yes	Yes	When the priority flows has data to transmit, it has access to the physical link.
II	Two priority CBR flows, *with* competition	No	Yes	Yes	The injection at fixed intervals serves first the flow which is nearer to the congestion area. Consequently, this flow has near to minimum latency, while the second flow has its latency significantly increased.
III	Two priority VBR flows, *with* competition	Yes	No	Yes	The injection at random intervals results in near to minimum latency, but jitter is increased.
IV	Three priority CBR flows, *with* competition	No	Yes	Yes	Idem to Experiment II
V	Three priority VBR flows, *with* competition	Yes	No	Yes	Idem to Experiment III

5.3   DP-NoC priority mechanism analysis

This Section compares *DP-NoC* and *SP-NoC*. The following performance figures are evaluated: latency, jitter and latency spreading. **Fig. 11** shows the results obtained in Experiment I, where a priority flow is transmitted without competing with any other priority flow, but competing with BE flows. The performance of the *DP-NoC* is inferior to the *SP-NoC*. Two reasons may be advanced to explain this:

1. The minimal latency for the SP-NoC is 100 clock cycles ((5*(10)+50), where 5 is the arbitration/routing delay, 10 is the number of hops and 50 is the packet length), while in *DP-NoC* is 120 clock cycles ((7*(10)+50), due to the two extra clock cycles in the arbitration/routing delay).
2. Even if the *DP-NoC* privileges higher priority flows, there is no lane reservation for priority packets. Thus, if there is no higher priority packet being transmitted, BE flows may use all lanes, blocking priority packets until a lane is freed.

This behavior leads to unpredictable jitter values. Here, the average jitter of F2 (without priority) is smaller than F1 (with priority). The second reason advanced above leads to an important latency spreading, since priority packets are blocked.

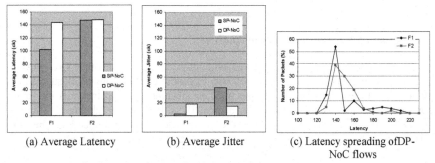

(a) Average Latency   (b) Average Jitter   (c) Latency spreading ofDP-
                                                             NoC flows

Fig. 11. Results for flows F1, F2, Experiment I.

Fig. 12 and **Fig. 13** show the results obtained when flows with the same priority compete for resources (output links). For both experiments, the performance of the *DP-NoC* is again inferior to the *SP-NoC*, for the same reason: absence of resource reservation. Increasing the number of different priorities could be effective with more lanes; however, the router area grows quadratically with the amount of lanes.

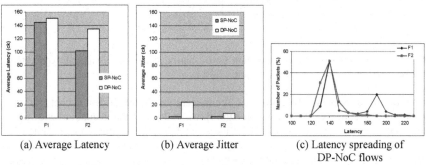

(a) Average Latency   (b) Average Jitter   (c) Latency spreading of
                                                             DP-NoC flows

Fig. 12. Results for flows F1, F2, Experiment II, CBR Flows.

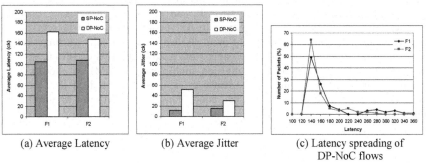

(a) Average Latency   (b) Average Jitter   (c) Latency spreading of
                                                             DP-NoC flows

Fig. 13. Results for flows F1, F2, Experiment III, VBR Flows.

Whenever the number of flows competing for a same channel is smaller or equal to the number of available virtual channels the DP-NoC can effectively guarantee QoS requirements.

5.4   Circuit Switching Mechanism Analysis

If a QoS flow has to be transmitted without competing with other QoS flows, circuit switching mechanism is the surest way to guarantee QoS. **Fig. 14** illustrates the amount of time required for connection establishment, data transmission and connection release, using flows of Experiment II, with F1 and F2 being GT flows, competing for the same lane. The time to establish and release a connection, small in this experiment, varies with network traffic, as BE packets control these actions.

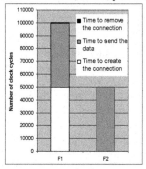

Fig. 14. Evaluation of time to connection establishment, data transmission and connection release for F1 and F2 in Experiment II using CS-NoC.

Both flows transmit 100,000 flits (equivalent to 2,000 50-flit packets of the previous experiments). As the rate for the flows is 20% of the available bandwidth, the total time to transmit all 100,000 flits is 500,000 clock cycles. As illustrated in **Fig. 14**, F2 establishes its connection first. The flow F2 spends 148 clock cycles to create the connection, plus 500,000 clock cycles to transmit data, and 73 clock cycles to remove the connection. Flow 1 waits all these clock cycles to start transmission. The, the total transmission time for both flows is approximately 1,000,000 cycles.

If packet switching is used, as in BE, SP, and DP NoCs, channels are shared among flows, resulting in a smaller time to deliver all flits (in the present case, approximately 500,000). This shows the main disadvantage of circuit switching: static reservation of resources, potentially wasting NoC bandwidth. This disadvantage can be partially minimized using time division multiplexing (TDM) to allocate the bandwidth in fixed size time slices. However, it should be noticed that regular behavior of the traffic is required when using TDM (as CBR flows) to adjust the incoming data rate to the reserved time slots. Otherwise the risk of wasting bandwidth is again present, possibly coupled to the risk of losing data.

5.5   Rate-based scheduling results

In this Section, the Rate-based NoC (*RB-NoC*) is compared to the *SP-NoC*. **Table 4** presents latency, jitter and throughput values for Experiment II (2 CBR flows with the same priority). Both scheduling policies guarantee throughput close to the inserted rate (20%). Analyzing the priority scheduling, F2 has average latency near to ideal, while F1 flow has higher latency (average latency is 77% greater than the ideal latency). Flows F1 and F2 insert packets at fixed intervals. As the F2 source node is closer to the region disputed by the flows, it is always served first. This experiment demonstrates that priority-based scheduling is inefficient for QoS when flows with the same priority compete for the same resources. In rate-based scheduling, the priority is dynamically updated according to the used rate, not as a function of the arrival time of the packets in the router. Therefore, as both flows have the same required rate, bandwidth is equally divided between the flows, resulting in almost the same latency values for both flows, near to ideal values. Jitter is slightly increased when compared to priority-based scheduling, due to the higher minimal latency of the router. This result demonstrates the efficiency of the method.

Table 4. Results for flows F1 and F2, Experiment II, CBR traffic using SP-NoC and RB-NoC.

Performance Figures		SP-NoC		RB-NoC	
		F1	F2	F1	F2
Latency	Ideal (ck)	250,00	250,00	330,00	330,00
	Minimum (ck)	441,00	250,00	330,00	330,00
	Average (ck)	**443,40**	**251,86**	**333,54**	**332,42**
	Maximal (ck)	450,00	258,00	350,00	346,00
Jitter (ck)		2,14	1,78	4,07	3,01
Average throughput (%)		19,80	19,80	19,80	19,80

Table 5 displays results for Experiment III, where F1 and F2 are VBR flows. Here, packets are inserted at variable intervals, using a 40% load for the ON period. The ON-OFF traffic model randomizes packet injection instants, which inserts jitter. Thus, jitter is not showed in **Table 5**. In both scheduling methods, F1 has average latency near to the ideal one. In priority scheduling, F2 has average latency 56% higher than the ideal latency, and the rate-based scheduling only 33% higher. Despite the fact they have similar behavior, rate-based is superior to priority-based scheduling, since it is able to reduce the percentage of deviation from the ideal latency.

Table 5. Results for flows F1 and F2, Experiment III, VBR traffic using SP-NoC and RB-NoC.

Performance Figures		SP-NoC		RB-NoC	
		F1	F2	F1	F2
Latency	Ideal (ck)	250,00	250,00	330,00	330,00
	Minimum (ck)	250,00	250,00	330,00	330,00
	Average (ck)	**253,40**	**321,96**	**337,58**	**440,00**
	Maximal (ck)	266,00	390,00	477,00	545,00
Average throughput (%)		38,82	39,26	38,86	39,40

5.6   Area Results

Table 6 details the router area mapped to a 0.35µm CMOS standard cell library (TSMC). Router area is similar for the BE-NoC and the SP-NoC. DP-NoC area is superior to others, since its arbitration/routing logic needs more comparators. SC-NoC has the smallest area, since simple registers replace the input buffers of the circuit switching lane. Results point to the fact that static priority (SP-NoC) and circuit switching (CS-NoC) do not significantly increase area, compared to the BE-NoC. These mechanisms may be used to force the NoC to respect QoS requirements without increasing total area. The area for all implementations is dominated by the buffers. It is recommended to use memory generators to optimize area. Considering real IPs (with 200,000 gates), an area overhead of around 10% per IP is expected.

Table 6. Router area results targeting a 0, 35µm CMOS standard-cell library (flit size=16, 2 virtual channels, buffer depth=8), using the Leonardo synthesis tool.

	BE-NoC	SP-NoC	DP-NoC	CS-NoC
Number of equivalent gates	18,657	18,621	21,080	12,792
Estimated clock frequency (MHz)	160	168	147	175

Table 7 presents router areas obtained with the Synplify synthesis tool, targeting FPGA devices. The results follow the same proportion as the ASIC mappings, with a little area penalty for the DP-NoC, and the smallest area for the CS-NoC.

Table 7. Router area results for 2V1000 FPGA (flit size=16, 2 virtual channels, buffer depth=8).

Resource	Mapping to Xilinx XC2V1000 FPGA device								
	Used				Available	Used /Available			
	BE-NoC	SP-NoC	DP-NoC	CS-NoC		BE-NoC	SP-NoC	DP-NoC	CS-NoC
Slices	1071	1158	1383	967	5.120	20,92%	22,62%	27,01%	18,89%
LUTs	1984	2150	2529	1622	10.240	19,38%	21,00%	24,70%	15,84%
Flip Flops	513	479	646	467	11.212	4,56%	4,27%	5,76%	4,17%

The area for the RB-NoC router is not available because the HDL description is not optimized for synthesis. A small increase in area can be expected here, because only a small table and few counters were added to the NoC router.

6   Conclusions and Future Work

This work evaluated different methods to provide QoS for NoCs. Dynamic priority is inefficient to guarantee QoS, due the absence of resource allocation. Static priority and connection establishment methods may guarantee QoS. However, both present limitations, especially when flows with QoS requirements compete for network resources. As shown in Experiment I, if no flows with a same priority compete for resources, static priority mechanisms are effective. When flows with a same priority compete for resources, the static priority mechanism does not provide rigid guarantees to any of the flows. An alternative to this, increasing the number of priorities, implies increasing the amount of virtual channels, which can be prohibitive in terms of silicon area. In connection establishment methods, all QoS requirements are guaranteed after connection establishment. However, if some other flow not using connection establishment has deadlines to send data as QoS requirement then this method will be not able to guarantee this requirement.

The state of the art in NoCs still does not provide efficient solutions to achieve QoS for applications when the network traffic is not known in advance. The proposed rate-based scheduling policy adjusts the flow priority w.r.t. the required flow rate and current rate used by the flow. Good results were obtained with CBR flows, with flow latencies near to ideal values. Rate-based scheduling overcomes the problem of flows with a same priority competing for resources, by balancing flows according to their required rates. With VBR traffic, where packets are randomly injected into the network, the proposed approach is also superior to priority-based scheduling. However, in this case rate-based scheduling does not currently achieves minimal latencies when QoS flows compete. One clear advantage of rate-based scheduling concerns high priority flows with differentiated QoS requirements. The experiments discussed in Section 5.5 assumed priority flows with the same throughput requirement, 20% of the available bandwidth. This was done for coherence with the other experiments. Other experiments were conducted over the RB-NoC only. In one of these, two competing CBR flows require 10 and 30% of the available bandwidth and receive 9,61 and 28,81% respectively, under the same conditions of noise traffic.

As future work it is possible to enumerate: (*i*) reducing the RB-NoC router minimal latency, responsible by increases in jitter and latency; (*ii*) evaluating the proposed method when more than three flows compete for resources; (*iii*) evaluating area overhead of the RB-NoC; (*iv*) implementing congestion control mechanisms.

7   References

[1]   Rijpkema, E.; Goossens, K.; Rădulescu, A. "*Trade-offs in the Design of a Router with Both Guaranteed and Best-Effort Services for Networks on Chip*". In: DATE'03, pp. 350-355.

[2]   Benini, L.; De Micheli, G. "*Networks on chips: a new SoC paradigm*". Computer, v.35(1), Jan. 2002, pp. 70-78.

[3]   Arteris. "*Arteris Network on Chip Company*". 2005. Available at http://www.arteris.net.

[4]   Duato, J.; Yalamanchili, S.; Ni, L. "Interconnection Networks". Elsevier Science, 2002, 600 p.

[5]   Bolotin, E; Cidon, I.; Ginosar R.; Kolodny A. "*QNoC: QoS Architecture and Design Process for Network on Chip*". Journal of Systems Architecture, v.50(2-3), Feb. 2004, pp 105-128.

[6]   Bertozzi, D.; Benini, L. "*Xpipes: A Network-on-chip Architecture for Gigascale Systems-on-Chip*". IEEE Circuits and Systems Magazine, v.4(2), 2004, pp. 18-31.

[7]   Goossens, K.; Dielissen, J.; Radulescu, A. "*Æthereal Network on Chip: Concepts, Architectures, and Implementations*". IEEE Design and Test of Computers, v.22(5), Sep./Oct. 2005, pp. 414-421.

[8]   Liang, J.; Swaminathan, S.; Tessier, R. "*aSOC: A Scalable, Single-Chip communications Architecture*". In: IEEE International Conference on Parallel Architectures and

Compilation Techniques, 2000, pp. 37-46.

[9] Karim, F.; Nguyen, A.; Dey S. *"An interconnect architecture for network systems on chips"*. IEEE Micro, v.22(5), Sep.-Oct. 2002, pp. 36-45.

[10] Millberg, M.; Nilsson, E.; Thid, R.; Jantsch, A. *"Guaranteed Bandwidth Using Looped Containers in Temporally Disjoint Networks Within the NOSTRUM Network on Chip"*. In: DATE, 2004, pp. 890-895.

[11] Wiklund, D.; Liu D. *"SoCBUS: Switched Network on Chip for Hard Real Time Systems"*. In: IPDPS, 2003, 8p.

[12] Véstias, M.; Neto, H. *"A Reconfigurable SoC Platform Based on a Network on Chip Architecture with QoS"*. In: XX DCIS, 2005, 6 p.

[13] Andreasson, D.; Kumar, S. *"Improving BE Traffic QoS Using GT Slack in NoC Systems"*. In: NORCHIP, 2005, pp. 44-47.

[14] Harmanci, M.D.; Escudero, N.P.; Leblebici, Y.; Ienne, P. *"Quantitative Modelling and Comparison of Communication Schemes to Guarantee Quality-of-Service in Networks-on-Chip"*. In: ISCAS, 2005, pp. 1782-1785.

[15] Shin, J.; Lee, D.; Kuo, C.-C. *"Quality of Service for Internet Multimedia"*. Prentice Hall, 2003, 204 p.

[16] Dally, W.J.; Towles, B. *"Principles and Practices of Interconnection Networks"*. Morgan Kaufmann Publishers, 2004, 550p.

[17] Kumar, S.; Andreasson, D. *"Slack-Time Aware Routing in NoC Systems"*. In: ISCAS, 2005, pp. 2353-2356.

[18] Bjerregaard, T.; Mahadevan, S. *"A survey of research and practices of Network-on-chip"*. ACM Computing Surveys, v.38(1), 2006, pp. 1-51.

[19] Moraes, F.; Calazans, N.; Mello, A.; Möller, L.; Ost, L. *"Hermes: an Infrastructure for Low Area Overhead Packet-switching Networks on Chip"*. Integration the VLSI Journal, v.38(1), Oct. 2004, pp. 69-93.

[20] Mello, A.; Tedesco, L.; Calazans, N.; Moraes, F. *"Virtual Channels in Networks on Chip: Implementation and Evaluation on Hermes NoC"*. In: 18th SBCCI, 2005, pp. 178-183.

[21] Giroux, N.; Ganti, S. *"Quality of Service in ATM Networks: State-of-Art Traffic Management"*. Prentice Hall, 1998, 252 p.

[22] Lee, J.W.; Kim, C.K.; Lee, C. W. *"Rate-based scheduling discipline for packet switching networks"*. Electronic Letters, v.31(14), 1995,1130-1131.

[23] Kumar, A.; Manjunath, D.; Kuri, J. *"Communication Networking: An Analytical Approach"*. Morgan Kaufman Publishers, 2004, 929 p.

[24] Pande, P.; Grecu, C.; Jones, M.; Ivanov, A.; Saleh, R. *"Performance Evaluation and design Trade-Offs for Network-on-Chip Interconnect Architectures"*. IEEE Transactions on Computers, v.54(8), Aug. 2005, pp. 1025-1040.

Accurate Performance Estimation using Circuit Matrix Models in Analog Circuit Synthesis

Almitra Pradhan and Ranga Vemuri

Department of ECE, University of Cincinnati, Cincinnati, OH 45221, USA
pradhaa@ececs.uc.edu, ranga@ececs.uc.edu

Abstract. Optimization based sizing methods allow automating the synthesis of analog circuits. Automated analog circuit synthesis techniques depend on fast and reliable estimation of circuit performance. This paper presents a highly accurate method of estimating performances by constructing models of the circuit matrix instead of the traditionally used performance models. Device matching in analog circuits is utilized to identify identical elements in the circuit matrix and reduce the number of elements to be modeled. Experiments conducted on benchmark circuits demonstrate the effectiveness of the method in achieving correct performance prediction. Results show that the performances can be predicted within a mean error of 0.1% compared to a SPICE simulation. Techniques such as hashing and near neighbor searches are proposed to expedite the matrix model evaluation procedure. These techniques avoid recomputations by saving previously visited solutions. The procedure is used for synthesizing analog circuits from various specifications such as performance parameters, frequency response. The proposed method gives accurate results for synthesis for various types of circuit specifications.

1 Introduction

Fast and accurate sizing of analog circuits has been a challenging problem in the EDA industry. Circuit sizing is the process of determining device dimensions and biasing of a given topology to achieve the desired performance goals. Automated synthesis methods are either knowledge based or optimization based. The former rely on expert knowledge for generating automated design plans or design equations. The latter methods on the other hand, construct sizing as a weighted cost minimization problem. Design variables $(v_1,.., v_m)$ including device lengths and widths, biasing sources are identified for the circuit being sized. The design variable values that minimize the weighted performance cost is accepted as the sizing solution. Thus, the sizing problem can be formulated as follows:

$$minimize \sum_{i=1}^{N} Weight[i] * (Perf[i] - Perf_{spec}[i])$$

(1)

$$where, \text{Perf} = \text{F}(v_1, ..., v_m)$$

Please use the following format when citing this chapter:

Pradhan, A. and Vemuri, R., 2009, in IFIP International Federation for Information Processing, Volume 291; *VLSI-SoC: Advanced Topics on Systems on a Chip*; eds. R. Reis, V. Mooney, P. Hasler; (Boston: Springer), pp. 131–150.

An optimization algorithm such as Simulated Annealing (SA) or Genetic Algorithm (GA) proposes device sizes and bias from a search range and the evaluator verifies if the performance goal is met. The evaluator has to be both fast and accurate. Spice simulation, symbolic analysis and regression models have been used by researchers for performance evaluation. Spice simulation is the most accurate but requires a large runtime. Using symbolic analysis provides a faster alternative but suffers from term explosion for larger circuits. With macromodels, the relation between the design variables and circuit performance is captured by a black box abstraction. These evaluate much faster than direct simulation and can achieve speedy synthesis. However, the performance parameters are extremely difficult to model. Macromodels can suffer from inaccuracies and research efforts are directed at using complex modeling strategies to achieve good accuracy.

2   Related Work

This section reviews some of the methods proposed for optimization based sizing of analog circuits in recent years. Krasnicki *et al.* [1, 2] propose a sizing flow with a SPICE level simulator for predicting the circuit performance. Although, using a simulator gives highly accurate results, it proves expensive in terms of runtime. Symbolic analyzers used for performance prediction are also highly accurate as well as faster than spice [3, 4]. However, the limitation of symbolic models is the exponential increase of symbolic terms with circuit size making them less scalable.

Performance macromodeling has emerged as faster sizing technique compared to exact spice-like optimization approaches. Here, data for some chosen performance parameters is gathered at a number of sample points in the circuit design space. Regression models are then developed for each performance parameter. During sizing, these fast evaluating regression models are used instead of simulation to speed up the synthesis process. Wolfe *et al.* [5], Doboli *et al.* [6] used neural networks for regressing over performance parameters. Support Vector Machines were used for the same by Kiely *et al.* [7], Bernanandinis *et al.* [8] and Ding *et al.* [9]. Other techniques used for modeling include adaptive splines [10, 11], boosted regressors [12]. A review of several performance modeling methods proposed in recent years can be found in [13, 14].

3   Introduction to Circuit Matrix Models

To obtain performance parameters of an analog circuit at a given point in the search space, the system matrix of the circuit is generated. This matrix, also called the circuit matrix, is derived based on the Modified Nodal Analysis (MNA) formulation. The circuit matrix can be represented as follows:

$$(G + sC)x = B;$$
$$y = L^T x$$

here, G: conductance submatrix, C: susceptance submatrix, B: input vector, L: output vector, x: unknown state vector, y: output vector

Pre-defined MNA stamps for all circuit elements allow circuit matrix generation to be quite straightforward. The MNA stamp of a mosfet is written in terms of its small signal values such as transconductance (gm), output conductance (gds), capacitance (cgs, cgd, cgb) etc., whereas for other circuit elements stamps are in terms of the component values. The small signal values of mosfets are obtained by linearizing the circuit around the operating point. The circuit matrix is solved to obtain the frequency response of the circuit. Performance parameters such as the low frequency gain, Unity gain frequency (UGF), Gain Margin (GM), Phase Margin (PM) are calculated from the frequency response. In simulation based synthesis, the spice engine generates and solves the circuit matrix. Macromodeling approaches use fast evaluating models and eliminate the use of spice. As shown in fig. 1 macromodeling is possible at *two* places in the synthesis flow:

1. Modeling the performance parameters
2. Modeling the circuit matrix

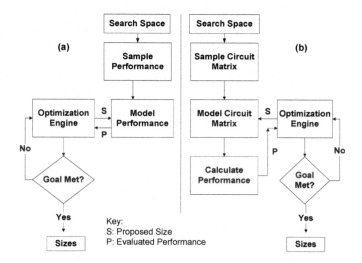

Fig. 1. (a) Performance Modeling Approach (b) Matrix Modeling Approach

Most of the existing macromodeling techniques use the first approach i.e. they model the performance parameters directly. Such methods greatly concentrate on the performance estimation speed, but suffer a tradeoff with accuracy. This paper presents an *alternative method* of estimating performance characteristics of linear analog circuits by constructing a model of the circuit matrix. The advantage, as will be seen, is that the matrix can be very accurately modeled even with simpler modeling approaches such as multivariate polynomial regression. Since it is possible to accurately estimate performance values, true design convergence is obtained by this method.

Performance is not directly modeled but it is calculated from the matrix model. Although this requires some extra computation time, the speed loss is not significant and is offset by the gain in accuracy and advantage of true convergence. The matrix model generation time is dependent on the circuit size. We have significantly reduced the number of models to be built by utilizing device matching properties of analog circuits. When matrix models are used in optimization based synthesis, partial model evaluation is done to speed up the matrix computation in successive iterations.

4   Comparison of Circuit Matrix Models and Performance Models

Performance estimation of analog circuits can use either system level models or performance level models. It is known that the relation between performance parameters such as UGF, PM and device sizes is extremely nonlinear [15, 5]. Sophisticated modeling approaches such as posynomials, neural networks are needed for modeling these severely nonlinear responses. However, these approaches too give significant errors [13]. We have observed that system matrix elements have lesser nonlinearity and can be accurately modeled.

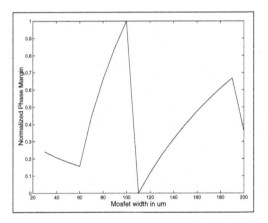

Fig. 2. Phase Margin vs. Device Width of OTA

Consider the operational Transconductance Amplifier (OTA) in fig. 4(a) as an example. We generated plots of performance parameters against device sizes and matrix elements against device sizes. Figures 2, 3 are representative plots of performance (PM) and matrix element (gds_M4). We can intuitively state from the figures that the matrix element is less nonlinear. The qualitative observation that matrix elements have less nonlinearity is now backed with two quantitative measures:

1. entropy of response curves
2. variance of local differentials

Entropy measures the complexity of a response curve [16], higher the entropy more complex the response. Entropy is calculated by definition from [17]. Variance of local first order differentials measures smoothness of a response, with lesser variance indicating greater smoothness. A response that has low entropy and is smooth is less complex to model. Worst case entropy and local variance values among all matrix elements is

Table 1. Entropy and Local Differential Variation of OTA

Response Variable	Variance of Local Differential	Entropy
Matrix Element (Worst Case)	0.0316	0.8565
Gain	0.0369	0.8072
UGF	0.0422	0.7076
Gain Margin	0.2318	1.5674
Phase Margin	0.4248	3.8017
Results are on a dataset of 2000 points		

shown in Table 1. The table also shows the entropy and local variance for performance parameters. Phase and Gain Margins have entropy and local variance an order greater than the matrix elements. From these qualitative and quantitative measures we can infer that matrix elements are less nonlinear and can be modeled with greater accuracy than their performance counterparts.

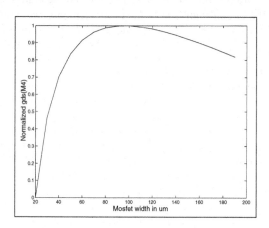

Fig. 3. Matrix Element vs. Device Width of OTA

5   Modeling Methodology

The matrix elements show a linear or curvilinear variation with respect to design variables. We model the response matrix by polynomial regression. The input variables of the model, usually the transistor widths, are normalized on a [0,1] range using eq.(2), since for polynomial regression it is important that higher order terms do not have high collinearity with lower order terms [18].

$$x_{transformed} = \frac{x - x_{min}}{x_{max} - x_{min}} \qquad (2)$$

The response is modeled using a least squares (LS) polynomial fit given by the following equation:

$$Y(x_1...x_n) = \beta_0 + \beta_1 x_1 + .. + \beta_n x_n + \beta_{11} x_1^2 + \beta_{12} x_1 x_2 + .. \tag{3}$$

(where β_is are coefficients of the polynomial fit.)

It is observed that the capacitance sub-matrix terms are highly collinear with respect to the design variables, and lower order polynomials are sufficient for modeling them. The conductance sub-matrix containing terms such as gm, gds etc are more nonlinear and are modeled by higher order polynomials. Once the response model within acceptable error limits is obtained by a LS fit, the regression coefficients are saved. The response at any unknown design point within the model bounds can now be predicted by simply plugging the input variable values in the model given by eq.(3). This makes response prediction extremely fast.

5.1   Circuit Matrix Generation

The first step in matrix macromodeling is generation of the circuit matrix. Subsequently values for the matrix are obtained in the design space and the matrix is modeled. Since we want to model the circuit matrix in terms of its elements, we would like to reduce the number of matrix elements to be modeled to as few as possible. To enable this reduction, we take advantage of:

– *matched* element identification
– *reverse* element identification

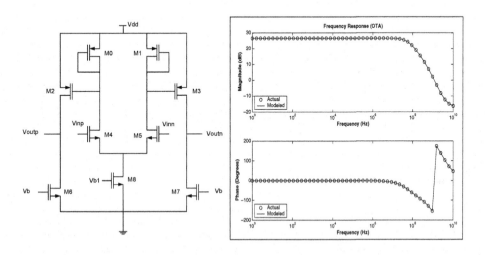

Fig. 4. (i) OTA schematic (ii) Actual vs. Modeled Frequency Response of OTA

In the OTA circuit fig 4, we can see that the transistor pairs $M0 - M1, M2 - M3, M4 - M5$ and $M6 - M7$ are matched. Using the half circuit concept [19] we know that the small signal values of the matched pairs will be equal. Thus, if the matrix elements are linear combinations of small signal values of matched elements, even these matrix elements will be identical. As a simple example, in the OTA the pairs $M0 - M1$ and $M2 - M3$ are matched and $gm0 = gm1$ and $gm2 = gm3$. If the circuit matrix has two elements, one being $gm0 + gm2$ and the other being $gm1 + gm3$, we know that these two elements will always have the same value. Thus a single model will be sufficient for both these matrix elements. With the MNA formulation we have seen that such identical elements occur at many places in the circuit matrix.

It is also observed that in the MNA matrix, some elements appear only with a reversal of polarity. For example, one matrix element is $gm4$ and the other is $-gm4$. It is possible to use a single model for elements that occur with opposite signs. Thus, we observed two properties of the circuit matrix elements which will help us reduce the number of elements to be modeled.

When the circuit matrix is generated through its MNA formulation, the matrix coefficients are first generated in a symbolic form to identify identical and reverse polarity elements. For our benchmarks, the number of non-zero coefficients in the original matrix versus the number of coefficients that need modeling after reduction is depicted in Table 2. The achievable reduction depends on the topology and the number of matched elements.

Table 2. Reduction of Matrix Elements

Benchmark	Original Matrix Elements	Elements after Reduction	Percentage Reduction
TSO	43	24	44
OTA	39	14	64
Differential Amplifier	145	61	58

5.2   Data Generation and Modeling

As with any modeling approach, we first need to generate raw data on which the model will be built. The data is obtained by performing a spice operating point analysis at a number of design points and storing values of circuit matrix elements. We have used random numbers drawn on a uniform distribution of the device ranges to sample the entire design space. About 2000 random data points are sampled for circuits with smaller design space such as the two stage amplifier, OTA and about 4000 points for circuits such as the differential amplifier with a larger design space . We have used high order polynomial response surface models for the circuit matrix as these give adequate accuracy.

For polynomial models it is important to choose the order appropriately since choosing a lower order than necessary will give an erroneous model, whereas choosing a higher order will cause overfitting. In our benchmark circuits we find that polynomials

Table 3. Modeling Accuracy for OTA

Matrix Element	Polynomial Model Order	Max Error (%)	Mean Error (%)	Std Dev (%)
C_{11}	2	0.0667	0.0129	0.0094
C_{13}	2	0.0439	0.0107	0.0085
C_{16}	3	0.0467	0.0122	0.0089
C_{33}	3	0.0908	0.0153	0.0155
C_{35}	1	0.0409	0.0102	0.0085
C_{55}	1	0.0430	0.0104	0.0081
C_{66}	3	0.0488	0.0115	0.0087
G_{11}	2	0.0641	0.0179	0.0119
G_{13}	6	0.2016	0.0207	0.0266
G_{15}	6	0.1879	0.0198	0.0252
G_{51}	7	0.3574	0.0602	0.0508
G_{55}	6	0.1888	0.0196	0.0254
G_{61}	4	0.1423	0.0202	0.0192
G_{66}	4	0.1256	0.0268	0.0206

with order 8 and beyond tend to overfit. We predefine the maximum order as 7 for our models. The model error is calculated using eq.(4). We define an error of 0.5% as the allowable model error.

Starting with a linear model, if the model error is less than the allowable error, that order is chosen, else we fit a polynomial with one higher order. This is done till the maximum order of 7 is reached. In some cases, increasing the order, gives very little return in terms of error reduction (the adjusted R^2 regression criterion), in which we use a lower order model to avoid complexity. Algorithm 1 shows the entire modeling procedure. Table 3 shows the modeling accuracy for each matrix element of the OTA matrix. The frequency response of the OTA with the original system matrix versus the modeled matrix at a random design point is shown in fig. 4. It is seen that the two frequency responses match extremely well.

$$ModelError = \left| \frac{ActualValue - PredictedValue}{ActualValue} \right| * 100\% \qquad (4)$$

After the model has been generated using sample data, the next step is model validation. Validation is necessary to ensure that the regression model obtained holds good for the entire design space and not just the sample data used to build the model. Validation of the model involves assessing the effectiveness of the model against an independent set of data and is essential if confidence in the model is to be expected [20]. For the purpose of validation we generate an independent set of random data points, 1000 data points for smaller circuits and 2000 points for larger circuits. The validated matrix model is used for estimating the performance of the analog circuit.

Algorithm 1 Generate Matrix_Model

Input: circuit.spice
Output: regression coefficients for all matrix elements
$Generate\_System\_Matrix()$;
$Identify\_Unique\_Elements()$;
$Generate\_Data()$;
$\forall$ Unique Elements do:
$order = 1$;
$done = false$;
while (!done) **do**
   polyfit(response, variables, order);
   Error(order) = Calc_Model_Error(order);
   if (error(order) $<=$ max allowed err) **then**
      Save_Reg_Coeffs(element);
      done = true; break;
   end if
   if ((error(order)-error(order-1)) $<= 1\%$) **then**
      Save_Reg_Coeffs(element);
      done = true; break;
   end if
   if (order $<=$ max allowed ord) **then**
      Increment(order,1);
   else
      Save_Reg_Coeffs(element);
      done = true;
   end if
end while

---

6   Experiments and Results

We have used three benchmark circuits: the two stage amplifier (TSO), the operational
transconductance amplifier (OTA) and the high gain differential amplifier (DA) for testing the accuracy of our models. The TSO [5] is a 8 transistor circuit with five design
variables (fig. 5), the OTA is a 9 transistor circuit with four variables (fig. 4)and the
differential amplifier [21] is a 33 transistor circuit with five variables (fig. 6). Design
space reduction was done as explained in [5] to obtain the design variables. The design
variables and their ranges used for the experiments (Table 4) are selected similar to
earlier published performance macromodeling work of [5] to enable a comparison of
results for the two methods. The design variable ranges are such that all design points
lie in a valid pocket i.e. all transistors are in saturation in the given range.

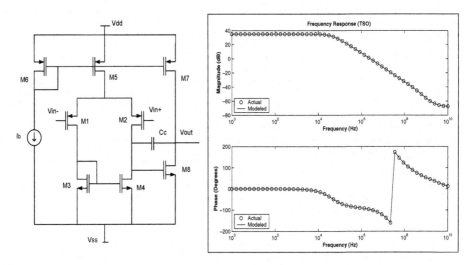

Fig. 5. (i) TSO schematic (ii) Actual vs. Modeled Frequency Response of TSO

Operating point analysis is done using Synopsys®Hspice and values for the elements of the matrix are obtained. For generating and evaluating the polynomial regression models the Matlab®Statistics Toolbox running on a 1.7GHz Pentium®M with
512 MB RAM is used.

Table 5 shows the time required to build the models and the time to estimate performance values for a given size. Table 6 shows the maximum matrix modeling errors
for the benchmarks. It is seen that the elements are modeled very accurately with the
maximum error about 0.5-4%. Figures 5, 7 compare the ac frequency response obtained
from actual circuit matrix and the modeled circuit matrix for the TSO and Differential
amplifier for a randomly chosen circuit size. The modeled response matches the actual
response extremely well. We compare our model building and estimation time with a
performance macromodeling approach [9] that uses support vector machines. As performance is directly modeled in the second case the estimation time is lower, but the
maximum error is 10.1%.

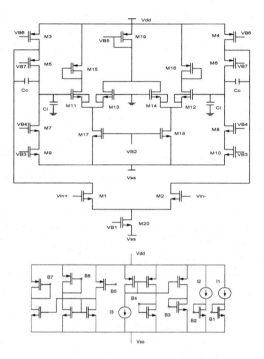

Fig. 6. DA schematic [21]

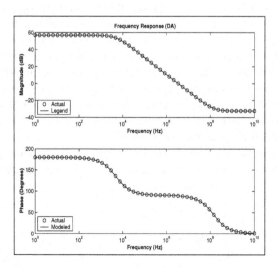

Fig. 7. Actual vs. Modeled Frequency Response of Differential Amplifier

Table 4. Design variable ranges for Benchmarks

Benchmark	Mosfet Count	Number of Variables	Ranges
TSO	8	5	M1-M5,M7:20-80um, Cc:2-10pF, l:2um
OTA	9	4	M2-M5:20-200um M0,M1,M6,M7:20-35um, l:2um
DA	33	5	M1-M10, 4*M25, 4*M26, 2*M23, 2*M27, 2*M28, 2*M32: 40-200um, Cc: 10-50pF, l: 4um

Table 5. Modeling and Estimation Time

Benchmark	Modeling Time	Performance (All) Estimation Time
Matrix Modeling Approach		
TSO	$3.7min$	$0.033sec$
OTA	$16sec$	$0.021sec$
DA	$31.7min$	$0.104sec$
Competing Approach [9]		
TSO	$131.15min$	$0.01sec$
OTA	$50.085min$	$0.001sec$

The performance parameters are calculated from the generated matrix models and results are compared with a spice simulation. Table 7 shows the maximum, mean and standard deviation of the performance estimation error for all benchmarks. The maximum error with matrix models is about 3% and the highest mean error is about 0.1%. To enable a comparison with performance macromodeling, polynomial regression models were built on the performance parameters directly. Table 8 comprises the results of directly modeling the performance. As would be expected, the errors are higher. The TSO and Differential Amplifier circuits are identical to the work of [5] which uses neural networks for performance estimation. The maximum performance estimation error in [5] is 45% and highest mean error is about 5%.

As the circuit matrix is modeled, the time for an operating point analysis is saved which can be upto 70% of the total analysis time [3]. Although the performance is not

Table 6. Worst Case Validation Error

Benchmark	Validation Dataset Size	Worst case Error (%)
TSO	1000	1.8
OTA	1000	0.51
DA	2000	4.37

Table 7. Performance Estimation Accuracy with Proposed Approach

Benchmark	Max Error (%)	Mean Error (%)	Std Dev
Two Stage Op-Amp			
Gain	0.3231	0.0301	0.0370
UGF	0.6234	0.0544	0.0623
GM	1.2944	0.0900	0.1220
PM	0.7848	0.0521	0.0833
CMRR	0.7372	0.0668	0.0818
Operational Transconductance Amplifier			
Gain	0.1555	0.0134	0.0168
UGF	0.3111	0.0232	0.0320
GM	0.3199	0.0363	0.0367
PM	1.2864	0.0597	0.1068
Differential Amplifier			
Gain	3.2670	0.1214	0.1490
UGF	2.2863	0.1473	0.1820
PM	0.7970	0.0648	0.0666

available directly and needs an extra step for its computation, the performance calculation time is much smaller than a spice evaluation. The added advantage with our method is that since the entire ac behavior is modeled, any related performance can be evaluated. Thus, if a performance parameter is required, it simply needs to be evaluated from the matrix model and a new model need not be generated for that parameter.

7   Synthesis Using Circuit Matrix Models

This section describes circuit sizing using the developed circuit matrix models. An optimization algorithm such as Simulated Annealing (SA) used for sizing works by perturbing the current solution to propose a new solution. With incremental perturbation a single parameter of the current solution is varied in every iteration. An important observation is that a design parameter affects only some elements of the circuit matrix. Thus during an SA move only the affected matrix elements are re-evaluated.

Synthesis is explained using the Differential Amplifier as an example. The Differential Amplifier has 61 matrix elements and 5 design variables. The design variables are four mosfet widths $(w_1 - w_4)$ and capacitance C_c. The correlation coefficient between matrix elements and design variables is calculated. If the p value of the correlation is less than 0.1, the correlation is considered significant. Based on the p values it is seen that w_1 affects 8 matrix elements, w_2 affects 30, w_3 and w_4 affect 30 and 36 elements respectively whereas 11 elements are dependent on C_c. Thus, with a maximum of 36 elements are evaluated when w_4 changes and only 8 elements need to be evaluated if w_1 changes.

During synthesis, new solutions are proposed by incrementally updating the current solution. Based on the design variable that is perturbed, the affected matrix elements are calculated from their models. The circuit matrix is then solved for various values

Table 8. Estimation Accuracy by Direct Performance Modeling

Benchmark	Polynomial Order	Max Error (%)	Mean Error (%)	Std Dev
Two Stage Op-Amp				
Gain	4	0.2523	0.0285	0.0272
UGF	7	14.06	1.4307	1.2449
GM	5	3.4894	0.6363	0.4933
PM	6	2.6748	0.3855	0.3463
CMRR	5	0.4704	0.0512	0.0555
Operational Transconductance Amplifier				
Gain	5	0.7582	0.0784	0.0878
UGF	6	8.4583	1.3731	1.0731
GM	7	7.1955	0.6016	0.7836
PM	7	3.3e3	186.31	411.50
Differential Amplifier				
Gain	4	6.2527	1.2365	1.1651
UGF	2	35.8732	9.9997	9.3995
PM	4	0.5234	0.0490	0.0567

of the frequency variable 's'. This gives the frequency response for the circuit. Values such as gain, bandwidth are calculated from the frequency response and compared with the given specification. The sizing algorithm terminates when a solution satisfying the required specifications is found or if no solution can be found in reasonable amount of time. Circuit sizing results for the Differential Amplifier by Simulated Annealing are given in Table 9. The target specifications are given in column 1. Column 2 gives the predicted values for performance at the sizing solution, and column 3 is the actual spice verified values for the sizing solution. It can be seen that the predicted and actual performance values match very well. Thus circuit matrix models are very accurate and can be used for performance prediction during synthesis.

Table 9. Differential Amplifier Synthesis with Partial Model Evaluation

Performance Specification	Estimated	Actual
Gain $\geq$ 78 dB	78.86	79.04
UGF $\geq$ 25 MHz	25.38	24.95
Phase Margin $\geq$ 88 Deg	88.43	88.72

8   Techniques for Faster Synthesis

This section describes two techniques to speed up the synthesis of analog circuits using circuit matrix models. Both techniques are based on reducing the time required to evaluate matrix elements from their models during each iteration of the synthesis run.

8.1   Speedup by Hashing

Here we store computed matrix elements in hash tables which are fetched when required to reduce model evaluation time. The SA algorithm used for synthesis starts with an initial random sizing solution and continuously makes incremental changes to the solution till the target specifications are satisfied. Although exactly same solutions are rarely encountered during the synthesis run, sub-solutions often get repeated. For example, for a circuit with 4 design variables two solutions proposed at different SA iterations are $v_1 = 10$, $v_2 = 20$, $v_3 = 30$, $v_4 = 40$ and $v_1 = 10$, $v_2 = 40$, $v_3 = 60$, $v_4 = 40$. Although, the solutions proposed are different, the sub-solution $v_1 = 10$, $v_4 = 40$ is the same in both cases. Thus, if we save matrix elements dependent on v_1, v_4 computed at the earlier iteration, they can be simply fetched and model evaluation time is saved.

Each matrix element is a function of a subset of design variables. We group all matrix elements that depend on the same design variable subset into a class called *hash class*. One hash table is constructed for each hash class. The sub-solution and the corresponding matrix element values for each hash class are stored in the hash table. During synthesis, the hash table is queried to check if the sub-solution was encountered previously. If the sub-solution was visited earlier, all the hash class elements can be obtained *at once* from the hash table, otherwise they are evaluated from their models and stored.

Thus, the steps involved in using hash tables for faster model evaluation are:

– group matrix elements into hash classes
– initiate one hash table for each hash class
– retrieve matrix elements from the hash table when possible

For example, the 61 matrix elements of Differential Amplifier circuit are divided into 9 different hash classes. The largest hash class has 16 matrix elements while the smallest has 1 element. Hash tables are constructed using a R-B tree data structure [22]. Both insertion and querying is performed in O(log n) time. Using hash tables to avoid matrix element recomputation gives an average synthesis speedup of 2.8x measured over a set of 35 synthesis experiments of the DA. Details of the procedure of using hashing for expedited synthesis and further experimental results can be found in [23].

8.2   Speedup by Near Neighbor Searches

Hash tables store and reuse matrix element values, thus reducing the time required to evaluate the matrix from its element models. Hashing is useful only when a newly proposed sub-solution *exactly* matches a previously visited one. However, during a synthesis run there may be many sub-solutions close to previously visited solutions without matching exactly. In such cases, computing values of matrix elements incrementally from a close (neighboring) previously visited design point helps in saving matrix model evaluation time.

For example, consider a matrix element M dependent on variables v_1, v_2, v_3, therefore M = f(v_1, v_2, v_3). A first order Taylor series expansion for M is given by:

$$dM = \frac{\partial M}{\partial v_1} \cdot dv_1 + \frac{\partial M}{\partial v_2} \cdot dv_2 + \frac{\partial M}{\partial v_3} \cdot dv_3 \tag{5}$$

If the value of M is already calculated at some design point ($v_1 = x$, $v_2 = y$, $v_3 = z$), its value can be quickly obtained at the neighboring design point ($v_1 = x + \Delta x$, $v_2 = y + \Delta y$, $v_3 = z + \Delta z$) using eq.(5). Thus instead of evaluating a higher order polynomial model, the element evaluation is done using the linear equation above making the computation faster. For all design points visited during synthesis, the value of the computer matrix element M and its associated differentials $\partial M/\partial v$ are stored and reused to compute matrix value at many neighboring points. Thus, computing matrix element values using the above method require the following steps:

– find a previously evaluated neighbor of the currently proposed sub-solution
– obtain the matrix element value and the value of differentials at the neighboring point
– calculate the matrix element value at the new point using eq.(5)

A good neighbor searching algorithm is essential for the success of this method. An optimal (near) neighbor search algorithm proposed by Arya *et al.* [24] can be successfully applied for this purpose. Since only few of the matrix elements require actual evaluation from their models the speedup by this method is much more than hashing alone. For the Differential Amplifier synthesis, computing matrix elements incrementally from its neighbors results in a speedup of about 13x over simple matrix element evaluation whereas with hashing it was only 2.8x. Further details of this method and experimental results can be found in [25].

9 Synthesizing circuit with different specifications

In the case of performance macromodels, performance data is gathered for certain parameters. Models are developed for these parameters and are used for synthesis. Using models makes performance evaluation faster than simulation and expedites the synthesis process. However, only the parameters for which performance models have been developed can be included in the synthesis. On the other hand, with circuit matrix models the target specifications need not be known beforehand. Performance parameter values required are calculated from the frequency response obtained from solving the circuit matrix. This is demonstrated with a band pass filter circuit.

9.1 Additional specifications for synthesis

Fig. 8 shows a 2nd order band pass filter with a Sallen Key implementation. Design variables identified for the filter synthesis are widths of mosfets M9, M7, resistor R3, capacitors C1, C2. The filter is to be synthesized with target specifications for gain, bandwidth and center frequency. The synthesis engine proposes sizes for design variables. For each set of sizes, the circuit matrix is obtained from evaluating the element models. Substituting the 's' variable with frequency values gives the frequency response of the circuit. The values of gain, bandwidth and center frequency are calculated from the frequency response till a sizing solution meeting the specifications is obtained. The synthesis results are shown in table 10.

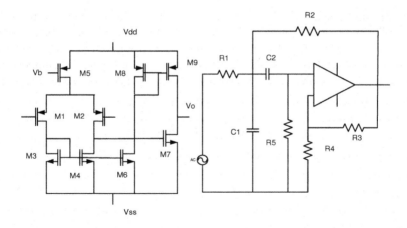

Fig. 8. (i) Amplifier used in bpf (ii) Active band pass filter schematic

Suppose, the filter has to be synthesized for another application where target specification include FP1 (frequency at the edge of the start of the pass band), FP2 (frequency at the edge of the end of the pass band) in addition to gain, bandwidth and center frequency. With circuit matrix models, synthesizing circuit with these additional specifications is simple. The cost function is changed to include the additional specifications. Both FP1 and FP2 are calculated from the frequency response along with the other specifications and synthesis procedure is the same as before. Table 10 shows the synthesis results.

Table 10. Synthesis results for the band pass filter

Performance Specification	Estimated	Actual
Gain ≥ 14 dB	15.18	15.44
Bandwidth ≥ 2000 Hz	2409	2417
Center Frequency ≥ 2500 Hz	2590	2592
FP1 ≥ 200 Hz	273	273
FP2 ≤ 15000 Hz	12109	12103

9.2 Alternate forms of target specifications

With circuit matrix models, circuits can be synthesized with alternate forms of target specifications and not necessarily performance parameters alone. In the next experiment, we synthesize the filter circuit with the specifications given in the form of a frequency response instead of parameters such as gain, bandwidth. The input specifications are in terms of the magnitude response at different frequencies (phase response specifications can be added similarly). The cost function is changed to include frequency response parameters instead of performance parameters. The rest of the synthesis process remains the same. Figure 9 shows the synthesis results. The blue line shows the specified response. The red dots show the frequency response achieved by the target circuit and the green dots are the SPICE frequency response for the sized circuit. Thus synthesis is possible with alternate specifications only by changing the cost function.

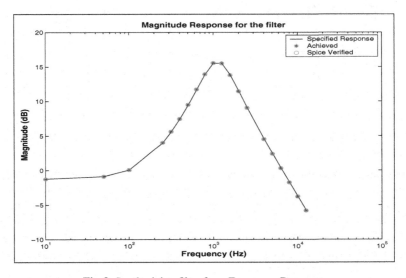

Fig. 9. Synthesizing filter from Frequency Response

10   Conclusion

Two methods for performance estimation of analog circuits, performance modeling and circuit modeling, are compared. It is demonstrated that the circuit matrix can be accurately modeled using polynomial regression. The number of coefficients that need to be modeled are significantly reduced by taking advantage of transistor matching. The accuracy of the proposed method is validated through experiments on three operational amplifier benchmarks. Techniques such as hashing and near neighbor searches can significantly speed up the synthesis process. Using circuit matrix models, synthesis can be performed for different types of specification such as performance parameters or frequency response.

References

1. M. Krasnicki, R. Phelps, R. A. Rutenbar, and L. R. Carley, "MAELSTROM: Efficient simulation-based synthesis for custom analog cells," in *Proc. - 36th Design Automation Conference*, pp. 945–950, 1999.

2. M. J. Krasnicki, R. Phelps, J. R. Hellums, M. McClung, R. A. Rutenbar, and L. R. Carley, "ASF: a practical simulation-based methodology for the synthesis of custom analog circuits," in *Proceedings of the IEEE/ACM International Conference on Computer-Aided Design*, pp. 350–357, 2001.

3. M. Ranjan, W.Verhaegen, A.Agarwal, H.Sampath, R.Vemuri, and G.Gielen, "Fast, layout-inclusive analog circuit synthesis using pre-compiled parasitic-aware symbolic performance models," in *Proc. DATE*, p. 10604, 2004.

4. T. McConaghy and G. Gielen, "Double-strength CAFFEINE: Fast template-free symbolic modeling of analog circuits via implicit canonical form functions and explicit introns," in *Proceedings of the conference on Design, Automation and Test in Europe*, pp. 269–274, 2006.

5. G. Wolfe and R. Vemuri, "Extraction and use of neural network models in automated synthesis of operational amplifiers," *Computer-Aided Design of Integrated Circuits and Systems, IEEE Transactions on* **22**, pp. 198–212, Feb. 2003.

6. S. Doboli, G. Gothoskar, and A. Doboli, "Extraction of piecewise-linear analog circuit models from trained neural networks using hidden neuron clustering," in *Proceedings of the conference on Design, Automation and Test in Europe*, p. 11098, 2003.

7. T. Kiely and G. Gielen, "Performance modeling of analog integrated circuits using least-squares support vector machines," in *Proceedings of the conf. on Design, Automation and Test in Europe*, p. 10448, 2004.

8. F. D. Bernardinis, M. I. Jordan, and A. S. Vincentelli, "Support vector machines for analog circuit performance representation," in *Proc. DAC '03*, pp. 964–969, 2003.

9. M. Ding and R.Vemuri, "A combined feasibility and performance macromodel for analog circuits," in *Proc. 42nd Design Automation Conference*, pp. 63–68, 2005.

10. D. Han and A. Chatterjee, "Adaptive response surface modeling-based method for analog circuit sizing," in *Proceedings. IEEE International SOC Conference*, pp. 109–112, 2004.

11. G. Wolfe and R. Vemuri, "Adaptive sampling and modeling of analog circuit performance parameters with pseudo-cubic splines," in *Proceedings of the IEEE/ACM International Conference on Computer-Aided Design*, pp. 931–938, 2004.

12. H. Liu, A. Singhee, R. A. Rutenbar, and L. R. Carley, "Remembrance of circuits past: macro-modeling by data mining in large analog design spaces," in *Proc. DAC '02*, pp. 437–442, 2002.

13. T. McConaghy and G. Gielen, "Analysis of simulation-driven numerical performance modeling techniques for application to analog circuit optimization," in *Proc. - ISCAS*, pp. 1298–1301, May 2005.

14. R. Rutenbar, G. Gielen, and J. Roychowdhury, "Hierarchical modeling, optimization, and synthesis for system-level analog and RF designs," *Proceedings of the IEEE* **95**(3), pp. 640–669, March 2007.

15. P. Mandal and V. Visvanathan, "Macromodeling of the A.C. characteristics of CMOS op-amps," in *Proc. International Conference on Computer-Aided Design.*, **7**, pp. 334–340, Nov. 1993.

16. France, Michel Mendes and Henaut, Alain, "Art, therefore entropy," *Leonardo* **27**(3), pp. 219–221, 1994.

17. A. Denis and F.Cremoux, "Using the entropy of curves to segment a time or spatial series," in *Mathematical Geology*, **33**, pp. 899–914, Nov. 2002.

18. M. Kutner, C. Nachtsheim, W. Wasserman, and J. Neter, *Applied Linear Regression Models*, McGraw-Hill/Irwin, 2003.

19. B. Razavi, *Design of Analog CMOS Integrated Circuits*, McGraw-Hill, Inc., 2000.

20. J. Rawlings, S. Panstula, and D. Dickey, *Applied Regression Analysis : A Research Tool*, Springer, 2001.

21. J. M. Cohn, *Analog Device-Level Layout Automation*, Kluwer Academic Publishers, Norwell, MA, USA, 2000.
22. T. H. Cormen, C. E. Leiserson, and R. L. Rivest, *Introduction to algorithms*, MIT Press, 2001.
23. A. Pradhan and R. Vemuri, "On the use of hash tables for efficient analog circuit synthesis," in *Proceedings of the International Conference on VLSI Design*, Jan 2008.
24. S. Arya, D. M. Mount, N. S. Netanyahu, R. Silverman, and A. Y. Wu, "An optimal algorithm for approximate nearest neighbor searching in fixed dimensions," *Journal of the ACM* **45**(6), pp. 891–923, 1998.
25. A. Pradhan and R. Vemuri, "Fast analog circuit synthesis using sensitivity based near neighbor searches," in *Proceedings of the conference on Design Automation and Test in Europe (To Appear)*, Mar 2008.

Statistical and Numerical Approach for a computer efficient circuit yield analysis

Lucas Brusamarello[1], Roberto da Silva[1], Gilson I. Wirth[2], and Ricardo Reis[1]

[1] UFRGS - Universidade Federal do Rio Grande do Sul - Instituto de Informática
Av. Bento Gonçalves, 9500. CEP 91501-970. Porto Alegre, Brazil
[2] UFRGS - Universidade Federal do Rio Grande do Sul - Departamento de Engenharia Elétrica
Av. Osvaldo Aranha, 103. CEP : 90035-190, Porto Alegre, Brazil

Abstract. In nanometer scale CMOS parameter variations are a challenge for the design of high yield integrated circuits. Statistical Timing Analysis techniques require statistical modeling of logic blocks in the netlist in order to compute mean and standard deviate for system performance. In this work we propose an accurate and computer efficient methodology for statistical modeling of circuit blocks. Numerical error propagation techniques are applied to model within-die and die-to-die process variations at electrical level. The model handles co-variances between parameters and spatial correlation, and gives as output the statistical parameters that can be applied at higher level analysis tools, as for instance statistical timing analysis tools. Moreover, we develop a methodology to compute the quantitative contribution of each circuit random parameter to the circuit performance variance. This methodology can be employed by the designer or by an automatic tool in order to improve circuit yield.

The methodology for yield analysis proposed in this work is shown to be a solid alternative to traditional Monte Carlo analysis, reducing by orders of magnitude the number of electrical simulations required to analyze memory cells, logic gates and small combinational blocks at electrical level. As a case study, we model the yield loss of a SRAM memory due to variability in access time, considering variance in threshold voltage, channel width and length, which may present both die-to-die and within-die variations. We compare results obtained using the proposed method with statistical results obtained by Monte Carlo simulation. A speedup of $1000\times$ is achieved, with mean error of the standard deviate being 7% compared to MC.

1 Introduction

Performance and reliability of deep-sub-micron technologies are being increasingly affected by process variations and leakage current [24]. Variability in the manufacturing process imposes limitations to the design of circuits in recent technologies. Process variations are related to machinery limited precision and process methodology variations like temperature and lithography exposure time, and discreteness of the material. These variations are stochastic and the prediction of the percentage of manufactured circuits which will achieve a given performance becomes a major problem for the circuit designer. Therefore, the use of statistical methods in circuit design is of increasing relevance.

Please use the following format when citing this chapter:

Brusamarello, L., Silva, R.da., Wirth, G.I. and Reis, R., 2009, in IFIP International Federation for Information Processing, Volume 291; *VLSI-SoC: Advanced Topics on Systems on a Chip*; eds. R. Reis, V. Mooney, P. Hasler; (Boston: Springer), pp. 151–174.

Electrical parameter variability may be decomposed into die-to-die variations (D2D) and within-die variations (WD) [27]. Within-die variations may arise from different sources, for instance the discreteness of matter and energy (dopant atoms, photo resist molecules, and photons). A well known example of a WD parameter is threshold voltage (VtMahmoodi2005Estimation-of-d. Random Dopant Fluctuations (RDF) is mainly caused by the irregular distribution of doping atoms in the channel, and this effect nowadays represents one of the greatest challenges for the industry [10]. Consider σ_{vt0} the standard deviation in threshold voltage for minimum sized transistors, then the dependence of σ_{vt} on transistor size is given by [25]:

$$\sigma_{vt} = \sigma_{vt0} \sqrt{\frac{L_{min} \times W_{min}}{L \times W}} \qquad (1)$$

Die-to-die variations may arise from equipment asymmetries (like asymmetries in chamber gas flows, thermal gradients and so on) or imperfections in equipment operation and process flow. These asymmetries and imperfections affect the average value of a parameter from die to die, wafer to wafer, and lot to lot. Variations may also be originated by the pattern or layout induced deviation of a parameter from its nominal value [6]. Parameters such as oxide thickness, transistor channel length and channel width may show systematic variations [12]. In the case of a D2D parameter k, transistors close to each other are affected by the same constant fluctuation δk.

Statistical Static Timing Analysis (SSTA) gives at logic level a quantitative risk management for the design as a function of the circuit topology, the electrical parameters and the variations [26]. In order to apply a SSTA methodology, the cell libraries are characterized at electrical level, for which nowadays Monte Carlo simulation is commonly employed. Larger designs, composed by many hundreds of transistors, may be decomposed in functional blocks and treated at different levels of abstraction. A block may be a simple or complex gate, a sequential block (e.g. flip-flop) or a memory cell. At the block level the variability may be evaluated using the methodology proposed in this manuscript. The result provided by this methodology (mean, standard deviation) may then be used by higher abstraction level techniques, as for instance Statistical Static Timing Analysis (SSTA), to provide risk management at this higher abstraction levels.

In [12] cell characterization using numerical error propagation is proposed. However, their cell modeling methodology does not include D2D variation, although their proposed SSTA algorithm considers spatial correlation at gate level. Furthermore, the quantitative contribution of each random parameter to the circuit performance variance is not analyzed. As shown further in our work, this analysis may help to improve yield. Finally, in that work only first order approximation for numerical derivatives is employed, and the algorithm complexity and accuracy are not analyzed. In our work we show that the model accuracy may be very sensitive to numerical derivative approximation. Higher order approximations may lead to a better accuracy.

Yield analysis of SRAM memories using Monte Carlo has been studied in [2], [3] and [4]. Error propagation at electrical level for yield analysis of SRAM memory has been explored in [14] and [15], but Vth is the only random variable analyzed (Monte Carlo is performed to simulate D2D). Sensitivities are computed using first order numerical approximation. In these works failures in SRAM cell are statistically modeled (access time failure, read failure, write failure and hold failure), and yield of SRAM memory is given as a function of redundant columns employed in the design. Simulations in these works show that the most significant source of failures in SRAM cell is access time failure. In [9] an electrical-level analysis of SRAM cell static noise margin is presented, which is based in the extraction of the electric parameters by an atomistic device simulator. This method is robust because the transistor cards are the most consistent and closely related to the device variations, but still a huge number of device and electric-level simulations must be run (200 runs in that case).

This manuscript presents a general methodology for analysis of circuit blocks at electrical level which is able to consider WD and D2D variations, as well as co-variances between electrical parameters. Also, we implement a method to point out the parameters which most contribute to circuit performance variance. The methodology is general because it is independent of circuit topology (SRAM cell, multiplexer block, complex gate, etc), and circuit performance parameter of interest (delay, leakage current, power, etc). It maintains the generality of the traditional Monte Carlo techniques, still largely employed in commercial electrical simulators [23].

As a case study we discuss yield analysis and optimization of a SRAM memory. SRAM memory is a good case study because memory yield is directly dependent on SRAM cell yield, and SSTA is not required to analyze critical paths and signal correlations. For this case study we develop a methodology of yield improvement based on the analysis of parameter contribution to variability. We resize the transistors that present the major contribution to the access time variance.

The paper is organized as follows. Section 2 presents a high-level introduction to the methodology. Sections 3 and 4 formally define the problem of statistical analysis of integrated circuits at electrical level and describe the mathematical foundations of the proposed methodology. Section 5 exposes a formulation for the sensitivity of the variance to the electrical parameters. Section 6 gives formulations for numerical computation of derivatives using higher order approximations. Section 7 details the proposed algorithm, and presents a study on its complexity. Section 8 focuses on the methodology applied to yield analysis and yield maximization of a SRAM memory, considering variability in the SRAM cell access time. Finally, last section presents our conclusions.

2   Methodology

This work describes a framework to compute variability in circuit electrical behavior and its dependency on the design and process parameters. The methodology is based on the computation of variance using error propagation, where derivatives are numerically computed using electrical simulations – in this work HSPICE[23] is employed.

Both circuit netlist and the set of circuit parameters which are modeled as random variables are user inputs. Each random variable has its mean and standard deviation, as well as its kind (WD or D2D).

A first script generates a set of runs for the electrical simulator – in our the case HSPICE .DATA command [23]. This library is included in the netlist file, and HSPICE is run in SWEEP mode.

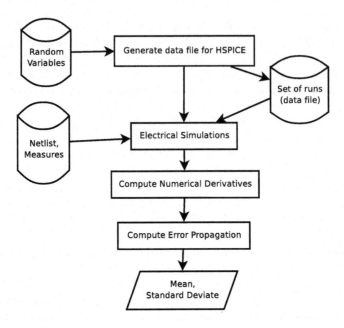

Fig. 1. High level flowchart

One value (circuit response) is computed at each run. These values are gathered in order to compute the partial derivatives for each electrical parameter. Finally, error propagation is employed to compute the variance. An approximation for the mean is obtained by simulation using nominal values.

3   Model

Consider an electric circuit denoted by ω, composed of n transistors represented as components of the vector $\overrightarrow{\tau} = (\tau_1, \ldots, \tau_n)$, interconnected according to a topology Γ. By definition, the circuit response is given by the function $F(\overrightarrow{\alpha}_1, \ldots, \overrightarrow{\alpha}_n, \overrightarrow{\beta}_1, \ldots, \overrightarrow{\beta}_n, \omega)$, where the vectors $\overrightarrow{\alpha}_i = (\alpha_i^{(1)}, \ldots, \alpha_i^{(p)})$ and $\overrightarrow{\beta}_i = (\beta_i^{(1)}, \ldots, \beta_i^{(q)})$ represent respectively the WD and D2D parameters of transistor i, p is the number of WD parameters and q the number of D2D parameters. For instance, the case $\overrightarrow{\alpha}_3 = (V_t)$ and $\overrightarrow{\beta}_3 = (T_{ox}, L, W)$ represents typical input parameters for transistor τ_3, including oxide thickness (T_{ox}), threshold voltage (Vt) and dimensions (L and W) of the transistor.

In the presence of variability in the fabrication process, electrical characteristics and physical dimensions of the circuit can be considered random variables and consequently the output is a random variable. Consider, without loss of generality, that parameters (as for instance T_{ox}, Vt, L, W) are Gaussian variables with mean (μ) and variance (σ^2), i.e, $\alpha_i^{k_1} = N\left(\mu(\alpha_i^{k_1}), \sigma^2(\alpha_i^{k_1})\right)$ and $\beta_i^{k_2} = N\left(\mu(\beta_i^{k_2}), \sigma^2(\beta_i^{k_2})\right)$, where $i = 1, \ldots, n$, $k_1 = 1, \ldots, p$ and $k_2 = 1, \ldots, q$.

The circuit statistical response S is a function that depends on $N = n \times (p+q)$ random variables (including WD and D2D parameters), given by the functional relation

$$S = F(\vec{\alpha}_1, \ldots, \vec{\alpha}_n, \vec{\beta}_1, \ldots, \vec{\beta}_n, \omega) \tag{2}$$

3.1 D2D and WD random variables

In order to model the impact of process variations on the electric circuit response, D2D and WD are treated differently. In the case of a D2D parameter, the same fluctuation affects transistors close to each other. Still their absolute values may be different because they may have distinct averages.

Other random variables are modeled as Gaussian random variables, which are denoted in this work as WD parameters. A WD variable assumes a random value for each transistor, although it can be subject to covariance coefficients (σ_{ij}).

Notice that both D2D and WD parameters are random variables. The difference between them is the randomness context: each instance of a WD variable assumes a different random value, while a D2D parameter has a single random fluctuation that applies to a set of devices.

D2D parameters Spatial correlation impels the D2D electrical parameter of all transistors to change in a synchronized way. For instance, if the dimension W is assumed to present D2D variations and W_1 of transistor τ_1 changes by a quantity δW, the dimension W_2 of a transistor τ_2 changes by the same quantity δW although their mean ($\mu(W_1)$ and $\mu(W_2)$) in the standard sampling process can be different. The parameter W is then defined as a variable that presents

1. exactly the same variation δW inside an single electrical block;
2. but different variation in different electrical blocks, as for instance variation δW_1 in block 1 and variation δW_2 in block 2.

The reader should notice that the position (x,y) of a device is not taken into account. Parameters that present D2D variations can be modeled as

$$\beta_i^j = \mu(\beta_i^j) + \xi_j \cdot \sigma(\beta^j)$$

where $\xi_j = N(0,1)$ is a standard normal variable which is independent of the transistor $1 \le i \le n$. It means that the same variable j will have the same shift of magnitude $\xi_j \cdot \sigma(\beta^j)$ independent of the transistor to which it is applied. In other words, the variables $\beta_1^j, \ldots, \beta_n^j$ are the same random variable except by their mean values. Looking at the contribution of this variables for error estimation, it is important to define the general variable $\beta^j = \mu(\beta^j) + \xi_j \cdot \sigma(\beta^j)$, where $\mu(\beta^j)$ is a transistor-independent constant. Then it can be written as

$$\beta_i^j(k) = \mu(\beta_i^j) + \xi_j \cdot \sigma(\beta^j) = \mu(\beta_i^j) + \beta^j - \mu(\beta^j) \tag{3}$$

Which leads to suitable simplification
$F(\vec{\alpha}_1,\ldots,\vec{\alpha}_n,\vec{\beta}_1,\ldots,\vec{\beta}_n,\omega) = F(\vec{\alpha}_1,\ldots,\vec{\alpha}_n,\beta^1,\ldots,\beta^q,\omega)$ and using the chain rule
the computation of partial derivatives becomes

$$\frac{\partial F}{\partial \beta^j} = \sum_{i=1}^{n} \frac{\partial F}{\partial \beta_i^j} \frac{\partial \beta_i^j}{\partial \beta^j} \tag{4}$$

$$= \sum_{i=1}^{n} \frac{\partial F}{\partial \beta_i^j} \tag{5}$$

because according to equation 3 it is true that $\partial \beta_i^j / \partial \beta^j = 1$, for all $i \in \{1,\ldots,n\}$.

4   Error propagation and Monte Carlo

When measuring a quantity denoted by f which depends of n variables, $x_1, x_2, \ldots, x_n$, an important point is to determine the uncertainty in f given the uncertainty in each variable. A general formula is known if we suppose that $\{x_i\}_{i=1}^n$ are random Gaussian variables, which is a widely accepted procedure [6]. In this case the uncertainty in f (this is an error estimate, including systematic and statistical sources) is given by the classical error propagation formula [21]:

$$\sigma_f^2 = \sum_{i=1}^{n} \left(\frac{\partial f}{\partial x_i}\bigg|_{x_i=\bar{x}_i} \right)^2 \sigma_{x_i}^2 + 2\sum_{i=1}^{n}\sum_{j=i}^{n} \left(\frac{\partial f}{\partial x_i}\bigg|_{x_i=\bar{x}_i} \frac{\partial f}{\partial x_j}\bigg|_{x_j=\bar{x}_j} \right) \sigma_{x_i,x_j} \tag{6}$$

where $\sigma_{x_i}^2$ is the variance (error estimate of variable x_i) while σ_{x_i,x_j} is the covariance between variables x_i and x_j.

For highly non-linear parameters the methodology may lead to significant errors in the yield estimation. However, for most of the practical situations, the parameter distributions are expected not to be highly non-linear. The study of the shape of the actual distribution (and linearity) of the parameters is a topic of intense research, and general models are not yet available. It is out of the scope of this work to provide such models. What can be said is that if the parameters are not highly non linear, the proposed methodology is expected to provide an appropriate yield estimation methodology.

The general error propagation formula (equation 6) applied to the model for WD and D2D variations in an electric circuit, considering co-variances, is:

$$
\sigma_S^2 = \sum_{i=1}^{n} \sum_{j=1}^{p} \left(\frac{\partial F}{\partial \alpha_i^j} \bigg|_{\alpha_i^j = \mu(\alpha_i^j)} \right)^2 \sigma^2(\alpha^j) + \sum_{j=1}^{q} \left(\sum_{i=1}^{n} \frac{\partial F}{\partial \beta_i^j} \bigg|_{\beta_i^j = \mu(\beta_i^j)} \right)^2 \sigma^2(\beta^j)
$$

$$
+ 2 \sum_{i=1}^{n} \sum_{j=1}^{p} \sum_{k=j}^{p} \left(\frac{\partial F}{\partial \alpha_i^j} \bigg|_{\alpha_i^j = \mu(\alpha_i^j)} \frac{\partial F}{\partial \alpha_i^k} \bigg|_{\alpha_i^k = \mu(\alpha_i^k)} \right) \sigma(\alpha^j, \alpha^k)
$$

$$
+ 2 \sum_{i=1}^{n} \sum_{j=1}^{q} \sum_{k=j}^{q} \left(\frac{\partial F}{\partial \beta_i^j} \bigg|_{\beta_i^j = \mu(\beta_i^j)} \frac{\partial F}{\partial \beta_i^k} \bigg|_{\beta_i^k = \mu(\beta_i^k)} \right) \sigma(\beta^j, \beta^k)
$$

$$
+ 2 \sum_{i=1}^{n} \sum_{j=1}^{p} \sum_{k=1}^{q} \left(\frac{\partial F}{\partial \alpha_i^j} \bigg|_{\alpha_i^j = \mu(\alpha_i^j)} \frac{\partial F}{\partial \beta_i^k} \bigg|_{\beta_i^k = \mu(\beta_i^k)} \right) \sigma(\alpha^j, \beta^k) \tag{7}
$$

The reader should notice that covariances between electrical parameters do not imply in any overhead in the number of simulations.

The non-biased sampling estimator to the standard deviation computed from a sample of n_{sample} experimental measures of S, denoted as $S_1, S_2, ..., S_{nsample}$, is calculated by the expression

$$
\delta_S = \sqrt{ \frac{1}{(n_{sample} - 1)} \sum_{i=0}^{n_{sample}} (S_i - \langle S_i \rangle)^2 }
$$

must be numerically equal to σ_S for a n_{sample} sufficiently large, i.e.,

$$
\delta_S \approx \sigma_S
$$

Monte Carlo simulation [5] is often employed in order to obtain the probability density function (PDF) of some circuit output (delay, power consumption, leakage current, ...). Usually, a run with a large number of samples n_{sample} is generated, aiming the convergence of the standard deviation. However, the error in a Monte Carlo simulation is hardly reduced, once it is $O(1/\sqrt{n_{sample}})$.

The inputs in the error propagation formulation are 1) the partial derivatives of the circuit response to the random parameters; 2) standard deviation of the random parameters; and 3) the correlation between random parameters. Standard deviations and correlation coefficients are technology dependent and are given by the foundry. According to what will be shown in section 6, as $F(k_1, ..., k_N)$ is an arbitrary function that can be computed by electrical simulation, the numerical estimates for derivatives $\frac{\partial F}{\partial k_i} \big|_{k_i = \bar{k}_i}$ also can be computed by electrical simulation.

5 Sensitivity of the circuit variability to the electrical parameters

When dealing with the challenges imposed by design for manufacturability, it is essential to have a methodology capable of identifying which parameters contribute most to the circuit variability. Once error propagation decomposes the circuit response variance into its components, it can be used to point out which devices of the circuit could be re-designed in order to optimize yield.

Error propagation uncovers the quantitative contribution of each transistor to the variability in circuit performance. Revisiting equation 7, the sensitivity of the circuit response variance to a within-die parameter α^k is given by

$$K(\alpha^k) = \left(\frac{\partial F}{\partial \alpha^k}\right)^2 \sigma_{\alpha^k}^2. \tag{8}$$

For D2D components, a re-weighted function can be defined as

$$p_{ik} = \left(\frac{|\partial F/\partial \beta_i^k|}{\sum_{j=1}^m |\partial F/\partial \beta_j^k|}\right) \tag{9}$$

where $\sum_{i=1}^m p_{ik} = 1$ for m synchronized variables. For a parameter β_i^k that presents D2D variation the sensitivity is given by

$$K(\beta_i^k) = p_{ik} \times \left(\frac{\partial F}{\partial \beta^k}^2 \sigma_{\beta^k}^2\right) \tag{10}$$

6   Numerical estimate of partial derivatives

Numerical approximations of derivatives is applied in order to present a generic methodology independent of circuit topology. Linear approximations using 1, 2 and 4 points around the nominal values are exploited, aiming to obtain the sensitivity of circuit response for the random variables. The difference between these formulas is the accuracy in the numerical estimates and the number of electric simulations needed: higher order approximations require more simulations, but are more accurate.

Problem Formulation: *Consider a general function of n variables $f = f(x_1, x_2, x_n)$, such that numerical values for the variables are $x_1 = \overline{x_1}, \ldots, x_n = \overline{x_n}$. By error propagation we have $\sigma_f^2 = (\partial f/\partial x_1)_{x_1=\overline{x_1}}^2 \sigma_{x_1}^2 + \ldots + (\partial f/\partial x_n)_{x_n=\overline{x_n}}^2 \sigma_{x_n}^2$. Find a numerical approximation for $\partial f/\partial x_i$ $(i = 1, \ldots, n)$.*

6.1   1st Order Approximation

Expanding the n-dimensional Taylor series around point $f(\overline{x_1}, \ldots, \overline{x_i}, \ldots, \overline{x_n})$ up to order 2 we obtain:

$$f(\overline{x_1}, \ldots, \overline{x_i} + \varepsilon, \ldots, \overline{x_n}) = f(\overline{x_1}, \ldots, \overline{x_i}, \ldots, \overline{x_n}) + \varepsilon \frac{\partial f(\overline{x_1}, \ldots, \overline{x_i}, \ldots, \overline{x_n})}{\partial x_i} + O(\varepsilon^2) \tag{11}$$

The numerical value of $f(x_1, \ldots, x_n)$ is computed by electrical simulation. Thus, one can calculate the sensitivity at point $f(\overline{x_1}, \ldots, \overline{x_i} + \varepsilon, \ldots, \overline{x_n})$, rewriting 11 and assuming $\varepsilon \ll 1$ as follows

$$\frac{\partial f}{\partial x_i}(\overline{x_1},\ldots,\overline{x_i},\ldots,\overline{x_n}) = \frac{f(\overline{x_1},\ldots,\overline{x_i}+\varepsilon,\ldots,\overline{x_n}) - f(\overline{x_1},\ldots,\overline{x_i},\ldots,\overline{x_n})}{\varepsilon} + O(\varepsilon)$$

(12)

Complexity of 1st order approximation: For this case 2 electrical simulations are required to compute each partial derivative: one is required to compute $f(\overline{x_1},..,\overline{x_i}+\varepsilon,\ldots,\overline{x_n})$ and another one for $f(\overline{x_1},..,\overline{x_i},...\overline{x_n})$. However, as $f(\overline{x_1},..,\overline{x_i},...\overline{x_n})$ is the same for all partial derivatives, it needs to be computed only once. Thus, computation of all partial derivatives using first order approximation requires $n+1$ runs.

6.2   2nd Order Approximation

In order to obtain a more precise approximation, algebraic manipulations over Taylor expansion results in a formula with accuracy $O(\varepsilon^2)$. Consider Taylor expansions around the points $f(\overline{x_1},\ldots,\overline{x_i}+\varepsilon,\ldots,\overline{x_n})$ and $f(\overline{x_1},\ldots,\overline{x_i}-\varepsilon,\ldots,\overline{x_n})$, and a better approximation for $\frac{\partial}{\partial x_i}f(\overline{x_1},\ldots,\overline{x_i},\ldots,\overline{x_n})$ can be computed according to:

$$\frac{\partial}{\partial x_i}f(\overline{x_1},\ldots,\overline{x_i},\ldots,\overline{x_n}) = \frac{f(\overline{x_1},\ldots,\overline{x_i}+\varepsilon,\ldots,\overline{x_n}) - f(\overline{x_1},\ldots,\overline{x_i}-\varepsilon,\ldots,\overline{x_n})}{2\varepsilon} + O(\varepsilon^2)$$

(13)

Complexity of 2nd order approximation: this formulation requires 2 electrical simulations for each variable of interest: one to evaluate $f(\overline{x_1},\ldots,\overline{x_i}+\varepsilon,\ldots,\overline{x_n})$ and another one to evaluate $f(\overline{x_1},\ldots,\overline{x_i}-\varepsilon,\ldots,\overline{x_n})$. Therefore, to calculate n partial derivatives over all the variables – 2nd order approximation requires $2n$ runs.

6.3   4th Order Approximation

An $O(\varepsilon^4)$ approximation can be obtained for the numerical estimate of the derivative, as in (please refer to Appendix A for detailed algebraic manipulations) :

$$\frac{\partial f}{\partial x_i}(\overline{x_1},\ldots,\overline{x_n}) = \frac{1}{3}\cdot\frac{[-f(\overline{x_1},\ldots,\overline{x_i}+2\varepsilon,\ldots,\overline{x_n}) + f(\overline{x_1},..,\overline{x_i}-2\varepsilon,\ldots,\overline{x_n})]}{4\varepsilon}$$
$$+ \frac{4}{3}\cdot\frac{f(\overline{x_1},..,\overline{x_i}+\varepsilon,\ldots,\overline{x_n}) - f(\overline{x_1},..,\overline{x_i}-\varepsilon,\ldots,\overline{x_n})}{2\varepsilon} + O(\varepsilon^4)$$

(14)

Complexity of 4th order approximation: for each variable 4 electrical simulations must be run. Hence, an $O(\varepsilon^4)$ approximation requires $4n$ electrical simulations.

7   Algorithm

Algorithm 1 presents the general methodology developed along the last section. The numerical method for derivatives is the one which gives and error of $O(\varepsilon^2)$. Notice that algorithm for other approximations are very similar – in fact the unique difference would be the formula for derivative computation (l. 5-6 and 12-13).

Consider a circuit net-list ω which has a vector of transistors $\vec{\tau}$ connected according to the specified topology. The circuit response F is specified in the net-list of ω, for instance it can be a DC or a transient analysis. The vector of random variations $\vec{\alpha}$ and vector of systematic variations $\vec{\beta}$ are related to the model of variability that will be implemented. The vector of mean values $\vec{\mu}$ is in accordance to nominal transistors parameters in ω. The vector of standard deviations $\vec{\sigma}$ depends on the foundry and technology node, and the vector of steps $\varepsilon(\beta)$ are as small as possible (in this work the steps are assumed to be equal to the standard deviations). Finally, C is the matrix of co-variances between the electrical parameters.

At line 2 of the algorithm the nominal value is computed, which will be an approximation for the average.

First, for all the transistors (lines 3-24), numerical derivatives for WD parameters (lines 4-10) and D2D parameters (lines 11-23) are computed. Notice that the approach for derivative computation requires 2 HSpice runs for each parameter, since the algorithm being studied employs a $O(\varepsilon^2)$ approximation for the computation of derivatives.

For WD parameters, electrical simulations are computed (l. 5 and 6) and in the next step the derivative is calculated using these values (l. 7). Then the sensibility of variance to the parameter is computed in l. 8, and added to the circuit variance.

For D2D parameters, electrical simulations are run (l. 12 and 13) and next the derivative is computed (l. 14). As the contribution of D2D parameters is given in function of the sum of these parameters ($\zeta(\beta^j)$ at line 16) to all transistors (eq. 10), the actual contribution is computed at line 22 (at l. 15 K is employed as a temporary variable).

Correlations are added to the circuit variance in lines 25-41. For all transistors, add correlation between WD to WD parameters (l. 26 - 30), D2D to D2D (l. 31-35), and WD and D2D (36-40). The reader should notice that the number of correlation coefficients given as input does not affect the number of HSpice simulations needed. Thus, the covariances do not affect the running time of the method.

The algorithm computes the following outputs:

1. matrix of contributions K, which represents the contribution of the parameter $1 \leq j \leq (p+q)$ of the transistor $1 \leq i \leq n$;
2. variance of circuit response σ_F^2 and
3. approximation for the average value of the response μ_F.

7.1   Complexity

The proposed tool runs as a front-end for HSpice and computational complexity of each electrical simulation depends on the kind of analysis – DC, AC, transient, ... – and the

---

Algorithm 1 Error propagation using numerical derivatives

Require: $\omega, \overrightarrow{\tau} = (\tau_1, ..., \tau_n), \overrightarrow{\alpha} = (\alpha_1^1, ..., \alpha_n^p), \overrightarrow{\beta} = (\beta_1^1, ..., \beta_n^q),$
    $\overrightarrow{\mu} = (\mu(\alpha_1^1), ..., \mu(\alpha_n^p), \mu(\beta_1^1), ..., \mu(\beta_n^q)),$
    $\overrightarrow{\sigma} = (\sigma(\alpha_1^1), ..., \sigma(\alpha_n^p),$
    $\sigma(\beta_1^1), ..., \sigma(\beta_n^q)), \overrightarrow{\varepsilon} = (\varepsilon(\alpha^1), ..., \varepsilon(\alpha^p), \varepsilon(\beta^1), ..., \varepsilon(\beta^q)), C_{p+q}^{p+q}$

1: $\sigma_F^2 \leftarrow 0; \zeta(\overrightarrow{\beta}) \leftarrow 0$

2: $\mu_F \leftarrow F(\alpha_1^1 = \mu(\alpha_1^1), ..., \alpha_n^p = \mu(\alpha_n^p), \beta_1^1 = \mu(\beta_1^1), ..., \beta_n^q = \mu(\beta_n^q), \omega)$

3: **for all** i such that $1 \leq i \leq n$ **do**

4:     **for all** j such that $1 \leq j \leq p$ **do**

5:         $s_\downarrow \leftarrow F(\alpha_1^1 = \mu(\alpha_1^1), ..., \alpha_i^j = \mu(\alpha_i^j) - \varepsilon(\alpha^j), ..., \alpha_n^p = \mu(\alpha_n^p), \beta_1^1 = \mu(\beta_1^1), ..., \beta_n^q = \mu(\beta_n^q), \omega)$

6:         $s_\uparrow \leftarrow F(\alpha_1^1 = \mu(\alpha_1^1), ..., \alpha_i^j = \mu(\alpha_i^j) + \varepsilon(\alpha^j), ..., \alpha_n^p = \mu(\alpha_n^p), \beta_1^1 = \mu(\beta_1^1), ..., \beta_n^q = \mu(\beta_n^q), \omega)$

7:         $s_i^j \leftarrow s_\uparrow - s_\downarrow$

8:         $K_i^j \leftarrow \left(\frac{s_i^j}{2\varepsilon(\alpha_i^j)}\right)^2 \sigma^2(\alpha^j)$

9:         $\sigma_F^2 \leftarrow \sigma_F^2 + K_i^j$

10:    **end for**

11:    **for all** j such that $1 \leq j \leq q$ **do**

12:        $s_\downarrow \leftarrow F(\alpha_1^1 = \mu(\alpha_1^1), ..., \alpha_n^p = \mu(\alpha_n^p), \beta_1^1 = \mu(\beta_1^1), ..., \beta_i^j = \mu(\beta_i^j) - \varepsilon(\beta^j), ..., \beta_n^q = \mu(\beta_n^q), \omega)$

13:        $s_\uparrow \leftarrow F(\alpha_1^1 = \mu(\alpha_1^1), ..., \alpha_n^p = \mu(\alpha_n^p), \beta_1^1 = \mu(\beta_1^1), ..., \beta_i^j = \mu(\beta_i^j) + \varepsilon(\beta^j), ..., \beta_n^q = \mu(\beta_n^q), \omega)$

14:        $s_i^{p+j} \leftarrow s_\uparrow - s_\downarrow$

15:        $K_i^{p+j} \leftarrow \left(\frac{s_i^{p+j}}{2\varepsilon(\beta^j)}\right)$

16:        $\zeta(\beta^j) \leftarrow \zeta(\beta^j) + K_i^{p+j}$

17:    **end for**

18: **end for**

19: **for all** j such that $1 \leq j \leq q$ **do**

20:    $\sigma_F^2 \leftarrow \sigma_F^2 + \zeta(\beta^j)^2 \sigma^2(\beta^j)$

21:    **for all** i such that $1 \leq i \leq n$ **do**

22:        $K_i^{p+j} \leftarrow (\frac{K_i^{p+j}}{\varepsilon(\beta_j)})(\zeta(\beta_j)^2 \sigma^2(\beta_i^j))$

23:    **end for**

24: **end for**

25: **for all** i such that $1 \leq i \leq n$ **do**

26:    **for all** j such that $1 \leq j \leq p$ **do**

27:        **for all** k such that $j \leq k \leq p$ **do**

28:           $\sigma_F^2 \leftarrow 2 \times s_i^{p+j} \times s_i^{p+k} \times C_j^k$

29:        **end for**

30:    **end for**

31:    **for all** j such that $1 \leq j \leq q$ **do**

32:        **for all** k such that $j \leq k \leq q$ **do**

33:           $\sigma_F^2 \leftarrow 2 \times s_i^j \times s_i^k \times C_{p+j}^{p+k}$

34:        **end for**

35:    **end for**

36:    **for all** j such that $1 \leq j \leq p$ **do**

37:        **for all** k such that $j \leq k \leq p$ **do**

38:           $\sigma_F^2 \leftarrow 2 \times s_i^j \times s_i^{p+k} \times C_j^{p+k}$

39:        **end for**

40:    **end for**

41: **end for**

Ensure: K, μ_F, σ_F^2

---

algorithms implemented by the simulator. For a suitable study about transient and DC analysis performed by spice refer to [17] and its references.

The number of electrical simulations required to compute the circuit variance is a function of the following inputs:

n: number of transistors
p: number of parameters that present WD variations
q: number of parameters that present D2D variations
d: numerical method employed to compute the derivatives
ω: spice netlist

Section 6 introduced 3 linear approximations for the computation of partial derivatives. Each one has a different accuracy order and each requires a given number of electrical simulations to compute partial derivative for a variable. Let d be the number of electrical simulations required to compute the derivative using each numerical method. Therefore, d is related to the desired accuracy as follows:

Accuracy	d	Equation
$0(\varepsilon)$	1	12
$0(\varepsilon^2)$	2	13
$0(\varepsilon^4)$	4	14

One electrical simulation is run using nominal values in order to compute the nominal response, which is an approximation for the average.

The complexity required to compute variance using numerical error propagation is exactly

$$C(n,d,p,q,\omega) = [d \times n \times (p+q)+1]C_{spice}(n,p,q,\omega)$$

where $C_{spice}(n,p,q,\omega)$ is the computational complexity of one spice run for the given netlist and the parameters n,p,q.

8   Case Study: Yield Analysis of a SRAM Memory

In the last sections the mathematical foundations of the proposed parametric yield analysis methodology were exposed. This section presents a case study, describing the application of the method to yield analysis and yield improvement of a SRAM memory based on cell access time failure [7]. The transistors nomenclature employed in this work is as shown in picture 2. Electric simulations were run in HSpice, using the 70nm node Berkeley Predictive Technology Model [8].

Variations in threshold voltage, channel width and channel length are modeled. The electrical parameters which are assumed to show variability are as follows:

Parameter	Type	nominal	3σ
Length	WD	70 nm	3.5 nm
Length	D2D	70 nm	3.5 nm
Width	WD	100 nm	7.5 nm
Width	D2D	100 nm	7.5 nm
Vt(PMOS)	WD	-0.22 V	40 mV
Vt(NMOS)	WD	0.2 V	40 mV

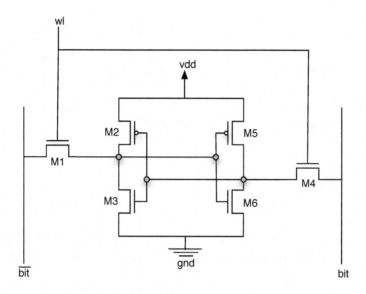

Fig. 2. 6-transistors SRAM cell

This data is in accordance to the ITRS [11] and [19]. In our case study, we assume that there is no correlation between parameters, but we consider the functional dependence given by equation 1.

Access time is the time needed to read the data stored in a cell, computed as the time needed to discharge the bit line (*bit*) or the negated bit line ($\overline{bit}$) to 0.5VDD, if a zero or an one is stored in the cell, respectively. Access time failure is assumed to occur if the access time of a given cell is greater than the maximum value allowed for the design. For the results presented in this section, both bit line (bit) and negated bit line ($\overline{bit}$) are assumed to be pre-charged to VDD. After pre-charge, signal *wl* is set to *VDD* and transistors M1 and M4 are switched to on. *Bit* is maintained at *VDD* if an one is stored in the cell, or is discharged to *gnd* if the cell stores a zero.

The access time may be written as a function of the random variables, where considering the cell symmetry we have:

$$T_{AC} = T_{AC}(L_{M1}, \ldots, L_{M3}, W_{M1}, \ldots, W_{M3}, Vt_{M1}, \ldots, Vt_{M3},)$$

Channel width and channel length will be considered to present WD and D2D variations. Thus, according to equation 4 access time can be written as
$$T_{AC} = T_{AC}(L_{M1}^{wd}, \ldots, L_{M3}^{wd}, L^{d2d}, W_{M1}^{wd}, \ldots, W_{M3}^{wd}, W^{d2d}, Vt_{M1}, \ldots, Vt_{M3}).$$
Rewriting equation 7 we have:

$$
\sigma_{T_{AC}}^2 = \sum_{i=1}^{3} \left(\frac{\partial T_{AC}}{\partial W_{Mi}^{wd}} \bigg|_{W_{Mi}^{wd} = \overline{W_{Mi}^{wd}}} \right)^2 \sigma_{W^{wd}}^2 + \left(\sum_{i=1}^{3} \frac{\partial T_{AC}}{\partial W_{Mi}^{d2d}} \bigg|_{W_{Mi}^{d2d} = \overline{W_{Mi}^{d2d}}} \right)^2 \sigma_{W^{d2d}}^2
$$

$$
+ \sum_{i=1}^{3} \left(\frac{\partial T_{AC}}{\partial L_{Mi}^{wd}} \bigg|_{L_{Mi}^{wd} = \overline{L_{Mi}^{wd}}} \right)^2 \sigma_{L^{wd}}^2 + \left(\sum_{i=1}^{3} \frac{\partial T_{AC}}{\partial L_{Mi}^{d2d}} \bigg|_{L_{Mi}^{d2d} = \overline{L_{Mi}^{d2d}}} \right)^2 \sigma_{L^{d2d}}^2
$$

$$
+ \sum_{i=1}^{3} \left(\frac{\partial T_{AC}}{\partial Vt_{Mi}} \bigg|_{Vt_{Mi} = \overline{Vt_{Mi}}} \right)^2 \sigma_{Vt}^2 \tag{15}
$$

Considering T_{MAX} a design constraint related to target circuit clock, then the probability p of a SRAM cell do not present access time violation failure is given by

$$
p = P(T_{AC} \leq T_{MAX}) = \frac{1}{\sigma_{T_{AC}} \sqrt{2\pi}} \int_{-\infty}^{T_{MAX}} e^{-\frac{(x - \mu_{T_{AC}})^2}{2\sigma_{T_{AC}}^2}} \, dx \tag{16}
$$

Next sections expose the algorithm 7 applied to a SRAM memory, using the specific formulations in order to provide a comprehensive explanation. Circuit partial derivatives are computed using electric simulations. Derivatives and variances are inputs for equation 15, which gives SRAM cell access time variance. The PDF is plotted by using the standard deviate obtained applying error propagation and mean value approximated by simulation using nominal values for input parameters. After, the yield of the entire memory chip is computed. In the last section of this case study, we analyze the contribution of each parameter to the circuit variability, and improve yield resizing critical transistors.

8.1   Yield of the SRAM cell

The access time variance is computed by error propagation, which has as input the numerical estimates of derivatives and the standard deviates. The derivatives can be computed using equation 12, 13 or 14, according to the desired trade-of between accuracy and run-time. Higher number of points implies in higher order accuracy and running time increases. Figure 3 shows a comparison between PDF obtained using values computed using error propagation (using 1, 2 and 4 points around mean) and histogram given by Monte Carlo. The yield of the SRAM cell considering access time failure as a function of the design constraint T_{MAX} is shown by figure 4.

Numerical error propagation using 1, 2 or 4 points requires respectively 10, 19 or 37 electrical simulations, while we run Monte Carlo using 10^4 runs. Monte Carlo simulation with 10^4 runs has a running time of $\tilde{3}4000$ seconds, while the running time for error propagation with numerical derivatives using 2 points is less than 80 seconds in a dual processor Sun Fire V240 (UltraSPARC IIIi 1 GHz).

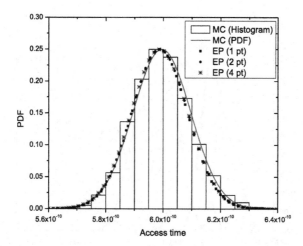

Fig. 3. Monte Carlo histogram (10^4 Spice simulations) compared to PDF obtained by error propagation using 1 point (10 Spice simulations), 2 points (19 Spice simulations) and 4 points (37 Spice simulations)

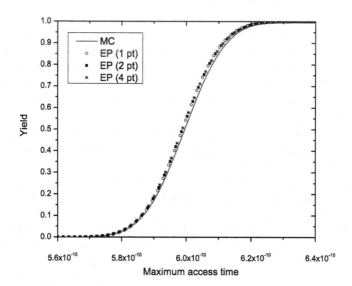

Fig. 4. Yield of the SRAM cell as a function of T_{MAX} computed using Monte Carlo (10^4 runs) compared to error propagation using 1 point (10 runs), 2 points (19 runs) and 4 points (37 runs)

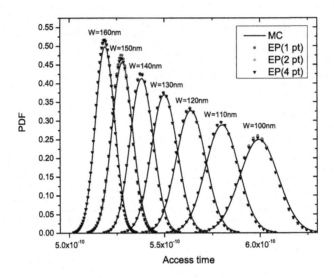

Fig. 5. Influence of Transistors Width in Access Time Variability

8.2   Resizing of the critical transistors

Once the sensitivity and contribution of each electric parameter are computed, the design can be optimized in order to diminish the effect of these parameters, decreasing the variance. Although this work presents an yield optimization based in the access time failure only, there are of other issues which need to be taken into account during yield optimization (for instance read margin, write margin and hold margin in the case of SRAM cells).

By resizing the transistors, three components of access time variance are affected. While W_{wd} and W_{d2d} are directly affected, Vt variance decreases because of the functional relation given by equation 1.

Figure 5 presents the access time PDFs for several transistor channel widths varying from 100nm to 160nm (in these experiments we assume $W_{M1} = \ldots = W_{M6} = W$). The PDFs were computed using MC (10^4 runs) and EP (9 runs for 1 point, 19 runs for 2 points and 37 runs for 4 points). SRAM cell access time variance and average are inversely proportional to transistors channel width. Thus, memory yield can be increased by properly sizing the transistors which more contribute to access time variance.

Figure 6 reports the sensitivity of the access time variance to each parameter (in percentage). The transistors are shown in pairs because of the symmetry of the SRAM cell. The transistor which contributes most to the variance is M1-M4($\tilde{6}5\%$), and the second most preponderant is M3-M6 ($\tilde{3}5\%$). The most significant parameter is Vt of transistor M1-M4: 27% of the access time variance is caused by this parameter.

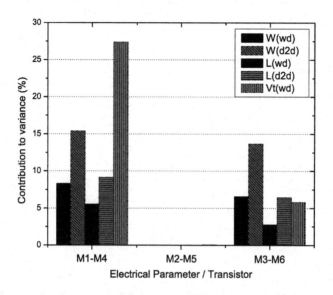

Fig. 6. Sensitivity of the access time variance to each parameter

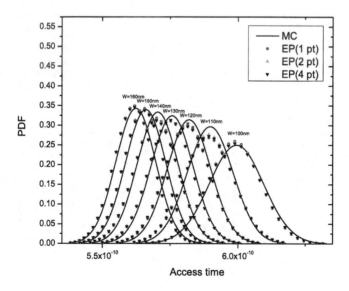

Fig. 7. Impact of transistors M1 and M4 in access time variability by Monte Carlo (10^4 runs) compared to error propagation using derivatives with 1 (10 runs), 2 (19 runs) and 4 points (37 runs)

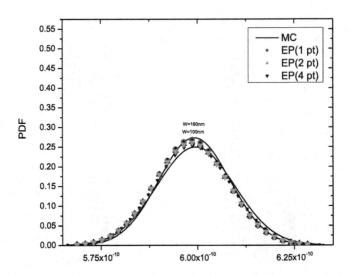

Fig. 8. Impact of transistors M2 and M5 in access time variability by Monte Carlo (10^4 runs) compared to error propagation using derivatives with 1 (10 runs), 2 (19 runs) and 4 points (37 runs)

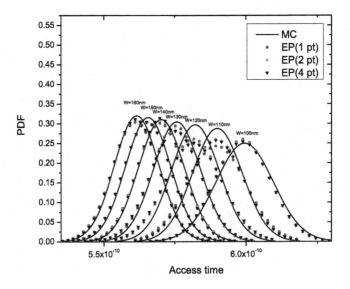

Fig. 9. Impact of transistors M3 and M6 in access time variability by Monte Carlo (10^4 runs) compared to error propagation using derivatives with 1 (10 runs), 2 (19 runs) and 4 points (37 runs)

Figure 7 reveals the access time PDFs obtained from experiments where $W_2 = W_3 = W_5 = W_6 = 100nm$ and $W_1 = W_4$ varies from $100nm$ to $160nm$ in increments of 10nm. By sizing these transistors the standard deviate decreases 35% (comparing $W_1 = W_4 = 160nm$ against $W_1 = W_4 = 100nm$) while average decreases 7%. Skewness and average decrease as W increases.

Figure 8 points out the impact of resizing transistors M2 and M5. As the previous analysis of the contribution of these parameters indicated, they do not impact in the access time variance. Thus, the skewness is not correlated to W. Figure 9 presents the impact of resizing transistors M3 and M6. The standard deviate decreases by 20% and average decreases by 7% increasing these transistors by 60%.

The above simulations indicate that Monte Carlo and error propagation both present similar results which corroborate the hypothesis that the skewness can be decreased by optimizing the parameters pointed out by the methodology. The average difference between standard deviate computed by error propagation using 1 point and the one computed by Monte Carlo is 7%. For the simulations using 1 point around mean for derivatives, a total of 10 electrical simulations must be computed. Thus, this approach means to improve running time $1000\times$ compared to MC using 10^4 runs. Computation of partial derivatives for access time using 2 points gives and adjustment of $O(\varepsilon^2)$, and in this case 17 electrical simulations are required. Using this approach the average difference between standard deviate computed using MC and EP is 6%, and the speedup is up to $580\times$. Derivatives using 4 points requires 37 simulations, but for our case study the precision $O(\varepsilon^4)$ does not significantly improve solution accuracy (average difference is 6%, which is similar to approach using 2 points). In this case, approach using 2 points for numerical derivatives conciliates running time and solution quality, but for some application a higher order approach may be necessary.

8.3 Yield Analysis of the SRAM memory

SRAM memories present a regular architecture in which most of the chip area is dedicated to regularly disposed SRAM cells. Consider a memory grid designed with N_{COL} columns, N_{ROW} rows of SRAM cells and N_R redundant columns, as figure 10 illustrates. If process fabrication variability causes at least one memory cell to fail in a column, that column must be discarded and replaced by a redundant column – this can be done during circuit test phase, setting a set of fuses. If process variability causes more than N_R (at least $N_R + 1$) columns to fail, than the circuit is considered faulty and must be discarded, reducing yield and increasing product cost.

Denoting p as the probability of the SRAM cell to work properly in the presence of process variability, $P_{COL} = (p)^{N_{ROW}}$ is the probability that none cell fails in the column. We are interested in the probability to manufacture N_{COL} working columns in a total of $N_{COL} + N_R$ designed columns. Thus, the yield (percentage of working chips) of a SRAM memory design is given by a binomial distribution, [13]:

$$P_{MEM} = \sum_{i=N_{COL}}^{N_{COL}+N_R} \binom{N_{COL} + N_R}{i} (P_{COL})^i (1 - P_{COL})^{N_{COL}+N_R-i} \qquad (17)$$

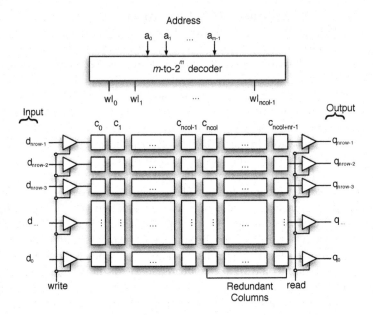

Fig. 10. Scheme of a SRAM memory

Consider a 2 Kbytes SRAM memory for which the architectural parameters are $N_{COL} = 512$ and $N_{ROW} = 32$ (rows of 4 bytes without redundancy in the row). Also assume $N_R = 24$ (4% of total number of columns). Figure 11 shows the memory yield as a function of T_{MAX} for the design where all transistors have $W = 100$ and for the design which transistors M1-M4 are re-sized to $W = 160$. The figure presents points computed using equation 17 (squares) as well as the fit of its points to a logistic function (line) given by

$$yield(T_{max}) = a_2 + \frac{(a_1 - a_2)}{1 + (T_{max}/T_0)^p} \tag{18}$$

where a_1, a_2, T_0 and p are parameters.

The logistic function fit to the design with W=100 for all transistors has $T_0 = 6.28 \times 10^{-10}$ and $p = 1702.7$, while the design where transistors M1-M4 are re-sized to W=160 presents $T_0 = 5.8^{10} - 10$ and $p = 2151.1$. Thus, the re-sized circuit presents a smaller mean for the access time and a yield that grows faster as function of T_{MAX}, if compared to the original design.

9   Conclusions

In this work we present a computer-efficient method for electrical yield simulation of combinational and sequential circuit blocks. The method is based on error propagation. The numerical methods employed for the computation of derivatives assures the independence of topology and parameters to be analyzed. The main contributions of this

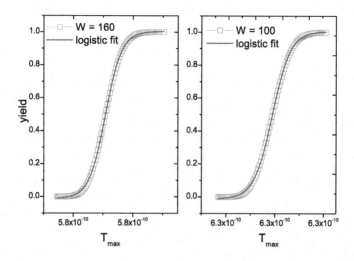

Fig. 11. SRAM memory yield. Increasing W of transistor M1-M4, the memory yield increases for the same T_{MAX}

work are (1) support for WD and D2D variations, as well as co-variances; (2) yield analysis based solely on numerical formulations (no analytical formulations are needed), including the study of accuracy, numerical complexity and higher order numerical approximations; (3) analysis of the sensitivity of the variance to the electrical parameters; and (4) development of a general method (algorithm) which can be employed for yield analysis of combinational or sequential blocks.

We studied the three numerical formulations for the computation of derivatives. They differ in the upper bound of the numerical error as well as the number of electrical simulations required to compute the derivatives. We verify an accuracy increase of 1% in the formulation which has $O(\varepsilon^2)$ in comparison to $O(\varepsilon)$. No significant improvement is observed when using the $O(\varepsilon^4)$ formulation. This is due to the limited precision of the electrical simulations, since the function being modeled is not smooth.

Based on an error propagation formulation, we derived the sensitivity of the circuit response variance as a function of each electrical parameter. This analysis plays a fundamental role when dealing with any kind of electrical block – memories, library cells, sequential and combinational blocks –, because it can guide the designer to figure out what parameters are the most preponderant to the variance in circuit behavior. During the yield optimization phase, this data can lead to a better understanding of how to improve circuit yield. This is an advantage of using error propagation instead of sampling techniques.

The proposed methodology keeps the generality of electrical (Spice) level simulations, and can thus be applied to yield analysis in many CMOS circuits. The method shows results that are statistically equivalent to the usual sampling techniques, like Monte Carlo simulation, while increasing simulation speed by orders of magnitude.

References

1. A. Agarwal, D. Blaauw, and V. Zolotov. Statistical timing analysis for intra-die process variations with spatial correlations. In *Proc. International Conference on Computer Aided Design*, pages 900–907, Nov. 2003.

2. A. Agarwal et al. A process-tolerant cache architecture for improved yield in nanoscale technologies. *IEEE Transactions on Very Large Scale Integration (VLSI) Systems*, 13(1):27–38, 2005.

3. A. Agarwal et al. Process variation in embedded memories: failure analysis and variation aware architecture. *IEEE Journal of Solid-State Circuits*, 40(9):1804–1814, Sept. 2005.

4. A. Agarwal, B. C. Paul, and K. Roy. Process variation in nano-scale memories: failure analysis and process tolerant architecture. In *Proceedings of Custom Integrated Circuits Conference*, pages 353–356, 2004.

5. Jacques G. Amar. The monte carlo method in science and engineering. *Computing in Science and Engineering*, 8(2):9–19, 2006.

6. K. Bernstein, D. J. Frank, A. E. Gattiker, W. Haensch, B. L. Ji, S. R. Nassif, E. J. Nowak, D. J. Pearson, and N. J. Rohrer. High-performance cmos variability in the 65-nm regime and beyond. *IBM J. Res. Dev.*, 50(4/5):433–449, 2006.

7. Yang Byung-Do and Kim Lee-Sup. A low-power sram using hierarchical bit line and local sense amplifier. *IEEE Journal of Solid-State Circuits*, 40(6):1366–1376, June 2005.

8. Y. Cao et al. New paradigm of predictive mosfet and interconnect modeling for early circuit design. In *Proc. Custom Integrated Circuit Conference*, pages 201–204, June 2000.

9. B. Cheng, S. Roy, G. Roy, F. Adamu-Lema, and A. Asenov. Impact of intrinsic parameter fluctuations in decanano mosfets on yield and functionality of sram cells. *Solid-State Electronics*, 49(5):740, 2005.

10. Kim Hyun-Woo et al. Experimental investigation of the impact of lwr on sub-100-nm device performance. *IEEE Transactions on Electron Devices*, 51(12):1984–1988, Dec. 2004.

11. ITRS. *International Technology Roadmap for Semiconductors*, 2005. Available at ¡http://www.itrs.net¿. Visited on Nov. 2006.

12. Kunhyuk Kang, B. C. Paul, and K. Roy. Statistical timing analysis using levelized covariance propagation. In *Proceedings Design, Automation and Test in Europe*, pages 764–769 Vol. 2, 2005.

13. H. Mahmoodi, S. Mukhopadhyay, and K. Roy. Estimation of delay variations due to random-dopant fluctuations in nanoscale cmos circuits. *IEEE Journal of Solid-State Circuits*, 40(9):1787–1796, 2005.

14. S. Mukhopadhyay, H. Mahmoodi, and K. Roy. Statistical design and optimization of sram cell for yield enhancement. In *Proc. IEEE/ACM International Conference on Computer Aided Design*, pages 10–13, Nov. 2004.

15. S. Mukhopadhyay, H. Mahmoodi-Meimand, and K. Roy. Modeling and estimation of failure probability due to parameter variations in nano-scale srams for yield enhancement. In *Proc. Symposium on VLSI Circuits*, pages 64–67, Piscataway, NJ, June 2004.

16. N. S. Nagaraj et al. Beol variability and impact on rc extraction. In *Proc. Design Automation Conference*, pages 758–759, Anaheim, California, USA, June 2005.

17. Lawrence W. Nagel. *SPICE2: A Computer Program to Simulate Semiconductor Circuits*. University of California, Electronics Research Laboratory, College of Engineering, Berkeley, CA, 1975.

18. Sani R. Nassif. Modeling and forecasting of manufacturing variations. In *Proc. International Workshop on Statistical Metrology*, 2000.

19. S.R Nassif. Design for variability in dsm technologies [deep submicron technologies]. In *Proc. IEEE International Symposium on Quality Electronic Design*, pages 451–454, 2000.

20. M. Orshansky et al. Impact of spatial intrachip gate length variability on the performance of high-speed digital circuits. *IEEE Transactions on Computer-Aided Design of Integrated Circuits and Systems*, 21(5):544–553, 2002.

21. L. G. Parrat. *Probability and Experimental Errors on Science*. John Wiley and Sons, New York, NY, USA, 1961.

22. Rajeev R. Rao et al. Parametric yield estimation considering leakage variability. In *Proc. Design Automation Conference, 41.*, pages 442–447, 2004.

23. SYNOPSYS INC. *HSPICE Simulation and Analysis User Guide*, 2005.

24. Yuan Taur et al. Cmos scaling into the nanometer regime. *Proceedings of the IEEE*, 85(4):486–504, Apr. 1997.

25. Yuan Taur and Tak H. Ning. *Fundamentals of modern VLSI devices*. Cambridge University Press, New York, NY, USA, 1998.

26. Chandu Visweswariah. Death, taxes and failing chips. In *Proc. Design and Automation Conference, DAC, 40.*, pages 343–347, Anaheim, CA, USA, 2003. New York: ACM Press.

27. P. S. Zuchowski et al. Process and environmental variation impacts on asic timing. In *Proc. IEEE/ACM International Conference on Computer Aided Design, ICCAD*, pages 336–342, 2004.

A 4th **Order Derivative**

By expansion in Taylor Series we have:

$$f(\overline{x_1},\ldots,\overline{x_i}+2\varepsilon,\ldots,\overline{x_n}) = f(\overline{x_1},\ldots,\overline{x_i},\ldots,\overline{x_n}) + 2\varepsilon f'(\overline{x_1},\ldots,\overline{x_i},\ldots,\overline{x_n})$$
$$+ \frac{4\varepsilon^2}{2!}f''(\overline{x_1},\ldots,\overline{x_i},\ldots,\overline{x_n}) + \frac{8\varepsilon^3}{3!}f'''(\overline{x_1},\ldots,\overline{x_i},\ldots,\overline{x_n})$$
$$+ \frac{16\varepsilon^4}{4!}f^{(4)}(\overline{x_1},\ldots,\overline{x_i},\ldots,\overline{x_n}) \tag{19}$$

$$f(\overline{x_1},\ldots,\overline{x_i}+\varepsilon,\ldots,\overline{x_n}) = f(\overline{x_1},\ldots,\overline{x_i},\ldots,\overline{x_n}) + \varepsilon f'(\overline{x_1},\ldots,\overline{x_i},\ldots,\overline{x_n})$$
$$+ \frac{\varepsilon^2}{2!}f''(\overline{x_1},\ldots,\overline{x_i},\ldots,\overline{x_n}) + \frac{\varepsilon^3}{3!}f'''(\overline{x_1},\ldots,\overline{x_i},\ldots,\overline{x_n})$$
$$+ \frac{\varepsilon^4}{4!}f^{(4)}(\overline{x_1},\ldots,\overline{x_i},\ldots,\overline{x_n}) \tag{20}$$

$$f(\overline{x_1},\ldots,\overline{x_i}-\varepsilon,\ldots,\overline{x_n}) = f(\overline{x_1},\ldots,\overline{x_i},\ldots,\overline{x_n}) - \varepsilon f'(\overline{x_1},\ldots,\overline{x_i},\ldots,\overline{x_n})$$
$$+ \frac{\varepsilon^2}{2!}f''(\overline{x_1},\ldots,\overline{x_i},\ldots,\overline{x_n}) - \frac{\varepsilon^3}{3!}f'''(\overline{x_1},\ldots,\overline{x_i},\ldots,\overline{x_n})$$
$$+ \frac{\varepsilon^4}{4!}f^{(4)}(\overline{x_1},\ldots,\overline{x_i},\ldots,\overline{x_n}) \tag{21}$$

$$f(\overline{x_1},\ldots,\overline{x_i}-2\varepsilon,\ldots,\overline{x_n}) = f(\overline{x_1},\ldots,\overline{x_i},\ldots,\overline{x_n}) - 2\varepsilon f'(\overline{x_1},\ldots,\overline{x_i},\ldots,\overline{x_n})$$
$$+ \frac{4\varepsilon^2}{2!} f''(\overline{x_1},\ldots,\overline{x_i},\ldots,\overline{x_n}) - \frac{8\varepsilon^3}{3!} f'''(\overline{x_1},\ldots,\overline{x_i},\ldots,\overline{x_n})$$
$$+ \frac{16\varepsilon^4}{4!} f^{(4)}(\overline{x_1},\ldots,\overline{x_i},\ldots,\overline{x_n}) \tag{22}$$

Combining the equations 19 and 22 we obtain:

$$f(\overline{x_1},\ldots,\overline{x_i}+2\varepsilon,\ldots,\overline{x_n}) - f(\overline{x_1},\ldots,\overline{x_i}-2\varepsilon,\ldots,\overline{x_n}) = 4\varepsilon f'(\overline{x_1},\ldots,\overline{x_i},\ldots,\overline{x_n})$$
$$+ \frac{16\varepsilon^3}{3!} f'''(\overline{x_1},\ldots,\overline{x_i},\ldots,\overline{x_n}) + O(\varepsilon^5) \tag{23}$$

Similarly, from equations 20 and 21 we can write:

$$f(\overline{x_1},\ldots,\overline{x_i}+\varepsilon,\ldots,\overline{x_n}) - f(\overline{x_1},\ldots,\overline{x_i}-\varepsilon,\ldots,\overline{x_n}) = 2\varepsilon f'(\overline{x_1},\ldots,\overline{x_i},\ldots,\overline{x_n})$$
$$+ \frac{2\varepsilon^3}{3!} f'''(\overline{x_1},\ldots,\overline{x_i},\ldots,\overline{x_n}) + O(\varepsilon^5) \tag{24}$$

Multiplying equation 24 for (-8) we have:

$$\frac{16\varepsilon^3}{3!} f'''(\overline{x_1},\ldots,\overline{x_i},\ldots,\overline{x_n}) = -16\varepsilon f'(\overline{x_1},\ldots,\overline{x_i},\ldots,\overline{x_n}) + 8f(\overline{x_1},\ldots,\overline{x_i}+\varepsilon,\ldots,\overline{x_n})$$
$$- 8f(\overline{x_1},\ldots,\overline{x_i}-\varepsilon,\ldots,\overline{x_n}) + O(\varepsilon^5) \tag{25}$$

and substituting $\frac{16\varepsilon^3}{3!} f'''(\overline{x_1},\ldots,\overline{x_i},\ldots,\overline{x_n})$ given by equation 25 on equation 23, then an $O(\varepsilon^4)$ approximation can be derived as follows:

$$\frac{\partial f}{\partial x_i}(\overline{x_1},\ldots,\overline{x_n}) = \frac{1}{3} \cdot \frac{[-f(\overline{x_1},\ldots,\overline{x_i}+2\varepsilon,\ldots,\overline{x_n}) + f(\overline{x_1},\ldots,\overline{x_i}-2\varepsilon,\ldots,\overline{x_n})]}{4\varepsilon}$$
$$+ \frac{4}{3} \cdot \frac{f(\overline{x_1},\ldots,\overline{x_i}+\varepsilon,\ldots,\overline{x_n}) - f(\overline{x_1},\ldots,\overline{x_i}-\varepsilon,\ldots,\overline{x_n})}{2\varepsilon} + O(\varepsilon^4)$$
$$\tag{26}$$

SWORD: A SAT like Prover
Using Word Level Information

Robert Wille, Görschwin Fey, Daniel Große, Stephan Eggersglüß, and
Rolf Drechsler

Institute of Computer Science, University of Bremen,
28359 Bremen, Germany
{rwille,fey,grosse,segg,drechsle}@informatik.uni-bremen.de

Abstract. Solvers for Boolean *Satisfiability* (SAT) are state-of-the-art
to solve verification problems. But when arithmetic operations are considered, the verification performance degrades with increasing data-path
width. Therefore, several approaches that handle a higher level of abstraction have been studied in the past. But the resulting solvers are still
not robust enough to handle problems that mix word level structures
with bit level descriptions.

In this paper, we present the satisfiability solver SWORD – a *SAT* like
solver that facilitates *word* level information. SWORD represents the
problem in terms of modules that define operations over bit vectors.
Thus, word level information and structural knowledge become available
in the search process. The experimental results show that on our benchmarks SWORD is more robust than Boolean SAT, K*BMDs or SMT.

1 Introduction

The number of elements integrated within digital circuits grows exponentially
and this trend is going to continue for at least another 10 years. Already today
millions of gates are integrated in a single circuit. Throughout the design flow
for such complex systems, techniques to represent and manipulate the function
are needed. In particular, to formally verify the correctness of a circuit with
respect to all design states and input sequences, techniques for symbolic function
manipulation are applied.

Current state-of-the-art tools for formal verification use Boolean techniques
like *Binary Decision Diagrams* (BDDs) [1], *AND-Inverter-Graphs* [2] and provers
for *Boolean Satisfiability* (SAT) [3, 4]. No word level information such as knowledge about arithmetic operations or structural knowledge is directly used for
function manipulation. As a result, the performance of verification tools degrades with increasing data-path width. Especially handling data paths is a
difficult problem.

For this reason, approaches to exploit such high level information have been
proposed in the past [5–7]. But pure word level approaches suffer from complexity problems when irregularities in the word level structure occur, e.g. bit
slicing [8]. The recent concept of *Satisfiability Modulo Theories* (SMT) [9–12] is

Please use the following format when citing this chapter:

Wille, R., Fey, G., Große, D., Eggersglüß, S. and Drechsler, R., 2009, in IFIP International Federation for Information Processing,
Volume 291; *VLSI-SoC: Advanced Topics on Systems on a Chip*; eds. R. Reis, V. Mooney, P. Hasler; (Boston: Springer), pp. 175–191.

more powerful since multiple provers are combined, but still structural information is not available. Related work is discussed in more detail in Section 2 and empirically compared in Section 6.

In this paper, we propose SWORD – a *SAT*-like prover that uses *word* level information and also resembles the structure of the original problem. Internally, the problem is represented as a composition of modules; each module is defined over bit vectors and enforces the constraints for a word level operation on the corresponding Boolean variables. The main advantages of this approach are the following:

- *Compact problem representation:*
  The composition of word level modules is a much more compact representation than the transformation to Boolean constraints.
- *Knowledge about structure and semantics:*
  This knowledge is determined by the position of a module within the problem instance and the type of a module. Such information helps to predict the impact of a decision or of learned information during the search process more accurately.
- *Efficient reasoning:*
  Different types of modules require different reasoning procedures and decision heuristics to allow for an efficient search procedure. These procedures are designed for each type of module individually in the proposed framework.

Thus, SWORD combines the advantages of a Boolean proof procedure with the power of word level knowledge. The proposed solver is empirically compared to K*BMDs [6] as a word level decision diagram, the Boolean SAT solver MiniSat [4] and the SMT solver Yices [11, 12].

The paper is structured as follows: Related work is discussed in more detail in the next section. The preliminaries and limits regarding Boolean SAT are reviewed in Section 3. Then, the basic algorithm of SWORD and the use of modules to effectively model a problem are introduced in Section 4. Section 5 discusses the advantages of this approach. Experimental evidence for the efficiency of SWORD in comparison to other prover paradigms is provided in Section 6. Finally, a summary and the conclusions are presented in Section 7.

2   Related Work

Several approaches to incorporate word level information in the proof process have been proposed so far. BDDs have been generalized to the word level quite early [5] resulting in K*BMDs [6] as a very general form. These diagrams can represent word level multiplications very efficiently, but whenever bit nibbling occurs – as is common practice in circuit descriptions – the performance degrades. In fact, *BMDs may be exponentially large for certain functions [8].

A different approach is the transformation of the problem into *Integer Linear Programming* (ILP) constraints [7]. But the same limitations to pure word level descriptions have been observed. A pure ILP-based approach is often too slow for real world applications.

Combining Boolean provers and word level provers seems to be more promising. The framework proposed in [13] is based on an ATPG engine that is enhanced by arithmetic word level primitives. An arithmetic constraint solver is applied to validate bit level assignments on the circuit. But the powerful learning concepts known from Boolean SAT are not incorporated.

Due to the tremendous improvements in the performance of provers for Boolean SAT in the recent past [14–16, 4], several researchers investigated the combination of SAT with other proof techniques, i.e. *Satisfiability Modulo Theories* (SMT) [9–12]. An SMT solver integrates a Boolean SAT solver with another solver (or multiple solvers) for specialized theories. Usually, the SAT solver works on an abstract representation of the problem and steers the overall search process. Each satisfiable assignment for the Boolean SAT problem has to be validated on the concrete problem using the theory solver. The solver proposed in [17] can be seen as a specialized SMT solver for bit vector logic. Tightly coupling the different solvers, especially to enforce learning due to conflicts resulting from partial assignments and to efficiently carry out implications, is a challenge in this area. Usually, validating a given SAT assignment by using the theory solver is very time consuming. Therefore, the overall performance is limited by the performance of the theory solver. In our framework no theory solvers are needed. Moreover, structural information about the original problem is available.

A very general theoretical framework for hierarchical SAT solving was presented in [18]. There, the problem is also decomposed into modules, where each module may have different implication procedures. But no experimental evidence was given and no hints for an implementation were provided.

Nonetheless our solver works similar to such a hierarchical solver. Besides specialized implication procedures also dedicated decision heuristics are applied to different types of modules.

3   Boolean SAT Solving

Our algorithm inherits the basic structure of a classical algorithm to solve a problem instance of Boolean *Satisfiability* (SAT) [14]. Therefore, we briefly review the techniques applied in Boolean SAT solvers.

3.1   Definition

The *Boolean satisfiability problem* (SAT problem) is to determine whether there exists an assignment α to an Boolean function f such that $f(\alpha) = 1$ (i.e. f is satisfiable) or to prove that no such assignment exists (i.e. f is unsatisfiable).

A SAT instance is represented as a Boolean formula in *Conjunctive Normal Form* (CNF) which is given as a set of clauses; each clause is a set of literals and each literal is a propositional variable or its negation. The CNF formula is satisfied if all clauses are satisfied. A clause is satisfied if at least one of its

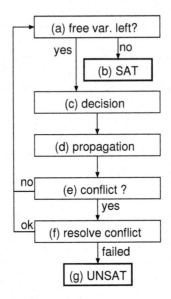

Fig. 1. DPLL algorithm in modern Boolean SAT solvers

literals is satisfied. A variable is satisfied when 1 is assigned to the variable, the negation of a variable is satisfied under the assignment 0.

3.2   Basic Algorithm

The basic search procedure to find a satisfying assignment is shown in Fig. 1 and has the structure of the DPLL algorithm [19, 3]. Instead of simply traversing the complete space of assignments, intelligent decision heuristics [16], conflict based learning [14] and sophisticated engineering of the implication algorithm [15] lead to an effective search procedure. The description follows the implementation of the procedure in modern SAT solvers. While there are free variables left (a), a decision is made (c) to assign a value to one of these variables. Then, implications are determined due to the last assignment by *Boolean Constraint Propagation* (BCP) (d). This may cause a conflict (e) that is analyzed. If the conflict can be resolved by undoing assignments from previous decisions, backtracking is done (f). Otherwise, the instance is unsatisfiable (g). If no further decision can be done, i.e. a value is assigned to all variables and this assignment did not cause a conflict, the CNF is satisfied (b). In the following, the *decision level d* denotes the number of variables assigned by decisions in the current partial assignment, i.e. neglecting variable assignments due to implications.

3.3   Limits of Boolean SAT

Due to the translation of the problem into CNF, the power of BCP as an implication engine and the efficiency of learning are limited. In the verification domain, the original problem is usually given at the word level. Operations are defined over bit vectors. Each Boolean variable that is visible in a bit vector at this level is called *module variable* in the following. The translation of word level operations over bit vectors of *module variables* into CNF involves the creation of a large number of *auxiliary variables* [20]. The dependencies between these variables are modeled by constraints in terms of clauses.

Example 1. Consider an $n \times n$-multiplier. On the word level, $4n$ module variables are needed for the bit vectors of the operands and the result.

On the other hand, the multiplier can be represented by n^2 AND gates [21], i.e. the number of auxiliary variables is in $\theta(n^2)$. A single gate can be modeled by three clauses for each element. Therefore, the multiplier can be represented by a CNF with $\theta(n^2)$ clauses[1].

Simplified, all these auxiliary variables have to be considered during BCP; but implications on auxiliary variables do not yield a reduction of the search space for the original problem. Moreover, conflict clauses may be derived that are defined over auxiliary variables only – again without pruning the search space of the original problem. In principle, this problem can be prevented by introducing additional clauses that describe the implications on module variables directly, but then the translation becomes inefficient due to a large number of clauses.

4 Using Word Level Information

In this section, we describe the architecture of SWORD and how word level information is used during the solve process. Therefore, we first explain the representation of the problem and present the overall algorithm. Afterwards the utilization of word level information in decision making, the implication engine and conflict analysis are explained in more detail.

4.1 Representation

SWORD represents the problem in terms of so called *modules*. Each module defines an operation over bit vectors of *module variables*. Each module variable is a Boolean variable. By this, structural and semantical knowledge is available and can be exploited during the search process by special algorithms for each kind of module (we will explain this in more detail later).

Example 2. Fig. 2 shows an equivalence checking problem in terms of a miter circuit. A multiplier is compared to a realization that sums up the partial products.

SWORD represents this problem by using one module representing a multiplier, $n-1$ modules representing an adder, n modules representing a multiplexor and one module representing a comparator. No auxiliary variables are needed.

---

[1] More efficient translations may be available, but in principle, the problem instance still grows.

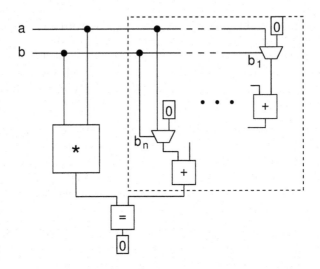

Fig. 2. Miter example of a multiplier

Besides providing word level information the representation in terms of modules has another advantage: The problem description of SWORD is much more compact than a CNF. To represent it for a classical SAT solver we need $\theta(n^2)$ clauses (see Example 1). Our representation consists of $2n + 2$ modules, only. Furthermore we need no auxiliary variables in total.

4.2 Overall Algorithm

The overall algorithm of SWORD is shown in Fig. 3. This algorithm is similar to the DPLL procedure as applied in standard SAT solvers (see Section 3.2): While free variables remain (a) a decision is made (c), implications resulting from this decision are carried out (d), and if a conflict occurs, it is analyzed (f). The important difference is that SWORD has two operation levels: the *global* algorithm controls the overall search process and calls the *local* procedures of modules for decision and implication. Thus, decision making and implication engine can be adjusted for each type of module.

In more detail, the solver first chooses a particular module based on a *global decision heuristic* (c.1). Then, this module chooses a value for one of its variables according to a *local decision heuristic* (c.2). Afterwards, the solver calls the *local implication procedures* (d.2) of all modules that are potentially affected (d.1) by the previous decision or implication. Here a *variable watching scheme* similar to the one presented in [15] is used which can efficiently determine these modules. The chosen modules imply further assignments and detect conflicts.

In the following, the global and local algorithms are described in more detail, respectively.

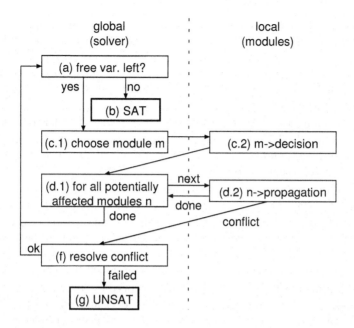

Fig. 3. Algorithm

4.3   Decision Strategies

Global Decision. The global decision procedure chooses a module that assigns a value to one of its connected module variables. So the global decision procedure has to decide which module will make the best decision, i.e. which decision of a module leads to as many implications as possible. Therefore, a (global) heuristic is employed to decide which modules are "more important" than others. To determine the importance of a particular module, semantical information such as the type or structural information such as the position within the overall problem are available.

Example 3. Again, consider the miter circuit shown in Fig. 2. In this example the primary inputs and the outputs of the multiplier module are considered more important than, for example, the select input of one of the multiplexors. Therefore, the global decision heuristic selects the multiplier module first.

To realize this efficiently, the global decision heuristic currently uses a static priority based on the type of the module. Here, more complex modules (e.g. multipliers) are considered as being more important and, therefore, are selected for a decision with a higher priority than less complex modules. The complexity is measured in the number of two-input gates needed to describe a module. Furthermore, the priority of a particular module can be increased/decreased when it is located near to the primary inputs/outputs or the objective. By this, each global decision can be done very efficiently, because no complex data manipulation is necessary.

Local Decision. The local decision procedure of a module assigns a value to one of its module variables. The impact of a particular decision depends on the type of a module. Therefore, different strategies are applied for different types of modules. For example, a module representing a multiplier uses a different heuristic than a module representing an AND gate. In the following, an adder exemplifies the local decision procedures of SWORD.

An n-bit adder ADD : $\mathbb{B}^n \times \mathbb{B}^n \to \mathbb{B}^{n+1}$ is considered which is represented by a module in SWORD. The module variables connected to this module are given by $a_{n-1}, \ldots, a_0$ and $b_{n-1}, \ldots, b_0$ that represent the inputs of the adder and $o_n, \ldots, o_0$ that represent the outputs.

For an adder, assigning some variables a_i, b_i or o_i (with $n > i \geq 0$) while variables a_j, b_j or o_j (with $i > j \geq 0$) are still unassigned, often does not allow to imply values for the outputs since then, the value of the respective carry bits are unknown, too. In contrast, when all of the least significant bits of both operands are given, the corresponding bits of the outputs can be determined. Therefore, the variable representing the least significant unassigned bit is assigned first.

In the implmentation, the local decision procedure is realized as a *Finite State Machine* (FSM). This allows to carry out decisions efficiently. The FSM has $n + 1$ states and is in state i ($n > i \geq 0$) when all variables with lower significance than i are assigned, i.e. a_j, b_j and o_j ($i > j \geq 0$) are assigned. Thus, if the FSM is in state i, only the variables a_i, b_i and o_i are considered. If all of these variables are assigned, the FSM proceeds to state $i + 1$. Otherwise, at least two of these variables are unassigned (because an implication is carried out when only one variable is unassigned, as explained in the next section).

An additional state R is needed to recalculate the state when it was invalidated: Due to backtracking the state of the local FSM of a module may be invalidated because currently assigned variables may become unassigned. This is recognized by tracking the decision level. The decision level of the last state transition, i.e. since the last change of a state, is stored in d_{ch} and the lowest decision level that has been reached after a backtrack intermediately is stored in d_{bt}. The state of the FSM may only be invalidated when $d_{bt} < d_{ch}$.

Example 4. Fig. 4 illustrates this mechanism. The global search tree is indicated by the plain line and the decision levels that are reached are also shown. A transition of the FSM of a module is indicated by a cross. The table shows the values of d_{ch} and d_{bt} before the transition is done. The first transition occurs at A and d_{ch} is changed from 0 to d; d_{bt} is uninitialized. At B the decision level has increased; the state is still valid; d_{ch} is updated to $d + 1$. Due to a backtrack d_{bt} is set to $d + 2$. Thus, at C the state from decision level $d + 1$ is still valid. In contrast, when transition D is done, the state is potentially invalid and has to be recalculated.

The resulting FSM for a 3-bit adder is shown in Fig. 5; only state transitions are indicated, internal variables are not shown.

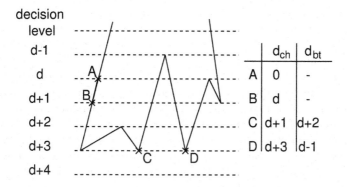

Fig. 4. Search tree and decision levels

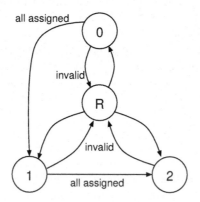

Fig. 5. FSM for an adder

4.4   Implication Engine

The implication engine is also divided into a global part and local procedures that are dedicated to the type of a module.

Detection of Affected Modules. Globally, those modules that may be affected by a previous decision or implication have to be identified. This is done by a variable watching scheme. Currently, a conservative approach is applied: the local propagation procedure of each module that contains a variable that has been assigned is called. Such a static scheme is efficient, because module variables usually only connect to a few modules – often only two modules.

Local Implication. The local implication procedures only consider the connected module variables for the propagation of values. For efficiency these procedures do not determine all implications that are possible, but only those that can be derived efficiently. Again, the local implication procedure of an adder exemplifies the local implication procedures.

The implication procedure works similar to the decision procedure: If, for example, the input bit a_i and the output bit o_i and all less significant input bits (a_j and b_j with $i > j \geq 0$) are assigned, then the third variable (b_i in the example) can be implied. This implication procedure does not guarantee to detect implications on higher significant bits and is therefore not too powerful. But in most cases implications on these bits are improbable.

The implication procedure relies on the same FSM that is used for decisions. Additionally, the carry bits $c_{n-1}, \ldots, c_0$ are internally updated at each state transition. In state i ($n > i \geq 1$) carry bit c_{i-1} is also given. Therefore, an implication can be carried out efficiently based on the current state i, the value of the carry bit c_{i-1} and the values of the module variables a_i, b_i, o_i.

Note, due to the implication procedure a conflicting assignment may not be detected directly. But when the FSM reaches state n, i.e. all module variables are assigned, the consistency of the assignment will be validated. However, due to the order of decisions conflicts are usually detected early. The mechanisms for conflict analysis are explained in detail in the next section.

4.5   Conflict Analysis

In SWORD, conflict analysis and learning are quite similar to the classical approach of a SAT solver. Upon detection of a conflict, the module returns the conflicting variables to the global solve process. Then, conflict analysis is carried out. Currently, we adapted the implementation of MiniSat [4]. Because SWORD does not work in terms of clauses, a separate *implication graph* is stored globally. Each module updates this graph when an implication is carried out. The learned information is stored in terms of clauses as in standard SAT solvers. Therefore, an additional clause module exists which handles all clauses generated by conflict analysis (and applies the known state-of-the-art SAT techniques).

Note, that the implication graph itself is more compact than the one of a Boolean SAT solver, because there are no auxiliary variables contained in the graph. As a result all clauses derived by conflict analysis consist of module variables and prune the search space of the original problem domain directly.

The conflict graph keeps track of the reasons for a particular assignment. Thus, the identification of a reason is crucial in this context. The smaller the reason, the smaller the conflict clauses and the more effectively the search space is pruned. Again, an adder is used to give an idea of how the implication graph is created.

Example 5. Assume, o_i is implied based on the internal value of c_{i-1} and the module variables a_i and b_i. Furthermore, due to previous assignments $a_{i-1} = 0$ and $b_{i-1} = 0$, the reasons for these assignments are already stored in the implication graph. In this case input bits with lower significance than $i - 1$ do not influence the value of o_i, because no carry bit is propagated beyond $i - 1$. Thus, the four variables a_i, b_i, a_{i-1} and b_{i-1} are identified as the reason for the implication on o_i. The four edges (a_i, o_i), (b_i, o_i), (a_{i-1}, o_i) and (b_{i-1}, o_i) are added to the implication graph. Note, that the reasons for $a_{i-1} = 0$ and $b_{i-1} = 0$ are already stored in the graph.

Like in standard SAT solvers, only conflict clauses up to a certain length are learned. The ratio behind this heuristic is that short clauses prune a large part of the search space while longer clauses are less valuable.

Semantical knowledge is also exploited in this process. For example, a conflict clause is not learned if it contains variables that are associated to a complex module like a multiplier – in this case only backtracking is carried out. This heuristic is motivated by the observation that usually a large number of clauses is learned that describe the behavior of a multiplier which causes memory overhead but does not speed up the search.

5   Discussion

The first observation is that SWORD represents problems in a much more compact way than a CNF based solver. In contrast to modeling the internal structure of a module by clauses, the functionality is described on an algorithmic level. As already explained, this leads to a smaller number of variables and less constraints that have to be handled.

At the same time, this representation enables more efficient implications. Instead of a large number of clauses usually only the connecting modules have to be considered to imply a value for a particular variable. The implication procedures of particular modules are not as strong as possible (using the notation of [18] they are not *maximally implicative* and in the notation of constraint programming they are not *fully arc-consistent*). Of course, it is possible to create stronger implication procedures, but only at the cost of more complex modules and higher computation time. Currently, the implication procedures are crafted manually and exploit the knowledge about the decision order. By this, it is possible to trade-off between implicative power and efficiency. Investigating more powerful procedures that are automatically generated remains future work. One promising approach that starts from BDDs has been suggested in [22].

Implications and decisions are restricted to module variables. Therefore, in contrast to CNF based SAT, no auxiliary variables can occur in the implication graph. Thus, the size of the implication graph is reduced and, as a result, the time needed to traverse the implication graph is reduced. Similarly, the conflict clauses consist of module variables only. Therefore, instead of learning a large number of locally conflicting assignments, the overall search space is pruned.

Finally, structural information about predecessors or successors of modules is available within SWORD. Currently, this information is not fully exploited. Only the global decision heuristic evaluates the position of modules in a static preprocessing step. For Boolean SAT dynamic decision procedures have proven to be much more efficient. Thus, combining structural knowledge with heuristics from Boolean SAT is another direction for future work.

6   Experimental Results

This section provides experimental results for SWORD in comparison to the Boolean SAT solver MiniSat [4], K*BMDs [6] using the package of [23] as a representative of pure word level approaches, and the SMT solver Yices using the theory of bit vectors [11, 12]. All experiments have been carried out on an AMD Athlon64 3500+ (Linux, 2.2 GHz, 1 GB). Unless mentioned otherwise the time out was set to 500 CPU seconds.

We considered different benchmark problems. In the following, the name indicates the type of the problem. The prefix *ec_* indicates equivalence checking of a multiplier (*mul_*) on the word level with another multiplier that is given as word level module (*mul_*), as sum of partial products (*pp_*), or as gate level description (*gt_*), respectively. Thereby, a miter circuit is used. In some cases, the least significant bit was ignored in the miter (indicated by *li_*) and in other cases a fault was injected at the gate level to create a satisfiable instance (indicated by *ft_*). The prefix *pc_arith* indicates a property checking problem that contains arithmetic modules. Finally, a number indicates the bit width of the data path.

6.1   Parameter Studies

For selected representative instances Table 1 reports run times in CPU seconds to evaluate different features of SWORD. To demonstrate the influence of the parameters, alternative configurations are used. The last column *DEF* provides the run times of SWORD in the current configuration. The influence of the decision heuristic is studied in columns *RAND* and *MSB*. If the modules in the global decision heuristic are randomly selected, the numbers in column *RAND* are obtained. Column *MSB* gives the results, if the arithmetic modules are assigned from the higher to the lower bits, what is typically not clever. As can be seen, both approaches lead to high run times and even time outs in comparison with the heuristic shown in column *DEF*. In the remaining columns, learning strategies are evaluated. Column *CCLS* reports results for learning all conflict clauses regardless of the length and the origin. In column *30%* only short conflict clauses are learned that consist of up to 30% of the variables contained in the problem instance; clauses including variables from a multiplier are learned as well. The maximum relative length of 30% for learned clauses was experimentally determined. Finally, column *DEF* gives the run time of SWORD using all features: the global decision heuristic using priorities, the local decision heuristic that assigns least significant bits first, and conflict based learning of short clauses together with neglecting clauses coming from complex modules, like multipliers. As can be seen, *DEF* is the most robust approach and clearly outperforms all others. Therefore, this setting was used for the experiments in the following.

6.2   Comparison to Boolean SAT solver

Table 2 shows results in comparison to MiniSat. For each benchmark the number of variables to represent the problem, the number of clauses for MiniSat and

Table 1. Parameter studies

circuit	Heuristic		Learning		
	RAND	MSB	CCLS	30%	DEF
ec_mul_mul_10	53.97	47.95	>500	36.88	37.09
ec_mul_pp_9	125.83	187.06	45.51	45.29	15.54
ec_mul_gt_10	>500	>500	>500	>500	113.84
ec_mul_mul_li_10	59.32	48.19	>500	36.93	37.01
pc_arith_a_9	>500	>500	>500	37.57	37.83
pc_arith_b_13	>500	>500	363.42	30.68	30.91

the number of modules for SWORD are given in columns *var*, *cls* and *mod*, respectively. The memory requirements (in MB) and the CPU time (in seconds) are provided in columns *mem* and *time*. The improvement in run time of SWORD over MiniSat (i.e. the run time of SWORD divided to the run time of MiniSat) is shown in column *imp*. An *x* in column *sat* indicates whether the problem instance is satisfiable. Since for most satisfiable instances both solvers had small run times, we mainly report numbers for unsatisfiable instances here (satisfiability is studied in more detailed below).

SWORD is quite efficient regarding memory consumption. This is due to the problem representation. Especially word level problems are much more compact than a corresponding SAT instance. This benefit decreases only slightly when the problem is partially converted to gate level. Moreover, in contrast to the SAT solver, SWORD is quite robust with respect to larger bit widths of the data path. Considering run time, except for *pc_arith_b[10-13]*, SWORD significantly outperforms MiniSat on all benchmark circuits. For benchmarks in the table the improvement is always larger than a factor of two and in one case even three orders of magnitude.

Furthermore, we studied in more depth satisfiable instances. The instances are generated by removing or substituting a single Boolean gate in a multiplier circuit, i.e. all instances were derived from *ec_mul_gt_16*. In this manner over 4000 instances were generated. For all of them MiniSat and SWORD were started with a time out of 5 CPU seconds. Table 3 summarizes the results by giving in the number of instances where the solver took less than 0.01 seconds and where a time out occurred in row two and three, respectively.

Here, it can clearly be seen that SWORD solves most of the instances in almost no time and in addition has fewer time outs than MiniSat. For all instances where both solvers computed a solution within the given limit, Fig. 6 graphically shows the results. As can clearly be seen in the lower half of the diagram, there are many more instances that SWORD can handle in very low run time.

6.3   Comparison to Word Level Solvers

Table 4 provides run times for K*BMDs, SWORD and Yices. As expected K*BMDs performs very well on pure word level problems and outperform SWORD

Table 2. Comparison to MiniSat

circuit	sat	MiniSat				SWORD				imp
		var	cls	mem	time	var	mod	mem	time	
ec_mul_mul_7		519	1766	3.98	2.02	43	3	2.73	0.35	5.77
ec_mul_mul_8		687	2348	4.50	10.79	49	3	2.73	1.67	6.46
ec_mul_mul_9		879	3014	5.65	54.96	55	3	2.73	8.02	6.85
ec_mul_mul_10		1095	3764	8.45	461.44	61	3	2.73	37.09	12.44
ec_mul_pp_7		1012	3381	4.24	3.98	228	17	2.73	0.62	6.41
ec_mul_pp_8		1331	4460	5.00	25.76	292	19	2.73	3.10	8.30
ec_mul_pp_9		1694	5689	6.93	189.24	364	21	2.73	15.54	12.17
ec_mul_pp_10		2101	7068	>10.16	>500	444	23	2.86	59.85	>8.35
ec_mul_gt_7		519	1766	3.98	2.02	274	246	2.73	0.91	2.21
ec_mul_gt_8		687	2348	4.50	10.79	360	328	2.86	4.69	2.30
ec_mul_gt_9		879	3014	5.65	54.96	458	422	2.86	23.20	2.36
ec_mul_gt_10		1095	3764	8.45	461.44	568	528	2.86	113.84	4.05
ec_mul_mul_li_7		518	1761	3.99	2.03	43	3	2.73	0.34	5.97
ec_mul_mul_li_8		686	2342	4.36	7.95	49	3	2.73	1.66	4.78
ec_mul_mul_li_9		878	3009	5.90	88.88	55	3	2.73	7.95	11.17
ec_mul_mul_li_10		1094	3759	8.11	409.51	61	3	2.73	37.01	11.06
ec_mul_gt_ft_18	x	3687	12788	17.16	70.58	1880	1808	3.12	<0.01	>7058.00
ec_mul_gt_ft_19	x	4119	14294	16.84	54.88	2098	2022	3.29	0.01	5488.00
ec_mul_gt_ft_21	x	4575	15884	20.10	73.91	2328	2248	3.30	<0.01	>7391.00
ec_mul_gt_ft_22	x	5055	17558	24.91	111.03	2570	2486	3.43	0.03	3701.00
pc_arith_a_6		572	1980	4.11	3.78	55	10	2.73	0.36	10.50
pc_arith_a_7		740	2562	5.00	28.52	61	10	2.73	1.72	16.58
pc_arith_a_8		932	3228	6.93	196.98	67	10	2.73	8.21	23.99
pc_arith_a_9		1148	3978	>10.16	>500	73	10	2.73	37.83	>13.21
pc_arith_b_10		250	852	3.60	0.01	77	17	3.89	1.42	<0.1
pc_arith_b_11		268	911	3.61	0.01	82	17	4.68	4.68	<0.1
pc_arith_b_12		286	970	3.59	0.01	87	17	6.70	12.24	<0.1
pc_arith_b_13		304	1029	3.59	0.01	92	17	7.70	30.91	<0.1

in this case (e.g. benchmark set *ec_mul_mul*). But when the description is provided at the bit level the performance degrades significantly (*ec_mul_gt*). Furthermore, bit level operations cannot be handled efficiently (*ec_mul_mul_li*). Yices also handles the pure word level problems extremely efficient. But again, when word level and lower level descriptions are mixed, the performance degrades. On these benchmarks SWORD is more robust.

6.4 Summary

SWORD is very efficient in comparison to the most powerful available SAT solver on our verification benchmarks. This especially holds if the word level structure can be exploited. Furthermore, in contrast to other word level approaches that break down if Boolean operations are used, SWORD is very robust also in this

Table 3. Data for satisfiable instances

time	MiniSat	SWORD
<0.01	50	2183
>500	708	565

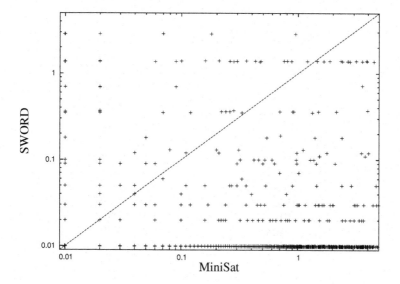

Fig. 6. Run time for satisfiable instances

case. This can be seen in the comparison with K*BMDs and Yices which often do not finish within the given time out.

7   Conclusions

We presented the solver SWORD that uses a SAT like algorithm and exploits word level information in the search process. SWORD works on a representation of the problem in terms of modules. This yields a powerful framework for decision making, implications and conflict analysis. Considering a problem directly at the word level significantly reduces the size of the instances. Moreover, the word level information is exploited in all steps of the search process. In contrast to other word level solvers, SWORD is robust with respect to bit level operations on our benchmarks.

In future work, the efficiency of SWORD will be further improved by investigating more powerful decision heuristics and engineering the watching mechanisms for implication and backtracking. Furthermore, the local procedures for different types of modules are currently coded manually; an automatic approach to generate this code could be applied to study different version of the procedures for a single type of module. Finally, the application to other problem

Table 4. Comparison to K*BMDs and SMT

circuit	K*BMD	SWORD	Yices
ec_mul_mul_7	<0.01	0.35	<0.01
ec_mul_mul_8	<0.01	1.67	<0.01
ec_mul_mul_9	<0.01	8.02	<0.01
ec_mul_mul_10	<0.01	37.09	<0.01
ec_mul_pp_7	0.01	0.62	15.83
ec_mul_pp_8	0.01	3.10	105.56
ec_mul_pp_9	0.01	15.54	>500
ec_mul_pp_10	0.01	59.85	>500
ec_mul_gt_7	3.48	0.91	10.93
ec_mul_gt_8	13.60	4.69	82.40
ec_mul_gt_9	53.45	23.20	>500
ec_mul_gt_10	202.31	113.48	>500
ec_mul_mul_li_7	>500	0.34	0.29
ec_mul_mul_li_8	>500	1.66	1.96
ec_mul_mul_li_9	>500	7.95	58.15
ec_mul_mul_li_10	>500	37.01	>500
pc_arith_a_6	0.5	0.36	<0.01
pc_arith_a_7	2.1	1.72	<0.01
pc_arith_a_8	8.7	8.21	<0.01
pc_arith_a_9	35.8	37.83	<0.01
pc_arith_b_10	1.69	1.42	0.07
pc_arith_b_11	3.18	4.68	0.15
pc_arith_b_12	6.36	12.24	0.34
pc_arith_b_13	12.82	30.91	0.96

domains than verification is an important topic. As one example logic synthesis for reversible circuits with SWORD was introduced in [24].

Acknowledgments

We wish to thank João Marques-Silva and Paulo Jorge Matos for many helpful discussions in the area of SMT.

References

1. Bryant, R.: Graph-based algorithms for Boolean function manipulation. IEEE Trans. on Comp. **35** (1986) 677–691
2. Kuehlmann, A., Paruthi, V., Krohm, F., Ganai, M.: Robust Boolean reasoning for equivalence checking and functional property verification. IEEE Trans. on CAD **21** (2002) 1377–1394
3. Davis, M., Logeman, G., Loveland, D.: A machine program for theorem proving. Comm. of the ACM **5** (1962) 394–397
4. Eén, N., Sörensson, N.: An extensible SAT solver. In: SAT 2003. Volume 2919 of LNCS. (2004) 502–518

5. Bryant, R., Chen, Y.A.: Verification of arithmetic functions with binary moment diagrams. In: Design Automation Conf. (1995) 535–541

6. Drechsler, R., Becker, B., Ruppertz, S.: K*BMDs: A new data structure for verification. In: European Design & Test Conf. (1996) 2–8

7. Brinkmann, R., Drechsler, R.: RTL-datapath verification using integer linear programming. In: ASP Design Automation Conf. (2002) 741–746

8. Thathachar, J.: On the limitations of ordered representations of functions. In: Computer Aided Verification. Volume 1427 of LNCS., Springer Verlag (1998) 232–243

9. Seshia, S.A., Lahiri, S.K., Bryant, R.E.: A hybrid SAT-based decision procedure for separation logic with uninterpreted functions. In: Design Automation Conf. (2003) 425–430

10. Ganzinger, H., Hagen, G., Nieuwenhuis, R., Oliveras, A., Tinelli, C.: DPLL(T): Fast decision procedures. In: Computer Aided Verification. Volume 3114 of LNCS. (2004) 175–188

11. Dutertre, B., Moura, L.: A fast linear-arithmetic solver for DPLL(T). In: Computer Aided Verification. Volume 4114 of LNCS. (2006) 81–94

12. Dutertre, B., L.Moura: The YICES SMT Solver. (2006) Available at http://yices.csl.sri.com/.

13. Huang, C.Y., Cheng, K.T.:   Using word-level ATPG and modular arithmetic constraint-solving techniques for assertion property checking. IEEE Trans. on CAD **20** (2001) 381–391

14. Marques-Silva, J., Sakallah, K.: GRASP: A search algorithm for propositional satisfiability. IEEE Trans. on Comp. **48** (1999) 506–521

15. Moskewicz, M., Madigan, C., Zhao, Y., Zhang, L., Malik, S.: Chaff: Engineering an efficient SAT solver. In: Design Automation Conf. (2001) 530–535

16. Goldberg, E., Novikov, Y.: BerkMin: a fast and robust SAT-solver. In: Design, Automation and Test in Europe. (2002) 142–149

17. Parthasarathy, G., Iyer, M., Cheng, K.T., Wang, L.C.: An efficient finit-domain constraints solver for circuits. In: Design Automation Conf. (2004) 212–217

18. Novikov, Y., Brinkmann, R.: Foundations of hierarchical SAT-solving. In: Int'l Workshop on Boolean Problems. (2004) 103–141

19. Davis, M., Putnam, H.: A computing procedure for quantification theory. Journal of the ACM **7** (1960) 506–521

20. Tseitin, G.: On the complexity of derivation in propositional calculus. In: Studies in Constructive Mathematics and Mathematical Logic, Part 2. (1968) 115–125 (Reprinted in: J. Siekmann, G. Wrightson (Ed.), Automation of Reasoning, Vol. 2, Springer, Berlin, 1983, pp. 466-483.).

21. Mano, M.M., Kime, C.R.: Logic and Computer Design Fundamentals. 3rd edn. Pearson Education (2004)

22. Höreth, S.: Compilation of optimized OBDD-algorithms. In: European Design Automation Conf. (1996) 152–157

23. Herbstritt, M.:   wld: A C++ library for decision diagrams, Institute of Computer Science, Albert-Ludwigs-University, Freiburg im Breisgau. (2000) http://ira.informatik.uni-freiburg.de/software/wld.

24. Wille, R., Große, D.: Fast exact Toffoli network synthesis of reversible logic. In: Int'l Conf. on CAD. (2007) 60–64

A new analytical approach of the impact of jitter on continuous time delta sigma converters

J. Goulier*, E. Andre*, M. Renaudin**

*STMicroelectronics, 850 Rue Jean Monnet, 38926 Crolles Cedex, France
julien.goulier@st.com

**TIMA Laboratory, 46 Avenue Felix Viallet, 38031 Grenoble Cedex, France
marc.renaudin@imag.fr

Abstract. The performances of continuous time delta sigma converters are severely affected by clock jitter and no generic technique to predict the corresponding degradations is nowadays available. This paper presents a new analytical approach to quantify the power spectral density of jitter errors. This
generic computational method can be applied to all kind of continuous time
delta sigma converters. Furthermore, clock imperfections are described by
means of phase noise spectrum, consequently all possible type of jitters can be
taken into account. This paper also describes the temporal non ideal clock models that have been created to simulate the impact of jitter on delta sigma converters and validate the theoretical results.

1. INTRODUCTION

The current attractiveness for low pass continuous time delta sigma converter is
largely due to the fact that it is possible to make them work at higher frequencies than
their equivalent discrete time implementation. This specificity is widely used in order
to increase the bandwidth or the resolution of the converters. This uninterrupted aug-
mentation of sampling frequency induces an amplification of the ratio between jitter
and clock period, making less and less negligible the influence of jitter on the converter performances.

Jitter impact on continuous time delta sigma converter is a tricky problem. The
need of a better comprehension of the phenomena and an accurate estimation of the
jitter degradations is nowadays still high. In the present paper, our new approach of
the jitter problem will be described.

In section 2, after a quick reminder of the jitter impact on discrete time delta sigma
converters, we will focus on the specificity of continuous time implementation regarding clock jitter and explain our approach to analyze this problem. Hence, we will
derive the complete set of equations describing the impact of jitter on a 2nd order
modulator and discuss about the possibility to extend this result to more complex ar-

Please use the following format when citing this chapter:

Goulier, J., Andre, E. and Renaudin, M., 2009, in IFIP International Federation for Information Processing, Volume 291; *VLSI-Soc:
Advanced Topics on Systems on a Chip*; eds. R. Reis, V. Mooney, P. Hasler; (Boston: Springer), pp. 193–208.

chitectures. Finally in section 4, the equations accuracy will be verified via some numerical comparisons with simulations.

2. INFLUENCE OF JITTER ON DELTA SIGMA CONVERTERS

In a discrete time delta sigma (DTΔΣ), the input signal is sampled before being converted. So analyzing clock jitter on those converters is equivalent to the investigation of irregular sampling problem [1]. This assumption can be done as long as the imperfections of the clock do not perturb the transfer function of the converter loop. Under the assumption of a white phase noise for the clock signal, the maximum achievable signal to noise ratio (SNR) of a discrete time converter is given by:

$$SNR_{dB} = 10\log\left(\frac{OSR}{(2\pi f_{max})^2 \sigma^2}\right) \qquad (1)$$

In this well known formula, σ is the standard deviation of the Gaussian distribution of jitter at each clock edge; OSR is the oversampling ratio of the converter and f_{max} is the maximal input frequency. Despite the important restrictions for the application of this equation, white phase noise and sinusoidal input, this formula is widely used for the design of DTΔΣ.

Unfortunately, in continuous time delta sigma converters (CTΔΣ) the jitter impact can not be reduced to the irregular sampling problem, and so (1) is inappropriate. The main reason why this equation is not valid any more is the fact that the sampling element in CTΔΣ is not in front of the loop but inside it, see figure 1. Moreover, in continuous time implementation the quantization noise introduced by the inner ADC is also responsible of losses linked to the clock imperfections. This phenomenon makes continuous time delta sigma converter much more sensible to clock jitter than discrete time analog-to-digital converters.

Several articles have already been published on the specific topic of jitter in CTΔΣ [2]-[4], giving us some interesting clues to understand the phenomena. In our approach of the jitter problem, we have decided not to make any initial assumption on the impact of this imperfection. So the first step of the study is to identify all possible errors introduced by jitter; only after this phase a mathematical estimation of the errors will be practicable.

If we consider that clock jitter has an impact on every continuous time function or signal, two kinds of jitter errors can be identified in a CTΔΣ. The first error, called sampling error, relates to the continuous input signal x(t) whereas the second one is introduced by the continuous time loop filter H(s). This second type of error is called integration error and is specific to continuous time delta sigma converters.

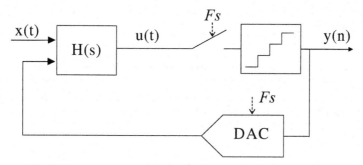

Figure 1. Typical block diagram of a $\Delta\Sigma\_CT$

2.1   Sampling error

The source of this error is the continuous time input signal x(t). Thus this error happens in both discrete and continuous time $\Delta\Sigma$. However the quantity of noise introduced by sampling errors is quite different whether the implementation is continuous or discrete. In a $CT\Delta\Sigma$, the input signal is processed by the loop filter before being sampled.

2.2   Integration error

This kind of error is specific to continuous time delta sigma converters and is related to the couple DAC/loop filter. Indeed, the processing of the jittered DAC output by the loop filter is responsible for the introduction of errors.

It is obvious that every clock non ideality modifies the timing diagram provided by the DAC. Those slight timing variations, normally processed by the continuous time filter, introduce voltage errors on every stage of the loop filter. The errors introduced in the loop filter by the variation of the integration period are defined by the term "integration errors". The number of integration errors is equal to the modulator order since there is one voltage error at each integrator output.

In spite of the localization of integration errors inside the loop filter, the DAC implementation has a strong influence on those errors. Indeed the DAC is the triggering element of integration errors, so every modification of its implementation induces important changes in the resulting errors. It is for example well known that $CT\Delta\Sigma$ using switched capacitor DAC are less sensitive to jitter than those with non return-to-zero (NRZ) DAC.

To conclude this phase of identification of the jitter errors, the impact of clock imperfections can be summarized as the introduction of N+1 errors for an Nth order modulator: one sampling error and N integration errors.

3. ANALYTICAL   EVALUATION   OF   JITTER DEGRADATION

In the previous section, the errors introduced by jitter have been identified; we now need to quantify them in order to derive a mathematical expression of the performance degradations. First the complete set of equations for a 2nd order $\Delta\Sigma$ modulator with NRZ feedback will be established. Then we will show that it is possible to extend those formulas to other architectures.

3.1   Second order $\Delta\Sigma$ with NRZ feedback

The architecture of the considered converter and the localization of the integration errors are given on figure 2. For the following calculations the classical linear model of $\Delta\Sigma$ modulators will be used. This means that the non-linear quantizer is replaced by a white noise adder.

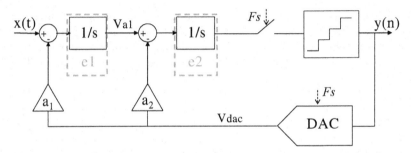

Figure 2. Second order $\Delta\Sigma$ with NRZ feedback

Estimation of integration errors

The input signal is continuous and directly applied to the loop filter; it is thus correctly processed by all the continuous time blocs preceding the sampler without introducing integration errors. Therefore to estimate the integration errors we simply assume that the input signal is nil.

Consider Δt the jitter error during the Nth clock period, that is to say from the instant t=nTS to t=(n+1)TS+Δt. Throughout the period, the voltage Vdac is constant and sent back to the loop filter trough a1 and a2, which is the principle of NRZ feedback DAC. The perturbation of the integration time due to the jitter Δt introduces two integration errors, e1 in the first integrator and e2 in the second stage of the modulator.

The error $e1$ is due to the fact that $a1*V_{dac}$ is integrated during $Ts+\Delta t$ instead of Ts. At the end of the nth clock period, that is to say at $t = (n+1)T_S + \Delta t$, the error introduced by jitter is equal to:

$$e1 = a_1 V_{dac} * \Delta t \qquad (2)$$

This error is generated within the first stage of the $\Delta\Sigma$ thus an equivalent voltage error $Ve1$ at the input of the first integrator can be computed.

$$\int_{nT_S}^{(n+1)T_S + \Delta t} a_1 * V_{dac}\ dt = \int_{nT_S}^{(n+1)T_S} \left(a_1 * V_{dac} + a_1 * V_{dac} * \frac{\Delta t}{T_S} \right) dt \qquad (3)$$

Therefore, we can write :

$$Ve1 = a_1 V_{dac} * \frac{\Delta t}{T_S} \qquad (4)$$

In order to derive the power spectral density (PSD) of this error S_{ve} (f), we can calculate the Fourier transform of its autocorrelation function. The autocorrelation function r_{Ve} of the error $Ve1$ is given by:

$$r_{Ve1}(mT) = E\left[Ve1(T) \cdot Ve1(T + mT) \right]$$
$$= \left(\frac{a_1}{T_S} \right)^2 r_{Vdac}(mT) \cdot r_{\Delta t}(mT) \qquad (5)$$

where E denotes the expectation operator, r_{Vdac} and $r_{\Delta t}$ are respectively the autocorrelation functions of the feedback voltage and timing jitter. By applying the Fourier transform to (3), the error spectrum can be found:

$$S_{Ve1}(f) = \left(\frac{a_1}{T_S} \right)^2 S_{Vdac}(f) \otimes S\ (f) \qquad (6)$$

The symbol $\otimes$ represents the convolution operator.

If we multiply this spectrum by the signal transfer function STF of the modulator and replace the temporal jitter spectrum $S_{\Delta t}$ by the phase noise spectrum S_θ, the equation of the PSD of the error $e1$ at the output of the converter can be computed.

$$S_{\Delta t}(f) = \left(\frac{T_S}{2\pi} \right)^2 S_\theta(f) \qquad (7)$$

From equations (6) and (7), the expression of S_{Ve} at the output of the converter can be derived.

$$S_{Ve1}(f) = \left(\frac{a_1}{2\pi}\right)^2 [S_{Vdac}(f) \otimes S_\theta(f)] * STF(f)$$

(8)

Of course, the same calculation method can be applied to the error $e2$, introduced within the second stage of the modulator. The equation is just a little bit more complex because $e2$ has got two components, the first part of the error is due to the single integration of a_2*V_{dac}, and the second one to the double integration of a_1*V_{dac}.

$$e2 = a_2 V_{dac} * \Delta t \left(1 + \frac{a_1}{a_2} T_s + \frac{a_1}{a_2}\frac{\Delta t}{2}\right) + V_{a1} * \Delta t$$

(9)

where V_{a1} is the output voltage of the first integrator, which is the integral of V_{dac}.

From this equation an equivalent second stage voltage error $Ve2$ can be derived. Furthermore, the quantities Ts and Δt are quite smaller than 1; consequently two terms of (9) can be neglected and $Ve2$ approximated to:

$$Ve2 \approx (a_2 V_{dac} + V_{a1})\frac{\Delta t}{T_s}$$

(10)

Finally, if the Fourier transform of the autocorrelation function of $Ve2$ is calculated and multiplied by the transfer function TF_{e2} between the input of the second stage and the output of the modulator, we can derive an expression for the PSD of $Ve2$.

Furthermore, we know that $Va1$ is the continuous time integral of $Vdac$. The relation between those two signals is:

$$S_{Va1}(f) = \frac{a_1^2}{(2\pi f)^2} S_{Vdac}(f)$$

(11)

So, the PSD of $Ve2$ is given by:

$$S_{Ve2}(f) = \frac{1}{(2\pi)^2}\left[\left[\left(a_2^2 + \frac{a_1^2}{(2\pi f)^2}\right)S_{Vdac}(f)\right] \otimes S_\theta(f)\right] * TF_{e2}(f)$$

(12)

In this chapter, the PSD expressions of the two integration errors have been calculated, in the special case of a second order delta sigma modulator with NRZ feedback DAC.

Estimation of the sampling error

In section 2, we have stated that one part of the jitter error is linked to the discretization of the input signal by the CTΔΣ. Even though this jitter degradation is easily understandable, the input signal being sampled when it gets through the modulator, we lack a detailed explanation of the phenomenon allowing us to analytically define an exact formula of the sampling error PSD.

From extensive observations and simulations of jitter in CTΔΣ it comes out that, in NRZ feedback ΔΣ, the errors introduced by jitter in relation with the input signal are equal to the errors that would happen if the input signal was filtered by the STF of the modulator before being sampled. This behavioral analysis has no physical meaning since modeling a CTΔΣ by a STF equivalent block followed by a sampler is irrelevant. However it allows us to quantify the sampling error and to give an easy and under-standable equation.

The PSD of the errors introduced by an isolated sampler is given in [5]:

$$S_{error}(f) = \left[\left(\frac{f}{F_s} \right)^2 S_X(f) \right] \otimes S_\theta(f) \tag{13}$$

If this equation is applied to our specific case, the following mathematical equation is obtained. This formula gives us the PSD of the errors introduced by clock jitter in re-lation with the input signal.

$$S_{Vin+jitter}(f) = \left[\left[\left(\frac{f}{F_s} \right)^2 S_{Vin}(f) \cdot STF(f) \right] \otimes S_\theta(f) \right] \tag{14}$$

From the three PSD equations, (6) (12) and (14), two essential remarks can be made. First, the dependency of jitter degradations to quantization noise, which is a specificity of CTΔΣ, is confirmed by (6) and (12). The second remark relates to the importance of phase noise profile. All formulas present a convolution involving phase noise, so the knowledge of the clock imperfections is a prerequisite for a good estima-tion of jitter degradations.

With the estimated PSD of all the errors introduced by the jitter in the CTΔΣ, it is quite simple to find the SNR degradation. Indeed, we just have to integrate (6), (12) and (14) on the right range of frequencies.

In section 4, we will express in figure some examples in order to attest of the for-mulas accuracy. First, the possible extension of those equations to generic converter architectures is discussed.

3.2 N^{th} order CTΔΣ with NRZ feedback

The above calculations have been conducted in the special case of a 2nd order con-verter to facilitate the comprehension of the phenomena; it is obviously possible to do exactly the same work with other architectures. However, the computation of the jitter equations, already time-consuming with the second order modulator, is becoming al-most endless as soon as the order of the loop filter is increased.

In reality, it is not necessary to extract the whole set of equations every time the modulator architecture is changed. In fact, in high order modulators, the errors introduced by the integration stages that are close to the quantizer have a small influence on performances because there are shaped by the loop. Thus the set of equations, defined in the preceding section can be considered as a good approximation of the impact of jitter for every modulator with NRZ feedback DAC.

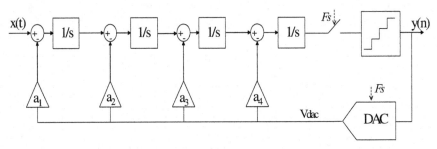

Figure 3. *4th order ΔΣ converter with NRZ feedback*

Let's consider a 4th order continuous time delta sigma converter with NRZ feedback DAC. We know from section 2 that this modulator owns one sampling error and 4 integration errors.

The conversion principle of this particular converter is comparable to the second order modulator described previously (feedback structure and NRZ DAC). Thus the formulation of the sampling error PSD is not changed. Therefore, equation (14) can be used again to estimate the impact of jitter, related to the input signal, for the considered 4th order modulator.

This result does not mean that the power of the sampling error introduced by the clock imperfections is similar. It is well known that the transfer function STF(f) of a CTΔΣ modulator depends on the loop filter architecture. So, the signal transfer function of a 4th order modulator is different from the STF of a second order modulator. Therefore, the numerical value of the sampling error PSD will be different as soon as the modulator is changed.

The number of integration error is equal to the number of integrators used to realize the continuous time loop filter. So, in the considered 4th order modulator, there is 4 integration errors.

The errors introduced inside the third and fourth stages of the loop filter will have a really small impact on the performances of the modulator in comparison with the integration errors of the first two stages. Integration errors are shaped by the loop transfer functions. Thus, the jitter error computation can be wisely reduced to the calculation of the first two integration errors only. The expressions for those two integration errors have already been derived in section 2, see equations (6) and (12).

So the set of equations derived for the second order modulator can be used without any modification to compute the degradations introduced by jitter for every CTΔΣ converter with NRZ feedback DAC.

3.3   Jitter compensation techniques : Switched Capacitor feedback and Finite Impulse Response DAC

In the last decade, different methods have been proposed to reduce the jitter sensitivity of CTΔΣ. Switched Capacitor (SC) DAC [6]-[8] and FIRDAC [9] [10] are two techniques which have proven their efficiency. If the computation principle previously described is applied to ΔΣ using those correction systems, the resultant benefit can be evaluated.

The main idea behind those two correction techniques is to reduce the impact of jitter by making the feedback DAC completely independent of the clock imperfections. In a continuous time delta sigma converter, the outputs of DACs are integrated by the loop filter. Therefore, the important parameter in a CTΔΣ is not the value of the current sent back in the conversion loop but the quantity of charges integrated during the clock period by the continuous time filter.

Switched capacitor DAC

Let's consider again the case of the second order modulator with a feedback architecture, see figure 2. But this time the NRZ feedback scheme is replaced by a switched capacitor DAC.

With this kind of digital to analog converter, the quantity of charges sent back in the loop during a clock period is controlled by the charge and the discharge of a capacitor. If the SC DAC and the loop filter are designed neatly, that is to say that time constants for the charge and discharge of the capacitors are quite smaller than the clock period, the quantity of charge sent back in the loop is independent of jitter. Therefore, the error $e1$ introduced in the first integrator is nil and the integration error of the second stage $e2$ is strongly reduced. No details of the computation of the following equations are given here, because the derivation of those two formulas is really similar to the work presented in section 3.1.

$$S_{Ve1}(f) = 0 \tag{15}$$

$$S_{Ve2}(f) = \frac{1}{(2\pi)^2}\left[\left[\frac{a_1^2}{(2\pi f)^2} S_{Vdac}(f)\right] \otimes S_\theta(f)\right] * TF_{e2}(f) \tag{16}$$

The power spectral density of the sampling error is modified too by the introduction of the SC DAC. Contrarily to the modulator with NRZ feedback, the sampling error is not sent back integrally in the conversion loop when SC technique is used. Therefore, the PSD of the sampling error is shaped by the loop filter:

$$S_{Vin+jitter}(f) = \left[\left[\left(\frac{1}{2\pi}\right)^2 S_{Vin}(f) \cdot STF(f)\right] \otimes S_\theta(f)\right] * TF_{e2}(f) \tag{17}$$

If the equations (15), (16) and (17) are compared with the equations derived in section 3.1 (formulas (6), (12) and (14)), the benefit from the utilization of switched capacitor DAC is clearly visible. Indeed the integration errors are reduced and the sampling errors are shaped by the conversion loop. However, the PSD of clock jitter errors is not equal to zero; this correction system is therefore not perfect.

In this paragraph, the case of switched capacitor ADC has been analyzed in details and the set of equations providing the jitter errors PSD has been derived. This study has shown that the calculations are really comparable to those detailed in paragraph 3.1. Some numerical results for a 3rd order modulator with a SC DAC will be given in section 4.

Finite impulse response DAC

The principle of this jitter correction is again to reduce the impact of jitter on the signal sent back in the loop filter by the DACs. However the strategy employed is completely different from the one used with SC DAC. The idea here is to spread the feedback current over several periods in order to limit the jitter influence. With the FIRDAC technique, the impact of clock imperfections are not corrected on each period, as it is the case with SC DAC. Nevertheless, jitter error PSD is reduced by a simple effect of averaging.

The modifications on the NRZ feedback DAC structure are really small. The digital to analog converters are just split in smaller elements in order to reduce the instantaneous current sent back in the loop during each clock period. On figure 4, a temporal diagram example of DAC currents is represented with a classical NRZ feedback and with a 4 stages FIRDAC correction.

FIRDAC technique is definitely less efficient than SC DAC, because it only realize an averaging of jitter errors. However, its implementation is easier and the impact on the analog loop filter is usually lower than the integration of switched capacitor DAC.

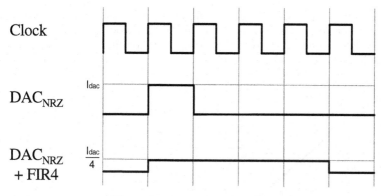

Figure 4. FIRDAC impact on the feedback current

4. VALIDATION OF THE ANALYTICAL JITTER ERRORS ESTIMATION

In the previous sections, our approach to estimate the impact of clock jitter on the output signal of CTΔΣ has been explained. To prove the accuracy of the given formulas, they will now be compared with simulations.

4.1 Clock jitter modeling

In order to simulate the impact of jitter on CTΔΣ, temporal models of non-ideal clocks are needed. To realize clock signals presenting different phase noise profile, a voltage controlled oscillator (VCO) has been modeled. This frequency synthesis circuit has been chosen because it is simple enough to be accurately modeled and it allows us to generate a wide range of jittered clocks. This non ideal clock model has been created with Matlab Simulink blocks and used to drive CTΔΣ modulators.

The phase noise profile of our VCO model is characterized by a -20dB/decade slope and a phase noise floor. The decreasing phase noise slope is a classical feature of an oscillator while the phase noise floor represents the bufferization of the clock signal. Thus, this model possesses two tuning parameters, the levels of the noise slope and noise floor, allowing us to generate different non ideal clocks. Moreover this VCO has been included in a phase locked loop (PLL) to create a more complex jittered clock.

The VCO phase noise profile can be easily translated to temporal imperfections using the classical relations between phase noise and temporal jitter [11]. In fact, the phase noise slope of the VCO corresponds to an accumulated Gaussian timing error while phase noise floor relates to an independent Gaussian temporal error. It is those two temporal imperfections that have been used to create the Matlab Simulink model of VCO.

The model accuracy has been validated using phase noise profile comparisons. Figure 5 shows a validation example of the VCO model. The black curve is the theoretical phase noise level while the grey one is the phase noise profile extracted from the simulation of the Matlab VCO model.

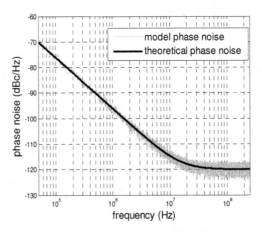

Figure 5. *VCO phase noise model validation*

4.2   Jitter equations comparisons with simulations

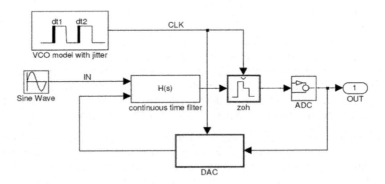

Figure 6. *CTΔΣ simulation with non ideal clock*

From the equations stated in section 3, we know that jitter degradations are related to the architecture of the converter, the phase noise profile and the input signal PSD. To prove the precision of our jitter impact computation, formulas and simulations have been compared for different CTΔΣ architecture and several phase noise profiles. The comparisons have focused on two criterions, the converter output PSD and the SNR value. To simulate the impact of jitter on the performances of CTΔΣ, the VCO model described in the preceding paragraph has been used to drive different converters, see figure 6.

To explore the architecture dependency, three different converter architectures have been used:

- A 2nd order feedback modulator with NRZ DAC
- A 4th order feedback modulator with NRZ DAC
- A 3rd order feedback modulator with Switched capacitor DAC

All modulators used a 4-bits internal quantizer. Moreover, two sinusoidal signals with the same amplitude but different frequencies, Fin1=5MHz and Fin2=25MHz, have been used to illustrate the relation between the jitter degradation and the input PSD.

Finally, to demonstrate how the clock phase noise profile modifies the errors introduced by jitter, two dissimilar clocks have been defined. The frequency of both clocks is 500MHz. The first clock has a flat phase noise profile at -120dBc/Hz, whereas the second clock is a type 1 PLL, with a 500kHz cut off frequency. The PLL phase noise is equal to -90dBc/Hz at 500kHz and the phase noise floor is located at -120dBc/Hz. The phase noise profiles of those two clocks are represented on figure 7.

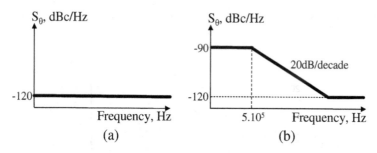

Figure 7. Clocks phase noise profiles, (a) white noise, (b) PLL

For all the possible combinations of architecture, input signal and clock, the converter output PSD and the SNR from 0 to 10 MHz have been derived from equations and simulations.

For each test case, the correct superposition of the simulated PSD with the calculated one demonstrates the reliability of our jitter impact estimation method. PSD comparison examples, with the two non ideal clocks, are shown in figures 8 and 9. The out of band PSD is not shown on those figures because it is dominated by quantification noise. The curves correspond to the output signals of the 2nd order feedback modulator with NRZ DAC and a sinusoidal input signal at 5MHz.

The PSD superpositions are evident, and they are confirmed by the calculation of SNR values. For the white phase noise clock comparison case, the SNR achieved by the simulated converter is equal to 64.82dB and the SNR given by the equation is 64.50dB. In the second test case, the SNR values are respectively 62.63dB and 62.59dB.

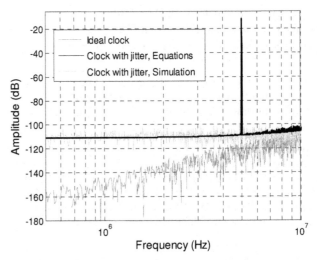

Figure 8. *Output spectrum comparison of a 2nd order CT$\Delta\Sigma$ controlled by the white phase noise clock*

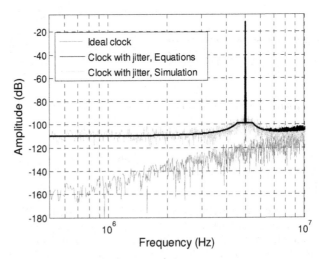

Figure 9. *Output spectrum comparison of a 2nd order CT$\Delta\Sigma$ controlled by the PLL clock*

The same PSD and SNR comparisons have been done with the others converters and clocks and resulted in comparable conclusions on the accuracy of the jitter estimation method. The SNR values of the 12 test cases described above are summarized in table 1. The SNR from simulations are in regular characters, while those from formulas are in bold font. For information, the SNR value of the input signal sampled by non ideal clocks is also given in table 1. Those numbers correspond to the degradations introduced by a jittered clock if a DT$\Delta\Sigma$ was used.

The SNR comparison, encapsulated in table 1, illustrates the accuracy of the mathematical jitter error estimation method presented in this paper. The discrepancies between calculated and simulated SNR values are indeed really small, always less than 1 dB.

Moreover, the jitter degradation dependence to the three key parameters (modulator architecture, phase noise and input signal) is highlighted by both simulations and equations. The validity of our approach of the jitter problem and the accuracy of the equations are clearly demonstrated by the given results.

	Ideal Clock	Clock 1 : white noise		clock 2 : PLL	
		Fin1	Fin2	Fin1	Fin2
Sampled input signal	∞	87.06dB **87.02dB**	73.17dB **73.04dB**	66.81dB **67.10dB**	72.21dB **72.99dB**
2nd order modulator with NRZ feedback	72.5dB	64.82dB **64.50dB**	63.73dB **63.94dB**	62.63dB **62.59dB**	63.64dB **63.91dB**
4th order modulator with NRZ feedback	95dB	71.05dB **70.65dB**	69.10dB **68.96dB**	65.20dB **65.53dB**	68.90dB **68.92dB**
3rd order modulator with SC return	86.6dB	80.80dB **81.25dB**	83.58dB **83.96dB**	66.17dB **66.81dB**	83.25dB **83.91dB**

Table 1. SNR comparisons

5.   CONCLUSION

In this paper, a new analytical approach to solve the problem of clock jitter in CT$\Delta\Sigma$ is presented. By focusing on continuous time components and signals, two kinds of jitter errors have been identified and mathematical equations of those errors PSD have been derived. Finally, the accuracy of the jitter errors formulas has been proven with exhaustive comparisons with simulated converters controlled by non ideal clocks.

The provided results quite clearly confirm the relation between the jitter errors and the converter architecture. This strong relationship automatically draws aside the possibility to derive a single and simple jitter error equation as it is the case for discrete time converters. However, the presented work provides an efficient mathematical method to specify the clock phase noise profile needed to achieve the targeted performances of $CT\Delta\Sigma$ converters.

6. REFERENCES

[1]   B. E. Boser, B. A. Wooley, "The design of sigma-delta modulation analog-to-digital converters", IEEE Journal of Solid-State Circuits, vol . 23, December 1988.

[2]   J. A. Cherry, W.M. Snelgrove, "Clock jitter and quantizer metastability in continuous-time delta-sigma modulators", IEEE Transaction on Circuits and Systems-II, vol. 46, June 1999.

[3]   E. J. Van Der Zwan, E. C. Dijkmans, "A 0.2 mW CMOS $\Sigma\Delta$ modulator for speech coding with 80 dB dynamic range", IEEE Journal of Solid-State Circuits, vol 31, December 1996.

[4]   M. Ortmanns, F. Gerfers, Y. Manoli, "Fundamental limits of jitter insensitivity in discrete and continuous-time sigma delta modulators", International Symposium on Circuits and Systems, ISCAS 2003.

[5]   N. Da Dalt, M. Harteneck, C. Sandner, A. Wiesbauer "On the jitter requirements of the sampling clock for analog-to-digital converters", IEEE Trans. Circuits and Systems-I, vol. 49, September 2002.

[6]   M. Ortmanns, F. Gerfers, Y. Manoli, "A continuous-time $\Sigma\Delta$ modulator with reduced sensitivity to clock jitter through SCR feedback", IEEE Trans. Circuits and Systems-I, vol 52, May 2005.

[7]   R. Van Veldhoven, "A tri-mode continuous-time $\Sigma\Delta$ modulator with switched-capacitor feedback DAC for a GSM-EDGE/CDMA2000/UMTS receiver", International Solid State Circuits Conference, ISSCC 2003.

[8]   S. Ouzounov et al., "A 1.2V 121-mode CT $\Delta\Sigma$ modulator for wireless receivers in 90nm CMOS", International Solid State Circuits Conference, ISSCC 2007.

[9]   O. Oliaei, "Continuous-time sigma-delta modulator incorporating semi-digital FIR filters", International Symposium on Circuits and Systems, ISCAS 2003.

[10]   B. M. Putter, "A $\Sigma\Delta$ ADC with Finite Impulse Response Feedback DAC" , International Solid State Circuits Conference, ISSCC 2004.

[11]   T. C. Weigandt, "Low phase noise, low timing jitter design techniques for delay cell based VCOs and frequency synthesizers", Ph.D. thesis, University of California, Berkeley, 1998, pp 17-30.

An adaptive genetic algorithm for dynamically reconfigurable modules allocation

Vincenzo Rana, Chiara Sandionigi, Marco Santambrogio and Donatella Sciuto

chiara.sandionigi@dresd.org,
{rana, santambr, sciuto}@elet.polimi.it

Politecnico di Milano - Dipartimento di Elettronica e Informazione
Via Ponzio 34/5 - 20133 Milano, Italy

Abstract. This paper aims at defining an adaptive genetic algorithm tailored for the allocation of dynamically reconfigurable modules. This algorithm can be tuned at run-time with a set of parameters to best characterize different architectural scenarios (i.e., single device or multi-FPGAs characterized by several kinds of communication infrastructures) and to adapt the performance of the algorithm itself to the scenario in which it has to operate.

The proposed approach has been validated on a large set of meaningful combinations of parameters (i.e. changing the mutation or the crossover probability), in order to demonstrate the possibility of performing either a fast or an accurate allocation phase.

1 Introduction

Nowadays, thanks to reconfigurable devices (such as FPGAs), it is possible to dynamically tailor the hardware to a specific application, in order to dramatically improve its performance. One of the most suitable approaches in the development of reconfigurable systems is the module-based approach (see [1]), in which the original application is partitioned into several functions, each one of them implemented as a single module. These modules, thus, can be either dynamically loaded into the system or removed from the system, in order to change its overall functionality. The most recent Xilinx design flow, the Early Access Partial Reconfiguration (EAPR) flow, is based on the same approach, as described in [2].

One of the most interesting challenges in such a scenario is the allocation of requested modules in the free space of the reprogrammable device. The allocation phase has to take into account the fragmentation of the device in order to keep the maximum set of contiguous free slots, able to contain bigger modules. On the other hand, this phase has to be executed in a very short time, since it is not desirable to further increase the overhead due to the reconfiguration processes.

The approach presented in [5] trades the execution time for quality of placement, introducing a placement algorithm that is a hybrid solution of the best-fit

Please use the following format when citing this chapter:

Rana, V., Sandionigi, C., Santambrogio, M. and Sciuto, D., 2009, in IFIP International Federation for Information Processing, Volume 291; *VLSI-SoC: Advanced Topics on Systems on a Chip;* eds. R. Reis, V. Mooney, P. Hasler; (Boston: Springer), pp. 209–226.

and first-fit algorithm. Another feasible solution to this problem is represented by the adaptive genetic algorithm proposed in this paper. This algorithm can be tuned for different scenarios of dynamic reconfiguration. In fact, since it can be executed with a different combination of parameters, it can perform the allocation task either in a very short time or in a very accurate way, as shown by the presented experimental results.

This paper deals with the application of an adaptive genetic algorithm to the allocation of dynamically reconfigurable modules, introducing a very flexible approach to perform the allocation phase. In particular, the next section presents the scenario in which the genetic algorithm can be applied. Section 4 introduces the genetic algorithm on which the adaptive genetic algorithm presented in this paper is based. Section 5 describes the details of the adaptive genetic algorithm and all the parameters that it is possible to tune in order to achieve different levels of performance. Section 6 presents the experimental results that prove the effectiveness of the proposed approach. Finally, conclusions are drawn in Section 7.

2   Module based reconfiguration approach

As previously hinted, one of the more widely used approaches to reconfiguration is the module based approach, that has been proposed by Xilinx in [1]. This approach consist of splitting the reconfigurable device into two different parts:

- a static part, and
- a reconfigurable part.

The reconfigurable part has to be furthermore partitioned in a set of reconfigurable slots, as shown in Figure 1 (2). Both the size of the static part and the number of reconfigurable slots (that strictly depends on reconfigurable modules size) can be tuned in order to adapt the system to the particular design.

In order to change the functionality of the implemented system, it is possible to develop a set of reconfigurable modules, as shown in Figure 1 (3). These modules can be of different size, but they have to span the whole height of the device in order to be compliant with Xilinx Virtex 2 and Xilinx Virtex 2 Pro reconfigurable devices (while the newest Xilinx Virtex IV and Xilinx Virtex V devices also support rectangular modules of any size).

Each reconfigurable module can be dynamically placed on one or more reconfigurable slots (depending on its size), as shown in Figure 1 (4), where modules A, B and C have been configured on the reconfigurable part of the device.

When a module ends the computation, it can be unused for a unknown time interval (such as modules B and C in Figure 1 (5)); in this case, it is possible to remove the module from the system in order to free the resources occupied by the module itself. Another solution, presented in Figure 1 (6), consists of keeping the module configured on the device, implementing thus a sort of module cache. The latter solution occupies a larger amount of reconfigurable resources, but it

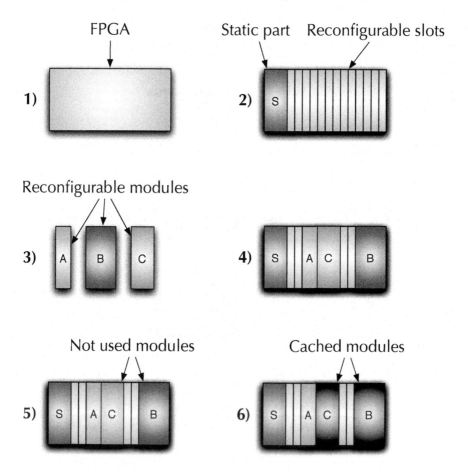

Fig. 1. Module based reconfiguration approach

makes it possible to avoid a reconfiguration (avoiding thus the reconfiguration time overhead) when a module that is cached is required. For instance, referring to Figure 1 (6), if either module B or module C is required, there is not the need to perform a reconfiguration, since they are both already configured in the system; this means that they can be used at any time without requiring any additional setup time.

3 Reconfiguration scenarios

One of the most general platforms on which a configurable or reconfigurable system can be developed is a multi-FPGA scenario where the reconfigurable resources are distributed on several interconnected FPGAs. In such a scenario it is common to have a master FPGA able to reconfigure, partially or totally, other slave FPGAs. These slave FPGAs can be divided into several slots that can be filled with IP-Cores (or modules) by the master FPGA.

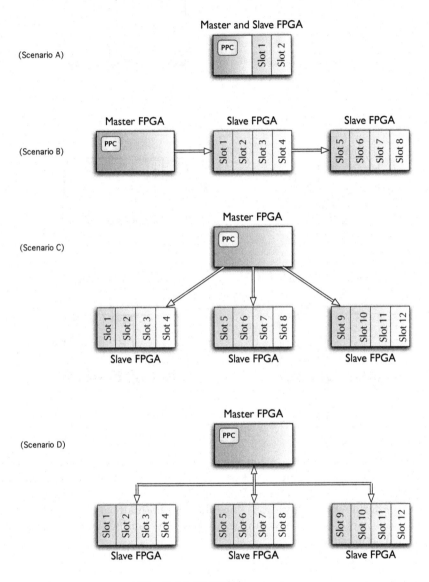

Fig. 2. Multi-FPGA scenarios

Figure 2 presents a collection of different scenarios. In all these scenarios, each master FPGA is characterized by the presence of an embedded PowerPC processor, on which the Operating System runs, in addition to the static hardware components such as a memory controller, general purpose inputs/outputs, and a reconfiguration manager.

The slave FPGAs, instead, hold the reconfigurable resources used to dynamically load hardware modules into the system. These resources are used according to a 1D-placement with a granularity of four CLB (Configurable Logic Block) columns [6]. This means that dynamic modules always use the full height of the FPGA, while their width is a multiple of four CLB columns, even if this scenario can be easily extended to the 2D scenario realized using Xilinx Virtex-4 [3] and Virtex-5 FPGAs [4].

In the first scenario, called Scenario A in Figure 2, there is one FPGA that is used both as a master and as a slave FPGA. An example of such a scenario can be found in [8]. This FPGA is logically divided into two different parts:

- a **xed part**, that is the part of the FPGA that contains the PowerPC processor and that acts as a single master FPGA;
- a **recon gurable part**, that is handled as a single slave FPGA, even if the number of slots that it is possible to configure is smaller.

On the other hand, in all the remaining scenarios each FPGA of the system acts either as a master or as a slave FPGA, without logical internal divisions.

The differences between these scenarios reside in the different ways in which the communication infrastructure is implemented. The second scenario (Scenario B) presents a chain communication in which the master FPGA can communicate with just one slave FPGA, and each slave FPGA can communicate just with the following one, for instance by using a communication module in the last slot.

Scenario C and Scenario D, instead, represent a point to point connection and a bus-based connection, respectively. In both these scenarios the master FPGA is able to communicate directly with each slave FPGA. [7] presents an architecture that can be represented using Scenario D.

Even if the presented scenarios differ in the logical partitioning of master and slave FPGAs sets and in their communication infrastructures, they can be reduced to the same class of platforms from the software point of view. For this reason they can be handled by the same software solution, as described in the following.

4   The genetic algorithm

A first version of the genetic algorithm that can be used for the allocation of dynamically reconfigurable modules has been first proposed in [9]. This approach proposes the encoding of a single chromosome (that has to contain the information about the solution that it represents) as a pair of arrays, the *Slots* and the *Modules* arrays:

- The *Slots* array consists of a collection of genes, which contain the information on which module is configured on each slot of the reprogrammable device. In particular, each gene directly corresponds to a single slot of a slave FPGA. Since on a device of n slots it is possible to configure not more than n modules (this is possible only when each configured module requires just one slot), the alleles of these genes are represented by a number between 0 and $n-1$. The numbers contained in the *Slots* array correspond to the position of a gene in the second array.

– The *Modules* array consists of a set of genes that represent hardware IP-Cores. The following numbers represent the coding of the alleles for this kind of gene:

  • 0: this number means that the module is not configured on the reprogrammable device, since it has not been placed yet or it has already been deleted from the system;

  • 1: this number indicates that the module has been already configured on the FPGA and it is still running, so at this time it cannot be directly unloaded from the system;

  • -2: a module characterized by this number is a cached IP-Core. In other words it is a module that has already been placed on the reprogrammable device but it is not currently used, thus it is possible to unload it to overwrite its slots with the configuration of a more useful IP-Core.

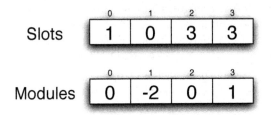

Fig. 3. Genetic algorithm chromosome

The example shown in Figure 3 represents a status of the system in which the second module (module 1) is configured on the first slot of the FPGA (slot 0) and the fourth module (module 3) is placed on the third and on the fourth slot (slot 2 and slot 3), while the second slot (slot 1) is free (since the first module, module 0, is not configured).

The *Slots* array gives further information, indicating that the second module (module 1) is cached, while the fourth module (module 3) is still running. This means that the largest module that is possible to configure starting from this status is a module that requires two slots, since it can be configureb on the first two slots of the FPGA (slot 0 and slot 1), by unloading the second module (module 1) that is currently cached.

After the choice of the proper coding for chromosomes, genes and alleles, it has to be defined a suitable fitness function. Main objective of the allocation manager is to handle the configurable space of the reprogrammable device to avoid both a waste of slots and the refusing of the configuration of an IP-Core, that happens when there is no place where it is possible to configure it. This means that it is desirable to keep the free slots all together, without breaking them in a lot of smaller separate set of free slots, since a large collection of contiguous slots allows to configure also bigger modules.

For this reason the fitness function has been defined as a number that increases of a small quantity for each free slot. This quantity starts from a default value, but it gets bigger when a free slot is followed by another free slot. On the opposite, when a free slot is followed by a slot containing a cached or a running module, the gain comes back to the default value. Moreover, to prefer solutions with a large number of cached modules, that are useful to speed up the reconfiguration process, a fixed reward is introduced for each cached IP-Core of the solution.

Figure 4 shows an example of the evaluation of the fitness function of three given chromosomes, with a default gain of 2 points, increased of 1 point for each contiguous free slot, and a fixed reward of 1 point for each cached module. The three chromosomes are very similar, but the seventh module (module 6) is placed in a different position in each solution. In the first example (A), the seventh module is located at the end of the FPGA, in the second example (B) it is configured to break the set of the last four free slots, while in the third example (C) it has been placed in the most suitable location, that is the second slot (slot 1). Even if the number of configured IP-Cores, the number of cached modules and the total number of free slots are the same for all the solutions, the first one presents two sets of free slots (whose sizes are 1 and 3 slots, respectively) with a fitness of 13, the second one 4 sets (with sizes of 1, 2 and 1 slots, respectively) with a fitness of 11, while the third one is a single set of 4 slots with a fitness of 16. Obviously the last solution is the most suitable, since it is the only one that allows the configuration of a new module that requires 4 contiguous slots, in fact it presents the largest fitness value within the class of the presented solutions.

The proposed genetic algorithm is performed each time a set of new modules has to be configured on the reprogrammable devices of the system. If each module can be placed in n positions, an exhaustive search with a set of m IP-Cores requires n^m evaluations of feasible solutions. With a genetic algorithm it is possible to considerably decrease the time required by the allocation process, since it works on a smaller set of solutions, trying to modify them to reach a good sub-optimum solution in a reasonable time.

In particular, the first step of the algorithm is the creation of an initial set of randomly generated chromosomes. Then, after the fitness evaluation, a subset of chromosomes is chosen to create a new population. These chromosomes are called parents of the offspring, that is formed through the crossover process.

The crossover task is performed by randomly choosing two parents. The new chromosome is generated by keeping the genes of the first part of the first parent, while the other genes are directly taken from the second parent. During this phase it is possible to introduce, with a random probability, a mutation.

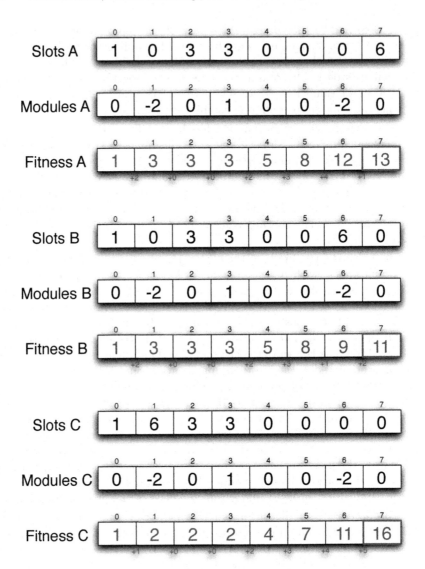

Fig. 4. Fitness evaluation examples

This is defined as a change in the partial solutions found by the parents, which means that the location inherited by the parents can be randomly modified, to prevent that all solutions in the population fall into a local optimum.

5 Adaptive genetic algorithm

The genetic algorithm described in Section 4 has been extended with a set of configurable parameters that make the algorithm dynamically adaptive with respect to the platform scenario where it has to work. These parameters provide the possibility of choosing either a fast or a very accurate allocation phase, depending on the timing performance and on the space constraints.

The parameters that can be tuned to tailor the solution onto a specific scenario are:

- **initial population size**, that is the initial size of the randomly generated population, as described in Section 5.1;
- **selection size**, the number of chromosomes that are chosen to create the new population, described in Section 5.2;
- **maximum number of rounds**, introduced in Section 5.3, that is the maximum number of generations that can be performed before stopping the execution of the algorithm;
- **minimum   tness**, described in Section 5.4, that is the fitness threshold;
- **crossover probability**, that is the probability of performing a crossover of two parents in order to generate a new offspring (otherwise the first parent is not modified), as presented in Section 5.5;
- **neutral mutation probability**, described in Section 5.6, that is the probability of performing a neutral mutation on the new chromosome;
- **positive mutation probability**, described in Section 5.7, that is the probability of performing a positive mutation on the new chromosome;
- **negative mutation probability**, described in Section 5.8, that is the probability of performing a negative mutation on the new chromosome.

Each parameter can be tuned in order to achieve the desired performance, both in terms of time and in terms of refused modules.

It is possible, in fact, that a particular scenario requires a fast allocation phase, for instance when the module that has to be deployed has to be available in a very short time. In this case it is possible to run the genetic algorithm with a set of parameters that provides a feasible position for the module in a fast way. The execution of the algorithm with this set of parameters affects the performance of the algorithm itself and increases the fragmentation of the reconfigurable device, but this negative effect can be kept under control by choosing the most suitable set of parameters, as shown in Section 6.

On the other hand, when a module is requested in advance with respect to its real utilization time (for instance when pre-fetching is performed), it is possible to execute the genetic algorithm with a set of parameters that allows the search for a solution that minimizes the fragmentation of the reprogrammable device. To achieve this result, it is necessary to know the right set of parameters that are able to reduce the average number of refused modules during the whole life of the system.

For these reasons, each parameter has been tested with a large set of significant values, as described in the following sections.

5.1   Initial population size

Each time a module is requested, the genetic algorithm has to create an initial population that consists of randomly generated individuals. Each one of these individuals has to satisfy all the constraints, since it has to represent a feasible solution. The single chromosome within the population will change its characteristics, but the total number of chromosomes will not change, since the population size is fixed to the value of the size of the initial population. The initial population size, then, will affect the whole execution of the genetic algorithm, since it represents the size of the population on which each operation (such as crossover and mutations) will be performed. The genetic algorithm has been tested with three different values, that are 10, 50 and 100 chromosomes.

5.2   Selection size

When the fitness of each chromosome of the population is evaluated in order to choose the chromosomes that will act as parents (that are, in other words, the chromosomes with the maximum fitness value) during the generation of the new population, it is possible to select a set of these chromosomes that will be kept, without any changes, in the next generation. The selection size is hence the number of chromosomes that will be kept without any changes, while the difference between the initial population size and the selection size represents the number of chromosomes that have to be created during the offspring generation phase. The selection size depends on the initial population size: for this reason the values of the selection size has been chosen as $1/4$, $1/2$ and $3/4$ of the initial population size, that represent three different situations, in which few, half or a lot is preserved from the previous generation.

5.3   Maximum number of rounds

The generation (that consists of the evaluation of the fitness, in the selection of the most suitable solutions and in the generation of the children) has to be performed either for the maximum number of rounds or until the minimum fitness is reached. In the first case, in which the minimum fitness is never reached, the value that represents the maximum number of rounds has to be chosen keeping into account that a big value requires a large execution time, while a small value can lead to a solution that is not optimal and that increases the fragmentation of the reconfigurable device. In particular, in our experiments, we used for this parameter the following values: 10, 20 and 50.

5.4   Minimum   tness

The minimum fitness represents the threshold that has to be exceeded in order to accept a chromosome as a final solution. This parameter is very important since it allows an early-stop of the algorithm when a good solution has been found. Obviously, with a small minimum fitness value, the final solution will not be optimized, while a big value of this parameter will probably bring the algorithm to execute for the maximum number of rounds, as described in Section 5.3. The minimum fitness is hence a measurement of the goodness of the desired soution. The goodness index will be explained more in details in Sextion 6. For our experiments we used three different values: 100, 1000 and 2000.

5.5   Crossover probability

The crossover task is performed by randomly choosing two parents within the set of the selected chromosomes, as introduced in Section 5.2. Each new chromosome is generated by keeping the genes of the first part of the first parent, while the other genes are directly taken from the second parent. When the crossover is not performed, the new chromosome is equal to one of the two parents, chosen randomly. In both cases, children always represent valid solutions for the given problem. The crossover parameter is hence responsible for the generation of an offspring that mixes the good characteristics of the most suitable solutions of the previous generation, in the hope to determine a better one. In our experiments we tested this probability with the following values: 25%, 50% and 75%.

5.6   Neutral mutation probability

Each time a new chromosome is generated it is possible to perform a neutral mutation by modifying the position of the requested module within the reconfigurable device (for this reason it has been called neutral mutation, since it preserves the status of the modules configured on the reconfigurable device). This mutation allows the generation of a new solution that was not present in the initial population, so it is an index of the difference between the solutions achieved by a population and the following one. The new location of the requested module has to be a feasible position, since each chromosome has always to represent a feasible solution. As with the other probabilities, we tested this parameter with the following values: 25%, 50% and 75%.

5.7   Positive mutation probability

With a positive mutation it is possible to free space on the reprogrammable device by deleting a module that was previously kept in cache. This mutation allows the increase of the number of positions where the requested module can be placed (as described in Section 6) without any penalization. The slots occupied by the deleted module are marked in a special way, since they have to be recognized at the end of the algorithm, when slots that have been deleted but that are not used by the requested module can be simply reintroduced without introducing any overhead and increasing the goodness of the final solution. Also this probability has been tested with the following values: 25%, 50% and 75%.

5.8 Negative mutation probability

A negative mutation, in which a module that has been removed from the cache will be reintroduced in the cache, can be introduced to increase the goodness of the solution at run-time. This kind of modules, in fact, can be reintroduced in the cache in order to avoid the placement of the requested module, without any penalization, in a location that will lead to delete a cached module. In our experiments, we used the following values for this probability: 25%, 50% and 75%.

6 Experimental results

Each combination of the values of the parameters presented in Section 5 has been tested in order to achieve the performance characterization of all the possible sets of parameters.

The base scenario on which these tests have been performed consists of a reconfigurable device that has been divided in fifty reconfigurable slots. Furthermore, the size of the single module that can be deployed on the system ranges from one to three slots.

Table 1. Parameters values

Parameter	First value	Second value	Third value
Initial population size (IPS)	10	50	100
Selection size	$\frac{1}{4} * IPS$	$\frac{1}{2} * IPS$	$\frac{3}{4} * IPS$
Maximum number of rounds	10	20	50
Minimum tness	100	1000	2000
Crossover probability	25	50	75
Neutral mutation probability	25	50	75
Positive mutation probability	25	50	75
Negative mutation probability	25	50	75

Table 1 presents all the possible values for each parameter. Since there are eight parameters and each parameter presents three different values, it is necessary to perform $3^8 = 6561$ experiments in order to evaluate all the possible combinations of the parameters values.

For each combination of parameters an experiment has been performed that consists of the following steps:

- fifty tests, consisting of fifty module requests each, have been performed. In particular, each test performs the following tasks:
  - a random module request is given as input to the genetic algorithm;
  - the result (success/fail) of this process and the time required for its execution are stored to calculate the fitness of the current solution;
  - randomly a module is deleted from the reconfigurable device (in order to avoid the saturation of the device itself);
- at the end of each test the status of the reprogrammable device has been reset and the average results of the simulations (number of refused modules, cash index and timing performance) have been updated.

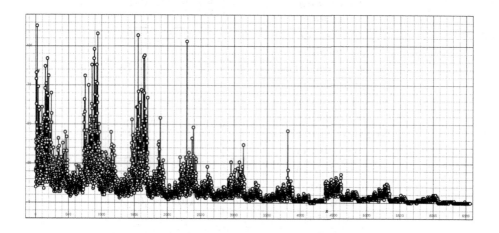

Fig. 5. Goodness index for all the solutions

Figure 5 shows the average goodness index (that represent the fitness of a given solution) for each combination of parameters (the test ow previously described has been performed two times in order to avoid erroneous results). The goodness has been evaluated as follows:

$$Goodness = \frac{CI}{ET*RM}$$

where:

- CI is the Cache Index: this index is inversely proportional to the fragmentation of the reprogrammable device ($CI = \frac{1}{Fragmentation}$);

222   Vincenzo Rana, Chiara Sandionigi, Marco Santambrogio and Donatella Sciuto

- *ET* is the Elapsed Time: it represents the time necessary to perform a whole experiment, that consists of 2500 module requests;
- *RM* is the number of Refused Modules. In other words, this index represents the number of modules that have not been placed during the execution of the algorithm.

Table 2. Top four experimental results

Combination number	22	942	1554	2289
Initial population size	10	10	10	10
Selection size	2	7	5	5
Maximum number of rounds	10	20	50	10
Minimum tness	100	100	100	1000
Crossover probability	25	50	25	25
Neutral mutation probability	75	75	50	75
Positive mutation probability	50	50	50	25
Negative mutation probability	25	75	75	75
Number of refused modules	250	230	175	262
Elapsed time (s)	0.5465	0.544	0.6885	0.5295
Cash index	15450	13540	12977	14399
Goodnes index	113	108	107	104

Table 2 chesh index and inversely proportional to both the number of refused modules and the elapsed time. It is also possible to tune this goodness function in order to give more importance to the first two components (for instance, by using this function for the goodness index, $Goodness = \frac{CI^2}{ET*RM^2}$,the result will be a solution optimized in terms of the number of refused modules) or to the last one (for instance, by using the following function, $Goodness = \frac{CI}{ET^2*RM}$, the result will be a solution optimized with respect to timing performance).

Table 3 presents two combinations of parameters that lead to a very small number of refused modules (both combinations have achieved less then 200 refused modules). In both these combinations the maximum number of rounds has been set to 50 and in the second one the initial population size has been set to 50 too.

Table 3. Refused modules optimization

Combination number	1554	1891
Initial population size	10	50
Selection size	5	37
Maximum number of rounds	50	50
Minimum tness	100	100
Crossover probability	25	50
Neutral mutation probability	50	25
Positive mutation probability	50	25
Negative mutation probability	75	25
Number of refused modules	175	180
Elapsed time (s)	0.6885	1.792
Cash index	12977	17381
Goodnes index	107	54

Table 5 shows the top three combinations that are able to perform the allocation of a requested module in a very short time. By using these combinations, in fact, it is possible to accomplish a single module request in less than 0.2 milliseconds, since 2500 modules requests require less than 0.5 seconds. All the combinations presented in Table 5 are characterized by an initial population size of 10, by a selection size of 7, by a maximum number of 10 and by a minimum fitness of 100.

Table 4. Timing optimization

Combination number	166	169	179
Initial population size	10	10	10
Selection size	7	7	7
Maximum number of rounds	10	10	10
Minimum tness	100	100	100
Crossover probability	25	25	25
Neutral mutation probability	25	25	50
Positive mutation probability	50	75	75
Negative mutation probability	25	25	50
Number of refused modules	522	546	335
Elapsed time (s)	0.473	0.476	0.477
Cash index	12579	11854	14770
Goodnes index	51	46	92

Finally, Figure 6 shows a comparison between timing performance of the genetic algorithm and an exhaustive approach. The experiment has been performed on a reconfigurable module 8 columns wide. Communication overhead (that is needed in order both to perform a module request and to know where the module has been placed) is around 1 ms. Since communication with the Reconfigurator Manager occurs two times, the total communication overhead is around 2 ms. These values, that can be found in Table 5, are the same for both the genetic algorithm and the exhaustive approach.

On the other hand, the Reconfigurator Manager overhead strictly depends on the algorithm that has been chosen. With an exhaustive approach, around 3 ms are needed in order to perform the allocation phase, while the genetic algorithm is able to decrease this value to 1 ms (introducing a negligible worsening in the quality of the output, as shown by the previous experimental results). Thus, the adoption of a Reconfigurator Manager based on the proposed genetic algorithm provides the possibility to achieve a total speedup of ~ 1.5, since the genetic algorithm makes it possible for the Reconfiguration Manager to perform the allocation phase around 3 times faster.

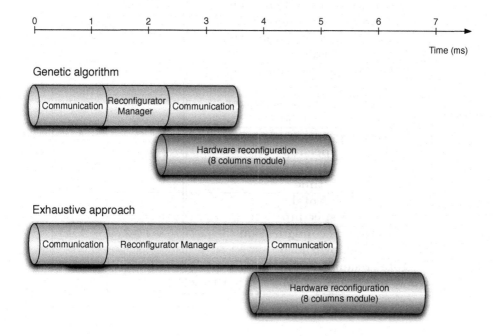

Fig. 6. Timing performance comparison

7   Conclusions

Figure 5 proves that the goodness index (Y-axis), evaluated for all the possible combinations of the parameters (X-axis), is a cyclic function and that it is significantly affected by the changes in the parameters value.

Furthermore, results presented in Section 6 have shown how it is possible to perform an allocation of a requested module with a different combination of parameters in order to achieve different optimizations. It is possible either to minimize the number of refused modules or to reduce the time required for the computation. It is also possible, finally, to use a combination of parameters that optimizes the goodness index; this makes it possible to achieve an optimal compromise between the three presented metrics.

The genetic algorithm presented in Section 4 and extended as described in Section 5 has been proved to be an effective solution for dynamically reconfigurable modules allocation.

Table 5. Timing performance comparison

Algorithm	Exhaustive	Genetic
Hardware reconfiguration (8 columns module)	$\sim 3\ ms$	$\sim 3\ ms$
Communication overhead (request)	$\sim 1\ ms$	$\sim 1\ ms$
Communication overhead (response)	$\sim 1\ ms$	$\sim 1\ ms$
Reconfiguration Manager overhead	$\sim 1\ ms$	$\sim 3\ ms$
Reconfiguration Manager speedup	~ 3	1
Total time	$\sim 5\ ms$	$\sim 7\ ms$
Total speedup	$\sim 1.5\ ms$	1
Total reconfiguration overhead	$\sim 2\ ms$	$\sim 4\ ms$
Total reconfiguration overhead w.r.t. hardware reconfiguration time	$\sim$66 %	$\sim$133 %

References

1. Xilinx Inc., Two Flows of Partial Reconfiguration: Module Based or Dif- ference Based, Tech. Report XAPP290, Xilinx Inc., November 2003.
2. Xilinx Inc., Early Access Partial Reconfiguration User Guide, Tech. Report UG208, Xilinx Inc., March 2006.
3. Xilinx Inc., Virtex-4 User Guide, Tech. Report UG070, Xilinx Inc., April 2007.
4. Xilinx Inc., Virtex-5 User Guide, Tech. Report UG190, Xilinx Inc., February 2007.
5. K. Bazargan, R. Kastner, M. Sarrafzadeh *Fast template placement for reconfig-urable computing systems*, IEEE design and test - Special issue on reconfigurable computing, pages 68-83, Volume 17, Issue 1, January 2000.
6. H. Kalte, M. Porrmann, U. Ruckert *System-programmable-on-chip approach en-abling online fine-grained 1D-placement*, IPDPS'04, Workshop 3, page 141.
7. H. Kalte, M. Porrmann, U. Ruckert *A Prototyping Platform for Dynamically Re-configurable System on Chip Designs*, Proceedings of the IEEE Workshop Hetero-geneous reconfigurable Systems on Chip (SoC), 2002.
8. Alberto Donato and Fabrizio Ferrandi and Marco D. Santambrogio and Donatella Sciuto *Coperating system support for dynamically reconfigurable SoC architectures.*, IEEE-SoCC, 2005.
9. Vincenzo Rana, Chiara Sandionigi and Marco Domenico Santambrogio, *A genetic algorithm based solution for dynamically reconfigurable modules allocation*, South-ern Conference on Programmable Logic, pages 183-186, 2007.

The Hazard-Free Superscalar Pipeline Fast Fourier Transform Architecture and Algorithm

Bassam Mohd   Earl E. Swartzlander, Jr.   Adnan Aziz

Abstract. This chapter examines the superscalar pipeline Fast Fourier Transform algorithm and architecture. The algorithm presents a memory management scheme that avoids memory contention throughout the pipeline stages. The fundamental algorithm, a switch-based FFT pipeline architecture and an example 64-point FFT implementation are presented. The pipeline consists of $\log_2 N$ stages, where N is number of FFT points. Each stage can have M Processing Elements (PEs.)   As a result, the architecture speed up is $M*\log_2 N$. The pipeline algorithm is configurable to any $M > 1$.

I. INTRODUCTION

THE FAST FOURIER TRANSFORM (FFT) ALGORITHM, presented in [1], is a standard method for computing the Discrete Fourier Transform (DFT). The FFT algorithm consists of $\log_2 N$ loops; where each loop executes N/2 complex operations. FFT processor design has been researched extensively in the last few decades for speed, area and power optimization. As a result, many implementations have been proposed and developed to address one or more of the following optimization areas: architecture, memory access and power consumption. A variety of *FFT architectures* have been proposed, which employ different techniques such as pipelining, multi-processing and cache-design, as shown in Figure 1 [2]. A *single memory* architecture consists of a scalar processor connected to a single N-word memory via a bidirectional bus. While this architecture is simple, its performance suffers from inefficient memory bandwidth. A *cache memory* architecture adds a cache memory between the processor and the memory to increase the effective memory bandwidth. A *dual memory* architecture uses two memories connected to a digital array signal processor. A memory controller generates addresses to memories in a ping-pong fashion. The *processor array* architecture consists of independent processing elements, with local buffers, which are connected using an interconnect network. Finally, the *pipeline FFT* architecture utilizes $\log_r N$ blocks; each block consists of delay lines and radix-r butterfly units.

Processor *memory access* is another area of optimization that has received considerable research. Several algorithms have been proposed to avoid memory contention. Specifically, the address generation algorithm and logic are optimized for speed and area. A memory address generation scheme was presented by Cohen in [3], that allows parallel organization of memory so that the pairs of data that are used at any instant reside in different memories. The address generation is based on a counter,

Please use the following format when citing this chapter:

Mohd, B., Swartzlander, E.E. and Aziz, A., 2009, in IFIP International Federation for Information Processing, Volume 291; *VLSI-SoC: Advanced Topics on Systems on a Chip*; eds. R. Reis, V. Mooney, P. Hasler; (Boston: Springer), pp. 227–248.

shifters and rotators. In [4], Pease proposed dividing the memory into sub-memories for overlapping the access. He observed that the operand addresses differ only in the (n-i)-th bit for the butterfly operand pair in stage i, where n is the number of address bits. A multi-bank memory address assignment for a radix-r FFT was developed in [5]. A fast address generation scheme is described in [6] with hardware cost comparable to the address generation scheme in [3]. Ma and Wanhammar presented an address generation scheme in [7] to reduce the hardware complexity and power consumption. Power is reduced by activating only half of the memory during memory access and by minimizing the number of memory accesses. The methods do not address conflicts for multi-processors accessing memory simultaneously.

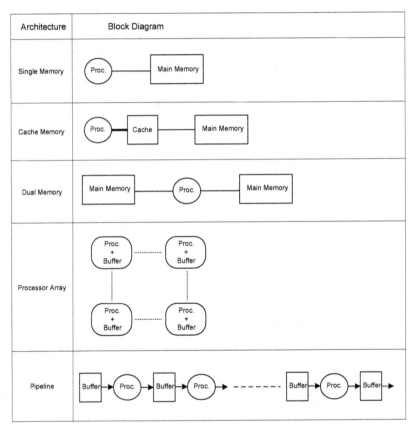

Fig. 1. FFT Processor Memory-System Architectures (after [2])

Lastly, several *power reduction* techniques were designed for energy-efficient processors; including techniques to reduce memory accesses. A cache-memory architecture was described in [8] to reduce communication energy between FFT processors and memories. In [9] and [10], Zhong, *et al.* described a power-scalable reconfigurable ring-architecture multiprocessor for a single chip FFT/IFFT processor.

The processor is capable of processing different FFT sizes with scalable power across
FFT sizes. However, while the use of the processor ring architecture seems to be an
interesting idea, the case for using the ring architecture to compute FFTs is weak. The
architecture seems to be better suited for more serialized computations such as FIR
filters. Also, large values of N require more complex processor programs. Further,
power does scale well for $N \leq 128$.

This chapter presents a superscalar pipeline architecture to achieve maximum speed
for FFT processing. A switch fabric controls and connects single-port memories and
processing elements (PEs). A memory management algorithm avoids memory access
contention. Rearranging data in the memories requires tracking them throughout the
pipeline to process the right pair of data for FFT computations. The ordering of data
elements is used to calculate the twiddle factors and other important indices. The
algorithm provides an implicit method to track data. The superscalar pipeline achieves
a speed up of $M*\log_2 N$.

The chapter is organized as follows. Section II discusses current pipeline designs.
Next, Section III explains the pipeline architecture and analyzes pipeline speedup
hazards and optimizations. Section IV discusses hazard conditions and resolutions. It
provides a pseudo code for the pipeline memory management algorithm. Section V
details the design of a 64-point FFT with emphasis on the data movement and storage
in the pipeline and memories. Section VI compares the proposed design with other
pipeline FFTs.

II. EXISTING PIPELINE FFT ARCHITECTURES

This section reviews the main pipeline FFT architectures. Groginsky and Works
developed an early pipeline FFT design [11]. Several pipeline FFTs have been
implemented [12]-[14]. Later, several pipeline architectures were proposed and
designed [15]-[17]. Pipeline FFT processors consist of $\log_r N$ stages, each stage
utilizes variable sizes of memories and complex multipliers/adders depending on the
pipeline type. Because it performs $\log_r N$ butterflies in parallel, the radix-r pipeline
FFT processor has as a speed-up of (at least) $\log_r N$ compared to an FFT performed on
a single radix-r FFT processor. Based on the number of paths between stages, FFT
pipelines are classified into Single-path Delay Feedback (SDF) and Multi-path Delay
Commutator (MDC). The modular pipeline constructs the pipeline from two smaller
pipelines to reduce power. The rest of this section will explain the SDF, MDC and
modular pipelines.

SDF Pipeline FFT

The SDF pipeline FFT has one path between stages, as shown in Figure 2. The
pipeline uses feedback registers in each stage. The feedback registers store previous
stage outputs for use by the butterfly. Figure 2 illustrates the SDF pipeline FFT for a

radix-r N-point FFT and shows an example of an 8-point radix-2 pipeline [15], [16]. Each SDF stage is comprised of:

- A radix-r FFT butterfly. Each butterfly is followed by a complex multiplier (shown explicitly in Figure 2), with the exception of the last stage.
- Shift registers to hold intermediate values. For stage i, the number of shift registers is $(r-1)(N/r^{(stage+1)})$, e.g., stage 0 has $(r-1)(N/r)$ registers.

The pipeline hardware complexity depends on the number of delay elements and multipliers. The total number of complex multipliers is $(\log_r N - 1)$ [15], [16]. Additionally, the total number of registers in the pipeline is N-1. A high radix SDF (i.e., r > 2) can be also implemented by cascading several radix-2 processing elements referred to as 2^s [15]. Calculating pipeline throughput and complexity is straightforward. The SDF pipeline accepts a new point each clock cycle. Further, it outputs one point per cycle. Therefore, the pipeline throughput is one point per cycle.

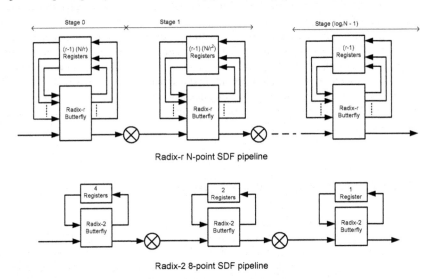

Radix-r N-point SDF pipeline

Radix-2 8-point SDF pipeline

Fig. 2. SDF Pipeline FFT (after [15])

MDC Pipeline FFT

The radix-r MDC pipeline FFT utilizes *r* paths between stages, as shown in Figure 3 [15], [16]. With the exception of one path, all paths utilize delays with different numbers of registers. Each stage receives *r* intermediate results from the previous stage, and passes *r* outputs to the next stage. An example of an 8-point radix-2 MDC pipeline FFT is shown in Figure 3. An MDC stage is comprised of:

- An *r*-input commutator,
- A radix-r butterfly which includes *(r-1)* complex multipliers

- Two sets of shift registers. The first set is located before the commutator (shown as
  D). This set does not exist in stage 0. The second set is situated after the
  commutator. Moreover, the number of registers in the j-th element of each set in
  stage i can be expressed as: $Di_j = DDi_j = j \times (N / r^{i+1})$. An example of the shift
  register sizes for a 1024-point radix-4 pipeline FFT is shown in Table 1.

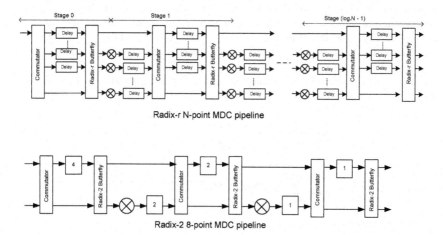

Radix-r N-point MDC pipeline

Radix-2 8-point MDC pipeline

Fig. 3. Radix -r N-point MDC Pipeline (after [16])

Table 1. DMC Delay Element Sizes for a 1024 Point Radix-4 FFT Processor

Stage	D size	DD size
0	N/A	64, 128, 192
1	16, 32, 48	16, 32, 48
2	16, 32, 48	16, 32, 48
3	4, 8, 12	4, 8, 12
4	1, 2, 3	1, 2, 3

The pipeline complexity is a function of the number and size of delay shift
registers, adders and multipliers. The total number of delay registers is (r+1)N/2 − r.
In addition, there are *(r-1) (log$_r$N -1)* complex multipliers and *2(r-1) (log$_r$N -1)*
complex adders in the pipeline [12], [16]. In contrast to the SDF pipeline, the MDC
pipeline receives r points and outputs r points in each clock cycle. Thus, the pipeline
throughput is r.

The Modular Pipeline

El-Khasahab, *et al.* developed the modular pipeline FFT detailed in [18]-[20]. The N-point modular pipeline FFT consists of two $\sqrt{N}$ -point FFT modules joined by a specialized center element. The center element contains coefficient and data memory as well as addressing, routing and control logic. The modular pipeline FFT significantly reduces the size of the shift registers. Moreover, the coefficient storage is concentrated within the center element, which can be implemented using energy-efficient RAM memories. Further, the throughput of the modular pipeline FFT is identical to that of the standard pipeline FFT, although the end-to-end latency is very slightly higher.

The modular pipeline FFT algorithm is expressed mathematically by the following equation, which demonstrates the two-stage N-point FFT:

$$X(\sqrt{N}k_1 + k_0) = \sum_{m_0=0}^{\sqrt{N}-1} W_N^{m_0 k_0} \left(\left(\sum_{m_1=0}^{\sqrt{N}-1} x(\sqrt{N}m_1 + m_0)W_{\sqrt{N}}^{m_1 k_0} \right) \times W_{\sqrt{N}}^{m_0 k_1} \right) \tag{1}$$

$$X(\sqrt{N}k_1 + k_0) = \sum_{m_0=0}^{\sqrt{N}-1} \sum_{m_1=0}^{\sqrt{N}-1} x(\sqrt{N}m_1 + m_0)W_N^{m_1 k_0 \sqrt{N} + m_0 k_1 \sqrt{N} + m_0 k_0}$$

where: $0 \le k_0, k_1 \le \sqrt{N} - 1$

To obtain the correct results, the transforms of the first stage are combined (in a fixed way) and fed to the second stage. Further, adjustment is made for intermediate results prior to second stage. Figure 4 shows how to construct a 16-point FFT with the second stage having same four FFTs as first stage. This demonstrates that the N-point FFT is now divided into two $\sqrt{N}$ point FFTs.

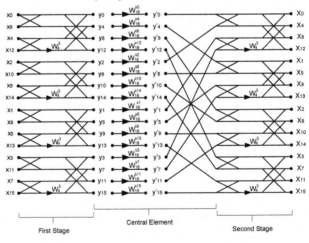

Fig. 4. 16-Point FFT Butterfly with Identical First and Second Stages [18]

Figure 5 shows the overall architecture of an N-point radix-2 modular pipeline
FFT. It consists of the two $\sqrt{N}$ -point FFT blocks and a center element. The center
element includes an address generator, RAMs for storing intermediate values and
ROMs for the coefficients. The design allows data to be both read and written
simultaneously to maximize performance. The pipeline operation can be explained as
follows. Two discrete inputs are received from the left side of the pipeline. The
address generation guarantees the two points have different parities, and hence they
reside in different memories. Once $\sqrt{N}$ points have been output from the first stage,
the control dispatches intermediate data to second stage. At the same time, the next
$\sqrt{N}$ points begin entering the first stage. Hence the pipeline is able to input and
output data every clock.

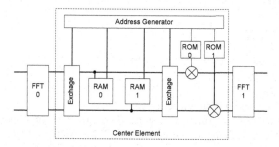

Fig. 5. Radix-2 Modular Pipeline Architecture [19]

Table 2 compares the modular pipeline with a conventional N-point pipeline FFT.
Despite the fact that it requires a larger memory; the modular pipeline has fewer shift
registers. The modular pipeline FFT requires an additional pre-rotation multiplication
and has very slightly higher latency than the standard pipeline FFT.

Table 2. Complexity of Radix-r Conventional and Modular Pipeine FFTs Using Optimum
Sized Stages

Parameter	STANDARD	Modular
ROM (Coefficient)	N-r	$2(\sqrt{N}-r)$
Shift Registers	N-r	$2(\sqrt{N}-r)$
Complex Multipliers	$\log_r(N)-1$	$\log_r(N)-1$
Central Element RAM	0	N
Throughput	r points / cycle	r points / cycle
Delay	$2\left(\dfrac{N}{r}\right)$	$\dfrac{2}{r}\left(N+\sqrt{N}\right)$

III. THE SWITCH-BASED ARCHITECTURE

This section describes the superscalar pipeline architecture for a radix-2 FFT.

Superscalar Pipeline Architecture

The pipeline architecture of an N-point radix-2 FFT consists of $\log_2(N)$ stages. Figure 6 shows a block diagram of the pipeline stage. Stage i of the pipeline executes the i-th loop of the Radix-2 decimation-in-frequency FFT algorithm.

Each stage consists of:

1. A switch fabric that connects PEs and memories.
2. PEs that have three inputs (a, b, w) and two outputs (c, d) and perform the radix-2 butterfly operation:

$$c = a + b$$
$$d = (a - b) * w \tag{1}$$

   (a, b) are inputs, *w* is the twiddle factor and *(c, d)* are outputs. There are *M* PEs per stage, where
   - $N/2 \geq M \geq 2$
   - $M = 2^p$, where *p* is an integer $p > 1$.

3. Memories that store intermediate results. There are 4*M single-port memories per stage, the size of each memory is equal to N/(2*M). Memories can be implemented as RAM, caches, register files or flip-flops, based on the size of the memory and cost constraints. One half of the input memories will be active per cycle, while the other half will be active in the following cycle

4. Memories that store twiddle factors. Since the twiddle factors do not change, the twiddle factor memories can be implemented as ROMs. There are M ROMs per stage, each with size equal to N/(2*M) words.

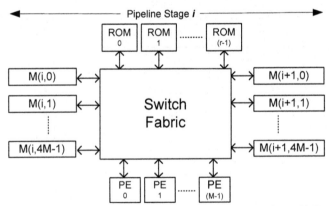

Fig. 6. Block Diagram of the Switch-Based Pipeline Stage [21]

Figure 7 shows an overview of pipeline architecture. Each stage is capable of
calculating M radix-2 butterfly results. Using the Instruction Level Parallelism (ILP)
classification from [22], the architecture is a superscalar machine with Instruction
Parallelism (IP) equal to M. It is also a super-pipeline where each cycle has $N/(2*M)$
minor-cycles. The architecture applies to the decimation-in-time FFT as well, where
the specifications of stage i in the decimation-in-time algorithm is the same as that of
stage $\log_2(N)$–i in the decimation-in-frequency algorithm. A scalar machine takes
$(N/2)*\log_2(N)$ steps to execute an N-point radix-2 FFT algorithm. The architecture
consists of $\log_2(N)$ stages, where each stage executes M operations. Therefore, the
pipeline speedup is: $M*\log_2(N)$. The maximum pipeline speedup is $(N/2)*\log_2(N)$,
when $M = N/2$. In this case memories are reduced to registers, and the switch fabric
connects each any register to any PE. Clearly, while this case provides the most speed
up, its hardware is expensive. The optimum value of M is decided by design
parameters: speed, area and power.

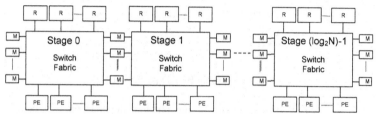

Fig. 7. Overview of the Pipeline Architecture [21]

Pipeline Design Optimization

Upon close examination of the FFT algorithm, it is clear that not all twiddle factors
are used in all stages. Also, the algorithm allows PEs to have identical twiddle factors
in some stages, and therefore, not all the ROMs are required. In fact, the number and
size of ROMs per stage can be reduced as outlined in Table 3.

Table 3. Number and Size of ROM Size Per Stage

Stage "i"	Number of ROMs	Size of ROM
0	M	$N/(2*M)$
$\log_2 M \geq i \geq 0$	M	$N/(M* 2^i)$
$i > \log_2 M$	$M/2^{(i- \log 2M)}$	1

If the pipeline is designed for a specific value of N, where N is fixed, the pipeline
connectivity and twiddle factors are fixed. As a result, the design implementation can
be optimized since the connectivity of each stage is predetermined. Figure 8 illustrates
the connectivity of 16-point 2-PE pipeline. Furthermore, in many computations the
value of the twiddle factor is one. A twiddle factor of one reduces the PE computation
to add/subtract operations. Also, several PEs execute specific sets of twiddle factors,
which can lead to design simplification.

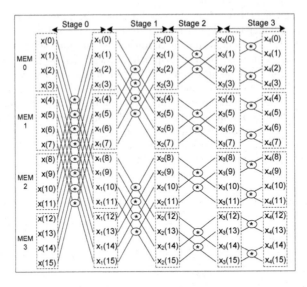

Fig. 8. Example FFT Data Flow [21]

As indicated earlier, the speed up of the pipeline depends on two factors: the number of PEs/stage (i.e., M) and the number of stages ($\log_2(N)$) since Speedup = $M*\log_2(N)$. One might ask, *"Given fixed target speedup (e.g., S), which factor should be increased to achieve more efficient design: the number-of-stages or the number-of-PEs/stage?"* Consider a pipeline with a speedup of S with two designs: Design A and design B, as shown in Table 4. Design A has one PE per stage, while design B has one stage. Clearly,

- Design B requires less memory than design A since the design A total memory is proportional to S.
- Design A switch fabric is simpler than that of design B. The complexity of the design B switch fabric is proportional to S^2.

Table 4. Analyzing Speed Up Factors

Parameter	Design A	Design B
Number of Stages	S	1
Number of PEs per Stage	1	S
Memory Size	N/2	N/(2*S)
Number of Memories	4*(S+1)	2*S
Total Memory	2*N*(S+1)	N
Switch Complexity	2*2	S*S

The main disadvantage of the increasing the number of stages is the increase in total memory. On the other hand, increasing the number of PEs per stage increases the complexity of the switch fabric. Hence, the tradeoffs between the two factors depend

on the constraints on the total memory and the maximum complexity of the switch.
Only specific design goals and technology processes can determine the optimum
solution.

Pipeline Hazards

The main source of hazards in the pipeline is memory contention. Memory
contention occurs when one or more PEs requests two or more accesses to a given
memory at the same time. Memory contention results in stalling the pipeline and
reduces the system speed. In the decimation-in-frequency FFT, memory contention
does not occur in the early stages, it occurs from stage $\log_2(M)+1$ to the last stage. In
the decimation-in-time FFT, contention affects stage 0 to stage $\log_2(N) - \log_2(M) - 1$.

Figure 8 shows an example of memory contention for N=16 and M=2. It is clear
that stage 0 and stage 1 have no contention. However, contention occurs in stage 2
and stage 3. Observe the following:

- In stage 2 the inputs for the top PE are $x_2(0)$ and $x_2(2)$, both of which reside in
  MEM0.
- In stage 3 the inputs for the top PE are $x_3(0)$ and $x_3(1)$, both of which reside in
  MEM0.

One solution for memory contention is to use a multi-port memory. However,
multi-port memories are expensive and can slow down the system performance. In
addition, the later stages of the pipeline have higher degree of contention which
requires more ports in the memory. Eventually, it becomes impractical to implement
the required multi-port memory. Moreover, the number of memory ports varies in the
memory hierarchy. Register files usually have more ports than caches and SRAMs.
Requiring a certain number of memory ports restricts where the intermediate results
can be saved in the memory system. Another solution to resolve memory contention
is to employ a memory management mechanism to mitigate the hazard, as discussed
in the next section.

IV. HAZARD FREE PIPELINE ALGORITHM

The main idea of the algorithm is resolve memory contention in the early stages of
the pipeline. The rest of the section describes the hazard conditions, memory
management operations and the algorithm.

Detecting Pipeline Hazards

From Figure 8, in stage 0, $x(0)$ and $x(8)$ go to PE_0. Similarly, $x(1)$ and $x(9)$ go to
PE_1,..., etc. Define stage distance as the index delta in each stage. The stage distance
for a 16-point pipeline FFT is shown in Table 5.

Table 5. Stage Distance For 16-point Pipeline FFT

Stage	Stage Distance	
	Decimation-In-Frequency	Decimation-in-Time
0	8	1
1	4	2
2	2	4
3	1	8

In general, for an N-point pipeline FFT, the stage distance for stage i is equal to $N/2^{(i+1)}$. Memory contention occurs when the stage distance falls in a single memory space. From Section III, the memory size is equal to $N/(2*M)$. Hence, memory contention occurs in stage i if the following condition is satisfied:

$$N/2^{(i+1)} \le N/(2^M)$$ (2)

$$i \ge \log_2(M)$$

A stage that satisfies condition (2) will be referred to as a hazard stage; the rest of the stages are safe stages. For instance, in Figure 8, stage 2 and stage 3 are hazard stages. Define memory pair $(i, j)_t$ as memory location $x(i)$ and $x(j)$ for stage t. In stage 2, the following memory pairs are hazard pairs: $(0, 2)_2$, $(1, 3)_2$, $(4, 6)_2$, $(5, 7)_2$. Other pairs will be referred to as safe pairs, for instance $(3, 5)_2$. The stage distance can be represented in binary form:

Stage-3 distance = 001

Define pair $(i, j)_t$ as a hazard pair if and only if:

1. t is a hazard stage
2. The bit wise Exclusive-OR of addresses i and j is equal to the stage t distance.

For example, the address pair $(5, 7)_2$ is a hazard pair since:

Stage-2 distance = 2_{10}

$5_{10} \oplus 7_{10} = 101_2 \oplus 111_2 = 010_2 = $ *Stage-2 distance*

On the other hand, address pair $(3, 5)_2$ is a safe pair because:

$3_{10} \oplus 5_{10} = 011_2 \oplus 101_2 = 110_2 \ne$ *Stage-2 distance*

Memory Management Operations

Let $x_i(t)$ and $x_j(t)$ be the i-th and j-th elements in stage t and $i < j$. Define the memory management operations as follows (see Figure 9):

- **Normal Operation**: Inputs $x_i(t)$ and $x_j(t)$ are provided to the first and second inputs of the PE: a, b. The results c and d are saved in $x_i(t+1)$ and $x_j(t+1)$.
- **Shuffle Operation** affects how PE results are saved back in memory. In shuffle operation, the results c and d are saved in $x_j(t+1)$ and $x_i(t+1)$
- **Swap Operation**: The swap operation affects the order of PE inputs. In swap operation, $x_i(t)$ is provided to b (instead of a) and $x_j(t)$ is provided to a (instead of b). The reason for the swap operation is because the PE is an asymmetric unit and the memory management algorithm changes the normal order of data in the

memory. If the algorithm detects a case with incorrect inputs, the swap operation is
performed.

- **Swap and shuffle operation**: A PE operation can have both swap and shuffle
memory operations at the same time.

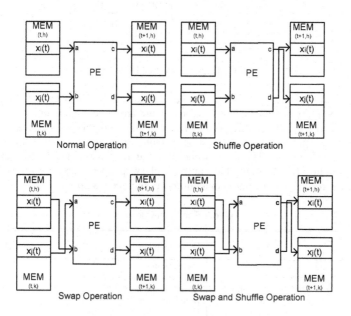

Fig. 9. Memory Management Operations [21]

The Algorithm

The main idea of the pipeline algorithm is to identify hazard pairs in early stages
and perform memory management operations to resolve the hazard. Because data is
rearranged in memory, the algorithm has to track where data is. One idea to track the
movement of data is to use a separate memory to store the data indexes (i.e., pointers),
as shown in Figure 10. This approach provides a great flexibility in moving data in
the memory. It also simplifies the reordering logic of the final stage hardware. The
downside of this approach is it increases memory size. Also, it increases loading the
operands in the PE by one cycle to retrieve pointers from memory. Another (less
flexible) solution is to move data in memory in a fixed way to simplify data tracking
in the pipeline. This approach resolves hazards for next stage only. As a result of
reordering data in the pipeline, results from the last stage in the pipeline should be
reordered.

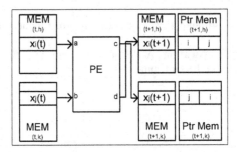

Fig. 10. Tracking Shuffled Data [21]

The algorithm utilizes several counters to calculate memory addresses and determine memory management operations. There are three main counters which are described in the upper three rows of Table 6. Other counters are derived from the main counters and described in the rest of the table. The flow of the algorithm of stage i is shown in Figure 11. The pseudocode of the algorithm is listed at the end of the section. Figure 12 illustrates the shuffle and swap operations performed by the algorithm to resolve the memory contentions in Figure 8 example.

Table 6. The Main Counters

Counter	Description/Usage
Current_Stage	Stage counter
Current_Stage_Cycle	Cycle counter within a stage
Current_Cycle_Operation	Operation counter within a cycle
Horizontal_op_index	Determines shuffle operations
Vertical_op_index	Used in generating RAM addresses
Group_Count	Determines swap operation
Current_Operation	Used in generating RAM addresses

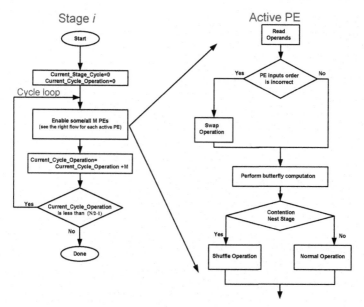

Fig. 11. Algorithm Flow in Stage *i*

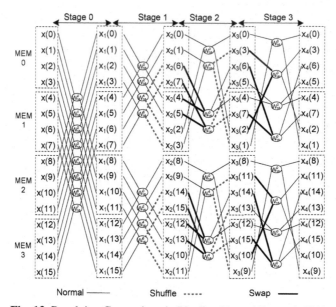

Fig. 12. Resolving Contentions in Pipeline Hazard Example [21]

Algorithm Pseudocode

```
// Preparation Step
Number_Of_Stages    = log₂NUMBER_OF_FFT_POINTS
Cycles_Per_Stage    = N/(2*NUMBER_OF_PE)
Memory_Size         = N/2^(NUMBER_OF_PE+1)
Safe_Stage          = log₂NUMBER_OF_PE
// Start main nester loops
for Current_Stage=0 to (Number_Of_Stages -1)
 Group_Size = N/2^(Current_Stage+1)
 for Current_Stage_Cycle=0 to (Cycles_Per_Stage -1)
  for Current_Cycle_Operation=0 to (NUMBER_OF_PE -1)
   // Calculate Operation Indices
   Horizontal_op_index = Cycles_Per_Stage *
                         Current_Cycle_Operation
                         + Current_Stage_Cycle
   Vertical_op_index   = NUMBER_OF_PE * Current_Stage_Cycle
                         + Current_Cycle_Operation
   Current_Stage_Rev = Number_Of_Stages - Current_Stage - 1
   Current_Group     = floor(Horizontal_op_index/
                         2^Current_Stage_Rev)
   Current_Operation = Horizontal_op_index mod 2^Current_Stage_Rev
   // Calculate Memory Address
   M0_addr = Current_Stage_Cycle
   If Current_Stage <= Safe_Stage
     M1_addr = M0_addr
   Else
     K = Safe_Stage +1
     L = Current_Stage
     M1_Addr = Reverse M0_Addr0 bits between K to L bits
   End
   // Calculate Memory Select
   If Current_Stage <= Safe_Stage
     Group_Offset = Current_Group * N /2^Current_Stage
     Group_Count  = Horizontal_op_index mod Group_Size
     Memory_Count = floor (Group_Count / Memory_Size)
     Offset       = Memory_Count * Memory_Size
     M0_Select    = Offset + Group_Offset
     M1_Select    = Offset + Group_Offset + Group_Size
   Else
     Memory_Count = Vertical_op_index mod NUMBER_OF_PE
     Offset    = 2 * Memory_Count * Memory_Size
     M0_Select = Offset;
     M1_Select = Offset + 2 * Memory_SiZe
   End
   M0_data = Memory(Current_Stage, M0_Select0) [ M0_addr ]
   M1_data = Memory(Current_Stage, M1_Select1) [ M0_addr ]
   // Determine if swap operation is required
   If  Current_Group is even
       AND Current_Sage <= Safe_Stage
     // Read data with no swap
     M0_data = Memory(Current_Stage, M0_Select) [ M0_addr ]
     M1_data = Memory(Current_Stage, M1_Select) [ M1_addr ]
   Else
     // Read Data and perform Swap
     M1_data = Memory(Current_Stage, M0_Select) [ M0_addr ]
     M0_data = Memory(Current_Stage, M1_Select) [ M1_addr ]
End
// Read Twiddle
```

```
ROM_SELECT  = Current_Cycle_Operation
ROM_Address = Current_Operation * 2^Current_Stage
  W    = ROM(Current_Stage, ROM_SELECT) [ROM_Address ]
// Enable PE to perform FFT butterfly operation
[Result1, Result0] =
       PE_Current_Cycle_Operation(M0_data, M1_data, W);
  // Perform shuffle operation
  Shuffle_Bit = log2NUMBER_OF_FFT_POINTS
                - Current_Stage - 2
  Shuffle_Flag = Horizontal_op_index [Shuffle_Bit]
  If  Current_Stage >= Sage_Stage  AND
    Shuffle_Flag == 1
    // Shuffle ResultsShuffle = 1
    Memory(Current_Stage+1, M0_Select) [ M0_addr ] = Result1
    Memory(Current_Stage+1, M1_Select) [ M1_addr ] = Result0
  Else
    // No Shuffling
    Memory(Current_Stage+1, M0_Select) [ M0_addr ] = Result0
    Memory(Current_Stage+1, M1_Select) [ M1_addr ] = Result1
  End
 end // Current_Cycle_Operation
 end // Current_Stage_Cycle loop
end // Current_Stage loop
```

V. 64-POINT PIPELINE FFT DESIGN

This section explains a 64-point pipeline FFT design using four PEs per stage.
Therefore, although there are 16 memories per stage, only eight memories will be
active memory at any time. The memory size is eight words. There are four ROMs
per stage, each with a capacity of eight words. The pipeline speed up equals 6*4=24.
The following tables detail the operation of the pipeline PEs and illustrate the memory
contents.

Table 7 gives the PE operand pairs for Stage 0. The rows give the operand pairs for
PE_0, PE_1, PE_2 and PE_3. The columns give the pairs for each micro-cycle in Stage 0
cycles. There are eight micro-cycles per stage. For example, at micro-cycle 0:

- PE_0 input operands will be MEM[0] and MEM[32]
- PE_1 input operands will be MEM[8] and MEM[40]
- PE_2 input operands will be MEM[16] and MEM[48]
- PE_3 input operands will be MEM[24] and MEM[56]

Tables 8-12 give the PE operand pairs for Stages 1-5. Underlined pairs indicate
shuffle operation. Since Stages 0-2 are safe stages, the first shuffle operation starts in
Stage 2 to prevent hazards in stage 3. Table 13 lists the memory contents for pipeline
stages. For example, the output of stage 2 has the memory contents for Memory 0 as
follows: 0, 1, 2, 3, 12, 13, 14, and 15.

Table 7. Pipeline Stage-0 Operand Paris

PE	Stage-0 Cycles							
	0	1	2	3	4	5	6	7
0	0,32	1,33	2,34	3,35	4,36	5,37	6,38	7,38
1	8,40	9,41	10,42	11,43	12,44	13,45	14,46	15,47
2	16,48	17,49	18,50	19,51	20,52	21,53	22,54	23,55
3	24,56	25,57	26,58	27,59	28,60	29,61	30,61	31,63

Table 8. Pipeline Stage-1 Operand Paris

PE	Stage-1 Cycles							
	0	1	2	3	4	5	6	7
0	0,16	1,17	2,18	3,19	4,20	5,21	6,22	7,23
1	8,24	9,25	10,26	11,27	12,28	13,29	14,30	15,31
2	32,48	33,49	34,50	35,51	36,52	37,53	38,54	39,55
3	40,56	41,57	42,58	43,59	44,60	45,61	46,62	47,63

Table 9. Pipeline Stage-2 Operand Paris

PE	Stage-2 Cycles							
	0	1	2	3	4	5	6	7
0	0,8	1,9	2,10	3,11	4,12	5,13	6,14	7,15
1	16,24	17,25	18,26	19,27	20,28	21,29	22,30	23,31
2	32,40	33,41	34,42	35,42	36,44	37,45	38,46	39,47
3	48,56	49,57	50,58	51,59	52,60	53,61	54,62	55,63

Table 10. Pipeline Stage-3 Operand Paris

PE	Stage-3 Cycles							
	0	1	2	3	4	5	6	7
0	0,4	1,5	2.6	3,7	12,8	13,9	14,10	15,11
1	16,20	17,21	18,22	19,23	28,24	29,25	30,26	31,27
2	32,36	33,37	34,38	35,39	44,40	45,41	46,42	47,43
3	48,52	49,53	50,54	51,55	60,56	61,57	62,58	63,59

Table 11. Pipeline Stage-4 Operand Paris

PE	Stage-4 Cycles							
	0	**1**	**2**	**3**	**4**	**5**	**6**	**7**
0	0,2	1,3	6,4	7,5	12,14	13,15	10,8	11,9
1	16,18	17,19	22,20	23,21	28,30	29,31	26,2	27,25
2	32,34	33,35	38,36	39,37	44,46	45,47	42,40	43,41
3	48,50	49,51	54,52	55,53	60,62	61,63	58,56	59,57

Table 12. Pipeline Stage-5 Operand Paris

PE	Stage-5 Cycles							
	0	**1**	**2**	**3**	**4**	**5**	**6**	**7**
0	0,1	3,2	6,7	5,4	12,13	15,14	10,11	9,8
1	16,17	19,18	22,23	21,20	28,29	31,30	26,27	25,25
2	32,33	35,34	38,39	37,36	44,45	47,46	42,43	41,40
3	48,49	51,50	54,55	53,52	60,61	63,62	58,59	57,56

Table 13. Pipeline Memory Content

MEM	Stages						
	Input	**0**	**1**	**2**	**3**	**4**	**5**
0	0	0	0	0	0	0	0
	1	1	1	1	1	3	3
	2	2	2	2	6	6	6
	3	3	3	3	7	5	5
	4	4	4	12	12	12	12
	5	5	5	13	13	15	15
	6	6	6	14	10	10	10
	7	7	7	15	11	9	9
1	8	8	8	8	8	8	8
	9	9	9	9	9	11	11
	10	10	10	10	14	14	14
	11	11	11	11	15	13	13
	12	12	12	4	4	4	4
	13	13	13	5	5	7	7
	14	14	14	6	2	2	2
	15	15	15	7	3	1	1
2	16	16	16	16	16	16	16
	17	17	17	17	17	19	19
	18	18	18	18	22	22	22
	19	19	19	19	23	21	21
	20	20	20	28	28	28	28
	21	21	21	29	29	31	31
	22	22	22	30	26	26	26
	23	23	23	31	27	25	25
3	24	24	24	24	24	24	24
	25	25	25	25	25	27	27
	26	26	26	26	30	30	30

	27	27	27	27	31	29	29
	28	28	28	20	20	20	20
	29	29	29	21	21	23	23
	30	30	30	22	18	18	18
	31	31	31	23	19	17	17
4	32	32	32	32	32	32	32
	33	33	33	33	33	35	35
	34	34	34	34	38	38	38
	35	35	35	35	35	37	37
	36	36	36	44	44	44	44
	37	37	37	45	45	47	47
	38	38	38	46	42	42	42
	39	39	39	47	43	41	41
5	40	40	40	40	40	40	40
	41	41	41	41	41	43	43
	42	42	42	42	46	46	46
	43	43	43	43	47	45	45
	44	44	44	36	36	36	36
	45	45	45	37	37	39	39
	46	46	46	38	34	34	34
	47	47	47	39	35	33	33
6	48	48	48	48	48	48	48
	49	49	49	49	49	51	51
	50	50	50	50	54	54	54
	51	51	51	51	55	53	53
	52	52	52	60	60	60	60
	53	53	53	61	61	63	63
	54	54	54	62	58	58	58
	55	55	55	63	59	57	57
7	56	56	56	56	56	56	56
	57	57	57	57	57	59	59
	58	58	58	58	62	62	62
	59	59	59	59	63	61	61
	60	60	60	52	52	52	52
	61	61	61	53	53	55	55
	62	62	62	54	50	50	50
	63	63	63	55	51	49	49

VI. Comparison with Other FFT Pipelines

The hardware complexity of a pipeline FFT is measured by the number of complex adders, complex multipliers and the memory size. A radix-2 butterfly consists of one complex multiplier and two complex adders which can be implemented using four real multipliers and six real adders. A radix-4 butterfly consists of three complex multipliers and eight complex adders and can be implemented using 12 real multipliers and 22 real adders. Less expensive (but slower) butterfly implementations exist especially for slow pipelines, e.g., SDF pipelines. The rest of this section uses counts of complex operations to compare different pipelines.

The SDF pipeline FFT has a total of $(log_r N -1)$ multipliers and $N-1$ delay elements. Further, the MDC pipeline FFT utilizes $(r+1)N/2 - r$ delay elements, and $(r-1)$ $(log_r N -1)$ real multipliers and roughly $2(r-1)$ $(log_r N -1)$ adders. Table 14 summarizes the hardware and timing complexities for FFT pipeline architectures discussed in references [18], [20]. The table also illustrates the complexities for the switch based architecture (shown in the last row of the table.) The other pipeline architectures require delay elements in the pipeline implementation. Delays are implemented by shift registers (which dissipate high dynamic power) or by RAMs with additional address generation hardware (which increases design complexity). The modular pipeline reduces number of delay elements to $2(\sqrt{N} -r)$. The switch-based pipeline uses SRAM memory arrays, which consume less power than registers and are easier to implement. Moreover, the throughputs of the other pipelines are limited to one (single-path) or a few (multi-path) data per clock, while the switch based implementation has a throughput of M. Unfortunately, the switch based pipeline requires larger memory size and more hardware in the data path.

Table 14. FFT Pipeline Architectures

FFT Pipeline	Multipliers	Adders	Memory Size	Speed up
Radix-2 SDF	$2(\log_4 N\text{-}1)$	$4 \log_4 N$	$N - 1$	$\log_2 N$
Radix-4 SDF	$\log_4 N\text{-}1$	$8 \log_4 N$	$N - 1$	$\log_2 N$
Radix-2 MDC	$2(\log_4 N\text{-}1)$	$4 \log_4 N$	$3N/2 - 2$	$\log_2 N$
Radix-4 MDC	$3(\log_4 N\text{-}1)$	$8 \log_4 N$	$5N/2 - 4$	$\log_2 N$
Radix-4 Single-path Delay Commutator	$\log_4 N\text{-}1$	$3 \log_4 N$	$2N/2 - 2$	$\log_2 N$
Radix-2^2 Single-path Delay feedback	$\log_4 N\text{-}1$	$4 \log_4 N$	$N - 1$	$\log_2 N$
Radix-2 Modular Pipeline	$2(\log_4 N\text{-}1)$	$4 \log_4 N$	N - 6 + 2*sqrt(N)	$\log_2 N$
Switch-Based Pipeline	$M*2(\log_4 N\text{-}1)$	$M*4 \log_4 N$	2*N* $(1+\log_2 N)$	$M* \log_2 N$

VII. CONCLUSION AND FUTURE WORK

This chapter extends results from [21]. It presents a switch-based architecture for FFT engine implementation. It also presents an algorithm to predict and resolve memory contentions. As a result the pipeline speedup is M*$\log_2$N, where N is the number of points and M is the number of processing elements. An implementation of a 64-point FFT machine using the proposed architecture is presented. The architecture compares favorably to other FFT pipelines. Future research should focus on reducing power consumption of the FFT pipeline.

References

[1] J. W. Cooley and J. W. Tukey, "An algorithm for the machine calculation of complex Fourier series," *Mathematics of Computation,* vol. 19, pp. 297-301, 1965.

[2] B. M. Baas, "A low-power high-performance 1024-point FFT processor," *IEEE Journal of Solid-State Circuits,* vol. 34, pp. 380–387, March 1999.

[3] D. Cohen, "Simplified control of FFT hardware," *IEEE Transactions on Acoustics, Speech, and Signal Processing*, vol. ASSP-24, pp. 577-579, 1976.

[4] M. C. Pease, "Organization of large scale Fourier processors," *JACM*, vol. 16, pp. 474-482, 1969.

[5] L. G. Johnson, "Conflict free memory addressing for dedicated FFT hardware," *IEEE Transactions on Circuits and Systems, II*, vol. 39, pp. 312-316, 1992.

[6] Y. Ma, "An effective memory addressing scheme for FFT processors," *IEEE Transactions on Signal Processing*, vol. 47, pp. 907-911, 1999

[7]   Y. Ma and L. Wanhammar, "A hardware efficient control of memory addressing for high-performance FFT processors," *IEEE Transactions on Signal Processing*, vol. 48, pp. 917-921, 2000.

[8]   B. M. Baas, "A generalized cached-FFT algorithm," *IEEE International Conference on Acoustic, Speech and Signal Processing*, 18-23 March 2005 pp. v/89 - v/92.

[9]   G. Zhong, F. Xu and A. N. Willson, Jr., "A power-scalable reconfigurable FFT/IFFT IC based on a multi-processor ring," *IEEE Journal of Solid-State Circuits*, Volume 41, Issue 2, Feb. 2006 pp. 483 - 495

[10] G. Zhong, F. Xu and A. N. Willson, Jr., "An energy-efficient reconfigurable FFT/IFFT processor based on a multi-processor ring," *XII European Signal Processing Conference (EUSIPCO)*, 2004, Vienna, Austria. pp. 2023-2026.

[11] H. L. Groginsky and G. A. Works, "A pipelined fast Fourier transform," *IEEE Transactions on Computers*, vol. C-19. pp. 1015-1019, 1970

[12] J. H. McClellan and R. J. Purdy, "Applications of Digital Signal Processing to Radar," in A. V. Oppenheim, ed., *Applications of Digital Signal Processing*, Englewood Cliffs, NJ: Prentice-Hall, pp. 239-329, 1978

[13] E. E. Swartzlander, Jr., "Systolic FFT Processors," in W. Moore, A. McCabe and R. Urquhart, eds., *Systolic Arrays*, Boston: Adam Hilger, 1987, pp. 133-140.

[14] S. M. Currie, P. R. Schumacher, B. K. Gilbert, E. E. Swartzlander, Jr. and B. A. Randall, "Implementation of a Single Chip, Pipelined, Complex, One-Dimensional Fast Fourier Transform in 0.25 µm Bulk CMOS," *IEEE International Conference on Application-Specific Systems, Architectures and Processors*, 2002, pp. 335-343.

[15] S. He and M. Torkelson, "Designing pipeline FFT processor for OFDM (de)modulation," *Proc. of URSI International Symposium on Signals, Systems, and Electronics*, 1998, pp. 257-262

[16] S. He and M. Torkelson. "Design and Implementation of a 1024-point Pipeline FFT Processor," *IEEE Custom Integrated Circuits Conference*, pp. 131–134, May 1998

[17] P.-Y. Tsai, T.-H. Lee and T.-D. Chiueh, "Power-Efficient Continuous-Flow Memory-Based FFT Processor for WiMax OFDM Mode," *International Symposium on Intelligent Signal Processing and Communication Systems (IPACS 2006)*, December 12-15, 2006.

[18] A. M. El-Khashab and E. E. Swartzlander, Jr., "The Modular Pipeline Fast Fourier Transform Algorithm and Architecture," *Proceedings of the Thirty-Seventh Asilomar Conference on Signals, Systems, and Computers*, November 9-12, 2003, Pacific Grove, CA, pp. 1463-1467.

[19] A. M. El-Khashab and E. E. Swartzlander, Jr., "A modular pipelined implementation of large fast Fourier transforms," *Proceedings of the Thirty-Sixth Asilomar Conference on Signals, Systems and Computers*, November 3-6, 2002, Pacific Grove, CA, pp. 995 – 999.

[20] A. M. El-Khashab and E. E. Swartzlander, Jr., "An architecture for a radix-4 modular pipeline fast Fourier transform," *IEEE International Conference on Application-Specific Systems, Architectures and Processors*, June 24-26, 2003, pp. 378 – 388

[21] B. J. Mohd, A. Aziz and E. E. Swartzlander, Jr. "The Hazard-Free Superscalar Pipeline Fast Fourier Transform Algorithm and Architecture," *15th Annual IFIP VLSI SoC 2007*, Atlanta, Oct, 2007

[22] J Shen and M Lipasti, *Modern Processor Design: Fundamentals of Superscalar Processors*, New York: McGraw-Hill, 2005, pp. 27-32.

System and Processor Design Effort Estimation

Cyrus Bazeghi   Francisco J. Mesa-Martinez   Jose Renau

University of California Santa Cruz
Dept. of Computer Engineering
http://masc.soe.ucsc.edu

Abstract. Design complexity is rapidly becoming a limiting factor in the design of modern high-performance digital systems. The increasing levels of design effort required to improve and implement critical processor and system structures have led to staggering design costs.

As we design ever larger and more complex systems, it is becoming increasingly difficult to estimate how much time it takes to design and verify them. Novel quantitative and optimization approaches are needed to understand and deal with the limiting effects induced by design complexity, which remain for the most part hidden from the architect. To address part of these shortcomings, this work introduces *μComplexity* and *μPCBComplexity*, a set of methodologies to measure and estimate design effort for modern processor and PCB (printed circuit board) designs.

1   Introduction

While the ability to fabricate ever larger and denser circuits is still increasing as predicted by Moore's Law, the semiconductor industry is facing several serious challenges. One of them is the cost of new processor development. Current development costs for top of the line designs are staggering, and are doubling every 4 years [10]. Another challenge is the growing difficulty to correctly design and verify the circuits — which has been called the Design and Verification Gaps [1]. As a result, according to the ITRS 2002 update [1], "the increasing level of risk that design cost and design quality present to the continuation of the semiconductor industry" is of serious concern. The design effort of modern digital systems is further compounded by the need to meet aggressive design constraints such as rising clock frequencies, thermal and power issues, reduced area, increasing number of layers, mixed signal devices, and the ever increasing component count and density.

All of these factors combined have made it increasingly difficult to estimate how much time would be required to design and verify these modern high-performance systems. Ironically, for such a resource-intensive endeavor, there is little systematic work (at least in the public domain) on measuring, understanding, and estimating the effort required by each step in the design of high-performance digital systems. If effort estimates were available early in the design process, they would help identify the critical paths in the whole design process,

Please use the following format when citing this chapter:

Bazeghi, C., Mesa-Martinez, F.J. and Renau, J., 2009, in IFIP International Federation for Information Processing, Volume 291;
VLSI-SoC: Advanced Topics on Systems on a Chip; eds. R. Reis, V. Mooney, P. Hasler; (Boston: Springer), pp. 249–269.

thus allowing resources to be more effectively allocated and procured. This is essential to keep design costs down and to increase the competitiveness of a company, as architects can access new quantitative approaches to make better design trade off decisions. This work focuses on two of the main areas of complexity in modern systems; circuit boards and processors.

Design effort is defined as the time required, in person-hours, to design and implement a given system. Design effort is equivalent to design time when the project has a single developer. For a given effort requirement, it is possible to reduce the design time by increasing the number of workers. However, as several studies in software metrics and business models have shown, increasing the number of workers may lead to decreases in overall productivity per worker. Since the conversion between design effort and design time can be approximated, the remainder of this work focuses only on design effort.

Different designs have different constraints, leading to specific challenges; typical design constraints are power, area, frequency, and manufacturing cost. For example, having area being a primary design constraint, may lead to a requirement for additional layers, more expensive package types, and/or more complex placement and routing. A design constrained by cost, on the other hand, may require a balance between number of layers, area, drill density, types of packages and possibly the number of different drill sizes. Having clear constraints is necessary in estimating layout effort as it can drastically affect complexity.

This work describes a set of methodologies for measuring and estimating the design effort for modern digital systems. These methodologies are based on the study and analysis of the correlation between multiple design statistics and the overall design effort required to implement these designs. Metrics or combinations there of with good correlation characteristics with overall design time are expected to be good design effort estimators.

This work estimates the design effort for a modern processor as being equivalent to the effort in person-months required to implement and verify the RTL (register transfer level) description of its design. This processor design estimation is based on the μ *Complexity* methodology [2], which consists of three parts: a procedure to account for the contributions of the different components of the design, accurate statistical regression of experimental measures using a nonlinear mixed-effects model, and a productivity adjustment to account for the differential in skills and productivity levels across different design teams.

In order to address some of the concerns related to PCB design time estimation, this work follows a similar approach taken in [2] as the principles that are applicable to microprocessors are also applicable to PCBs. In this work, design effort corresponds to the number of engineering-hours required for implementation (layout) of a PCB or microprocessor design.

To isolate good design metrics for PCB design effort, we explore statistics such as area, component count, pin count and device types and sizes for many PCBs. We analyze several of these statistics, and propose a metric, obtained after applying nonlinear regression over the different statistics, which we call

$\mu PCBComplexity$. In addition, we provide insights on the correlation between several statistics and the design effort for many systems with known layout times.

The evaluation shows that a simple statistics like PCB area size and number of components yield some correlation with design effort. With a 90% confidence, pins has a (0.47, 2.09) confidence interval. This means that roughly by looking at the number of pins, the typical design time error is half/double with a 90% confidence. Much better results can be achieved with the proposed $\mu PCBComplexity$ metric. In that case the confidence interval for a 90% confidence is (0.58, 1.72). This roughly means that less than 40% estimation error is achieved with a 90% confidence.

On the processor side, our data shows that any one of number of statements (Stmts), lines of code (LoC) or the fan in of logic cones (FanInLC) is a good single-metric estimator of design effort. Interestingly, this shows some similarity between hardware and software design efforts. On the other hand, it appears that the hardware estimators used elsewhere such as number of cells and transistor count used by the SIA Roadmap and Sematech are not so effective. Most of the other synthesis tools metrics such as area, power and frequency are not well correlated with design effort either. Further evaluation shows that the best estimator is a combination of the two most accurate, which we call Design Effort Estimator 1 (DEE1).

2   Overall Design Flow

The goal of this work is to develop a quantitative approach to estimate design effort based on several easily gathered statistics. This is important because being able to estimate/measure design effort is advantageous in helping to reduce design costs. In order to build a design complexity model, we analyze and gather data from several commercial PCB and processor designs. The layout times for the PCBs and the design times for the processors were well documented, which was a requirement for this analysis.

$\mu Complexity$ and $\mu PCBComplexity$ are methodologies to measure and estimate the design effort required for a processor design or PCB layout. They comprise three components. The first one is an accounting procedure whereby the design is partitioned into disjoint modules that can be measured individually. A quantification for the entire processor/PCB is obtained by aggregating all the module measurements. The second component is the application of statistical regression to these design measures to obtain an unscaled estimate of the design effort. The final component involves the multiplication of the unscaled effort estimation by a productivity factor, this is done to obtain the estimation of the design effort for a given design team.

In the following subsections, we first review a typical design flow and define the design effort that we are trying to estimate. Next, we discuss the three-component $\mu Complexity$ and $\mu PCBComplexity$ methodologies in detail. Finally, we examine some concerns about the methodologies.

2.1   Design Effort Defined

The system development timeline can be broken down into several overlapping stages as shown in Figure 1. Note that the duration of the different stages is not drawn to scale. The figure also shows an approximation of the size of the engineering team working on the processor portion of the project during each stage. For PCB design it is still fairly typical to have only small teams of 1 or 2 engineers working on the layout stage of the design, which is what we focus on in our PCB analysis.

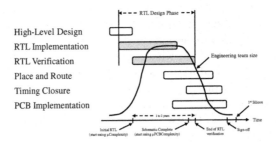

Fig. 1. System development timeline with the size of the IC engineering team. Note that the timeline is not drawn to scale.

In the *High-Level Design* stage, architects perform functional simulation and power estimation of multiple candidate designs. Based on that, they select one microarchitecture and produce a complete functional and interface description of each of its components. Examples of such components are the branch predictor, load-store queue, or floating-point unit. These components are then assigned to engineering teams for implementation. In the case of an ASIC, or if the processor is being designed for an embedded system, the PCB is also be planned during this stage. A Product Requirement Document (PRD) is produced which details the goals of the processor/ASIC and the system board (PCB).

In the *RTL Implementation* stage, engineering teams implement their assigned components in an HDL such as VHDL or Verilog. They continue refining the description until they reach an RTL-level implementation, which can be automatically translated to a gate-level netlist. Functional bugs are fixed as the verification teams discover them. Synthesis is performed to ensure that the timing, area, and power goals are being met.

In the *RTL Verification* stage, engineers create test cases to verify the functionality of individual components and of the whole chip. They perform cycle-accurate simulations and compare the results with the expected values. At this point, the verification team is only concerned with the functional correctness of the design — whether it produces correct answers in a logic-level simulation.

Circuit-level verification, in which electrical and timing parameters are verified, comes later. RTL verification is complete when the number of outstanding bugs reaches zero and stays there for a pre-agreed amount of time.

In the *Place and Route* stage, the synthesized netlist is physically placed within the chip-defined core area based on timing constraints. During the placement phase, gates are resized and some additional logical optimization may be performed. After the initial placement, the routing phase occurs and, if needed, minor placement changes are made. Once the design is successfully placed and routed, clock tree synthesis happens, whereby the clocks in the design have their buffer trees placed and routed.

In the *PCB Implementation* stage, engineers design the schematic and start the layout for the system board onto which the processor/ASIC resides. As chip interfaces become defined and stabilized the requirements for a system board design is gathered. This would include traces and foot prints for any IOs such as PCI, USB, or Ethernet. It would also include the memory system, either a bridge chip with memories, or possible just the memories if the processor/ASIC has a memory controller integrated on chip. A schematic is created and a BOM (bill of materials) is produced. These are then passed on to the layout person or team for implementation of a PCB design.

Finally, in the *Timing Closure* stage, engineers perform timing analysis of the gate-level implementation to determine the maximum clock speed of the design and to identify critical paths. A redesign may be required which could involve RTL or placement–and–route changes. A refine–test–refine loop exists between the Place-and-Route and Timing Closure stages.

As shown in Figure 1, the focus of this part of the work is the period that includes both the RTL Implementation and the RTL Verification stages. We define *Design Effort* as the number of person-months spent implementing the description of the processor in a hardware design language such as VHDL or Verilog, refining it to an RTL description, and verifying the latter for functional correctness. We exclude any additional time required to revise the design later, during the Timing Closure process. While the period considered excludes some design time, we believe that it includes the bulk of it.

In the following sections we describe the accounting procedure we use for the PCB and processor evaluations. In 2.2 we look at the accounting procedure stage of $\mu\,Complexity$, whereby the design is partitioned into disjoint modules that can be measured individually. In 2.3 we discuss the critical design parameters of a PCB and how the accounting for $\mu PCBComplexity$ is developed from them. A quantification for the entire processor is obtained by aggregating all the module measurements. In 2.4 we discuss the use of a productivity adjustment.

2.2   Approach to $\mu\,Complexity$

This assumes a processor design to represented as a collection of hardware description language (HDL) statements, thus ignoring certain design issues introduced to processor components implemented using custom layout and not standard cell designs. As described in Section 1 the design effort for a modern processor is directly proportional person-months required to implement and verify the RTL description of its design.

To measure overall design effort, estimates of the effort for each processor component must be obtained, and then added into a compounded index. However, components may be instantiated several times through any given design. Some components may also be *parameterized,* and different-sized instances could be generated. Parameters could be the width of the input or output buses, queue depth, or pipeline depth. To address these cases, we use the following two rules.

Account for a single instance of each component. When a design reuses a component (e.g., an ALU), we only count the design effort of one instance of it. The rationale is that, in accordance with the principles of modular design, the effort required to design and verify the component is a one-time cost. Once the component is designed and verified, it can be re-used elsewhere with negligible effort.

Minimize the value of component parameters. To estimate the design effort of a parameterized component, we set each parameter to the minimal value that does not result in a degenerate case. We refer to this minimization of parameters as *scaling*. The rationale is that, while different parameter values can drastically change the size of the component instance (in terms of chip area or number of gates), it is not much harder to write parameterized code than it is to write code for the smallest nontrivial instance.

More formally, consider a VHDL description where the parameterized component is implemented with GENERATE loops. We select for each parameter the smallest value that does not cause any loops or conditional statements in the RTL description to be optimized away by traditional program analysis techniques such as constant propagation and dead code elimination. The process for Verilog is more difficult to formalize because Verilog did not have an equivalent of the GENERATE construct until Verilog-2001 was introduced. However, the determination of what constitutes the minimal non-degenerate parameterization is conceptually the same.

Design Effort Estimator There are multiple metrics that may be related to design effort. Examples include the number of logic gates or the number of HDL lines in the design description. Consequently, for each component in the design (subject to the constraints of Section 2.2), we measure these metrics. Then, we select a single metric or a set of metrics (e.g., the number of gates and the number of HDL lines) and use statistical regression [11] to find how well they correlate with the person-months design effort reported by the processor designers. For each set of metrics $m_1, m_2, \ldots m_n$, we find the best values for the coefficients $w_1, w_2, \ldots w_n$ in Equation 1. The result is a *Design Effort Estimator* (*eff*):

$$\text{eff} = \frac{1}{\rho} \times \sum_{k=1}^{n} (w_k \times m_k) \qquad (1)$$

The regression model used is described in Section 3. In the equation, ρ is the productivity factor for the design team. It allows the same set of coefficients w_k to be used in different projects. The rationale for ρ is discussed next.

2.3   Approach to $\mu PCBComplexity$

Printed circuit board (PCB) design effort keeps growing due to such constraints as rising clock frequencies, thermal issues, reduced area, increasing number of layers, mixed signal devices, and the ever increasing component count and density. All of these factors combined have led to a steady rate of increase in development costs for current systems. As we design ever larger, denser and more complex systems, it is becoming increasingly difficult to estimate how much time would be required to design and verify them. To compound this problem, PCB design effort estimation still does not have a quantitative approach.

The lists of critical components of PCB designs is determined by [4]. These parameters contribute to the complexity of a design, and hence the time required to do layout. Some design parameters are dependent on other factors. For example, the size of the board is defined by the number of embedded and discrete passive components and total wiring requirements. However, the total wiring requirements are governed by the number of embedded and discrete passive components in the PCB. And furthermore, the total number of layers in the PCB depends on the size of the board, the number of embedded and discrete resistors and bypass capacitors [4].

These critical design parameters are focused towards manufacturability, not design effort estimation. We used them as a starting point in determining what parameters or metrics to analyze and include for correlation with design effort. None of the boards in our study have embedded passive components; instead we focus on the total number of all components (passive and discrete) and the pin count for them. These are easily obtainable values.

Since the routing data is not easily obtainable, the number of pins for all the components in the design is taken into account instead. While this is not an ideal metric since not all pins are used or have very short traces (VDD or GND), it is readily obtainable and does not hamper the focus of this paper, namely effort prediction starting from higher level design descriptions, such as a bill of materials (BOM) or schematics.

In order to find a metric highly correlated with design effort, several statistics were gathered from the existing designs. For each isolated board with a known design effort, we look at several statistics and apply nonlinear regression to find a highly correlated metric.

We present our design effort model as the aggregate of a set of statistics (S_i). Each of which has a specific constant (w_i), associated with it, which assigns a weight to the importance of every statistic used as input in the model. The aggregate of the statistics is inversely proportional to the productivity of a specific design team which is represented by a constant (ρ). The model is presented in Equation 2. In order to find suitable values for each of the data weights (w_i) we perform mixed nonlinear regressions on this equation. The design team productivity factor (ρ) is constant per design group, and it needs to be adjusted on a per company or design team basis. If the ρ is unknown, then the absolute design effort is invalid and only the breakdown inside the project is correct. Obtaining the value of ρ is simple; all that is needed is to have the design effort for a single project. Alternatively, it is possible to develop a productivity benchmark suite that calibrates ρ for a given company.

$$\text{Design Effort} = \frac{1}{\rho} \times \sum_{k=1}^{n} (w_k \times S_k) \tag{2}$$

In order to determine the weights that give a generalized solution to Equation 2, [2] proposes to use a mixed nonlinear regression model. If there are no productivity adjustments, it is possible to use a simpler nonlinear regression model. While the sum of a large number of random variables is distributed normally, the product of a number of random variables is distributed *lognormally* — a distribution where the logarithm of the variable is normally distributed [5]. Therefore, since the random variables have a log normal distribution an even simpler linear regression model can not be used.

To evaluate the accuracy of the model (Section 4.2), we use σ as a measure of error associated with the fit. Consequently, it is important to understand what different values of σ tell us about the quality of the estimate. For a given σ, we can find a *confidence interval* for the estimated effort. The $x\%$ confidence interval for a metric is defined to be the range of efforts ($Estimate_{low}, Estimate_{high}$) such that $P(Estimate_{low} < \text{metric prediction} < Estimate_{high}) = x/100$. For example, the 90% confidence interval gives us two values a and b such that there is a 90% chance that the actual effort is between metric prediction $\times a$ and metric prediction $\times b$.

2.4   Productivity Adjustments

In software development projects, it is well known that different development teams have different productivities. For example, it has been shown that the productivity difference between teams can be up to an order of magnitude [8]. We believe that a similar effect occurs between PCB and processor design teams. The productivity differences may be due to multiple factors, including the average experience of the designers in the team and the tools used. In our model, ρ captures this effect.

The designs under study in this analysis were produced either by a single manufacturer, or a just one design from a specific manufacturer was provided. Therefore the use of a productivity factor was not necessary as we did not obtained competing designs from multiple manufacturers of from multiple competing teams among a single manufacturer.

A Model Without Productivity Adjustments For the processor analysis, we can eliminate productivity adjustments by setting $\rho_i = 1$ for all i simplifies the statistical model. Instead of using the nonlinear mixed-effects model described in Section 3.1 to fit the weights, we can use a simpler multiple regression technique. Unfortunately, as we show in Section 4.1, the model without productivity factors fits the data poorly. We present it only for comparison with the recommended nonlinear mixed-effects model of Section 3.1.

A model without productivity adjustments may be acceptable for industrial practitioners with a very large single project, perhaps representing thousands of person-months of effort. In this case, they can set $\rho = 1$, since there is only one project and therefore no need to account for productivity differences across projects.

2.5 Issues

Ideally, we would like to use design effort estimators as soon as possible in the system design timeline. The earlier the estimations can be made, the more useful they are likely to be. After adjusting the coefficients w_i shown in Equation 1, early estimation presents a clear challenge: how to ensure that the values of the early metrics remain relevant (and valid) at later stages of the design.

To address this, we use metrics whose value changes little from initial stages of the design until completion of the RTL implementation and verification in the case of the processor, or pins and components, in the case of a PCB. Specifically, the metrics analyzed in this work can be measured once a module has been designed and before it starts to be verified. This corresponds to the point shown with an arrow in Figure 1, which is often 1 to 2 years before completing the RTL verification. The values of the metrics remain largely unchanged until the end of RTL/PCB verification. The exception is if the verification finds substantial bugs that require a major re-design.

One potential objection to the accounting procedure described is that counting each component only once regardless of its number of instances may not be appropriate. For example, at a very low level, we could consider that the entire processor is made out of logic gates, and that there are only a dozen or so types of gates. The analysis would clearly be inaccurate. However, at the high level of the functional components that we are discussing, the count-only-one heuristic is appropriate. Regardless, any given component is likely to have fewer than ten instances. At this level, scaling the effort estimate linearly with the number of instances does not seem appropriate.

In our discussion of parameter scaling in section 2.2, we argued that writing code for a parameterized component is no more difficult than writing code for the smallest nontrivial instance of it. In practice, however, the parameter values chosen for a given instance may affect the number of test vectors required for verification and, therefore, the verification time. For example, model checking and automatic theorem-proving tools may require more time to run with larger parameter values, since the size of the state space may be larger. However, this issue could be addressed, at least conceptually, by allocating more computational resources to the verification budget — not more engineer-hours.

The parameter scaling rule has another undesirable consequence. Specifically, varying the value of certain parameters may have implications on the difficulty of timing closure and, therefore, on the number of RTL redesign iterations. An example is the degree of associativity of a time-critical structure: higher associativity may make it hard to perform timing closure and may induce several redesigns. This issue suggests the need for future design effort estimators that are aware of back-end physical design and timing concerns.

Finally, our analysis has implicitly assumed that each component in the design is implemented from scratch. In practice, components are sometimes reused from older designs, often with little modifications. Integrating a reused component incurs some design effort, even if it requires no modification at all. The software engineering literature has discussed effort estimation for reused components [3]. We regard the study of reuse in hardware as a subject for future work.

Productivity Adjustments The volatility of ρ may make it difficult to use the model to make extrapolations across different projects. Once RTL coding is completed, all of the metrics are available, but it is still difficult to determine the productivity factor until after at least some of the components are completely verified. One option is to estimate ρ using data from a very recent project or to extrapolate the current value of ρ given a time series of previous values.

Unfortunately, we have no means of evaluating this approach. A second option is to assume $\rho = 1$ and use the model to make *relative* estimations only. Even without knowing ρ, we can still say that a component with an estimated design effort of $e = x$ is likely to take half as much effort to design as one with $e = 2x$. These relative estimates may be useful when allocating engineers to verification teams. They may also allow an early determination of which components are likely to delay project completion.

3   Regression Model

As indicated in Section 2.2, given a set of metrics m_1, m_2, ... m_n, the goal of the regression procedure is to find the w_1, w_2, ... w_n values for Equation 1 that provide the best fit for the person-months design effort reported by the designers. Each component in the design for which we know the design effort (e.g., fetch unit or load-store queue), is a data point consisting of the reported design effort and the measured metrics. The more data points we have, the more precise the determination of w_k is.

The data points for this work come from several small projects implemented by unrelated design teams at different times. Consequently, in addition to the usual statistical variation across data points, there is variation across teams. In statistical terms, this forces us to introduce a per-project *random effect* (represented by the productivity ρ). Therefore, we use a *nonlinear mixed-effects* model [15], which is able to deal with both *fixed* and *random* effects better than more conventional linear methods [7, 11].

In the following section, we describe the mixed-effects model that we use and then consider what would happen if we attempted to fit a simpler model without productivity adjustments.

3.1 A Nonlinear Mixed-Effects Model

When we use Equation 1 with data from multiple projects, we have one data point for each component j designed in project i. The estimated design effort eff_{ij} is given by Equation 3. Note that for each component j from project i, we have a set of n metrics m_{ijk}. There is a productivity factor ρ_i specific to each project. However, the coefficients w_k are assumed invariant across all data points. In reality, of course, the fit is not perfect and the actual (reported by designers) design efforts Eff_{ij} are different from the estimated ones eff_{ij} (Equation 4). The difference is accommodated by the ϵ_{ij} error term, which we assume is multiplicative.

$$\text{eff}_{ij} = \frac{1}{\rho_i} \times \sum_{k=1}^{n} (w_k \times m_{ijk}) \tag{3}$$

$$\text{Eff}_{ij} = \text{eff}_{ij} \times \epsilon_{ij} \tag{4}$$

To fit the mixed-effects model and determine the w_k, we need to treat ρ and ϵ as independent random variables. As such, we must provide a probability distribution for each. From software engineering, we know that productivity is determined by the product of a collection of variables (e.g., team cohesiveness, tool quality or process maturity) [3]. Since the sum of a large number of random variables is distributed normally, the product of a number of random variables is distributed *lognormally* — a distribution where the logarithm of the variable is normally distributed [5]. Similarly, software engineering studies tell us that the multiplicative error ϵ is also lognormally distributed [16]. Consequently, we use a lognormal distribution for both ρ and ϵ.

The lognormal distribution is described by two parameters: μ and σ. They represent, respectively, the mean and standard deviation of the *log* of the variable. For the ρ and ϵ distributions, we choose to set $\mu = 0$, and then let the fitting procedure determine the standard deviations σ_ρ and σ_ϵ. The result of setting $\mu = 0$ in both cases is that the median of the distributions is 1. Intuitively, this means that half of the projects have $\rho > 1$ and half have $\rho < 1$. Similarly, half of the estimations have $\epsilon > 1$ and half have $\epsilon < 1$. Figure 2 shows a lognormal distribution with $\mu = 0$, showing the difference between mean, median, and mode.

Our choice also means that the resulting estimated effort eff that we obtain is the *median* design effort. To determine the estimated mean design effort $\overline{\text{eff}}$ rather than the estimated median design effort, we would apply Equation 5.

$$\overline{\text{eff}} = \text{eff} \times e^{(\sigma_\epsilon^2 + \sigma_\rho^2)/2} \tag{5}$$

In Section 4.1, we use σ_ϵ as a measure of goodness of fit. Consequently, it is important to understand what different values of σ_ϵ tell us about the quality of

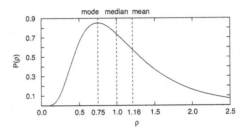

Fig. 2. Example of a lognormal distribution with $\mu = 0$.

the estimate. Specifically, we say that σ_ϵ determines a *confidence interval* for the estimated effort. The $x\%$ confidence interval for eff$_{ij}$ is defined to be the range of efforts (el_{ij}, eh_{ij}) such that $P(el_{ij} < \text{Eff}_{ij} < eh_{ij}) = x/100$. For example, the 90% confidence interval gives us two values a and b such that there is a 90% chance that the actual effort is between a and b. Figure 3 plots the 68% and 90% confidence intervals for a range of σ_ϵ. To compute the confidence interval for a given σ_ϵ and eff$_{ij}$, find the value y_h corresponding to the top of the interval and the y_l corresponding to the bottom of the interval. The confidence interval is then $(y_l \times \text{eff}_{ij}, y_h \times \text{eff}_{ij})$. For example, if $\sigma_\epsilon = 0.45$ then $y_h \approx 2.1$ and $y_l \approx 0.5$. Therefore, the 90% confidence interval for Eff$_{ij}$ is $(0.5 \times \text{eff}_{ij}, 2.1 \times \text{eff}_{ij})$.

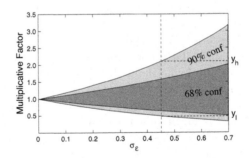

Fig. 3. 68% and 90% confidence intervals corresponding to $0 \le \sigma_\epsilon \le 0.7$. The figure demonstrates finding the multiplicative factors y_h and y_l for the 90% confidence interval corresponding to $\sigma_\epsilon = 0.45$.

We perform model fitting computation using the NLMIXED procedure from *SAS* [15], although we could also use the nlme package from *R* [19]. Equation 6 shows an alternative method for approximating rho_i given the w_k.

$$\frac{\sum_j \bar{e}_{ij}}{\sum_j E_{ij}} = 1$$

$$\rho_i \approx \frac{exp\left(\sigma_\epsilon^2/4\right) \sum_j \sum_{k=1}^n \left(w_k \times m_{ijk}\right)}{\sum_j E_{ij}} \tag{6}$$

4   Evaluation of Processor Designs

The evaluation of this work examines how accurately each of the software and synthesis metrics correlate with design effort. This section is divided into two parts, Section 4.1 shows processor design metrics and Section 4.2 shows PCB design metrics. For both cases, we also examine a few combinations of metrics.

4.1   Processor Designs

In our processor design analysis, we compare against some of the design effort estimators currently being used. Specifically, Sematech [10] and the SIA Roadmap [1] which use the number of cells and the number of transistors, respectively, to estimate effort. We also analyze other synthesis statistics which are often used to make effort estimations.

As indicated in Section 3.1, to assess the accuracy of an estimator, we report the standard deviation of its error (σ_ϵ). Lower values of σ_ϵ are better, and zero is the minimum possible value. Given a σ_ϵ, we can compute the interval for, say, 90% confidence for the true value. For the lognormal distribution used, the mapping between σ_ϵ and the 90% confidence interval.

In the following analysis, we first measure the accuracy of the different design effort estimators using our model. Then, we repeat the process without the productivity adjustment or without the $\mu Complexity$ accounting procedure.

Accuracy of Design Effort Estimators Table 1 shows the accuracy of various design effort estimators. First, Column 2 lists the reported design effort in person-months for each component of each design. Then, each of remaining columns shows data for one design effort estimator. Most of the estimators are simply the individual software or synthesis metrics. The only exception is the DEE1 estimator, which is the linear combination of two metrics — we analyze DEE1 in Section 4.1. For a given estimator, the column shows its value for each component of each design and, in the penultimate row, its σ_ϵ.

From Table 1, we see that there are a group of estimators that have a relative high accuracy (i.e., low σ_ϵ). They include Stmts, FanInLC, and Nets. For example, Stmts and FanInLC have σ_ϵ equal to 0.50 and 0.55, respectively, which, correspond to a 90% confidence interval of (0.44,2.28) and (0.40,2.47), respectively. Really, within the margin of error of our study, any one of Stmts or FanInLC has the same accuracy. The other estimators, namely Freq, *Power*, $Area_L$, $Area_S$, Cells, and FFs, have lower accuracy. For example, $Area_L$ has σ_ϵ equal to 1.23, which corresponds to a 90% confidence interval of (0.13,7.56). None of these metrics is a reasonable estimator.

Module Name	Effort (Months)	DEE1	Stmts	FanInLC	Nets	Freq (MHz)	$Area_L$ (μm^2)	Power (mW)	$Area_S$ (μm^2)	Cells	FFs
Leon3-Pipeline	24	12.8	2070	10502	4299	56	50199	80	68411	3586	1062
Leon3-Cache	6	7.3	1172	6325	1980	94	37456	57	12556	3	210
Leon3-MMU	6	4.4	721	3149	1130	84	60136	23	112765	246	699
Leon3-MemCtrl	6	5.4	938	2692	853	138	7394	5	11938	704	275
PUMA-Fetch	3	2.2	586	5192	1292	68	147096	226	555168	1809	1786
PUMA-Decode	4	6.2	1998	4724	5662	65	78076	11	47604	5189	464
PUMA-ROB	4	2.2	503	6965	9840	41	82527	733	1022	9709	922
PUMA-Execute	12	12.6	3762	18260	10681	49	92473	44	119746	10867	1725
PUMA-Memory	1	3.3	976	5034	1089	60	43418	80	115841	4337	1549
IVM-Fetch	10	8	1432	15726	4914	71	212663	8	135074	1859	1661
IVM-Decode	2	1.7	391	1044	504	104	2022	2	73	2	0
IVM-Rename	4	2.7	566	3307	1134	159	70146	1	26740	121	510
IVM-Issue	4	3.6	624	8063	4603	60	90388	2	68667	3414	2729
IVM-Execute	3	5.4	961	11045	4476	91	619561	5	154655	940	0
IVM-Memory	10	11.6	2240	19021	23247	54	267753	73	625952	12050	2510
IVM-Retire	5	5	1021	6635	3357	71	36100	2	50375	1923	924
RAT-Standard	0.6	0.7	64	3889	2905	137	34254	4	17603	2596	288
RAT-Sliding	1	1	78	5586	4936	119	52210	10	60713	4507	612
σ_e	–	0.46	0.50	0.55	0.67	0.94	1.23	1.34	2.07	2.09	2.14
σ_e $(\rho_i = 1)$	–	0.53	0.60	0.82	1.08	1.12	1.35	1.82	2.07	2.55	2.18

Table 1. Accuracy of various design effort estimators.

Freq has a 90% confidence interval as large as (0.21,4.69). While increasing processor frequency requires additional design effort, other metrics like Nets or FanInLC have higher correlation with design effort. The reason is that, to increase frequency, it is necessary to add extra pipeline stages or more complex logic. This increased effort is better measured by Nets and FanInLC.

Perhaps unsurprisingly, $Area_S$ and FFs are not well correlated with design effort. Their 90% confidence intervals are (0.03,30.11) and (0.03,33.78), respectively. The reason is that storage structures such as RAM banks are relatively simple to design. Similarly, $Area_L$ and Cells are not well correlated because simple to implement structures can occupy a lot of area and have large numbers of logic cells. Moreover, neither dynamic nor static power is well correlated with design effort as their confidence intervals are (0.11,9.06) and (0.09,10.68) respectively. Larger designs probably require more power, but are not necessarily more complicated to design.

Overall, our data shows that any one of Stmts or FanInLC is a good single-metric estimator of design effort. Interestingly, this shows some similarity between hardware and software design efforts. On the other hand, it appears that the hardware estimators used elsewhere such as Cells and transistors used by the SIA Roadmap and Sematech are not so effective. Most of the other synthesis tools metrics such as area, power and frequency are not well correlated with design effort either.

Design Effort Estimator 1 (DEE1) We have also analyzed the accuracy of estimators generated with the linear combination of groups of two metrics. As usual, we use Equation 1 from Section 2.2. We find that two-metric combinations that include Stmts, FanInLC, and Nets tend to have slightly more accuracy than those with a single metric. The ones that are the most accurate are Stmts plus

Nets, and Stmts plus FanInLC. They have the same accuracy, but we prefer the Stmts plus FanInLC estimator because, individually, the metrics are more accurate. We call the resulting estimator Design Effort Estimator 1 (DEE1).

As shown in Table 1, DEE1 has the lowest σ_ϵ, namely 0.46. This corresponds to a 90% confidence interval of (0.47,2.13). The slightly higher accuracy of DEE1 comes from the fact that its two component metrics measure slightly different underlying factors in the design.

To see the correlation between DEE1 and the reported design effort better, Figure 4 shows a scatter plot of DEE1 estimations versus reported design effort. The Figure has one data point per component and design. From the figure, we see that most of the DEE1 estimations are very close to the reported design effort. The exception is the data point for the Leon3 pipeline, where the DEE1 estimation is 12.8 months, and the reported effort is 24 months. In practice, most of the estimators in Table 1 underestimate the effort for the Leon3 pipeline. The reason is that this pipeline is more sophisticated than the other components and designs. Indeed, while IVM and PUMA only execute a subset of Alpha and PowerPC, respectively, Leon3 is a full SPARC V8 compliant processor. In addition, Leon3 is highly configurable, for example the user can select different processor and cache parameters.

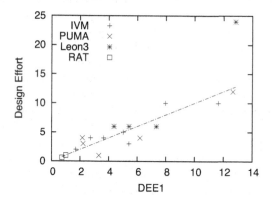

Fig. 4. Scatter plot of DEE1 estimations versus reported design effort.

Accuracy without the Productivity Adjustment The last row of Table 1 shows the σ_ϵ values that would be obtained if no productivity factor was used – in other words, if ρ_i was 1 for the Leon3, PUMA, IVM, and RAT teams. This approach was mentioned in Section 2.4.

From the values of σ_ϵ, we can see that practically all the estimators lose a significant amount of accuracy. For example, the σ_ϵ for Stmts and FanInLC becomes 0.60 and 0.82, respectively, which correspond to 90% confidence intervals of (0.37,2.68) and (0.26,3.85), respectively. Similarly, DEE1 expands its 90% confidence interval to (0.41,2.39).

The loss of accuracy for Stmts is due to several factors. Specifically, while Leon3 uses VHDL, the other designs use Verilog. Moreover, while RAT uses the more compact Verilog-2001, PUMA and IVM use the more verbose Verilog-95. Additionally, different coding styles add much noise to any correlation without productivity adjustment. To compound the problem, it is known from software projects that productivity across teams can vary by an order or magnitude [8].

The FanInLC and Nets estimators lose accuracy because each processor was designed under a different set of constraints and a different set of tools. For example, since Leon3 was designed for an area-constrained environment (FPGAs), a substantial effort was needed to reduce area and interconnections. On the other hand, PUMA's target was a high frequency CGaAs process. All these effects again add noise to any correlation.

Overall, we conclude that, to have good processor design estimation accuracy productivity adjustments are required.

4.2   Evaluation of PCB Designs

We analyze 12 different printed circuit boards from two separate companies. Table 2 shows the main results and characteristics for each of these. The first column corresponds to each of the statistics or metrics measured. Columns B1 to B12 correspond to each of the boards. The last column corresponds to the σ between the row and design effort. Since the boards either were designed by the same team, or we only had one board from a particular company, we do not evaluate the productivity factor (ρ). This simplifies the analysis, and we can use nonlinear regression instead of the mixed-effects nonlinear regression model. With σ we can compute the confidence interval. For the lognormal distribution used, the mapping between σ and the 90% confidence interval is shown in Figure 3. We use this chart to compare the accuracy of different estimators.

The design effort values were obtained by interviewing the original designers. Obviously, there is perfect correlation with itself so $\sigma = 0$. A zero σ results in a perfect $(1,1)$ confidence interval. We now proceed to analyze easily available statistics like number of components and pin count. These two sets of statistics are easily available before the PCB design starts. They are part of the PCB specification.

From the boards analyzed, we observe that it is best to use the total number of components to estimate design effort ($\sigma = 0.53$). Although traces for analog components and digital components are more difficult than traces for passive components, the low amount of digital and/or analog components on several of the boards make it difficult to use them as a method to estimate effort. Using Figure 3 and a $\sigma = 0.53$, the intersection between the components line and the confidence interval line is $(0.41, 2.39)$. This means that using the number of components on the specification, we have a 90% confidence that the design effort would be between 0.41 and 2.39 times the prediction.

	B1	B2	B3	B4	B5	B6	B7	B8	B9	B10	B11	B12	σ
Design Effort	68	35	43	21	48	48	24	40	32	24	12	400	–
Components													
# Passive	213	165	101	80	108	222	116	86	83	19	47	2643	0.56
# Digital	15	0	17	0	8	2	0	11	8	4	4	94	1.79
# Analog	35	24	8	10	24	53	28	4	16	1	11	91	1.18
Total #	263	189	126	90	140	277	144	101	107	24	62	2828	0.53
Total Area	6214	9053	6964	2719	9144	6579	8104	12193	12296	777	5430	38611	0.75
Pins													
Passive	563	429	365	182	414	578	414	194	188	39	109	5843	0.62
Digital	154	0	518	0	107	32	0	175	173	88	32	6889	1.88
Analog	360	208	216	98	72	448	150	25	53	14	65	924	1.10
Total	1077	637	1099	280	593	1058	564	394	414	141	206	13647	0.45
PCB Size	221	221	221	162	387	204	221	109	109	12	254	726	0.93
# of Sides	1	1	1	1	1	1	1	2	2	2	1	2	0.81
# of R. Layers	2	2	3	2	2	2	3	2	2	4	2	6	0.66
# of Layers	4	4	6	4	4	4	4	2	2	4	2	8	0.67
Comp. Density	70	50	33	33	21	80	38	27	29	55	14	115	0.60
Pin Density	54	32	55	19	17	57	28	40	42	122	9	207	0.64
$\mu PCBComplexity$	60	38	37	18	30	61	25	36	37	25	12	543	0.24

Table 2. Statistics, design effort, and correlation results of study boards.

Statistics about the pins are as easily available as components even before the design starts. The number of pins is a better predictor ($\sigma = 0.45$) than the number of components. The resulting 90% confidence interval for the number of pins is $(0.47, 2.09)$. This means that just by using the pins, we have a 90% confidence that the prediction is around half or double the expected design effort. Not shown in the table is the result of combining the number of pins and the components to predict design effort. The results did not improve because there is a high correlation between pins and components.

Area is not such an effective metric. Even assuming a perfect knowledge if the final dimension of the board, we can just estimate design effort with a $(0.21, 4.61)$ confidence interval. Table 2 also shows other statistics such as number of sides used, routing layers, and number of layers. Those statistics are not so useful by themselves because they are highly quantized, and this makes them difficult to use to predict effort.

To obtain the proposed $\mu PCBComplexity$ metric shown in Table 2, we analyzed multiple combinations of parameters and followed suggestions from experienced board designers. The best results were achieved when using the following equation:

$$\text{Effort} = w1 * \# \text{ Components} + w2 * \text{Comp. Density} + w3 * \text{Pin Density} \quad (7)$$

To capture component and pin density, we define them with equation 8 and equation 9 respectively.

$$\text{Component Density} = \frac{\# \text{ Components}}{\text{PCB Area} \times \# \text{ Sides w/ components}} \quad (8)$$

$$\text{Pin Density} = \frac{\# \text{ Pins}}{(\text{PCB Area})} \quad (9)$$

To obtain the factors on equation 7, we perform nonlinear regression as explained in Section 2.3. Although neither pin nor component density can achieve better predictions than the number of pins, when integrated together in the $\mu PCBComplexity$ metric we achieve a 0.24 σ. As Figure 3 shows, this represents a $(0.58, 1.72)$ confidence interval. This roughly means that by using the proposed $\mu PCBComplexity$ metrics, with a 90% confidence designers can predict design effort with less than 40% error.

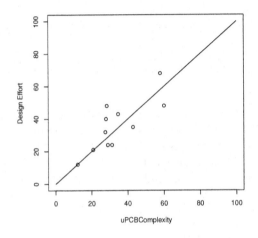

Fig. 5. Scatter-gather plot of design effort vs. PCB metric

Figure 5 shows a scatter-gather plot between design effort and $\mu PCBComplexity$. Each point corresponds to a different board. The plot does not include the B12 board to zoom on the area where most of the boards are located. This plot is an intuitive way to see that there is a high correlation between design effort and the metric proposed.

$\mu PCBComplexity$ works well because PCB design complexity increases as the component and pin density increases. Designers can increase the number of layers on the PCB to decrease the pin density or increase the area to reduce both densities. The problem is that both approaches require more costly boards. As a result, designers tradeoff between time to market and density.

5   Related Work

The work most related to ours in processor analysis is done by Numetrics, a company specializing in enterprise software and services product development [18].

They propose a "complexity unit" to measure the level of project difficulty and to quantify the development team's output. Patent 6,823,294 describes a method to estimate design effort. If we apply the method to our data, the result is considerably less accurate than DEE1. After discussions with Numetrics, they informed us that the patent represented preliminary work, and that their current models are more advanced. Unfortunately, little detail is available on these models because it is considered a technological advantage for their company.

Kahng [12] identifies the need for standards or infrastructures for measuring and recording the semiconductor design process. The author proposes improving design technology, time-to-market, and quality-of-result by addressing the Design Productivity Gap and the Design "Technology" Productivity Gap. However, this previous work focused mostly on the problems associated with the infrastructure and design tools related to the physical implementation of semiconductor designs, while the focus of this work is layout effort associated with PCB designs and design effort for processor flows.

In [17] introduces a weighting approach similar to the productivity factor described in our work. They use the "process productivity parameter" to tune the estimating process for software projects. They contend that if you know the size, time, and the process productivity parameter you can use it to make estimates for a new project. So long as the environment, tools, methods, practices, and skills of the people have not changed dramatically from one project to the next.

In [4] the issue of embedded passive components is discussed as a necessity to the smaller electronic devices requiring ever smaller PCBs. They note that board area is becoming so critical that to keep pace with the size constraints new techniques are required. Our goal would be to eventually develop a set of metrics and a model that estimates design effort by also taking into account manufacturing times.

Recently, some research has focused on reducing the number of RTL redesigns during the timing closure process. To streamline timing closure, new methods have been developed to predict logic criticality [13] and wire congestion [14] early in the RTL design phase. With these predictors, logic designers can focus their attention on the critical logic during the initial implementation, reducing the number of redesign cycles.

As process technology has improved, the major source of signal propagation delay has shifted from gates to wires. In [6] a new metric for evaluating interconnect architectures is proposed. The metric is computed by looking for an optimal assignment of wires from a given wire length distribution. This information is used to generate an interconnect architecture. That metric compares impacts of geometric parameters as well as process and material technology advances on designs.

Fornaciary et al. [9] propose a methodology to predict the final size of a VHDL project on the basis of a high-level description. With this, they seek some indication of development effort by estimating the number of lines of code from starting specifications. While their method is shown to be accurate in predicting lines of code, it dies not address design effort aspects, such as the number of engineering person-months required for the project.

6 Conclusions

Design complexity is rapidly becoming a limiting factor in the design of modern, high-performance microprocessors and systems. This work addresses the lack of quantitative approaches to estimate the design effort for modern systems and processors by making three major contributions:

First, we use the $\mu Complexity$ methodology to measure and estimate processor design effort. $\mu Complexity$ consists of three main parts, namely a procedure to account for the contributions of the different components, accurate statistical regression using a nonlinear mixed-effects model, and a productivity adjustment to account for the productivities of different teams.

Second, we apply $\mu Complexity$ to four designs and evaluating a series of estimators based on synthesis and software metrics. The evaluation uncovered a few simple, good design effort estimators, namely the number of lines of HDL code (or HDL statements) and the sum of the fan-ins of all the logic cones. A slightly more accurate estimator is DEE1, which is the linear combination of HDL statements and fan-ins of all the logic cones. We recommend this estimator, but using estimators that combine a larger number of metrics may make sense for a practitioner that has access to more data.

Third, we introduce a procedure, $\mu PCBComplexity$, to estimate PCB design effort. PCB design effort is estimated by correlating some easily obtained metrics from the design of a PCB, and the design time required during the layout stage of development.

The evaluation section reveals how multiple metrics, traditionally used by the design community to estimate design effort, are fairly uncorrelated with actual design time. These include dynamic or static power, logic or storage area, frequency, number of flip-flops and, somewhat surprisingly, the number of standard cells. The number of cells and transistors are two popular design effort estimators used by Sematech and the SIA roadmap. Finally, the evaluation shows that both the productivity adjustment and the $\mu Complexity$ accounting procedure are necessary to produce accurate estimators.

The PCB evaluation shows how simple statistics like the area size and number of components yield some correlation with design effort. With a 90% confidence, pins has a (0.47, 2.09) confidence interval. This means that roughly by looking at the number of pins, the typical design time error is half/double with a 90% confidence. Much better results can be achieved with the proposed $\mu PCBComplexity$ metric. In that case the confidence interval for a 90% confidence is (0.58, 1.72). This roughly means that less than 40% estimation error is done with a 90% confidence.

References

1. Semiconductor Industry Association. International Technology Roadmap for Semiconductors (ITRS), 2002.
2. C. Bazeghi, F. Mesa-Martinez, and J. Renau. μComplexity: Estimating Processor Design Effort. In *International Symposium on Microarchitecture*, Nov 2005.
3. B. Boehm. *Software Engineering Economics*. Prentice-Hall, 1981.
4. M. Chincholkar and J. Herrmann. Modeling the impact of embedding passives on manufacturing system performance. September 2002.
5. E.L. Crow and K. Shimizu. *Lognormal Distributions: Theory and Application*. Dekker, 1988.
6. P. Dasgupta, A. B. Kahng, and S. Muddu. A Novel Metric for Interconnect Architecture Performance. In *Design, Automation and Test in Europe Conference and Exhibition*, March 2003.
7. M. Davidian and M.D. Giltinan. *Nonlinear Models for Repeated Measurement Data*. Chapman & Hall, 1995.
8. T. DeMarco and T. Lister. *Peopleware Productive Projects and Teams*. Dorset House Publishing, 1999.
9. W. Fornaciari, F. Salice, and D.P. Scarpazza. Early Estimation of the Size of VHDL Projects. In *International Conference on Hardware/Software Codesign and System Synthesis*, pages 207–212, Oct 2003.
10. R. Goodall, D. Fandel, A. Allan, P. Landler, and H. R. Huff. Long Term Productivity Mechanisms of the Semiconductor Industry. www.sematech.org, 2002.
11. J.P. Hoffmann. *Generalized Linear Models*. Pearson, 2004.
12. A. B. Kahng. Design technology productivity in the dsm era (invited talk). In *Conference on Asia South Pacific Design Automation*, pages 443–448. ACM Press, 2001.
13. P. Kudva, B. Curran, S.K. Karandikar, M. Mayo, S. Carey, and S.S. Sapatnekar. Early Performance Prediction. In *Workshop on Complexity-Effective Design*, Jun 2005.
14. P. Kudva, A. Sullivan, and W. Dougherty. Metrics for Structural Logic Synthesis. In *International Conference on Computer-Aided Design*, pages 551–556, Nov 2002.
15. R.C. Littell, G.A. Milliken, W.W. Stroup, and R.D. Wolfinger. *SAS System for Mixed Models*. SAS Publishing, 1996.
16. T. Little. Value Creation and Capture: A Model of the Software Development Process. *IEEE Software*, 21(3):48–53, 2004.
17. L. H. Putnam and W. Myers. *Five Core Metrics: The Intelligence Behind Successful Software Management*. Dorset House Publishing, May 2003.
18. Numetrics Management Systems. Key Performance Indicators of IC Development Capability-A Framework. Technical report, Numetrics Management Systems, Inc., 2005. http://www.numetrics.com.
19. The R Development Core Team. *The R Reference Manual - Base Package*. Network Theory Limited, 2005.

Reconfigurable Accelerator with Binary Compatibility for General Purpose Processors

Antonio Carlos Schneider Beck, Luigi Carro

Universidade Federal do Rio Grande do Sul – Instituto de Informática
Av. Bento Gonçalves, 9500 – Campus do Vale – Porto Alegre/Brazil
{caco,carro}@inf.ufrgs.br

Abstract. Although transistor scaling keeps following Moore's law, and more area is available for designers, the clock frequency and ILP rate do not present the same level of growth anymore. This way, new architectural alternatives are necessary. Reconfigurable fabric appears to be one emerging possibility: besides exploiting the parallelism among instructions, it can also accelerate sequences of data dependent ones. However, reconfiguration wide spread usage is still withheld by the need of special tools and compilers, which clearly do not sustain the reuse of legacy code without any kind of modification. Based on all these facts, this work proposes a new Binary Translation algorithm, implemented in hardware and working in parallel to the processor, responsible for transforming sequences of instructions at run-time to be executed on a dynamic coarse-grain reconfigurable array, tightly coupled to a traditional RISC machine. Therefore, we can take advantage of using pure combinational logic to optimize even control-flow oriented code in a totally transparent process, without any modification in the source code or binary. Using the Simplescalar Toolset together with the MIBench embedded benchmark suite, we show performance improvements and area evaluation when comparing against a traditional superscalar architecture.

Introduction

The possibility of increasing the number of transistors inside an integrated circuit with the passing years, following Moore's Law, has been pushing performance at the same level of growth. However, high performance architectures as the diffused superscalar machines are now challenging well known limits of the ILP [1]: considering the Intel's family of processors, the IPC rate has not increased since the Pentium Pro [2]. This way, recent speed-ups in performance occurred mainly thanks to boosts in clock frequency through the employment of deeper pipelines. Even this approach, though, is reaching a limit. For example, the clock frequency of Intel's Pentium 4 processor only increased from 3.06 to 3.8 GHz between 2002 and 2006 [3].

Because of these reasons, companies are migrating to chip multiprocessors to take advantage of the extra area available, even though there is still a huge potential to speed up a single thread software. Hence, new architectural alternatives that can take

Please use the following format when citing this chapter:

Beck, A.C.S. and Carro, L., 2009, in IFIP International Federation for Information Processing, Volume 291; *VLSI-SoC: Advanced Topics on Systems on a Chip*; eds. R. Reis, V. Mooney, P. Hasler; (Boston: Springer), pp. 271–286.

advantage of the integration possibilities and that can address the performance issues stated before become necessary.

Reconfigurable fabric appears to be a serious candidate to be one of these solutions. By translating a sequence of operations into a combinational circuit performing the same computation, one could gain performance and reduce energy consumption at the price of extra area [4][5]. Furthermore, at the same time that reconfigurable computing can explore the ILP of the applications, it also speeds up sequence of data dependent instructions, which is its main advantage when comparing to traditional architectures. Dataflow architectures put this concept to the edge, achieving huge speed-ups [11].

Another advantage of reconfigurable architectures is their regularity: it is common sense that as the more the technology shrinks, the more important regularity becomes – since this will affect the reliability of printing the geometries employed today in 65 nanometers and below [6]. Besides being more predictable, regular circuits are also low cost, since as more customizable the circuit is, more expensive it becomes. This way, reconfigurable architectures based on regular fabric could solve the mask cost and many other issues such as printability, power integrity and other aspects of the near future technologies.

However, even with all these positive aspects cited before, reconfigurable architectures are still not largely used. The major problem precluding their usage is the necessity of special tools and compilers, modifying in somehow the source or binary code. As the old X86 ISA has been showing, keeping legacy binary code reuse and traditional programming paradigms are key factors to reduce the design cycle, allowing one to deploy the product as soon as possible on the market.

Based on all these facts, our work proposes the use of a technique called Dynamic Instruction Merging, which is a new binary translation approach implemented in hardware, used to detect and transform sequences of instructions at run time to be executed on a reconfigurable array, in a totally transparent process: there is no necessity of changing the code before its execution at all.

The employed array is coarse-grained and tightly coupled to the processor, composed of simple functional units and multiplexers. Therefore, it is not limited to the complexity of fine-grain configurations, making possible its implementation in any future technology, not just in FPGAs. Consequently, we can take all the advantages of the reconfigurable systems cited before, maintaining independence of technology and binary code reuse.

In this work we show some results concerning the potential of using such technique, demonstrating the binary translation algorithm, the structure of the reconfigurable hardware and how they interact with each other. Besides presenting the performance improvements and area overhead, we also compare our technique against a superscalar processor based on MIPS R10000.

This paper is organized as follows. Section 2 shows a review of the existing reconfigurable processors, some other approaches regarding dynamic translation of instructions and what is our contribution considering the whole context. Section 3 demonstrates the system, looking at the structure of the reconfigurable array and the algorithm itself. Section 4 presents the simulation environment and results. Finally, the last section draws conclusions and introduces future work.

Related Work

Reconfigurable Architectures

The well known ASIP circuits have specialized hardware that accelerates the execution of the applications they were designed for. A system with reconfigurable capabilities would have almost the same benefit without having to commit the hardware into silicon. A reconfigurable processor can be adapted after design, in the same way programmable processors can adapt to application changes. That is why reconfigurable systems have already shown to be very effective, implementing some parts of the software in a hardware reconfigurable logic, as shown in Figure 1. Huge software speedups [4] as well as a reduction in system energy have been achieved [5].

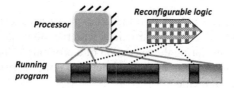

Fig. 1. An example of a reconfigurable system

Reconfigurable systems can be classified in different ways and aspects, considering coupling, granularity and instructions type [7]. A large range of systems with reconfigurable logic has already been proposed. For instance, processors like Chimaera [8], have a tightly coupled reconfigurable array in the processor core. The array is, in fact, an additional functional unit in the processor pipeline, sharing the same resources of the other units.

Reconfigurable fabric has also been applied in other levels of the architecture, imposing radical changes to the programming paradigm, involving the development of new compilers and tools. Putting this concept to the edge, an example of total dataflow architecture is the Wavescalar processor [11].

Binary Translation

The concept of binary translation (BT), illustrated in Figure 2, [12] is very ample and can be applied in various levels. BT is based on a system, which can be implemented in hardware or software, responsible for monitoring the running program. After the analysis, some transformation is done in the code, with the purpose of adapt an existing binary to be executed in a specific ISA, to provide means to enhance the performance or even both.

Fig. 2. The Binary Translation (BT) process

Existing optimizations include dynamic recompilation and caching of previous binary translation results. For instance, the Daisy architecture is based on a VLIW processor that uses binary translation at runtime to better exploit the ILP of the application [13]. One of the advantages of using this technique is that this process is transparent, since there is no need for any modifications in the binary code. Consequently, it requires no extra designer effort and causes no disruption to the standard tool flow used during the software development.

Reuse of Instructions

The idea of trace reuse is based on the principle of instruction repetition [14]. This principle relies on the idea that instructions with the same operands will be repeated a large number of times during the execution of a program. Hence, instead of executing the instruction again using an ordinary functional unit, the result of this instruction is fetched from a special memory.

Trace reuse is based on an input and an output context. For a given sequence of instructions, the context of the first instruction of this sequence is saved. The output context, in turn, is the set of results of all last instruction of this sequence. A context is composed by the program counter, registers and memory addresses. Each time that an instruction with the same input context previously found is executed again, the processor state is updated with the output context, avoiding the execution of all instructions that compose that trace. A special memory, called Reuse Trace Memory (RTM), is used for storing the values. Figure 3 summarizes this process.

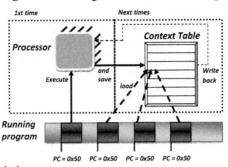

Fig. 3. The trace reuse technique

However, the context and trace sizes usually become huge, limiting the field of action of such approach, and increasing the complexity of the reuse detection algorithm. Good results are achieved just when using very optimistic assumptions, such as one cycle per trace reuse and the use of huge Reuse Trace Memories, not feasible even in future technologies because of power issues. The memory size grows too fast mainly because identical sequences of instructions, but with different contexts (as different input operands), must occupy different slots in this special memory.

Dynamic Detection and Reconfiguration

Trying to unify some of these ideas, Stitt et al. [15] presented the first studies about the benefits and feasibility of dynamic partitioning using reconfigurable logic, producing good results for a number of popular embedded system benchmarks. The structure of this approach, called warp processing, is a SOC. It is composed by a microprocessor to execute the software, another microprocessor where the CAD algorithm runs, a dedicated memory and an FPGA. Firstly, the microprocessor executes the binary, and a profiler monitors the instructions in order to detect critical regions. After that, the CAD software decompiles it to a control data flow graph, make the synthesis and maps the circuit onto a simplified FPGA structure.

However, although the CAD system is very simplified comparing to conventional ones, it remains complex: it does decompilation, CFG analysis, place and route etc, and, according to the work, 8 MB of memory are necessary for its execution, which is still huge for nowadays on-die memories. Another issue is the use of the FPGA itself: besides area consuming, it is also power inefficient because of the excessive switches and the considerable amount of static power. As a consequence, this technique is just limited to critical parts of the software, working well just in very particular programs, such as the ones based on filters.

In [16] it is also presented a very similar reconfigurable structure used in this work: a coarse-grain array, composed by very simple functional units, tightly coupled to an ARM processor. This array is called CCA. However, in the same way of the technique above, it relies on complex graph analysis, which is performed statically with compiler help. Moreover, it does not support memory operations or shifts, and has a very small number of input and outputs allowed, limiting its field of application.

Our Approach

Our work is based on a special hardware (Dynamic Instruction Merging Machine), designed in order to detect and transform sequences of instructions to be executed on the reconfigurable hardware. This is done concurrently while the main processor fetches valid instructions. When this unit realizes that there is a certain number of instructions that are worth being executed in the array, a binary translation is applied to this sequence. This translation transforms the original sequence of instructions to a configuration of the array, which performs exactly the same function. After that, this configuration is saved in a special cache, indexed by the PC register.

The next time the saved sequence is found, the dependence analysis is no longer necessary: the processor just needs to load the configuration from the special cache and the operands from the register bank, setting the reconfigurable hardware as active functional unit. Then, the array executes the configuration with that context and writes back the results, instead of executing everything in the normal flow of the processor. Finally, the PC is updated, in order to continue the normal operation.

Depending on the size of the special cache used to keep these configurations, the increase in performance can be extended to the whole software, not being limited to loop centered applications. By transforming any sequence of opcodes into a single combinational instruction in the array one can achieve great gains, since less access to program memory and less iterations on the datapath are required.

In a certain way, the approach saves the dependence information of the sequences of instructions, avoiding performing the same job for the same sequence of instructions as superscalar processors do. It is interesting to point out that almost half of the number of pipeline stages of the Pentium IV processor is related to dependence analysis [3]; and half of the power consumed by the core of the Alplha 21264 processor is also related to extraction of dependence information among instructions [17]. Moreover, both the DIM machine as the reconfigurable array work in parallel to the processor, bringing no delay overhead or increasing the critical path of the pipeline structure.

Comparing to the techniques cited before, our approach also takes advantage of a reconfigurable system, but a coarse grain one, so it can be implemented in any technology, not just FPGAs. Together with that, we use binary translation to avoid the need for code recompilation or the utilization of extra tools, making the optimization process totally transparent to the programmer. The algorithm for the detection and transformation of binary code is very simple, in the sense that it takes advantage of the hierarchal structure of the reconfigurable array. Hence, the use of complex on-chip CAD software or graph analyzers is not necessary, which usually makes use of another processor in the system just to perform this task.

Moreover, the proposed technique relies on the same basic idea of trace reuse, where sequences of instructions are repeated. However, it presents the advantage that just one entry in the special memory is needed for the same sequence of instructions, even when they have different contexts. This takes the pressure off from the cache system, making possible its implementation with a small memory footprint, with realistic assumptions concerning execution and accesses times, even for present days technologies. Figure 4 summarizes the technique and its similarities with the previous ones.

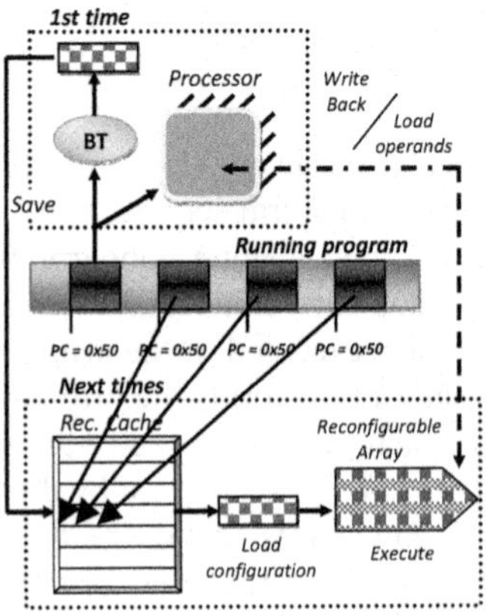

Fig. 4. The proposed approach

In the follow subsections we explain the architecture of the array, how it works together with the main processor, the detection and translation algorithm process and how the loading and execution of instructions inside the reconfigurable array are performed.

THE RECONFIGURABLE SYSTEM

Architecture of the Array

The reconfigurable unit is a dynamic coarse-grain array tightly coupled to the processor, working as another functional unit in the execution stage, using the same approach of Chimaera [8]. This way, no external accesses to the array are necessary (which in turn could increase the delay and power consumption). Furthermore, this makes the control logic simpler, diminishing the overhead required in the communication between the reconfigurable array and the rest of the system. The array is two dimensional, composed by rows and columns, where an intersection between one row and one column is represented by ordinary functional units (ALU, shifter, multiplier, etc), where each instruction is allocated. If two instructions do not have data dependence, they can be executed in parallel, in the same row.

A column is homogeneous, having always the same kind of functional unit. It is divided in groups, where each group takes a determined number of cycles to be executed, depending on the delay of each functional unit. The delay can vary depending on the technology and the way the functional unit was implemented. The detection algorithm can be adapted to different delays. For instance, according to the critical path of the processor, more sequential ALUs can be put together to be executed at the same cycle.

An overview of the general structure of the array is shown in Figure 5. Basically, there is a set of buses that receive the values from the registers. These buses will be connected to each functional unit, and a multiplexer is responsible for choosing which value will be used (Figure 5a). As can be observed, there are two multiplexers that will make the choice of which operand will be issued to the functional unit. We call them as input multiplexers. After that, there is a multiplexer for each bus line that will choose what result will continue through that line. These are the output multiplexers (Figure 5b). As some of the values of the input context or previous results generated by previous operations can be used by other functional units after it was already used, the first input of each output multiplexer is the previous result of that bus.

Note that in the simple example used in Figure 5, the first group supports up to two loads to be executed in parallel, while in the second group three simple logic/arithmetic operations are allowed. The reconfigurable array can not afford any kind of floating point operation.

Reconfiguration and Execution

As the detection for the address that will be used in the reconfiguration is done in the first stage of the pipeline, and the reconfigurable array is in the fifth stage, there are 4 cycles available between the detection and the use of the array. As one cycle is necessary to find the cache line that has the array configuration, three cycles are available for the reconfiguration, which involves the load of the values of all registers that will be used by that configuration, the load of immediate values, the configuration for the multiplexers and functional units and so on.

During the execution of the operations in the array, one issue is the load instructions. They stay in a different group in the array as shown in figure 5, and the number of columns of this group depends on the number of read ports available in the memory (which means the number of loads that can occur simultaneously). Operations that depend on the result of a load have already been allocated in the array during the detection phase, considering a cache hit as the total load delay. If a miss occurs, the whole array stops until it is resolved.

Finally, the results that need to be written back either in the memory or in the local registers are allocated in a buffer. The values will be allowed to be written back just when they are not used anymore for that configuration of the array. For instance, if there are two writes in the same register in a determined configuration, just the last one will be performed, since the first one was already consumed inside the array by other instructions.

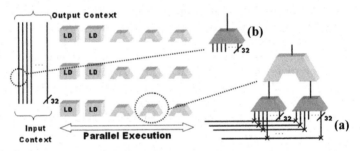

Fig. 5. The structure of the Reconfigurable Array

The Binary Translation Algorithm

Data structure

Some tables are necessary in order to perform the routing of the operands inside the reconfigurable array as well as the configuration of the functional units. Other intermediate tables are also needed, however, they are just used during the detection phase. These tables are:

Dependence table: Saves information of data dependence of each row. This table is in fact a small bitmap of 32 bits. It informs what registers in that row will be written.

Note that it is not necessary to store this information for each instruction. Summarizing the information in a bitmap for each row one can reduce the hardware necessary to check true data dependencies (RAW – read after write).

Resource Table: Stores what function each functional unit must perform.

Read Table: Informs what operand from the input context must be read. This table has two inputs, since there are two source operands for each functional unit. It is important to point out that the input context is basically an indirect table. In other words, not necessarily the first slot needs to store the value of the register R1.

Write table: This table informs what value each context slot will receive. This table is different when comparing to the read one. In the previous table the multiplexers were responsible for choosing what values from the context slots would be issued to each functional unit. This table informs what values from the whole set of the functional units that compose each row will continue in each slot of the context bus.

Context table: This table has two lines, the first one representing the input context, and will be used in the reconfiguration phase, and the second one called current table, that will be used during the detection phase. Its final state represents what values will be written when the execution of the array finishes.

How it works

To better explain the algorithm, we will start with its simplest version, considering that the array is composed just by adders. The following steps represent pipeline stages when considering the implementation in hardware.

Considering that

```
inst op_w, op_r1, op_r2
```

where `inst` is the current instruction and `op_w`, `op_r1` and `op_r2` are the target and the source operands, respectively, the follow steps are necessary.

1st) Decode the instruction, returning the target and source registers of the current instruction;

2nd) In the write table, for each row from 0 to N, verify if `op_r1` and `op_r2` exist. If any one of them or both exist in the line S, line O equals to $S + 1$. Considering a bottom-up search, the line s is the last one where `op_r1` or `op_r2` appears, since they may be found in more than one line. If nor `op_r1` neither `op_r2` exist in any line of this table, line O equals to 0.

3rd) In the resource table, search in the columns of row O, from left to right, if there is a resource available for use. If there exists, we call this free column as C, and row R equals to O. If there is no resource available in row O, increment the value of O in 1 and repeat the same operation, until finding the resource. This way, line R equals to O + N, where N was the number of increments necessary until finding an available resource. This resource table is also represented by a bitmap.

4th)
- Update the bitmap write table in line R with the value of `op_w`
- Update column C in row R of the resource table as busy
- Search in the current context table if there are `op_r1`, `op_r2` and `op_w`. For each one of these, if they exist, point $L1$, $L2$ and W to `op_r1`, `op_r2` and `op_w`

respectively, and disable the correspondent write signals. If one of them does not exist in the table, the correspondent signal of write is set and the correspondent pointer is set to the next free column available.

5th)

- Depending on the step 4c, the current context table is updated.
- The initial context table is also updated, if one of the write signals concerning op_r1 and op_r2 are set.
- In the write table, write the value of C in the row R, column W.
- In the read table, write the values of $L1$ and $L2$ in line R, column C (it is important to remember that each column of this table has two slots, as explained earlier)

Summarizing the algorithm, for each incoming instruction, the first task is the verification of RAW (read after write) dependences. The source operands are compared to a bitmap of target registers of each row. If the current row and all above do not have that target register equal to any of the source operands of the current instruction, this instruction can be allocated in that row, in a column as left as possible, depending on the group, as explained before.

When this is instruction is allocated in that row, the bitmap of target registers is updated. This way, for each instruction just one bitmap per line is necessary to be analyzed. Indirectly, such technique increases the size of the window of instructions, which is one of major limiting factors of ILP, exactly due to the number of comparators that is necessary [19]. For each row there is also the information about what registers can be written back or saved to the memory. This way, it is possible to write results back that will not be used anymore in the array in parallel to the execution of other operations. Figure 6 demonstrates an example of a sequence of instructions allocated in the reconfigurable array.

The complete version of the algorithm supports functional units with different delays and functions, and the use of immediate values in the input context; handles with false data dependencies among instructions; and performs speculative execution. For the speculative execution, each operand that will be written back has a flag indicating its depth concerning speculation. When the branch is taken, it triggers the writes of these correspondent operands.

The speculative policy is one of the simplest ones, based on bimodal branch predictor. For each level of the tree of basic blocks, the counter must achieve the maximum or minimum value (indicating the way of the branch). When the counter equals to this value, the instructions corresponding to this basic block are added to that configuration of the array. The configuration is always indexed by the first PC of the whole tree. If miss speculation occurs a determined number of times, achieving the opposite value of the respective counter, that entire configuration is flushed out and another one begins, starting everything again.

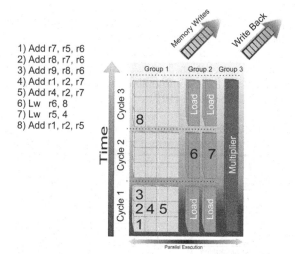

1) Add r7, r5, r6
2) Add r8, r7, r6
3) Add r9, r8, r6
4) Add r1, r2, r7
5) Add r4, r2, r7
6) Lw   r6, 8
7) Lw   r5, 4
8) Add r1, r2, r5

Fig. 6. An example of how a sequence of instructions is allocated inside the array

RESULTS

Performance

The Simplescalar toolset was employed for our experiments. We used the PISA instruction set, which is based on the MIPS IV ISA. Although the out-of-order simulator has some differences when comparing to the MIPS R10000 processor, we configured it to behave as close as possible to this processor. The configuration is summarized in Table 1a.

In Table 1b, we show three different configurations for the array that we used in the experiments. The last configuration was used in order to try to figure out what is the real potential of our technique. For each array configuration we also vary the size of the reconfiguration cache: 2 to 512 slots. Moreover, for each one of these configurations we evaluate the impact of doing speculation, up to three basic blocks ahead. Furthermore, we increased the cache memory in order to achieve almost no cache misses, so we can evaluate our results without the influence of it.

Table 1. Configurations

Out of Order
Fetch, decode and commit = up to 4 instructions
Register Update Unit = 16 Entries
Load/Store Queue = 16 entries
Functional Units = 2 Integer ALU, 1 multiplier, 2 memory ports
Branch Predictor = Bimodal/512 entries

(a)

	Reconfigurable Array		
	C #1	C #2	C #3
#Lines	27	54	99
#Columns	11	16	30
#ALU / line	8	8	11
#Multipliers / line	1	2	3
#Ld/st / line	2	6	8

(b)

Table 2a shows the IPC of the out-of-order processor cited before. This table can be used to compare the IPC of this processor against the IPC of the instructions that are executed inside the array, in different configurations. For each configuration, we vary the speculation: no speculation, 1 and 2 basic blocks ahead. We also change the number of slots available in the reconfigurable cache (4, 16, 64, 128 and 512). We are using a subset of the MIBENCH set [10].

Table 2. IPC in the Out-of-Order and average Basic Block size

Algorithm	IPC - Out-of-Order	BB size
Basicmath	1.43	5.8751
CRC	2.13	7.9954
dijkstra	1.76	5.6011
Jpeg decode	1.86	6.2554
patricia	1.40	4.4255
qsort	1.79	4.6243
sha	1.94	7.9381
stringsearch	1.60	4.8709
Susan Smoothing	1.64	15.8098
Susan Corners	1.83	13.4952
tiff2bw	1.90	22.5567
tiff2rgba	1.92	13.4952
tiffdither	1.56	18.9188
tiffmedian	1.91	30.686

(a)   (b)

As it is shown in Figure 7, we can achieve a higher IPC when executing instructions in the reconfigurable array in comparison to the out-of-order superscalar processor in almost all variations. However, the overall optimization when using our technique depends on how many instructions are executed in the reconfigurable logic instead of using the normal flow of the processor. Table 3 shows the overall speedup obtained when coupling the reconfigurable array to the out-of-order processor against the out-of-order without it.

The four benchmarks were chosen because they represent a very control-oriented algorithm, a dataflow one and a midterm between both, plus the CRC, which is the biggest benchmark in the set. In Table 2b the benchmarks are classified according to the average number of branches per instructions. It is important to notice that reconfigurable systems in general can just show improvements when the programs are very dataflow oriented. The proposed technique, on the other hand, can optimize control and data oriented programs, as it can be observed by the results.

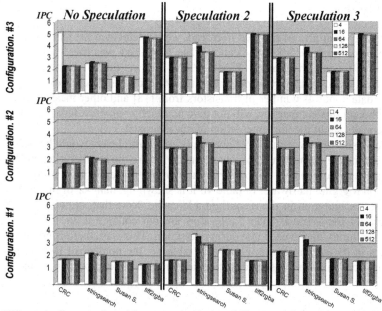

Fig. 7. IPC rate in the reconfigurable array considering different configurations and cache sizes.

Table 3. Speedups using the reconfigurable array coupled to the out-of-order processor

Algorithm	#Cycles in the Out-Of-Order	% of Speed Up - Out-of-Order coupled to array with configuration 1								
		No Speculation			Speculation 2			Speculation 3		
		4	64	256	4	64	256	4	64	256
Basicmath	111169924	5.03	13.75	17.85	3.52	14.49	21.79	3.40	15.22	23.31
CRC	399531928	-16.01	-16.03	-16.03	-5.20	-5.21	-5.21	9.03	9.03	9.03
dijkstra	31094638	-22.29	-24.31	-24.33	1.30	1.25	1.25	8.45	8.46	8.46
Jpeg decode	3942226	-9.15	-9.72	-9.77	4.63	3.24	3.29	7.11	7.45	7.61
patricia	95927575	4.41	13.30	13.72	3.99	14.42	21.52	3.26	14.22	21.96
qsort	23435690	-8.76	-11.69	-11.69	-0.58	4.18	4.18	0.37	-30.41	-30.21
sha	6800950	11.56	13.07	13.07	27.22	33.45	33.45	26.30	31.29	31.29
stringsearch	115917	16.32	20.16	21.23	28.95	35.20	35.24	28.50	35.39	35.38
S. Smoothing	15628090	-0.94	-3.22	-3.22	0.31	-0.99	-1.00	2.13	1.59	1.59
S. Corners	533870	2.16	1.79	1.79	4.40	4.29	4.28	1.13	4.29	4.28
tiff2bw	27391803	-4.24	-4.38	-4.42	0.88	0.82	0.82	-0.20	-0.20	-0.20
tiff2rgba	23796384	-10.94	-11.39	-11.40	-1.53	-1.75	-1.75	-1.19	-1.39	-1.40
tiffdither	188757828	1.48	8.88	8.92	6.65	9.34	9.41	4.47	-21.46	-23.52
tiffmedian	93254386	3.95	3.74	3.73	12.91	12.82	12.82	7.42	7.38	7.38

Algorithm	#Cycles in the Out-Of-Order	% of Speed Up - Out-of-Order coupled to array with configuration 3								
		No Speculation			Speculation 2			Speculation 3		
		4	64	256	4	64	256	4	64	256
Basicmath	111169924	5.76	19.27	26.40	4.63	19.83	30.33	4.86	20.52	32.14
CRC	399531928	3.97	3.97	3.97	8.12	8.14	8.14	20.75	20.77	20.77
dijkstra	31094638	-21.96	-20.08	-20.04	1.00	4.34	4.36	4.13	7.65	7.67
Jpeg decode	3942226	9.76	11.92	12.05	16.55	18.94	19.06	16.77	19.51	19.68
patricia	95927575	5.06	17.97	18.89	5.25	18.80	29.07	4.57	18.58	29.80
qsort	23435690	24.29	38.95	38.95	16.79	43.74	43.74	16.44	40.72	40.72
sha	6800950	22.57	25.48	25.48	39.91	48.66	48.66	41.27	50.28	50.28
stringsearch	115917	21.02	27.05	30.57	31.25	41.02	41.17	31.04	42.61	42.63
S. Smoothing	15628090	25.35	35.66	35.69	26.87	37.95	37.96	23.73	32.05	32.04
S. Corners	533870	32.69	41.44	41.44	37.53	41.44	41.45	33.89	37.13	37.12
tiff2bw	27391803	-5.65	-5.42	-5.39	19.08	19.60	19.60	24.41	25.22	25.22
tiff2rgba	23796384	57.19	57.83	57.83	58.29	59.69	59.69	47.30	48.87	48.87
tiffdither	188757828	4.33	18.15	18.30	10.73	19.33	19.57	7.95	14.31	14.60
tiffmedian	93254386	14.13	14.11	14.13	27.23	27.43	27.43	27.36	27.72	27.72

Area Evaluation

In order to give an idea of the area overhead, we implemented the hardware detection and the reconfigurable array in VHDL. The tool used was the Mentor Leonardo Spectrum [9], with the library TSMC 0.18u. As we do not have available any implementation of a superscalar processor in any Hardware Description Language, we took the data about its number of transistors from [18] and other measurements from [19]. Although this comparison will not give us exactly values, it will present realistic measurements about the implementation of our approach.

Table 4a shows how many functional units and multiplexers would be necessary to implement the configuration #1 of table 1, and what are the number of gates they take. In this same table one can also observe the number of gates taken by the Dynamic Instruction Merging hardware. In table 4b it is shown the number of bits necessary to keep one configuration in the reconfigurable cache. Note that, although 256 bits are necessary for the Write Bitmap Table, they are not counted in the final total. This table is temporary and is used just during detection. This way, there is no need to save its values in the special cache. Finally, in table 4c, the number of Bytes needed for different cache sizes is presented, depending on how much configurations they can store.

Table 4. Area evaluation

Unit	#	Gates
ALU	216	337,824
LD/ST	36	5,904
Multiplier	6	20,067
Input	510	327,420
Output	216	66,096
DIM Hardware		1,024
Total		735,223

(a)

Table	#bits
Write Bitmap Table	256
Resource Table	903
Reads Table	1,896
Writes Table	648
Context Start	40
Context Current	40
Immediate Table	128
Total	3655

(b)

#Slots	#Bytes
2	7,566
4	14,620
8	30,143
16	58,480
32	118,856
64	233,920
128	468,488
256	935,680

(c)

Finally, Figure 8a represents the MIPS layout with the reconfigurable array. According to [18], the total number of transistors of core in the MIPS R10000 is 2.4 million. As presented in table 4a, the array together with the hardware detection occupies 735,223 gates. We are considering that one gate (result given by the synthesis tool) is equivalent to 4 transistors, which would be the amount necessary to implement a NAND or NOR gates. This way, the reconfigurable array and DIM hardware would take 2,940,892 transistors. The area overhead is represented in Figure 6b. In this figure is also presented the area overhead concerning the reconfigurable cache, in number of different configurations supported.

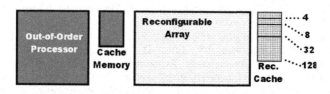

Fig. 8. Area overhead presented by the reconfigurable array and its special cache

CONCLUSIONS AND FUTURE WORK

Although there are some improvements concerning the algorithm and the structure of the reconfigurable array, this work demonstrated that it is possible to keep advantage of a reconfigurable architecture to speed up the system, in a totally transparent process and with a feasible area overhead. Using speculation in the array, we have obtained a mean speedup of up to 30% in the IPC using configuration 3, when comparing against a MIPS R10000 based superscalar processor. Now, we are working on finding the best shape for the reconfigurable array.

Another future work will be the measurement of the energy consumption of the system. Similar techniques applied to an embedded processor have already shown that such structures bring a huge energy saving [20] since, besides the fact that this technique trades sequential logic for combinational one to execute instructions, less accesses to the instruction memory are required, as well as less dependence analysis between instructions are necessary.

REFERENCES

[1] David W. Wall, "Limits of instruction-level parallelism", In Proceedings of the fourth international conference on Architectural support for programming languages and operating systems, p.176-188, April 08-11, 1991

[2] Sima, D., "Decisive aspects in the evolution of microprocessors". In Proceedings of the IEEE, vol. 92, pp.1896-1926, 2004

[3] Intel Pentium 4 Homepage – http://www.intel.com/products/processor/pentium4/index.htm

[4] Venkataramani, G., Najjar, W., Kurdahi, F., Bagherzadeh, N., Bohm W., "A Compiler Framework for Mapping Applications to a Coarse-grained Reconfigurable Computer Architecture. Conf. on Compiler". In Architecture and Synthesis for Embedded Systems (CASES), 2001

[5] Stitt, G., Vahid F., "The Energy Advantages of Microprocessor Platforms with On-Chip Configurable Logic". In IEEE Design and Test of Computers, 2002

[6] Or-Bach, Z., Panel: "(when) will FPGAs kill ASICs?", 38th Design Automation Conference, 2001.

[7] Compton, K., Hauck, S. "Reconfigurable computing: A survey of systems and software," ACM Computing Surveys, vol. 34, no. 2, pp. 171-210, June 2002.

[8]   Hauck, S., Fry, T., Hosler, M., Kao, J.: "The Chimaera reconfigurable functional unit". In Proc. IEEE Symp. FPGAs for Custom Computing Machines, pp. 87–96, Napa Valley, CA, 1997

[9]   Leonardo Spectrum, available at homepage: http://www.mentor.com

[10] Guthaus, M.R., Ringenberg, J.S., Ernst, D., Austin, T.M., Mudge T., Brown, R.B., "MiBench: A Free, Commercially Representative Embedded Benchmark Suite. 4th Workshop on Workload Characterization", Austin, TX, Dec. 2001

[11] Swanson, S., Michelson, K., Schwerin, A., Oskin. M., "WaveScalar". In MICRO-36, Dec. 2003

[12] Gschwind, M., Altman, E., Sathaye, P., Ledak, Appenzeller, D.: "Dynamic and Transparent Binary Translation". In IEEE Computer, pp. 54-59, vol. 3 n. 33, 2000

[13] Ebcioglu, E. A., "DAISY: Dynamic compilation for 100% architectural compatibility". In IBM T. J. Watson Research Center - Technical Report, Yorktown Heights, NY, 1996

[14] González, A., Tubella, J., Molina, C., "Trace-Level Reuse". In Int'l Conf. on Parallel Processing, Sep. 1999

[15] Stitt, G., Lysecky, R., Vahid, F., "Dynamic Hardware/Software Partitioning: A First Approach". In Design Automation Conference, 2003

[16] N. Clark, W. Tang, and S. Mahlke, "Automatically Generating Custom Instruction Set Extensions". In Workshop on Application Specific Processors (WASP). Turkey, 2002.

[17] K.Wilcox and S.Manne, "Alpha processors: A history of power issues and a look to the future". In CoolChips Tutorial An Industrial Perspective on Low Power Processor Design in conjunction with Micro-33(1999).

[18] Yeager, K.C. "The Mips R10000 Superscalar Microprocessor,"; IEEE Micro, Apr. 1996, pp. 28-40.

[19] Burns, J.; Gaudiot, J.-L., "SMT layout overhead and scalability". In Parallel and Distributed Systems, IEEE Transactions on Parallel and Distributed Systems, pp. 142-155, Volume: 13, Issue: 2, Feb 2002

[20] Beck, A. C. S., Carro, L., "Dynamic Reconfiguration with Binary Translation: Breaking the ILP barrier with Software Compatibility", In Design Automation Conference, 2005

FIRST ORDER, QUASI-STATIC, SOI CHARGE CONSERVING POWER DISSIPATION MODEL

Sameer Sharma and L G. Johnson

Oklahoma State University, Stillwater, OK 74075

Abstract. Conventional MOS models for circuit simulation assume that the channel capacitances do not contribute to net power dissipation. Numerical integration of channel currents and instantaneous terminal voltages however shows the existence of higher order dissipating terms. To overcome these limitations, we present a self-consistent, first order, quasi-static power dissipation model that is able to predict dissipative (transport) and conserved (charging) current components. Charge conservation is insured by using the current continuity equation. An analytical expression for energy stored in the channel is derived by separating out current components that contribute to net power dissipation. The power dissipation estimation is made computationally efficient by leaving out energy conserving terms.

1. INTRODUCTION

Modeling is a process of accurately representing the behavior of a device to be used in a circuit simulator. Designers need these reliable and accurate device models for circuit development. With the growth of CMOS technology, MOSFET modeling has become increasingly important. The accurate modeling of the MOSFET channel capacitance has been an ongoing effort for many decades. First, Meyer's [1] reciprocal capacitive model, then Ward's [2] charge-based non-reciprocal capacitance model have been used. Many papers have been written on the comparison of these models. Some [3-5] claim that Meyer's model fails due to charge non-conservation which justifies the usage of charge-based models, while others claim [6-7] that the charge non-conservation is mainly due to the incorrect mathematical modeling of non-linear capacitance by the simulation software. Recent papers on field-dependent mobility [8] and laterally asymmetrical doping [9] have now shown inconsistencies in Ward's model, which artificially partitions the channel charge into source and drain components. As pointed out by Fossum [10], it is not clear whether we have explored all other possibilities; we may be able to achieve a better result with a different channel partition or may be with no partition at all.

Many models have also been put forward to analyze the charging and the trans-capacitive current components. One of such models by Lim and Fossum [11] has a first order transient transport current and suggests the difference between non-reciprocal capacitive elements to be responsible for this current. We show that this model is correct for transistor current computation; however it is inconsistent and has some drawbacks when used to predict power consumption. These drawbacks are:

- Lim-Fossum's equations use Ward's channel charge partition model.

Please use the following format when citing this chapter:

Sharma, S. and Johnson, L.G., 2009, in IFIP International Federation for Information Processing, Volume 291; *VLSI-SoC: Advanced Topics on Systems on a Chip*; eds. R. Reis, V. Mooney, P. Hasler; (Boston: Springer), pp. 287–309.

- The MOS capacitors dissipate power and the trans-capacitive term used in the charge model includes both dissipating as well as conserved components which are not separated.

The charge partition model puts a constraint only on charge conservation. Even though the model predicts the channel charge correctly to first order, the device power is only predicted to zero order. The model may not include complete first order trans-capacitive currents due to the redistribution of the charges in the channel. This could cause the actual output waveform and delay to deviate from the simulation results [12]. In reality, the MOS channel is not purely an energy storage device [13]. Thus, it is not appropriate to leave out higher order dissipating terms due to charge redistribution as they become significant at higher frequencies.

Though many papers/chapters [3-5, 14-17] have been written on the transient transport current, no one has found a solution to separate the transport and charging current components. This makes our model and the closed form expressions for the dissipative and conserved currents significant. We have developed a self consistent, quasi-static, charge conserving, first order power dissipation model. It analyzes the first order power dissipation and computes the energy function for the conserved component of the charge storage. The existence of the energy function makes it possible to exclude energy conserving terms that do not contribute to power dissipation, making the total power estimation computationally efficient.

The rest of the paper is organized as follows. In the second section, we have used a one dimensional MOSFET transistor model with the current continuity equation to compute the channel currents and the channel charges as well as the currents at the source and the drain ends. In the third section, we have computed the power by integrating the power density over the entire channel. This leads to the derivation of an energy function in section five. In section five, we discuss the first order dynamic power dissipation model. Using the conserved power components, we have separated the conserved and dissipative current components in section six. Finally, we have developed an equivalent circuit by following the method used by Lim-Fossum and verified the results for current and charge. Even though they used a charge partition instead of solving exactly as we have, both models predict the same source and drain currents, and hence the same terminal capacitances. However, we are able to separate out these capacitances into conserved and dissipative components.

2. CHARGE DISTRIBUTION CALCULATION

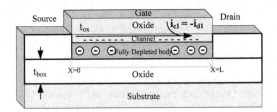

Fig. 1. SOI MOSFET Structure

In order to obtain an analytical solution, the current flow is considered in one dimension parallel to the surface of the device. It is assumed that the region under the channel is completely depleted of mobile charges. This fully depleted assumption for SOI MOSFET's helps us to make use of a linear relationship between the body and the surface potential to compute the stored energy function without partitioning the channel charge. The linear relation also provides a simplified charge model and terminal currents. It should be noted that solving these equations involves complicated algebraic calculations that are practically impossible without modern mathematics tools like "Mathematica" [18].

Fig. 1 shows NMOS SOI transistor. The charge per unit length (q_c) at a position x along the channel is given by

$$q_c(x) = -c_{ox}(v_{gb} - v_{fb} - v_{cb}(x) - \phi + q_b(x)/c_{ox})$$ (1)

Similarly, the body charge (back gate) per unit length (q_b) at x can be written as

$$q_b(x) = -c_{ox}(k_1 + \alpha v_{cb}(x))$$ (2)

where v_{fb}, v_{gb} and v_{cb} are the flat band, gate and channel voltages with respect to the body. k_1 and α are body effect coefficients. $c_{ox} = W(c_{ox}/A)$ is the oxide capacitance per unit length, where W is the channel width. Charge conservation is insured by defining the gate charge per unit length q_g as

$$q_g = -(q_b + q_c)$$ (3)

It will be convenient to define the channel charge per unit length at the source $(x = 0)$ q_s and the drain $(x = L)$ q_d and their time derivatives as

$$q_s = -c_{ox} v_{gst}$$ (4)

where $v_{gst} = v_{gb} - v_t - v_{sb}$

$$\frac{d}{dt}q_s = -c_{ox}\frac{d}{dt}v_{gst}$$ (5)

In equation (4), v_t is the threshold voltage. The body effect requires including the dependence of the threshold voltage on source terminal voltage and the substrate charge parameter [22].

$$v_t(v_{sb}) = v_{t0} + \alpha v_{sb}$$ (6)

where $v_{t0} = v_{fb} + k_1 + \phi$ is the threshold voltage at zero v_{sb}, and ϕ is the fermi potential. At the drain end,

$$q_d = -c_{ox} v_{gdt}$$ (7)

where $v_{gdt} = v_{gb} - v_t - v_{sb} - (1+\alpha)(v_{db} - v_{sb})$

$$\frac{d}{dt}q_d = -c_{ox}\frac{d}{dt}v_{gdt}$$ (8)

It is assumed that positive current flows into the drain and velocity saturation effects can be neglected. Assuming strong inversion, diffusion current in the channel is small. Drift current at a distance x along the channel can be written as

$$i_c(x,t) = q_c(x,t)\mu\frac{d}{dx}v_{cb}(x)$$ (9)

where μ is the charge carrier mobility in the channel. Charge conservation is assured using the one dimensional continuity equation

$$\frac{d}{dx}i_c(x,t) = -\frac{d}{dt}q_c(x,t) \tag{10}$$

Using (9) in (10) gives

$$\frac{d}{dx}[q_c(x,t)\mu\frac{d}{dx}v_{cb}(x)] = -\frac{d}{dt}q_c(x,t) \tag{11}$$

Taking the spatial derivatives of charge per unit length as a linear function of potential along the channel as in equation (1) and (2) gives

$$\frac{d}{dx}q_c(x,t) = (1+\alpha)c_{ox}\frac{d}{dx}v_{cb}(x) \tag{12}$$

Substituting $\frac{d}{dx}v_{cb}(x)$ in (11) and rearranging terms gives

$$\frac{d}{dx}[q_c(x,t)\frac{d}{dx}q_c(x,t)] = -\frac{(1+\alpha)}{\mu}c_{ox}\frac{d}{dt}q_c(x,t) \tag{13}$$

In the quasi-static approximation, equation (13) can be solved iteratively to compute the current and the charge in the channel by expanding $q_c = q_{c0} + q_{c1} + ...$ where q_{c0} is a function of terminal voltages only and q_{c1} is a linear function of first order time derivatives of terminal voltages. In terms of the steady state (zero order) charge per unit length at any position x along the channel, equation (13) reduces to

$$\frac{d}{dx}(q_{c0}\frac{d}{dx}q_{c0}) = 0 \tag{14}$$

Performing integration from the source $(x = 0)$ to the drain $(x = L)$, the zero order charge along the channel becomes

$$q_{c0} = -\sqrt{(q_s^2(1-x/L) + q_d^2 x/L} \tag{15}$$

and the steady state drift current component of equation (9) simplifies to

$$I_{c0} = \frac{\mu}{(1+\alpha)c_{ox}}q_{c0}\frac{d}{dx}q_{c0} \tag{16}$$

Equation (16) gives the usual equation for steady current neglecting velocity saturation, which is shown in Table I. The first order current and charge can be found by keeping terms of first order in time derivatives in equation (13)

$$\frac{d}{dx}(q_{c0}\frac{d}{dx}q_{c1} + q_{c1}\frac{d}{dx}q_{c0}) = -\frac{(1+\alpha)}{\mu}c_{ox}\frac{d}{dt}q_{c0} \tag{17}$$

Rearranging the terms, equation for the first order channel charge simplifies to

$$q_{c1} = -\frac{(1+\alpha)}{\mu}c_{ox}\frac{1}{q_{c0}}\frac{d}{dt}\int(\int q_{c0}[x]dx)dx) \tag{18}$$

and the first order current reduces to

$$i_{c1} = \frac{\mu}{(1+\alpha)c_{ox}}(q_{c0}\frac{d}{dx}q_{c1} + q_{c1}\frac{d}{dx}q_{c0}) \tag{19}$$

Finally, equation (19) can be solved to compute the first order channel current at the source $i_{s1} = i_{c1}(x = 0)$ and the drain $i_{d1} = -i_{c1}(x = L)$ ends in all regions of operation. We have assumed pinch-off saturation which occurs when $q_d = 0$ for $v_{ds} \geq \frac{(v_{gs} - v_t)}{(1+\alpha)}$. In cut-off, it is assumed that both $q_d = 0$ and $q_s = 0$. Table 1 summarizes the charge and current in all regions of operations.

2.1. Derivation of First Order Channel Charge and Channel Current

The equations for first order channel charge and first order currents were used in the previous section, however, the derivations were not shown, which is given in this section. These derivations are one of the most important findings of our research.

The first order channel charge allows calculating the first order channel current without the charge partition, which can be used to calculate the first order drain and source currents. The first order channel current also makes it possible to derive the conserved and dissipative power components.

Taking charge density as a function of potential along the channel, and keeping terms of first order in time derivatives, current continuity equation (17) can be rearranged to be written in terms of first order channel charge per unit length as

$$q_{c1} = -\frac{c_{ox}(1+\alpha)}{\mu} \frac{1}{q_{c0}} \frac{d}{dt} \iint q_{c0}[x]dxdx + c1x + c0 \tag{20}$$

where q_{c0} is the zero order channel charge density and is given by equation (15). $c1$ and $c0$ are constants of integration and can be calculated using the boundary condition $q_{c1} = 0$ at $x = 0$ and $x = L$

$$c0 = \frac{c_{ox}(1+\alpha)}{\mu} \frac{d}{dt} \iint q_{c0}[x]dxdx \Big|_{x \to 0}$$

$$c0 = \frac{4}{15} \frac{c_{ox}(1+\alpha)}{\mu} L^2 q_s \frac{(4q_d q_s \frac{d}{dt}q_d - 5q_d^2 \frac{d}{dt}q_s + q_s^2 \frac{d}{dt}q_s)}{(-q_d^2 + q_s^2)^3} \tag{21}$$

$$c1 = \frac{c_{ox}(1+\alpha)}{\mu} \frac{d}{dt} \iint q_{c0}[x]dxdx \Big|_{x \to L}$$

$$c1 = \frac{4}{15} \frac{c_{ox}(1+\alpha)}{\mu} L$$

$$\frac{(-q_d \frac{d}{dt}q_d(q_d^5 - 5q_d^3 q_s^2 + 4q_s^5) - q_s(4q_d^5 - 5q_d^2 q_s^3 + q_s^5)\frac{d}{dt}q_s)}{(-q_d^2 + q_s^2)^3} \tag{22}$$

Substituting the values of $c0$, $c1$ and q_{c0} in (20), the first order charge at any point x along the channel then becomes

$$q_{c1} = -\frac{1}{15\sqrt{\frac{q_s^2(L-x)+q_d^2 x}{L}} \cdot \mu}\{4C_cL(\frac{Lq_s^4(4q_dq_s\frac{d}{dt}q_d - 5q_d^2\frac{d}{dt}q_s + q_s^2\frac{d}{dt}q_s)}{(-q_d^2+q_s^2)^3} +$$

$$((q_d^5\frac{d}{dt}q_d - q_s^5\frac{d}{dt}q_s + 4q_d^3q_s^2(-\frac{d}{dt}q_d+\frac{d}{dt}q_s)+4q_d^2q_s^3(-\frac{d}{dt}q_d+\frac{d}{dt}q_s) -$$

$$q_dq_s^4(4\frac{d}{dt}q_d+\frac{d}{dt}q_s)+q_d^4q_s(\frac{d}{dt}q_d+4\frac{d}{dt}q_s))x)/(q_d-q_s)^2(q_d+q_s)^3) -$$

$$\frac{1}{(q_d^2-q_s^2)^3}\left(\frac{q_s^2(L-x)+q_d^2 x}{L}\right)^{3/2}(Lq_s(4q_dq_s\frac{d}{dt}q_d - 5q_d^2\frac{d}{dt}q_s + q_s^2\frac{d}{dt}q_s) -$$

$$(q_d-q_s)(q_d+q_s)(q_d\frac{d}{dt}q_d - q_s\frac{d}{dt}q_s)x)))$$

The first order channel current at any position x along the channel can now be estimated using equation (19). Taking derivatives of q_{c0} and q_{c1}, and substituting the corresponding values, equation (19) expands to

$$i_{c1} = \frac{L}{15(q_d-q_s)^2(q_d+q_s)^3}\{4(q_d\frac{d}{dt}q_d(q_d^4 + q_d^3q_s - 4q_d^2q_s^2 - 4q_dq_s^3 - 4q_s^4) +$$

$$q_d\frac{d}{dt}q_s(4q_d^4 + 4q_d^3q_s + 4q_d^2q_s^2 - q_dq_s^3 - q_s^4)\} - 10(q_d+q_s)(\sqrt{q_s^2(1-\frac{x}{L})+q_d^2\frac{x}{L}}$$

$$\{q_s(2q_d\frac{d}{dt}q_dq_s - (3q_d^2-q_s^2)\frac{d}{dt}q_s) - (q_d^2-q_s^2)(q_d\frac{d}{dt}q_d - q_s\frac{d}{dt}q_s)x\}$$

As mentioned above, this is one of the most important findings of our research and can be solved to find the first order drain $(-i_{c1} = i_{d1}, x \to L)$ and source $(i_{c1} = i_{s1}, x \to 0)$ current components, which are shown in Table 1. These results obtained without partitioning the channel charge are in agreement with previous results by Lim and Fossum, which were obtained using Ward's partition. Therefore we have verified that Ward's partition is correct when the body charge has a linearly dependence on channel potential.

3. CALCULATION OF MOSFET POWER

This section describes the detailed derivations of MOS power components. To not to confuse with the general definition of the static and dynamic power terms, channel power components are defined as the zero and the first order powers. It should be pointed out that the zero order power is different than the static power. In general, static power is defined as being independent of time (time invariant). However, the zero order power that has been used in this study is time variant. Although there is no explicit dependence, it depends on the terminal voltages that change in time. In fact it includes exactly the dynamic powers terms that are proportional or are the functions of the terminal voltages, and ignore the explicit terms proportional to dv/dt. The first order power on the other hand, depends on the time derivatives of the terminal voltages, while the dynamic power that has been used in the literature depends on energy stored in external capacitances which includes zero order and some of the first order power dissipated in the transistor.

The steady state current is usually used to determine power dissipation for MOS transistors. Charge redistribution in the channel causes additional power dissipation. In the quasi-static model, charge redistribution is assumed to happen instantaneously with no propagation delays. However, the channel charge density still changes as an indirect function of time through the dependence on time varying terminal voltages. This allows the use of the quasi-static model to predict the charge redistribution and the associated power dissipation.

The conventional charge model is based on the assumption that the MOSFET capacitors do not contribute any net power dissipation in the channel. But, the channel capacitances are not energy conserving [13]. They do have some higher order power dissipative terms due to the charge redistribution in the channel. These dissipative terms become significant at higher frequencies, which make it essential to include their effects for accurate power dissipation prediction.

Fig. 2 shows a MOS device. Considering a slice of thickness Δx, MOS channel can be thought of having two power components:

- Dissipative component (Fig. 2a): The current $i(x)$ flowing through the slice of thickness Δx having a potential Δv which looks like a series resistance and results in the power dissipation of $i\Delta v$.
- Conserved component (Fig. 2b): The rate of change of charge that is building in the slice due to the difference in current Δi. This power change $v\Delta i$ is the energy stored in the charge at the potential $v(x)$

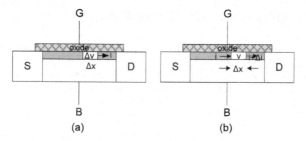

(a)   (b)

Fig. 2: MOS Channel Power Calculation

The instantaneous total power going into the transistor channel P_c can be estimated by integrating the power density over the channel length:

$$P_c = \int_0^L \frac{d}{dx}(i_c(x)v_{cb}(x))\,dx$$

$$= \int_0^L v_{cb}(x)(\frac{d}{dx}i_c(x))\,dx + \int_0^L i_c(x)(\frac{d}{dx}v_{cb}(x))\,dx \tag{23}$$

where the first integral represents change in stored energy and second term represents power dissipation. Keeping non-zero terms to first order in time derivatives, equation (20) can be expanded as:

$$P_c = P_{c0} + P_{c1,diss} + P_{c1,cons} \tag{24}$$

where

$$P_{c0} = \int_0^L I_{c0}(\frac{d}{dx}v_{cb0}(x))\,dx = I_{c0}(v_{db} - v_{sb}) \tag{25}$$

$$P_{c1,diss} = \int_0^L i_{c1}(\frac{d}{dx}v_{cb0}(x))\,dx \tag{26}$$

$$P_{c1,cons} = \int_0^L v_{cb0}(\frac{d}{dx}i_{c1})\,dx \tag{27}$$

The total instantaneous power P into the transistor is the sum of channel power P_c and gate power $P_{g1,cons}$.

$$P = P_c + P_{g1,cons} \tag{28}$$

where the gate power is

$$P_{g1,cons} = i_{g1}v_{gb} \tag{29}$$

Equation (25) represents the zero order power dissipation. Equation (26) represents the first order power dissipation due to the trans-capacitive transient current components and equation (27) represents the first order conserved power in the channel. Table 2 summarizes the power components.

4. ENERGY STORED IN THE CHANNEL

For the stored energy derivation, we have assumed that there is no charge leakage from the gate to the channel. However, energy is still supplied from the gate to drive the channel charges. It becomes necessary to add the conserved power contribution from the gate together with the channel conserved power. It is then possible to derive a closed form analytical solution for an energy function from the total conserved power.

4.1. Energy function validation for the channel

Clairaut's theorem states that, "*If two second order partials are continuous, they will be equal*". The same theorem can be used to check the equality of second order partial and verify the existence of the energy function.

Using equation (29), the conserved gate power can be written in terms of energy as

$$P_{g1,cons} = \frac{\partial E_g}{\partial v}\frac{dv}{dt} = \frac{\partial E_g}{\partial v_{gb}}\frac{dv_{gb}}{dt} + \frac{\partial E_g}{\partial v_{db}}\frac{dv_{db}}{dt} + \frac{\partial E_g}{\partial v_{sb}}\frac{dv_{sb}}{dt} \tag{30}$$

where E_g is the gate energy. Comparing (29) and (30), $\frac{\partial E}{\partial v}$'s can be derived from the coefficients of $\frac{dv_{jb}}{dt}$ as

$$\frac{\partial E_g}{\partial v_{sb}} = \frac{-2c_{ox}Lv_{gbt}v_{gst}(2v_{gdt}+v_{gst})}{3(v_{gdt}+v_{gst})^2}$$ (31)

$$\frac{\partial E_g}{\partial v_{db}} = \frac{-2c_{ox}Lv_{gbt}v_{gdt}(v_{gdt}+2v_{gst})}{3(v_{gdt}+v_{gst})^2}$$ (32)

$$\frac{\partial E_g}{\partial v_{gb}} = \frac{1}{6}c_{ox}Lv_{gbt}(6-\frac{2(v_{gdt}-v_{gst})^2}{K(v_{gdt}+v_{gst})^2})$$ (33)

As mentioned earlier, energy function exists if and only if the second order partials are equal. Taking partials and comparing equations (31-33), it is found that the second order partials are not equal. Hence, energy function does not exist for the gate.

4.2. Energy function validation for the channel

Taking similar approach, $\frac{\partial E}{\partial v}$'s are calculated from the coefficients of $\frac{dv_{jb}}{dt}$ in $P_{cl,cons}$ in (27) as

$$\frac{\partial E_c}{\partial v_{sb}} = \frac{-c_{ox}Lv_{gst}(3(v_{gdt}+v_{gst})^2-4v_{gbt}(2v_{gdt}+v_{gst})}{6(v_{gdt}+v_{gst})^2}$$ (34)

$$\frac{\partial E_c}{\partial v_{db}} = \frac{-c_{ox}Lv_{gdt}(3(v_{gdt}+v_{gst})^2-4v_{gbt}(v_{gdt}+2v_{gst})}{6(v_{gdt}+v_{gst})^2}$$ (35)

$$\frac{\partial E_c}{\partial v_{gb}} = \frac{c_{ox}L(3(v_{gdt}+v_{gst})^3-4v_{gbt}(v_{gdt}^2+4v_{gdt}v_{gst}+v_{gst}^2)}{6K(v_{gdt}+v_{gst})^2}$$ (36)

where E_c is the channel energy. It can again be shown that the second order partials are not equal and the channel also has no energy function from all of its conserved components.

4.3. Energy function validation for combination of the gate and the channel

Combining the conserved gate and channel power components, the first order conserved power can be written as

$$P_{cons} = (\frac{\partial E_c}{\partial v_{gb}}+\frac{\partial E_g}{\partial v_{gb}})\frac{dv_{gb}}{dt}+(\frac{\partial E_c}{\partial v_{db}}+\frac{\partial E_g}{\partial v_{db}})\frac{dv_{db}}{dt}+(\frac{\partial E_c}{\partial v_{sb}}+\frac{\partial E_g}{\partial v_{sb}})\frac{dv_{sb}}{dt}$$ (37)

which can again be solved to get $\dfrac{\partial E}{\partial v}$'s from the coefficients of $\dfrac{dv_{jb}}{dt}$ as

$$\frac{\partial E}{\partial v_{sb}} = \frac{-c_{ox}Lv_{gst}(3(v_{gdt}+v_{gst})^2 - 4v_{gbt}(2v_{gdt}+v_{gst}))}{6(v_{gdt}+v_{gst})^2}$$
$$+ \frac{-2c_{ox}Lv_{gbt}v_{gst}(2v_{gdt}+v_{gst})}{3(v_{gdt}+v_{gst})^2}$$

(38)

$$\frac{\partial E}{\partial v_{db}} = \frac{-c_{ox}Lv_{gdt}(3(v_{gdt}+v_{gst})^2 - 4v_{gbt}(v_{gdt}+2v_{gst}))}{6(v_{gdt}+v_{gst})^2}$$
$$+ \frac{-2c_{ox}Lv_{gbt}v_{gdt}(v_{gdt}+2v_{gst})}{3(v_{gdt}+v_{gst})^2}$$

(39)

$$\frac{\partial E}{\partial v_{gb}} = \frac{1}{6}c_{ox}Lv_{gbt}(6 - \frac{2(v_{gdt}-v_{gst})^2}{(1+\alpha)(v_{gdt}+v_{gst})^2})$$
$$+ \frac{c_{ox}L(3(v_{gdt}+v_{gst})^3 - 4v_{gbt}(v_{gdt}^2 + 4v_{gdt}v_{gst}+v_{gst}^2)}{6(1+\alpha)(v_{gdt}+v_{gst})^2}$$

(40)

In this case, second order partials are equal. It confirms that an energy function exists from all of the conserved components of the gate and the channel.

4.4. Energy Function Equation

The existence of an energy function was validated in previous section. In this section an energy function equation is derived solving the partial differentials using

$$\frac{\partial E}{\partial v_{jb}}(v_{gb},v_{sb},v_{db}) = \frac{\partial E_c}{\partial v_{jb}} + \frac{\partial E_g}{\partial v_{jb}}; j = g,s,d$$

(41)

This method however, is cumbersome as it involves lots of algebra. A simple solution is possible by separating the gate power into two components.

$$P_{g1,cons} = i_{g1}v_{gb} = i_{g1}v_{gbt0} + i_{g1}v_{t0}$$

(42)

where $v_{gbt0} = v_{gb} - v_{t0}$ and $i_{g1}v_{t0}$ is the threshold power. In terms of energy, the gate power becomes

$$P_{gl,cons} = (\frac{dE_{gbt}}{dv_{gb}} + \frac{dE_{t0}}{dv_{gb}})\frac{dv_{gb}}{dt} + (\frac{dE_{gbt}}{dv_{db}} + \frac{dE_{t0}}{dv_{db}})\frac{dv_{db}}{dt} + (\frac{dE_{gbt}}{dv_{sb}} + \frac{dE_{t0}}{dv_{sb}})\frac{dv_{sb}}{dt}$$

(43)

where E_{t0} and is the threshold energy function and E_{gbt} is the energy function from the remaining gate terms. Equation (41) now can be rewritten as

$$\frac{\partial E}{\partial v_{jb}}(v_{gb}, v_{sb}, v_{db}) = \frac{\partial E_c}{\partial v_{jb}} + \frac{\partial E_{gbt}}{\partial v_{jb}} + \frac{\partial E_{t0}}{\partial v_{jb}}; \; j = g, s, d$$

(44)

Though the total $\frac{\partial E}{\partial v}$ is same, the separation of the threshold component makes it possible to

derive two simple energy functions, one from the combination of $\frac{\partial E_c}{\partial v_{jb}} + \frac{\partial E_{gbt}}{\partial v_{jb}}$, and the other

from $\frac{\partial E_{t0}}{\partial v_{jb}}$. These two energy functions can then be combined to find the total energy

function.

4.4.1.   Threshold Energy Function (E_{t0}) Calculation

From (42) and (43), the threshold power can be written as

$$i_{g1}v_{t0} = \frac{\partial E_{t0}}{\partial v_{gb}}\frac{\partial v_{gb}}{\partial t} + \frac{\partial E_{t0}}{\partial v_{db}}\frac{\partial v_{db}}{\partial t} + \frac{\partial E_{t0}}{\partial v_{sb}}\frac{\partial v_{sb}}{\partial t}$$

(45)

where i_{g1} is the gate current. Since v_{t0} is constant, the threshold energy function can be estimated using

$$E_{t0} = \frac{d}{dt}(i_{g1}v_{t0}) = Q_g v_{t0}$$

(46)

where Q_g is the gate charge and is given in Table III.

4.4.2. E_{cgbt} Calculation

Leaving out the threshold terms, equation (44) reduces to

$$\frac{\partial E_{cgbt}}{\partial v_{jb}}(v_{gb}, v_{sb}, v_{db}) = \frac{\partial E_c}{\partial v_{jb}} + \frac{\partial E_{gbt}}{\partial v_{jb}}; \; j = g, s, d$$

(47)

which can be solved to find $\frac{\partial E}{\partial v}$'s as

$$\frac{\partial E_{cgbt}}{\partial v_{gb}} = \frac{1}{2}c_{ox}L(2v_{gbt} - v_{db} - v_{sb})$$

(48)

$$\frac{\partial E_{cgbt}}{\partial v_{sb}} = \frac{1}{2}c_{ox}L((1+\alpha)v_{sb} - v_{gbt})$$ (49)

$$\frac{\partial E_{cgbt}}{\partial v_{db}} = \frac{1}{2}c_{ox}L((1+\alpha)v_{db} - v_{gbt})$$ (50)

The second order partials of equations (48-50) are equal. It shows that an energy function also exist for the sum of remaining gate and channel components. This energy function E_{cgbt} can then be calculated solving the partial differentials with three independent voltage variables v_{gb}, v_{sb}, v_{db} respectively.

Solving with respect to the gate potential

$$E_{cgbt} = \int \frac{\partial E_{cgbt}}{\partial v_{gb}} dv_{gb} + E_1(v_{sb}, v_{db}) = \frac{1}{2}c_{ox}L(v_{gbt0}^2 - v_{gbt0}v_{db} - v_{gbt0}v_{sb}) + E_1(v_{sb}, v_{db})$$

Solving with respect to the drain potential

$$E_{cgbt} = \int \frac{\partial E_{cgbt}}{\partial v_{db}} dv_{db} + E_2(v_{gb}, v_{sb}) = \frac{1}{4}c_{ox}L(1+\alpha)v_{db}^2 - \frac{1}{2}c_{ox}Lv_{gbt}v_{db} + E_2(v_{gb}, v_{db})$$

Solving with respect to the source potential

$$E_{cgbt} = \int \frac{\partial E_{cgbt}}{\partial v_{sb}} dv_{sb} + E_3(v_{gb}, v_{db}) = \frac{1}{4}c_{ox}L(1+\alpha)v_{sb}^2 - \frac{1}{2}c_{ox}Lv_{gbt0}v_{sb} + E_3(v_{gb}, v_{db})$$

Comparing and combining equations for E_{cgbt}, the energy function reduces to

$$E_{cgbt} = \frac{1}{4}c_{ox}L((\alpha(v_{db}^2 + v_{sb}^2) + (v_{gbt0} - v_{db})^2 + (v_{gbt0} - v_{sb})^2)$$ (51)

The total energy function E can now be estimated using (46) and (51) as

$$E = E_{cgbt} + E_{t0}$$

and is shown in Table 3.

5. DYNAMIC POWER DISSIPATION MODEL

The basic idea of dynamic power estimation is that power dissipation comes from trapping the energy stored on a load capacitor by turning off a transistor very quickly. However, it does not make any sense as the first order dynamic power in those cases would be infinite. Also, the energy stored in the switching transistor should be included. In section 4, it was shown that an energy function was possible only from the combination of the gate and the channel conserved power components, which makes it very difficult to know the exact dissipation during the transients using the energy model alone. This is because the conserved components of channel currents are flowing in and out of the source and drain terminals during the transition. When the gate turns off, some of the energy supplied from the gate flows back to the supply through the source terminal while some of the energy gets dissipated from the drain terminal, and there is no way of telling what fraction goes to where without solving for the voltages and currents.

Charge based dynamic power estimation is an attractive alternate technique. Even though we do not know how much of the stored energy flows out the source and drain, we can always find the total drain charge, Q_d, and source charge, Q_s, from Ward's partition [2]. Q_s and Q_d are not physically separate but act as pseudo-charges, the sum of which constitutes the total channel charge. All they do is give a way to find the currents by taking their time derivatives. Even though there is no physical channel charge partition, it turns out that the current equations act as if they are the time derivatives of the charges. If currents are integrated over a time interval to get the total charges going in or out, it is exactly the same as the changes in Q_s and Q_d. Hence, we can figure out the total charge injected by a transistor without knowing the details of the waveform. All we need to know is the beginning and ending voltage of the transistor terminals and we can figure out ΔQ for each terminal. This ΔQ then gets added to the charge on the load capacitor and eventually all gets dissipated.

The total power dissipation is the sum of dynamic power and short circuit power. In contrast with dynamic power, short circuit power cannot be determined without an exact solution to the current and voltage waveforms. Short circuit power comes from the zero order component of the drain current from the turned off transistor. This current component is assumed to be zero in the following derivation.

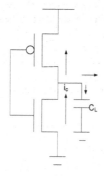

Fig. 3. Charge Based Dynamic Power Model

Fig. 3 shows the charge based dynamic power model. If we define the drain current as positive going in, then the total charge coming out is negative of the integral of the drain current. The zero order turn on current $i_0(on)$ going from the source to the drain terminal can then be estimated using

$$-\int i_0(on)dt = -\Delta Q_{DP} - \Delta Q_{DN} - \Delta Q_L \tag{52}$$

where ΔQ_L gives the charge going into the load capacitance. ΔQ_{DP} and ΔQ_{DN} are defined as the drain charges at the PFET and the NFET respectively and can be estimated from [11] as

$$Q_{DP} = -\frac{2}{3}Lc_{oxp}(1+\alpha_p)v_{ds}\left(-\frac{(u_p-1)^3}{2u_p-1} + \frac{2}{5}\frac{u_p^5-(u_p-1)^5}{(2u_p-1)^2} \right) \tag{53}$$

$$Q_{DN} = -\frac{2}{3} Lc_{oxn}(1+\alpha_n)v_{ds}\left(\frac{(u_n-1)^3}{2u_n-1} + \frac{2}{5}\frac{u_n^5-(u_n-1)^5}{(2u_n-1)^2}\right) \tag{54}$$

where $u_p = \dfrac{v_{gs}-v_{tp}}{(1+\alpha_p)v_{ds}}$, $u_n = \dfrac{v_{gs}-v_{tn}}{(1+\alpha_n)v_{ds}}$, c_{oxp} and c_{oxn} are the oxide capacitance per unit

lengths, α_p and α_n are the bulk charge coefficients and v_{tp} and v_{tn} are threshold voltages of PFET and NFET respectively. The change in charge at the ground or the supply can then be estimated using

$$\Delta Q = -\int i_0(on)dt - \Delta Q_S - \Delta Q_B \tag{55}$$

where ΔQ_S and ΔQ_B are defined as the changes in source and the substrate charges. Using this approach, the difference in charge at ground due to a falling transient can be estimate using

$$\Delta Q_f = -\Delta Q_{DPf} - \Delta Q_{DNf} - \Delta Q_{Lf} - \Delta Q_{SNf} - \Delta Q_{BNf} \tag{56}$$

and the difference in charge at ground due to the rising transient becomes

$$\Delta Q_r = -\Delta Q_{SNr} - \Delta Q_{BNr} = \Delta Q_{SNf} + \Delta Q_{BNf} \tag{57}$$

which is correct if the short circuit power is zero. For a rising transient, as mentioned above, zero order components are assumed to be zero. Hence we only get the reverse changes in ΔQ_S and ΔQ_B. The difference in charge ΔQ can then be rewritten as

$$\Delta Q = \Delta Q_r + \Delta Q_f = -\Delta Q_{DPf} - \Delta Q_{DNf} - \Delta Q_{Lf} \tag{58}$$

In equation (58), the last term represents the normal component present in the conventional dynamic power model, while our model adds two extra terms responsible for the first order power dissipation from charge stored in the channel. The dynamic power dissipation is then given by

$$P = \Delta Q\, V_{dd}\, f = \left(\Delta Q_r(final) - \Delta Q_r(initial)\right) + \left(\Delta Q_f(final) - \Delta Q_f(initial)\right)V_{dd}\, f \tag{59}$$

which can be solved for a falling transient as

For the PFET:

$$Q_{DP}(initial) = Q_{DP}\Big|_{V_{gs}\to 0} = 0 \tag{60}$$

$$Q_{DP}(final) = Q_{DP}\Big|_{V_{gs}\to -V_{dd}, V_{ds}\to 0} = \frac{1}{2}c_{oxp}(V_{dd}+V_{tp}) \tag{61}$$

From (60) and (61)

$$\Delta Q_{DP} = \frac{1}{2}c_{oxp}(V_{dd}+V_{tp}) \tag{62}$$

For the NFET:

$$Q_{DN}(initial) = Q_{DN}\Big|_{V_{gs}\to V_{dd}, V_{ds}\to 0} = -\frac{1}{2}c_{oxn}(V_{dd}-V_{tn}) \tag{63}$$

$$Q_{DN}(final) = Q_{DN}\Big|_{V_{gs} \to 0} = 0 \tag{64}$$

From (63) and (64)

$$\Delta Q_{DN} = \frac{1}{2} c_{oxn} (V_{dd} - V_{tn}) \tag{65}$$

<u>For the load:</u>

$$Q_L(initial) = C_L V_{db}\Big|_{V_{db} \to 0} = 0 \tag{66}$$

$$Q_L(final) = C_L V_{db}\Big|_{V_{db} \to v_{dd}} = C_L V_{dd} \tag{67}$$

From (66) and (67)

$$\Delta Q_L = C_L V_{dd} \tag{68}$$

From (62), (65) and (68)

$$\Delta Q = C_L V_{dd} + \frac{1}{2} c_{oxn} (V_{dd} - V_{tn}) + \frac{1}{2} c_{oxp} (V_{dd} + V_{tp}) \tag{69}$$

Substituting ΔQ in (59), the dynamic power equation reduces to

$$P = C_L V_{dd}^2 f + \left(\frac{1}{2} c_{oxn} (V_{dd} - V_{tn}) V_{dd} + \frac{1}{2} c_{oxp} (V_{dd} + V_{tp}) V_{dd} \right) f \tag{70}$$

Equation (70) shows the presence of extra dynamic power component to the conventional dynamic power equation.

6. FIRST ORDER CURRENT COMPONENTS

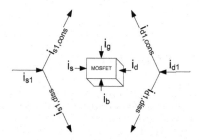

Fig. 4: First order dissipative and conserved current components

As seen from Table I, first order current is a function of terminal voltages and their time derivatives, and as mentioned above, the coefficient of dv/dt instead of representing purely storage capacitance, is also responsible for some of the power dissipation in the channel. This suggests that the first order drain and the source currents consist of two separate components, one that contributes to power dissipation in the channel, and another that is responsible for the energy storage. Taking this approach, i_{dl} and i_{sl} can be expanded as

$$i_{d1} = i_{d1,cons} + i_{d1,diss} \tag{71}$$

$$i_{s1} = i_{s1,cons} + i_{s1,diss} \tag{72}$$

Fig. 4 shows this concept where first order currents i_{dl} and i_{sl} are separated into two components. Since the gate and the substrate currents are non-dissipative in the absence of leakage, there is no need to separate them.

The dissipative current components in equations (71) and (72) are due to the first order power dissipation in the channel from the charge redistribution and is computed by dividing the power dissipated in the channel by the drain to source potential

$$i_{d1,diss} = \frac{P_{c1,diss}}{v_{ds}} = i_{tt,diss} = -i_{s1,diss} \tag{73}$$

$i_{tt,diss}$ in equation (73) is the trans-capacitive transport current that is responsible for the extra power dissipation in the channel, and is defined as positive going into the drain. The conserved drift component can now be computed by subtracting the dissipated component from the total first order current.

$$i_{d1,cons} = i_{d1} - i_{tt,diss} \tag{74}$$

$$i_{s1,cons} = i_{s1} + i_{tt,diss} \tag{75}$$

Separation of currents into conserved and dissipative terms helps to compute the true energy conserving capacitances. True in the sense that these capacitances are estimated simply from the conserved components of current using equations (74) and (75).

$$i_{i1,cons} = C_{cii} \partial_t v_{ib} - \sum_{j \neq i,b} (C_{cij} \partial_t v_{jb}) \; ; \; i,j = g,d,s,b. \tag{76}$$

where C_{cii}, C_{cij} are the conserved components of the capacitor. In equation (76) and all the subsequent equations, the subscript notation 'c' or 'd' is used for conserved or dissipative components. Table 4 and 5 summarize the conserved and dissipative components of currents and capacitances.

7. EQUIVALENT CIRCUIT

In this section, we develop an equivalent circuit by following the method used by Lim-Fossum [11]. Table IV showed that the capacitances were not reciprocal, which makes the capacitance representation using two terminal reciprocal capacitances impossible if these capacitances are made to represent the total first order drain current. However, equation (74) can be rewritten with reciprocal capacitors as

$$i_{d1,cons} = C_{gd} \partial_t v_{dg} + C_{bd} \partial_t v_{db} + i_{tt,cons} \tag{77}$$

where

$$i_{tt,cons} = (C_{gd} - C_{cdg}) \partial_t v_{gb} + (C_{csd} - C_{cds}) \partial_t v_{sb} + C_{csd} \partial_t v_{ds} \tag{78}$$

The dissipative component of current from equation (73) can also be written in terms of dissipative capacitances as

$$i_{d1,diss} = C_{ddd} \partial_t v_{db} - C_{ddg} \partial_t$$ (79)

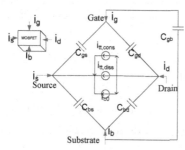

Fig. 5: Equivalent Circuit for a four terminal SOI MOSFET

Fig. 5 shows an equivalent circuit of a four terminal MOSFET. The model is equivalent to Lim-Fossum [11], but we have separated the trans-capacitive transport current, i_{tt} into conserved and dissipative components. There are three current components flowing from the drain to the source terminal. The current component responsible for the first order power dissipation in the channel is represented by $i_{tt,diss}$ the conserved current component is represented by $i_{tt,cons}$. I_{c0} represents the steady state zero order current. The two terminal reciprocal capacitances C_{gd}, C_{gs}, C_{bd}, C_{bs} and C_{gb} represents the conserved gate to drain, gate to source, substrate to source, substrate to drain and gate to substrate capacitances respectively. The two terminal capacitances do not conserve energy by themselves; the conserved component of i_{tt} must be included. C_{ddd}, C_{ddg}, C_{dds} in equation (79) represents the dissipative drain to drain, drain to gate and drain to source capacitances respectively.

8. MODEL VALIDATION AND COMPARISON

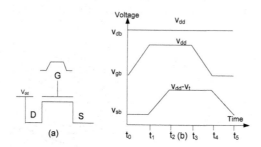

Fig. 6: (a) Pass transistor logic (b) Voltage Waveforms

In this section, we have shown that the gate is leakage free and does not contribute any net charge to the channel. We have also validated the fact that our first order power dissipation model is indeed a charge conserving, as the total charge over a complete cycle is conserved.

Fig. 6 shows the idealized voltage waveforms for the drain, gate and the source terminals used to pass the logic through the NFET. The drain terminal is assumed to be high during the entire simulation, while the gate and the source potentials goes through many transitions. In the first transition (t_0 to t_1), the gate terminal goes from low at t_0 to high at t_1, while the source potential remains low. The transistor enters the saturation as soon as the gate to source potential becomes greater than the threshold voltage v_t. The extra gate charge ΔQ_{g1}, is then given by

$$\Delta Q_{g1} = \left(c_{gg} \Delta v_{gb} \right)_{cutoff} + \left(c_{gg} \Delta v_{gb} \right)_{saturation}$$

$$= \frac{\alpha}{1+\alpha} c_{ox} v_{t0} + \left(\frac{1}{3} \frac{\alpha}{1+\alpha} + \frac{2}{3} \right) c_{ox} (v_{dd} - v_{t0})$$

(80)

During the second transition (t_1 to t_2), the gate terminal stays high (v_{dd}) and the pass transistor remains in the saturation. The source terminal on the other hand, goes from low (0) to high ($\frac{v_{dd} - v_t}{1+\alpha}$) and the extra gate charge ΔQ_{g2} becomes

$$\Delta Q_{g2} = -\left(c_{gs} \Delta v_{sb} \right)_{saturation} = -\frac{2}{3} c_{ox} \frac{v_{dd} - v_{t0}}{1+\alpha}$$

(81)

The transistor now enters the cutoff (at t_2) and remains there even though the gate and source terminals come back to its original states at t_4 and t_5. The extra gate charge during these transitions are given by

$$\Delta Q_{g3} = \left(c_{gg} \Delta v_{gb} \right)_{cutoff} = -\frac{\alpha}{1+\alpha} c_{ox} v_{dd}$$

(82)

The total gate charge ΔQ_g is then calculated by adding the extra gate contributions as

$$\Delta Q_g = \sum_{i=1}^{3} \Delta Q_{gi} = 0$$

(83)

For a complete cycle, charge is conserved and there is no extra non-zero contribution from the gate. Fig. 7 shows this concept using a two dimensional profile, where $v_{sb} = v_{gbt0}/(1+\alpha)$

sets a boundary between the cutoff and saturation regions. Simulation is started at some point A, and goes through transitions B, C and D, before settling back to its initial state at A.

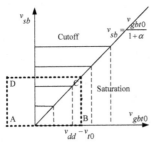

Fig. 7 : Charge Profile

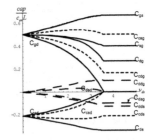

Fig. 8: Capacitance Plots vs. v_{ds}

Our model also verifies that Ward's method of charge partitioning works correctly as long as the body charge has a linear dependence on the channel potential. It predicts the same source and the drain currents, and hence the same terminal capacitances. However, we are able to partition these capacitances into conserved and dissipative components, as shown in Fig. 8. The partitioning approach to capacitances offers several advantages over conventional trans-capacitances.

- The energy stored in the conserved capacitances can be predicted.
- They can be made to agree with Meyer's capacitances [1] if the body effect and body bias are ignored.

Our other significant contribution has been in the power estimation. Our models have improved the device power measurements by implementing two important concepts:

- First order terms have to be included for power dissipation estimation as they become significant at higher frequencies.
- Stored components can be ignored for computationally efficient power dissipation estimation.

The average device power, $\overline{P}$, is then possible by taking dissipative current times voltage and integrating them over time. A simple simulation can be used to show the importance of first order power.

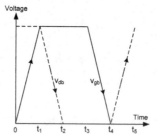

Fig. 9: v_{gb} and v_{db} waveforms

Fig. 9 shows the idealized voltage waveforms for the drain and the gate terminals used for simulation of turning a transistor on then off. The average first order dissipative power from the first transition $(v_{ds}=v_{dd})$ when v_{gb} goes from low at t_0 to high at t_1 is computed by

$$\overline{P}(t_0 \rightarrow t_1) = \frac{1}{(t_1-t_0)} \int_{t_0}^{t_1} (i_{d1,diss} v_{db} + i_{s1,diss} v_{sb}) dt \qquad (84)$$

If we assume the source and the substrate are at the same potential $(v_{sb}=0)$, equation (84) can be rewritten as

$$\overline{P}(t_0 \rightarrow t_1) = \frac{1}{(t_1-t_0)} \int_{t_0}^{t_1} (i_{d1,diss} v_{db}) dt \qquad (85)$$

In the second power dissipating transition, when the gate terminal is high, the drain swings from high at t_1 to low at t_2. The dissipative power equation (84) reduces to

$$\overline{P}(t_1 \rightarrow t_2) = \frac{1}{(t_2-t_2)} \int_{t_1}^{t_2} i_{d1,diss} v_{db} dt \qquad (86)$$

During the interval t_2 to t_4, there is no power dissipation in the channel ($v_{ds}=0$). The final power transition occurs when the drain waveform swings from low at t_4 to high at t_5. As the gate voltage has already reached a steady low value, the power equation becomes

$$\overline{P}(t_4 \rightarrow t_5) = \frac{1}{(t_5-t_4)}\int_{t_4}^{t_5} i_{d1,diss}{}^v db \, dt \qquad (87)$$

The total dissipative power for a complete cycle is computed taking the sum of all these powers as

$$\overline{P} = \overline{P}(t_0 \rightarrow t_1) + \overline{P}(t_1 \rightarrow t_2) + \overline{P}(t_4 \rightarrow t_5) \qquad (88)$$

For a complete cycle, energy is conserved. This allows us to leave out the conserved component from the power equation for computationally efficient power dissipation predictions [13]. Nonetheless, the total dissipative power includes the first order terms as predicted by equation (88). These first order dissipative components become significant at higher frequencies and modify the total power dissipated in the channel as shown in Fig. 10. The total power is no longer constant, and at high frequencies becomes dependent on the switching frequencies.

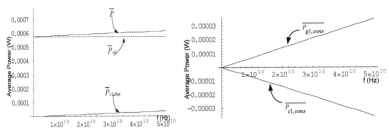

Fig. 10: Dissipative Power vs. Frequency **Fig. 11:** Conserved Power vs. Frequency

The result also shows that we need to be extra careful while doing the power measurements. It is not appropriate to look only at the channel dissipation; the first order power dissipation does have contributions from the gate. If the power dissipation is estimated by just considering the total channel power, there would be an extra negative component from the conserved energy. In that case, the channel could act as an energy generator. In reality, that is not the case. Power is pumped from the gate to the channel and when the contribution from the gate is added, the conserved terms cancel out (Fig. 11).

8. CONCLUSIONS

The development of a self consistent, quasi-static, first order power dissipation model for a fully depleted SOI MOSFET has been described. The Lim-Fossum current and charge model has been verified as correct to first order even though the Ward partition of source and drain charge was used. The transient current is separated into conserved and dissipative components. Significance of higher order power dissipation at higher frequencies is discussed. The existence of energy function also is validated to make the power dissipation estimation computationally efficient.

REFERENCES

[1]   J.E. Meyer, "MOS models and circuit simulation," RCA Rev., vol. 32, pp. 42-63, 1971.
[2]   D.E.Ward, "Charge-Based Modeling of Capacitance in MOS Transistors", Stanford Electronics Lab., Stanford University, Tech. Rep. F201-11, June 1981.
[3]   B. J. Sheu, D. L. Scharfetter, C. Hu and D. O. Pederson, "A compact IGFET charge model", IEEE Transactions on Circuits Systems, vol. CAS-31, pp 745-748, 1984.
[4]   K.A. Sakallah, Yao-Tsung Yen, and S.S.Greenberg, "A first-order charge conserving MOS capacitance model," IEEE Transactions on Computer-Aided Design, vol. 9, pp. 99-108, January 1990.
[5]   S. S. Chung, "A charge-based capacitance model of short-channel MOSFET's," IEEE Transactions on Computer-Aided Design, vol. 8, no. 1, January 1989.
[6]   M. A. Cirit, "The Meyer model revisited: why is charge not conserved?" IEEE Transactions on Computer- Aided Design, vol. CAD-8, pp. 1033-1037, October 1989.
[7]   P. Yang, B.D. Epler and P. K. Chatterjee, "An Investigation of the Charge Conservation Problem for MOSFET Circuit Simulation", IEEE Journal of Solid-State Circuits, Vol. SC-18, February 1983.
[8]   A. S. Roy, C. C. Enz and Jean-Michel Sallese, "Source-Drain Partitioning in MOSFET", IEEE Trans. On Elec. Devices, vol. 54, No. 6, June 2007.
[9]   A. Aarts, R. van der Hout, J. Paasschens, A. Scholten, M. Willemsen, and D. Klaassen, "New fundamental insight into capacitance modeling of laterally nonunion MOS devices, "IEEE Trans. Electron Devices, vol. 53, No. 2, pp. 270-278, Feb 2006.
[10] J.G. Fossum, H. Jeong, and S. Veeraraghavan, "Significance of the channel-charge partition in the transient MOSFET model," IEEE Transactions on Electron Devices, vol. Ed-33, no.10, October 1986.
[11] H. Lim and J. Fossum, "A charge-based large-signal model for thin-film SOI MOSFET's", *IEEE Journal of Solid-State Circuits*, Vol. Sc-20, no.1, February 1985.
[12] W. Lie, M. Chang, "Transistor Transient Studies Including Trans-Capacitive Current and Distributive Gate Resistance for Inverter Circuits", IEEE Trans. on Circuits and Systems, Vol. 45, April 1998.
[13] S. Sharma, "First Order, Quasi-Static, Charge Conserving MOSFET Channel Capacitance Model," PhD. Dissertation, Oklahoma State University, December 2007.
[14] S. Y. Oh, D. E. Ward and R. W. Dutton, "Transient analysis of MOS transistors", IEEE J. Solid-State Circuits, vol. SC-15, pp. 636-643, 1980.
[15] Y.Cheng and C. Hu, "MOSFET modeling and BSIM3 user's guide", Kluwer Academic Publishers, 1999.
[16] William Liu, "MOSFET models for SPICE simulation, including BSIM3v4 and BSIM4", John Wiley and Sons, Inc., 2001.
[17] Yannis Tsividis, "Operation and the Modeling of The MOS Transistors", Oxford University Press, June 2003.
[18] Wolfram Reseach, Inc., Mathematica, Version 5.2, Champaign, IL (2005).

Table 1: Charge and Current Equations for NMOS

	Linear	Saturation	Cut-Off
	$q_c < 0$ $v_{gdt} > 0$ $v_{gst} > 0$	$q_c < 0$ $v_{gdt} = 0$ $v_{gst} > 0$	$q_c = 0$ $v_{gdt} = 0$ $v_{gst} = 0$
q_s	$-c_{ox} v_{gst}$	$-c_{ox} v_{gst}$	0
q_d	$-c_{ox} v_{gdt}$	0	0
I_{c0}	$\dfrac{\mu c_{ox}}{2L(1+\alpha)}(v_{gst}^2 - v_{gdt}^2)$	$\dfrac{\mu c_{ox}}{2L(1+\alpha)} v_{gst}^2$	0
i_{s1}	$\dfrac{2c_{ox}L}{15(v_{gdt}+v_{gst})^3}[2v_{gdt}(\tfrac{d}{dt}v_{gdt})(v_{gdt}^2+3v_{gdt}v_{gst}+v_{gst}^2)+v_{gst}(\tfrac{d}{dt}v_{gst})(8v_{gdt}^2+9v_{gdt}v_{gst}+3v_{gst}^2)]$	$\dfrac{2}{5}c_{ox}L\dfrac{d}{dt}v_{gst}$	0
i_{d1}	$\dfrac{2c_{ox}L}{15(v_{gdt}+v_{gst})^3}\left(v_{gdt}(\tfrac{d}{dt}v_{gdt})(3v_{gdt}^2+9v_{gdt}v_{gst}+8v_{gst}^2)+2v_{gst}(\tfrac{d}{dt}v_{gst})(v_{gdt}^2+3v_{gdt}v_{gst}+v_{gst}^2)\right)$	$\dfrac{4}{15}c_{ox}L\dfrac{d}{dt}v_{gst}$	0

Table 2: Power Equations

	Linear	Saturation	Cut-Off
P_{c0}	$\dfrac{\mu c_{ox}}{2L(1+\alpha)}v_{ds}(v_{gst}^2 - v_{gdt}^2)$	$\dfrac{\mu c_{ox} v_{ds} v_{gst}^2}{2L(1+\alpha)}$	0
$P_{c1,diss}$	$c_{ox}L\dfrac{v_{ds}(v_{gst}-v_{gdt})}{30(v_{gdt}+v_{gst})^3}\left(3v_{gdt}^2\dfrac{d}{dt}v_{gdt}+3v_{gst}^2\dfrac{d}{dt}v_{gst}+7v_{gdt}(\dfrac{d}{dt}v_{gdt}+\dfrac{d}{dt}v_{gst})v_{gst}\right)$	$\dfrac{c_{ox}Lv_{ds}}{10}\dfrac{dv_{gst}}{dt}$	0
$P_{c1,cons}$	$\dfrac{-c_{ox}L}{6(1+\alpha)}\left(-3(v_{gdt}\dfrac{d}{dt}v_{gdt}+v_{gst}\dfrac{d}{dt}v_{gst})+\dfrac{4(v_{gdt}\tfrac{d}{dt}v_{gdt}(v_{gdt}+2v_{gst})+v_{gst}\tfrac{d}{dt}v_{gst}(2v_{gdt}+v_{gst}))v_{gbt0}}{(v_{gdt}+v_{gst})^2}\right)$	$-\dfrac{c_{ox}L}{6(1+\alpha)}\dfrac{d}{dt}v_{gst}\cdot$ $(4v_{gbt0}-3v_{gst})$	0

Table 3: Energy Function

	Linear	Saturation	Cut-Off
Q_g	$c_{ox}L\left(v_{gb}-v_{fb}-\phi-v_{sb}-\dfrac{v_{db}-v_{sb}}{2}+\dfrac{(1+\alpha)(v_{db}-v_{sb})^2}{12(v_{gst}-(1+\alpha)(v_{db}-v_{sb})/2)}\right)$	$c_{ox}L(v_{gb}-v_{fb}-\phi-v_{sb}-\dfrac{v_{gst}}{3(1+\alpha)})$	$c_{ox}L(v_{gb}$ $-v_{fb}-\phi$ $-\dfrac{v_{gbt0}}{(1+\alpha)})$
E_f	$\dfrac{1}{4}c_{ox}L\left(\alpha(v_{db}^2+v_{sb}^2)+(v_{db}-v_{gbt0})^2+(v_{gbt0}-v_{sb})^2\right)+Q_g v_{t0}$	$\dfrac{1}{4}c_{ox}L(\alpha(\dfrac{v_{gbt0}^2}{1+\alpha}+v_{sb}^2)$ $+(v_{gbt0}-v_{sb})^2)+Q_g v_{t0}$	$\dfrac{c_{ox}\alpha L}{2}\dfrac{v_{gbt0}^2}{1+\alpha}$ $+Q_g v_{t0}$

Table 4: Conserved and Dissipative Current Components

	Linear	Saturation	Cut-Off
$i_{tt,diss} =$ $-i_{s1,diss}$	$\dfrac{c_{ox}L(v_{gst}-v_{gdt})}{30(v_{gdt}+v_{gst})^3}\left(3\left(v_{gdt}^2\dfrac{d}{dt}v_{gdt}+v_{gst}^2\dfrac{d}{dt}v_{gst}\right)+7v_{gdt}v_{gst}\left(\dfrac{d}{dt}v_{gdt}+\dfrac{d}{dt}v_{gst}\right)\right)$	$\dfrac{c_{ox}L}{10}\dfrac{d}{dt}v_{gst}$	0
$i_{d1,cons}$	$\dfrac{c_{ox}L}{6(v_{gdt}+v_{gst})^2}\left(v_{gdt}\dfrac{d}{dt}v_{gdt}(3v_{gdt}+5v_{gst})+v_{gst}\dfrac{d}{dt}v_{gst}(3v_{gdt}+v_{gst})\right)$	$\dfrac{c_{ox}L}{6}\dfrac{d}{dt}v_{gst}$	0
$i_{s1,cons}$	$\dfrac{c_{ox}L}{6(v_{gdt}+v_{gst})^2}\left(v_{gdt}\dfrac{d}{dt}v_{gdt}(v_{gdt}+3v_{gst})+v_{gst}\dfrac{d}{dt}v_{gst}(5v_{gdt}+3v_{gst})\right)$	$\dfrac{c_{ox}L}{2}\dfrac{d}{dt}v_{gst}$	0

Table 5: Conserved and Dissipative Capacitances

	Linear	Saturation	Cut-Off
C_{gb}	$\dfrac{\alpha}{3(1+\alpha)}c_{ox}L\dfrac{(v_{gdt}-v_{gst})^2}{(v_{gdt}+v_{gst})^2}$	$\dfrac{\alpha}{3(1+\alpha)}c_{ox}L$	$\dfrac{\alpha c_{ox}L}{(1+\alpha)}$
C_{gd}	$\dfrac{2}{3}c_{ox}Lv_{gdt}\dfrac{(v_{gdt}+2v_{gst})}{(v_{gdt}+v_{gst})^2}$	0	0
C_{gs}	$\dfrac{2}{3}c_{ox}Lv_{gst}\dfrac{(2v_{gdt}+v_{gst})}{(v_{gdt}+v_{gst})^2}$	$\dfrac{2}{3}c_{ox}L$	0
C_{csg}	$\dfrac{1}{6}c_{ox}L\dfrac{(v_{gdt}^2+8v_{gdt}v_{gst}+3v_{gst}^2)}{(v_{gdt}+v_{gst})^2}$	$\dfrac{1}{2}c_{ox}L$	0
C_{csb}	αC_{csg}	αC_{csg}	0
C_{csd}	$-\dfrac{(1+\alpha)}{6}c_{ox}L\dfrac{v_{gdt}(v_{gdt}+3v_{gst})}{(v_{gdt}+v_{gst})^2}$	0	0
C_{cdg}	$\dfrac{1}{6}c_{ox}L\dfrac{(3v_{gdt}^2+8v_{gdt}v_{gst}+v_{gst}^2)}{(v_{gdt}+v_{gst})^2}$	$\dfrac{1}{6}c_{ox}L$	0
C_{cdb}	αC_{cdg}	αC_{cdg}	0
C_{cds}	$-\dfrac{(1+\alpha)}{6}c_{ox}L\dfrac{v_{gst}(3v_{gdt}+v_{gst})}{(v_{gdt}+v_{gst})^2}$	$-\dfrac{1+\alpha}{6}c_{ox}L$	0
C_{ddg}	$c_{ox}L(v_{gst}-v_{gdt})(3v_{gdt}^2+14v_{gdt}v_{gst}+3v_{gst}^2)/30(v_{gdt}+v_{gst})^3$	$\dfrac{1}{10}c_{ox}L$	0
C_{dds}	$-(1+\alpha)c_{ox}L(v_{gst}-v_{gdt})v_{gst}(7v_{gdt}+3v_{gst})/30(v_{gdt}+v_{gst})^3$	$-\dfrac{1+\alpha}{10}c_{ox}L$	0
C_{ddb}	$-\alpha C_{ddg}$	$-\dfrac{\alpha}{10}c_{ox}L$	0
C_{dsg}	$-C_{ddg}$	$-C_{ddg}$	0
C_{dsd}	$(1+\alpha)c_{ox}L(v_{gst}-v_{gdt})v_{gst}(3v_{gdt}+7v_{gst})/30(v_{gdt}+v_{gst})^3$	0	0
C_{dsb}	$-C_{ddb}$	$-C_{ddb}$	0